THE MONETARY AND FINANCIAL SYSTEM

Second Edition

by

David J. Goacher B.A.(Econ), Ph.D.

332   GOA

73329

First published 1990
Second edition 1993

BANKERS BOOKS LIMITED
c/o The Chartered Institute of Bankers
10 Lombard Street
London EC3V 9AS

CIB publications are published by The Chartered Institute of Bankers, a non-profit making, registered educational charity, and are distributed exclusively by Bankers Books Limited which is a wholly-owned subsidiary of The Chartered Institute of Bankers.

© Goacher, D., 1990

ISBN 0 85297 338 1

B|**L**| **British Library Cataloguing in Publication Data**

Goacher, David J.
The monetary and financial system – 2 Rev. ed
1. Monetary system
I. Title
332.4

Typeset in 10 on 11pt Times by Style Photosetting Ltd, Mayfield, East Sussex
Printed by Commercial Colour Press, London E7; text printed on 80gsm general purpose woodfree; cover printed on 240 gsm matt coated art.

CONTENTS

Tables

ABOUT THE AUTHOR

David J. Goacher was awarded a First Class Honours Degree in Economics in 1976 and a Ph.D. for his research work in the field of macro-monetary economics in 1982, both by the University of Sheffield. Between 1979 and 1982 he held the post of Esmée Fairbairn Research Fellow in Economics at the University of Sheffield, and was Tutor in Economics at that institution for six years. Since 1982 he has held the posts of Lecturer in Economics, Senior Lecturer in Banking, Principal Lecturer in Financial Studies, and Yorkshire Bank Reader in Financial Services at Sheffield Hallam University (formerly Sheffield City Polytechnic). He is currently Head of Research in the School of Financial Studies and Law at Sheffield Hallam University.

Dr Goacher is author of four other books on the subjects of monetary economics and financial institutions and markets, he has written distance learning packages for banking students, has contributed articles to leading journals, and has written a wide range of academic papers on monetary and financial topics. His teaching experience encompasses an array of undergraduate degree and diploma courses, postgraduate degree courses, and professional courses, including several preparing students for The Chartered Institute of Bankers Associateship and Financial Studies Diploma Examinations. Dr Goacher is currently an Assistant Examiner for The Monetary and Financial System (and formerly for Monetary Economics), and is the Academic Supervisor and an Examiner for the CIB's Financial Studies Diploma Practice of Banking 5 Project. He was formerly an Assistant Examiner for the CIB's Financial Studies Diploma course in Business Planning and Control, and has been Course Director of Institute Revision Seminars and local revision courses.

ACKNOWLEDGEMENTS

The author wishes to thank The Chartered Institute of Bankers for permission to reproduce questions from past examination papers, and also all the institutions and organisations which have provided the statistical data reproduced in this book; in particular, the Bank of England, the Central Statistical Office, and *The Economist* and *Financial Times* newspapers.

Special thanks must go to Mr Peter Gutmann FCIB, for reading the whole of the first edition of this book and making perceptive and, more important, constructive comments on its contents and structure. As former Chief Examiner for The Monetary and Financial System and for its predecessor, Monetary Economics, Peter's influence on this book has been immeasurable. Thanks are also due to my colleague Mr Paul Cowdell FCIB, DipFS, for his expert guidance on the contents of chapter 2 (Corporate Sector Finances). Finally, as ever, I wish to express my gratitude to Mrs Sheila Watts for the production of yet another accurate typescript from my increasingly untidy scrawl. Unfortunately, I must admit to sole property rights to the errors of omission and commission embodied within this book.

David J. Goacher
School of Financial Studies and Law
Sheffield Hallam University
September 1993

INTRODUCTION

This book has been written specifically for students preparing for The Chartered Institute of Bankers Associateship Examination in *The Monetary and Financial System*. However, it is hoped that many of the topics covered will be of interest to students studying for other professional and academic qualifications, and wishing to obtain a deeper knowledge of the operation of the UK monetary and financial system.

Each of the 10 chapters in this book covers one of the 10 topic areas specified by the syllabus for *The Monetary and Financial System,* and attempts to provide a thorough treatment of all relevant basic concepts, key issues and major practical problems. Each chapter also examines recent practical experience in respect of the operation of the UK monetary and financial system, and comments upon applied issues relating to other countries, wherever this is appropriate to aid understanding of the subject matter. For all students, the starting point for study should be the realisation that there are no 'short cuts' to passing the Associateship Examination in *The Monetary and Financial System.* Attempting to 'spot' questions and then memorise model answers is likely to prove fatal. The chances of success in the examination will be maximised only through structured and serious preparation, and this book is intended to provide a firm foundation for that purpose.

Having mastered the 'basics' of the subject, it is important for students to *keep up-to-date* with developments in the major topic areas. A few minutes each day spent reading the financial and business pages of a quality newspaper should provide at least a general impression of the current monetary and financial situation. *The Economist, Banking World,* and *The Banker* are excellent sources of more detailed information. A first class publication is the *Bank of England Quarterly Bulletin,* although in some of its more specialist sections the analysis is very detailed and rather advanced (but the returns to be obtained are well worth the effort involved in studying this material). Students should also get into the habit of consciously thinking about where particular 'real world' events fit in to the whole scheme of their course of study. At the end of each chapter there is a section entitled 'Further Study', which includes comments on specific sources of material for students wishing to develop their knowledge of particular subject areas and to maintain an awareness of relevant current developments.

The layout of this book is designed to help students obtain a clear focus on the essential issues for examination purposes. Thus, key words are printed in *italic type* and critical material is identified by *indentation*. By contrast, material which may be thought of as 'further reading' is reproduced in *small-size print* and is enclosed within *boxes*. This material is relevant to the syllabus, and involves knowledge which will attract bonus marks if used correctly within examination answers, but it is not essential for the examination and may be omitted without loss of continuity. Included within the 'further reading' sections are many of the detailed statistics which support the discussion on areas such as the operations of banks and building societies, economic policy and the balance of payments. The examiners do not expect students to memorise detailed economic and financial statistics; but a working knowledge of the *recent magnitudes of key variables* and the *broad trends* within the monetary and financial system is required. The level of detail which students should aim for is clearly visible within the main body of the text.

Many students fail examinations not through a lack of knowledge, but rather through an inability to apply their knowledge to *answering examination questions*. In order to address this problem, each chapter includes a section entitled 'Examination Practice', which students would be well advised to study carefully. Each of these sections includes either five or six examination questions, each with guidance notes highlighting the essential components of answers and their common weaknesses. There are also detailed references to the parts of the text where the material required to answer each question may be accessed. The majority of questions may be answered by drawing upon the chapter within which they are set. However, the nature of the syllabus and the form of the examination are such that students should be prepared for questions which straddle two or more topic areas. Therefore some questions are included in this book which draw upon material covered in two or more chapters. Questions marked † require reference to earlier chapters, but so long as the book is read in the normal sequence of chapters, this should present no undue difficulty. A small number of questions, marked ‡, require material from later chapters in order to answer some of their parts. Students may wish to return to these questions once the relevant part of the book has been studied.

The questions listed in the 'Examination Practice' sections of chapters 1 and 4 to 10 are drawn from past examination papers in *The Monetary and Financial System* and its predecessor *Monetary Economics*. However, as the topic areas covered by some of chapter 2 and all of chapter 3 were only introduced into the syllabus for *The Monetary and Financial System* in 1993, new questions have been formulated, which, it is hoped, will give students some impression of the form and standard of questions which are likely to be set in future examination papers on *The Monetary and Financial System*. Students are strongly recommended to use the 'Examination

Practice' sections as the basis for self-study and for revision. Before consulting the guidance notes, it may be a good idea to map out answers to the questions listed. Indeed, students might wish to set mock examinations for themselves by picking at random one question from each of eight chapters, and then attempting to answer four of these questions under examination conditions. (The examination is three hours in duration, and students have a free choice of four questions from nine, which will normally be spread across most topic areas within the syllabus.)

Despite having undertaken serious and well-planned courses of study, students may still experience difficulties as a result of not thinking through their approach to the examination paper before entering the examination room. Students are likely to benefit by bearing in mind the following general advice (which will probably be of relevance for all Associateship Examinations):

(a) *Read the questions carefully.* At first sight questions will often appear to be unfamiliar and sometimes students panic needlessly, for it must be remembered that all questions are based on the syllabus, upon which preparation for the examination should have centred. Thus, the initial problem is to identify the concepts and issues relevant to the question. Also questions are sometimes deliberately set to be ambiguous in order to test the student's insight into a particular problem. If there is doubt over the precise requirements of a question, then the particular approach taken should be justified in the answer, and, if time allows, comments should be made on other possible approaches.

(b) *Ensure that the questions are answered.* Students often lose marks by answering questions which they would like to see, rather than the ones that actually appear on the examination paper. However 'correct' the content of an answer may be, it will score few marks if it is not directed towards answering the examination question.

(c) *There is no such thing as an easy question; there are merely different types of questions.* A question which appears to be straightforward may have hidden dangers; in any event, it will most probably require a clear, detailed answer if good marks are to be obtained.

(d) *Note the instruction words carefully:* outline, describe, explain, assess, discuss, appraise, list, evaluate, and so on. Do not merely regurgitate paragraphs from textbooks or Examiners' Reports.

(e) *When an examination requires that four questions should be answered, then four questions should be answered.* Students answering too many questions waste their own time, as examiners will usually only consider the first four answers. Answering only three questions is very dangerous; remember that to obtain the overall 51% pass mark, an average of around 70% must be achieved on each of those answers.

(f) *Time should be allocated carefully.* There are often diminishing returns to effort in answering examination questions, and hence it is usually the case that answering three-quarters of four questions will pick up more marks than answering just three complete questions. In addition, the student who believes that he or she has finished within the time allowed should remain seated and think about the possible reasons for this. It may be that relevant items have been omitted from answers, or that a question has been misinterpreted. If time allows, the answers should be read through, necessary corrections made, and so on. Indeed, there is no reason why footnotes should not be included; in general examiners will take these into account, and an extra mark can make the difference between a pass and a fail.

(g) *It is important to plan answers.* A plan at the beginning of an answer will not gain marks in itself, and should not be allowed to absorb more than a few minutes of examination time. However, the structure of an answer is important, and a clear plan of attack will aid exposition. Students often possess the relevant knowledge, but appear incapable of using it in a coherent and logical manner in order to deal with an examination question.

(h) *It is a sad fact of life that marks are not given for the possession of knowledge or intellectual ability; they are only given for what is written down on the examination answer script.* Students are strongly advised to memorise this point.

(i) *Presentation, spelling and grammatical constructions* do not attract marks in themselves. However, it should be remembered that there may be instances of doubt over the interpretation of a student's answers, and a good quality of presentation can only help to sway the examiner in favour of the student.

Finally, when preparing for Associateship Examinations, students should remember that The Chartered Institute of Bankers produces a range of extremely useful study aids:

- *Lesson Programmes* set out in detail the material which needs to be covered for each syllabus and specify the boundaries of individual topics and the depth of knowledge required. This booklet also provides suggested schemes of work which may be used in conjunction with college courses or private study.

- *Examiners' Reports* contain question papers from previous examinations and the examiners' comments on candidates' answers, together with notes on the key points required of good answers. These booklets provide a mine of useful information on the trends within examinations and the examiners' thinking on major issues, and hence should be regarded as essential reading for all students.

- *Updating Notes* are published annually and offer concise summaries of important recent developments of relevance for each examination syllabus.
- 'Signpost' articles appearing in *Banking World* should be studied carefully by all students. These articles normally cover topical developments relating to specific areas of examination syllabuses, and are often written by the Chief Examiners for the subjects.

1 MONEY AND INFLATION

1.1 THE ECONOMIC IMPORTANCE OF MONEY

Modern economies are based on the principle of *specialisation* (division of labour). There are very few people who are self-sufficient in any meaningful sense, and the typical individual depends upon the production of goods and services by other people. In turn he or she is likely to specialise in the production of particular services or a fairly narrow range of goods, often in collaboration with other individuals also specialising in the same line of production. Without this specialisation living standards would be extremely low, as individuals would be unable to develop specific skills, instead having to spread their efforts over the production of basic items, such as food, shelter and clothing, required for survival. Also, the significant economies of scale, so vital to the efficiency of modern production processes, would be lost. However, despite the clear advantages arising from specialisation for society as a whole, it does not automatically follow that specialisation is without problems. Indeed, for both individuals and groups there is always the risk that they will be unable to sell the goods or services which they have decided to produce or to offer. Clearly, they could face great difficulties if they devoted all their time and efforts to producing output or to developing skills which are then not desired by other people, and hence which cannot be sold in exchange for other goods and services. Therefore, in general, specialisation will only be undertaken if there is some prospect for *trade* to take place. Today, however, in most Western countries, the inability to trade is rarely fatal, as state welfare systems stand ready to provide at least a minimum level of support to those individuals who are unable (or unwilling) to produce saleable output.

The most basic form of trade is pure *barter*. This occurs where goods or services are traded directly for other goods or services. The successful operation of this form of trade requires a *double coincidence of wants*. That is, it is not sufficient merely for the vendor of a product to find some other person who is willing to purchase that product; the prospective purchaser must also be willing to provide in exchange some other good or service which is acceptable to the vendor. The potential problems involved in completing a transaction may be great, especially as many goods are variable in quality, not easily divisible, and possibly perishable. Thus, barter trade is extremely inefficient, involves high transactions costs, and consequently undermines the willingness of people to specialise.

1

An important stage in economic development came with the evolution of the *market system*. The coming together of individuals at a particular time and place to trade specific types of goods served to reduce transactions costs, and hence the risks arising from specialisation. However, there still remained the need to establish a double coincidence of wants. The way to by-pass this requirement was found through the evolution of a generally acceptable intermediary substance in all trading processes. Thus, if it is known that in general people will always accept one specific commodity in exchange for goods and services, the vendor of a particular product merely has to find some other person willing to purchase his product in exchange for the generally acceptable commodity. The vendor may then use this commodity, at some other time and at some other place, to purchase the goods and services which he or she requires.

The introduction of a generally acceptable trading commodity greatly reduces transactions costs and encourages greater economic specialisation by reducing the risks associated with trading activity. This intermediary commodity, the existence of which is regarded as being crucial to the maintenance of high living standards in the Western world, is referred to as *money*.

1.2 A GENERAL DEFINITION OF MONEY

Money may be defined as any *generally acceptable medium of exchange*. Within any society it is necessary that the vast majority of people are willing to accept a particular substance in exchange for their goods or services before that substance may be regarded as being money. Clearly, people would be unwilling to give up their own products in exchange for a commodity that may be of little direct use to them, unless there is a reasonably good chance that it can be exchanged for goods and services as desired.

1.3 THE MAJOR TYPES OF MONEY

Money may exist in several different forms, each of which differs in terms of its physical nature and general acceptability, as well as the costs its utilisation involves for society:

(a) *Commodity monies.* These money substances have an *intrinsic use value,* in addition to their value as a medium of exchange, and this is likely to enhance their general acceptability. Gold and silver are, perhaps, the best examples of such money, but any valued commodities may be used in this role. As might be expected, early forms of money were invariably commodity monies.

(b) *Representative monies*. The value of these money substances is to be found largely in their *purchasing power*; they have little value in their own physical substance. Banknotes and coin in the modern economy are representative money, and widespread *confidence* in their purchasing power is vital to the successful operation of the monetary system. In most countries the acceptability of notes and coin is supported by the coercive powers of the state. Thus, in the UK, banknotes issued by the Bank of England and by the Scottish and Northern Ireland clearing banks are known as *legal tender*, in the sense that the law requires that they must be accepted in discharge of debt. Coins produced by the Royal Mint (and distributed by the Bank of England) are also legal tender up to certain maximum total values for each denomination.

(c) *Token monies*. These forms of money do not exist in any physical form, but rather involve *financial claims*, such as bank or building society deposits, which may be transferred via the chequing system as a means of discharging debt. The acceptability of token monies depends critically upon *confidence* in the financial system, and ultimately upon their convertability into representative or even commodity monies should this be desired by the holder.

1.3.1 The relative costs and benefits

Commodity monies are useful as a means of building confidence in the money concept; however they involve the withdrawal of commodities from their alternative uses, and hence are *wasteful* of resources.

The production of representative monies, which involves use of only small amounts of scarce resources, is clearly an improvement in respect of the costs to society of using money. However, the major problem with the utilisation of low cost money, such as banknotes, is that the producer, which is normally the country's central bank, may be tempted to produce *excessive amounts*, perhaps as a means of providing the government with purchasing power. This, in turn, is likely to have implications for the rate of *inflation* (as will be explained below), and hence for confidence in the money substance.

The possible problem of over-production of money becomes even more serious once private sector institutions are free to create token money. In consequence, the control of money supply growth is an important *policy issue* for the monetary authorities. The need for an adequate supply of money within the economy is without doubt, but so too is the need to avoid the generation of inflationary pressures which may be very damaging to the economy.

3

1.4 THE QUALITY OF MONEY

It is possible to assess the quality of different forms of money in terms of the characteristics which they possess:

(a) *Acceptability*. By definition a substance must be generally acceptable if it is to be regarded as money. However, the extent of this acceptability and the willingness of people to accept some forms of money in preference to others, are important indicators of the quality of money.

(b) *Portability*. Money should be easy to transport, and hence physically convenient for the user.

(c) *Divisibility*. In order that transactions of all values may be undertaken, it is necessary that money should be divisible into very small units of purchasing power.

(d) *Durability*. People will only accept a money substance in exchange for their own products if they believe that the substance will maintain its key physical characteristics, at least until after the time at which it is planned to spend the money. In addition, the less durable is the money substance the greater is the cost to society in maintaining the money stock.

(e) *Homogeneity*. Ideally, the individual components of the money stock should be of the same physical form, or, if a number of substances are used as money, they should be perfectly interchangeable. If this is not so, it is likely that confidence in the monetary system will be undermined, and the benefits arising from using money will be reduced.

(f) *Recognisability*. The requirement for special expertise or the expenditure of time and effort to identify a money substance would seriously detract from its usefulness as money. Clearly, the more easily recognised is the substance, the better will be its quality as money, other things being equal. There is also the related issue that money should not be easily forgeable.

In the light of the above-listed characteristics, it is not surprising that the grading of money according to its quality is extremely difficult. Indeed, over time and in differing circumstances, the relative qualities of money substances are also likely to differ. Thus, for example, a commodity money such as gold bullion may be quite appropriate for very large scale international transactions. It would be wholly inappropriate for the day-to-day payments made by the ordinary individual. In the latter case, the portability of banknotes or a cheque book, together with the associated divisibility and homogeneity of the representative or token money, normally make these forms of spending power far more attractive than the use of a commodity money. However, if political unrest or economic crises should occur, the intrinsic value of commodity money is likely to enhance its attractiveness relative to token monies which depend upon confidence in the financial system for their purchasing power.

Finally, it should be recognised that if the amount of goods or services which may be purchased with a given volume of money alters over time, this introduces a special sort of risk into the holding of money. In itself this is not the extreme risk that other people will not accept the substance in exchange for their products, but rather that they will only accept it on progressively more inferior terms. However, if the loss of purchasing power of the money substance becomes great, it may cause that substance to become unacceptable as a medium of exchange, and hence to lose its key money characteristic. Clearly, the stability of purchasing power of a money substance is not one of its inherent physical properties, rather it depends upon the economic environment within which the money is used. The relationship between the supply of money and the purchasing power of money (or the rate of inflation) is still somewhat controversial, and is examined in detail in sections 1.10.1 to 1.10.3 below.

1.5 FUNCTIONS OF MONEY

1.5.1 Medium of exchange

If a substance is not generally acceptable as a medium of exchange then it is not money. However, money performs a number of other functions, some or all of which may be performed by assets which are not generally acceptable as media of exchange, and hence which are not classed as money. These functions are: store of value, unit of account, and standard for deferred payment.

1.5.2 Store of value

Wealth may be held in the form of money. It is often the case that individuals and organisations do not wish to spend the whole of their income immediately on consumption or capital expenditures, and instead may accumulate financial wealth, with the view to making expenditures at a future date. A major advantage in holding money, for what is sometimes referred to as its *'asset' function*, is that this form of wealth is immediately spendable, and may be used directly to purchase other forms of wealth or goods and services. In most cases, wealth stored in the form of non-money financial assets (for example, government bonds or equity shares), real assets and commodities has to be turned into money before it can be used to make purchases, and this is likely to take time and effort, and is not without risk of capital loss when such wealth is liquidated.

A major disadvantage in holding wealth in the form of money is that it loses *real purchasing power* as prices rise. The higher is the rate of *inflation*, the greater is the loss of real wealth per period of time. There are only two exceptions to this statement: first, where a commodity money is used and the real intrinsic value of the commodity is maintained; secondly, where the money used attracts interest payments (for example, interest-bearing bank deposits) which more than compensate for the loss of purchasing power of the initial sum of money held.

Whilst the real (potential purchasing power) value of non-money financial assets is also affected by inflation, the return on the assets, in the form of interest or dividend payments, normally provides some *compensation* for the effects of inflation. However, it must be remembered that the resale market price of marketable financial assets may fall and there is always the possibility of outright default on securities and direct loans, and hence such non-money assets need not necessarily be better stores of value than money, even in times of inflation. A similar position exists in respect of wealth held in the form of physical assets, which may generate capital losses if they are sold.

1.5.3 Unit of account

Money acts as a *common denominator* for the valuation of goods, services and assets. By using money values it is easy to compare directly the relative values of all traded goods and services, irrespective of their absolute values. Consequently, trade is made much easier, and hence economic development is facilitated. Also, the valuation of assets for insurance or taxation purposes is made feasible. Nevertheless, it should be recognised that non-money commodities, such as barrels of oil, may be used to value transactions, although such occurrences are today rather rare. One possible advantage in using a non-money commodity for this purpose is that prices may be fixed in real terms independently of the effects of inflation.

1.5.4 Standard for deferred payment

Money is extremely useful where a transaction involves an agreement to make a payment at a future date. A promise to pay a certain amount of money in the future is likely to be more acceptable to a prospective creditor than a promise to hand over real goods or assets which might not even exist at the time of the initial transaction. Thus money is an important aspect of the credit mechanism, although once again the possibility of inflation occurring complicates the calculation of the terms upon which credit may be granted.

1.6 CONCEPT OF LIQUIDITY

The concept of liquidity is very closely related to the medium of exchange function of money. *Cash* is perfectly liquid and may always be used *immediately* for the purchase of goods and services. In general, a liquid asset is one which can be *turned into cash quickly and without capital loss or interest loss.* Thus, liquidity is a matter of degree, with cash at one end of the *liquidity spectrum* and physical assets, such as buildings and land, at the other end. The holders of relatively illiquid physical assets will normally incur transactions costs in turning them into cash, and may sometimes have to wait significant periods of time before finding buyers for the assets. There is also the risk of capital loss if an asset has to be sold at a time when market prices are low.

Financial assets may be placed on the liquidity spectrum between cash and physical assets, with their position depending upon their precise characteristics. Thus, any financial asset which is close to maturity may be regarded as being relatively liquid, irrespective of its original maturity. However, it is not sufficient that active markets exist for financial assets, as their sale prior to maturity may involve capital loss. It is the length of time taken to obtain the full nominal value of an asset which is the crucial factor in the strict interpretation of the liquidity concept. Thus, for example:

(a) *sight deposits* with banks or building societies constitute, for most purposes, near perfect liquidity;

(b) *seven-day time deposits* with banks are also very liquid, although strictly seven days' notice of withdrawal must be given by the holder if an interest penalty is to be avoided;

(c) *Treasury bills* issued with either a 91-day or a 63-day maturity can be thought of as being fairly liquid from their time of issue. 182-day bills are much less liquid at issue, but clearly the liquidity of all bills increases as their residual maturity decreases. The fact that Treasury bills may be sold on the money markets prior to maturity is not relevant for the strict definition of liquidity, although, depending upon market conditions, the shorter maturity bills may be sold quickly and with very little, if any, capital loss;

(d) *gilt-edged securities* usually have original maturities from five years upwards, with long-dated stock being in excess of 15 years. As these securities approach maturity their liquidity increases, but for most of their period in circulation they may be regarded as illiquid assets. In addition, although gilts are tradeable instruments, their generally long maturities make their market values extremely responsive to changes in market rates of interest, and thus serious capital loss may result from premature sale;

7

(e) *certificates of deposit* normally have original maturities ranging from 28 days to five years, and hence for liquidity purposes these negotiable instruments may be treated in the same way as either Treasury bills or gilt-edged securities;

(f) *building society term shares* are effectively deposits with building societies committed for fixed periods of time; they are not available on demand. Thus, these non-marketable assets cannot be considered as being liquid, but again the length of residual maturity will be crucial. It should also be noted that whilst some building society term shares may be cashed prior to maturity, this may be possible only with an interest penalty incurred;

(g) *ordinary equity shares in companies* are irredeemable except in special circumstances. Hence, whilst there is an active secondary market in company shares, they are not liquid according to the strict definition of liquidity. If a holder of equity shares requires cash at a time when the equity market is depressed, a capital loss may be made on the holding.

In the UK, the following assets are usually classed as being liquid:

- cash (banknotes and coin)
- sight and time deposits with banks
- building society deposits and shares (excluding term shares)
- National Savings Bank deposits and other National Savings instruments with easy access
- local authority deposits and bills
- Treasury bills
- certificates of tax deposit
- call money with discount houses (held by banks)
- commercial bills, sterling commercial paper and certificates of deposit (depending upon residual maturity).

1.7 MONEY IN THE MODERN ECONOMY

In the modern economy money is usually made up of *financial assets*, rather than real commodities. However, there is some ambiguity as to the precise components of the money supply, and the general uncertainty as to which assets should be included in the money supply for policy purposes has led to the evolution of a range of different definitions, as well as to considerable debate on the usefulness of such definitions.

1.7.1 Cash and sight deposits

Cash in circulation with the private sector is unambiguously an element of spending power; its legal tender status ensures its general acceptability. In addition, most people would include holdings of current account (sight) deposits at banks and building societies as part of the money supply. These deposits may be transferred through the cheque clearing system or by electronic means, and they are widely accepted in discharge of debt, especially when a cheque is backed by a cheque support card, effectively guaranteeing payment on the cheque by a bank or building society, up to a specified amount. However, it is important to understand that sight deposits are not legal tender; there is no legal duty to accept them in discharge of debt, and a creditor could insist on cash payment. The level of confidence in the financial system and in the ability of the payer to honour his cheque is extremely important. It must also be emphasised that the cheque itself is not money, it is merely a transfer document relating to money held in the form of sight deposits.

The possibility that payment by cheque may be refused makes sight deposits marginally less liquid than cash itself, but in the modern economy the difference is negligible. For practical purposes the total of cash and sight deposits gives a measure of immediate purchasing power.

1.7.2 Time deposits

The difficulties in determining the composition of the money supply begin to surface once we move beyond cash and sight deposits. Thus, whilst bank time deposits formally require seven days' notice of withdrawal, and whilst cheques may not be drawn directly on such deposits, UK banks will invariably transfer funds between time and sight accounts on demand. Consequently, given the time delay involved with the cheque clearing process, time deposits represent virtually immediate spending power, although a certain amount of inconvenience is experienced in organising the transfers between bank accounts. Therefore, it would seem to be appropriate to include bank time deposits in the measure of the money supply, due to their *high level of liquidity*. Indeed, very similar comments may be made in respect of savings deposits and shares with building societies which also offer full current account deposit facilities. In practice such assets are highly liquid, and may be regarded as part of private sector spending power.

1.7.3 Other financial assets

If the notion is accepted that liquid assets, which are somewhat less liquid than cash itself, may be included in the money measure, then the question arises as to which liquid assets, in addition to sight and time deposits, should be included. The answer to this question is obviously related to the liquidity of the assets involved, and to the precise reasons for holding the assets. Thus, it is generally agreed that *savings deposits and shares with building societies* should be included, even where the societies do not offer current account facilities. These assets may often be converted into cash or sight deposits on demand or at very short notice, and although it is not possible to draw cheques directly on these deposits and shares, the relatively long opening hours and convenient branch networks of many building societies make these funds virtually as good as bank time deposits for most people. By contrast, there is some controversy in respect of *National Savings Bank deposits, shorter-term National Savings instruments* and various *money market instruments* which, although not immediately spendable, are usually thought of as being relatively liquid assets.

It must be emphasised that there is *no obvious boundary* between liquid assets which are classified as money and other liquid assets which are not. The official definitions of the money supply (that is, the official monetary aggregates to be considered in 1.8 below) are not the only ones which may be specified. The extent to which the definitions are carried beyond the immediate purchasing power of cash and into what might be called *'near-money'* or *'quasi-money'* assets, appearing some way down the liquidity spectrum, will depend upon the reason for obtaining a money measure in the first place.

1.7.4 The need for definitions of money

The monetary authorities of most developed countries consider it to be necessary to *monitor*, and often to *target*, their nation's money supply growth. The reason for this action is a generally held belief that the rate of money supply growth has an *important influence on other key economic variables*. In particular, it is thought to be a major determinant of the *rate of inflation*, especially in the longer term. Also, either through its effect on the rate of inflation, or perhaps more directly through its influence on aggregate demand or the level of interest rates, the money supply may affect the *rate of economic growth*, the *level of unemployment* and the *balance of payments*. Consequently, it is probable that the authorities will seek to maintain the growth of the money supply within certain limits, and hence close monitoring of its progress is vital. The setting of targets for money supply growth is also seen as being important, both in terms of providing a *discipline* for the application of monetary controls, and in convincing those people responsible for the fixing of prices and wages that the authorities are serious about controlling inflation. Indeed, it may be argued that influencing *expectations of inflation* within the economy is a critical aspect of any anti-inflation policy, and that monetary targets are crucial in this respect.

Unfortunately, there is *disagreement* amongst economists as to the timing and precise nature of the effects of changes in monetary aggregates on economic activity, and *uncertainty* is expressed as to which group or groups of money assets should be the focus for official policy actions. Therefore, even if the authorities decide that there should be some control over the money supply, important questions remain as to which measure or measures of money should be controlled, and as to the optimal rate of money supply growth to aim for. It is largely due to this uncertainty, and to the widely held belief that *monetary conditions* should be controlled, rather than one specific set of money assets, that statistics relating to *several definitions* of the money supply are collected.

There is a clear need to develop measures of the money supply in the light of *practical experience* with existing measures and in the face of a *continually evolving financial sector*, where money assets may be introduced in response to the financial requirements of the private sector. Indeed, some developments in respect of official measures of monetary aggregates have attempted to introduce explicit recognition of why people hold specific money assets, rather than simply take all holdings of particular groups of assets as being homogeneous for money definition purposes.

1.8 BANK OF ENGLAND'S OFFICIAL MONETARY AGGREGATES

There are currently four official monetary aggregates used in the UK:

M0 = notes and coin in circulation outside of the Bank of England
+ banks' operational deposits with the Bank of England
M2 = M4 private sector holdings of notes and coin
+ M4 private sector holdings of sterling retail deposits with UK banks
+ M4 private sector holdings of sterling retail deposits and shares with UK building societies
M4 = M4 private sector holdings of notes and coin
+ M4 private sector holdings of sterling deposits (including sterling certificates of deposit) with UK banks
+ M4 private sector holdings of sterling shares and deposits (including sterling certificates of deposit) with UK building societies
M3H = M4
+ M4 private sector holdings of foreign currency deposits with UK banks and building societies
+ sterling and foreign currency deposits held by UK public corporations with UK banks and building societies

Notes:
  (i)   M4 private sector = UK non-bank non-building society private sector.
  (ii) Notes and coin relate exclusively to holdings of sterling.
  (iii) M2 is a sub-set of M4. Hence M4 may also be specified as: M4 = M2 + M4 private sector holdings of all other sterling deposits (including sterling certificates of deposit) with UK banks and all other sterling shares and deposits (including sterling certificates of deposit) with UK building societies.
  (iv) Banks' 'retail' deposits are defined as deposits which arise from a customer's acceptance of an advertised rate (including nil) for a particular product. Typically, banks' retail deposits are taken via their branch networks.
  (v)   Building societies' 'retail' shares and deposits include all shares held by, and sums deposited by, individuals. Also included are shares and deposits placed with societies in accordance with the terms of contractual savings schemes operated by banks and friendly societies acting as intermediaries for individuals and, where a building society has so elected, shares and deposits of under £50,000 from corporate bodies.
  (vi) The term M3H is used to describe an aggregate which embodies more components than M4 simply because of the Bank of England's desire to maintain consistency of terminology with that used for comparable aggregates measured in other EC countries.

During the late-1980s, the official definitions of the money supply used in the UK underwent a series of changes. Of particular note was the abandonment, in July 1989, of the M1, M3 and M3c measures, which comprised solely UK non-bank private sector holdings of notes and coin and various groupings of bank deposits. In April 1991, the Bank of England also ceased publication of M4c (M4 plus foreign currency deposits of the M4 private sector with UK banks and building societies) and M5 (M4 plus a range of money market and National Savings instruments held by the M4 private sector). However, recognising the potential importance for spending decisions of liquid asset holdings falling outside of the M4 definition, in April 1991 the Bank of England began the publication of statistics on a wide range of such assets, including M4 private sector holdings of sterling bank bills, foreign currency deposits with UK banks and building societies, Treasury bills, local authority debt, certificates of tax deposit, National Savings instruments, sterling commercial paper, short maturity gilts and sterling unused credit facilities. These assets, together with several others, are included in the Bank of England's list on account of their close substitutability for money assets.

1.8.1 Narrow and broad money

The different measures of the money supply may be divided into two groups:

(a) *Narrow measures of money* embody assets which may be used as immediate purchasing power. Narrow money is held for transactions (medium of exchange) purposes. It is normal to include the M2 measure in this group. M0 may also be included, although this measures base money, and does not relate directly to private sector purchasing power as it is normally defined.

(b) *Broad measures of money* embody the assets included under the narrow money heading, and in addition, assets which are held, at least partly, for their store of value characteristic, but which are also liquid. Thus, broad measures of money include assets such as bank time deposits and building society shares, which may be turned into purchasing power quickly, but which also earn interest and hence may be held as effective stores of values. Broad measures of money include M3H and M4.

1.8.2 The liabilities of financial institutions

As money assets held by individuals and organisations in the modern economy are financial assets, they have as their counterpart financial liabilities. Therefore, whilst it is normal to refer to measures of money as reflecting holdings of various groups of assets, it is equally acceptable to consider money definitions in terms of the liabilities of financial institutions. Table 1.1 classifies the relevant liabilities of the Bank of England, commercial banks and building societies according to the currently published measures of money within which they are to be found.

Table 1.1 Components of official monetary aggregates

	Narrow definitions	Broad definitions
Bank of England liabilities		
Banknotes*	M0, M2	M3H, M4
Banks' operational deposits	M0	—
Commercial bank liabilities		
Sterling retail deposits	M2	M3H, M4
Sterling non-retail deposits	—	M3H, M4
Sterling certificates of deposit	—	M3H, M4
Foreign currency deposits of UK residents and businesses	—	M3H

Building society liabilities

Sterling retail shares and deposits	M2	M3H, M4
Sterling non-retail shares and deposits	—	M3H, M4
Sterling certificates of deposit	—	M3H, M4
Foreign currency deposits of UK residents and businesses	—	M3H

Note:

*Coin is not a liability of the Bank of England; it is merely distributed by the Bank and is produced by the Royal Mint. It is included in all measures of the money supply, both narrow and broad.

1.8.3 Evolution of the official monetary aggregates

Between late 1976 and March 1987, the *M3* measure (initially referred to as £M3) was the major target of official monetary controls in the UK. However, in his 1987 Budget speech the Chancellor of the Exchequer announced that M3 was to be dropped as an official target. The authorities had experienced only limited success in controlling M3, but more fundamentally there were increasing difficulties arising in the interpretation of M3 and hence in determining its relevance for private sector expenditure decisions. One problem was that the M3 measure included bank balances held for *investment purposes*, which were unlikely to have a major influence on private sector expenditures. A more serious problem had been the increasing *substitutability* between *bank deposits* and *building society deposits and shares*, to the point where many people saw little difference between bank and building society current accounts, and between bank and building society savings accounts. Ultimately, the authorities accepted the view that the changes which had been taking place within the UK financial system during the 1980s, had caused M3 to become increasingly distorted as a measure of private sector purchasing power, and hence increasingly irrelevant for policy purposes. Consequently, in July 1989, the Bank of England ceased publication of both the M3 and M3c aggregates; although at the same time M4c was introduced. The immediate cause of the Bank's decision would appear to have been the conversion of Abbey National Building Society to the status of a retail bank.

The abandonment of the M3 and M3c measures may be viewed as a continuation of a process which was begun by the Bank of England in May 1987. At that time the Bank announced that the *broad measures of money* were to be *reclassified*. Specifically, £M3 was relabelled M3, and the former M3 (at that time the only aggregate to include foreign currency deposits) became M3c. But of much greater significance was the introduction of *M4*, embodying exclusively bank and building society liabilities. The former measure of private sector liquidity, PSL2, was relabelled M5, and the slightly narrower measure of liquidity, PSL1, was abandoned. Thus, the Bank of England established a series of monetary aggregates ranging from M0 to M5, which did not attempt to distinguish between the technical concepts of money and liquidity.

The reclassification was considered to be necessary in the light of the high degree of *deregulation* and *financial innovation*, which had been taking place since the early 1980s. Quite simply, it was believed that the then existing classification did not provide a true reflection of the range of financial assets available within the UK financial system, or of the changing activities of the major financial institutions. In particular, the authorities were concerned to recognise the rapid evolution of the building societies, which were increasingly moving into the provision of banking facilities. The greater freedom endowed upon the building societies by the Building Societies Act 1986, had merely served to accelerate the provision of full current account facilities (complete with cheque books and a range of money transmission services), and the distinction between the major building societies and the retail banks was becoming increasingly blurred. Consequently, the M4 aggregate was introduced as a means of bringing together all the private sector sterling bank deposits and building society deposits and shares, within a single measure of the money supply which would not be distorted by the switching of funds between the different groups of institutions. The importance of M4 for government *monetary policy* was formally recognised by the Chancellor of the Exchequer's Autumn Statement in November 1992. Here it was announced that the authorities would, in future, set a *monitoring range* (although not a formal target band) for the growth of M4. It was explained that deviations of M4 growth from this monitoring range would be taken into account in the setting of interest rates for monetary policy purposes.

The Bank of England's decision, in April 1991, to cease publication of the *M4c* and *M5* measures was motivated largely by unease as to the relevance of the assets included in addition to those embodied in M4. *The increasing flexibility and sophistication of financial instruments and markets* meant that there was a growing range of assets which could be converted into spending power fairly easily. Consequently, rather than maintain broader measures of money which were likely to become increasingly controversial, the authorities decided to begin the publication of a series of statistics relating to a *wide range of liquid assets* falling outside of the M4 measure. These statistics might be thought of as giving some indication of monetary conditions in general, and their publication allows for more detailed analysis of monetary trends to be undertaken.

Somewhat ironically, pressure for a consistent approach to be taken to the evaluation of *monetary trends across EC countries as a whole* caused the Bank of England, in August 1992, to introduce a new broad measure of money which bears great similarity to the previously abandoned M4c. The *M3H* measure (which was given its title purely on the grounds of consistency of terminology with similar measures adopted by other EC countries) reintroduced UK private sector holdings of foreign currency deposits with UK banks and building societies into an official broad monetary aggregate. It also includes sterling and foreign currency deposit holdings of UK public sector corporations, which makes it unique amongst official money measures. However, there must be some doubt as to the relevance of M3H for domestic policy purposes. The Government's privatisation programme and public sector funding rules mean that deposits held by the public sector corporations that remain are normally relatively small, whilst foreign currency balances are often used to finance overseas (as opposed to domestic) economic activities. In addition, evidence provided by the Bank of England would suggest that these components of M3H have tended to behave more erratically than have the components of M4.

Major changes in respect of the narrower measures of money were initiated when the Bank of England abandoned the *M1* aggregate in July 1989. Despite its use as a target for monetary controls between 1982 and 1984, the M1 measure had been the subject of widespread criticism for many years on a number of counts. In particular, the high proportion of non-interest-bearing elements within M1 tended to make its value quite *sensitive* to interest rate movements (as holders of such elements often switched to liquid assets not included within M1 when interest rates rose), whilst the effect on private sector spending power was often only very small. In addition, the *exclusion* of certain very liquid bank deposits and building society sight deposits meant that it gave a relatively distorted picture of immediate purchasing power held by the private sector. Therefore, the significance of M1 had been decreasing for a considerable period of time before its final abandonment.

The narrow measure of money M2 was introduced in June 1982, with the view to providing a measure which was more closely related to the value of *total transactions in goods and services* than were the then existing money supply measures. Initially, the Bank of England used the criteria of maturity, size and type of deposits in order to identify the private sector transactions balances to be included in M2. This approach was altered in December 1992 due to the increasing difficulty being experienced by banks and building societies in measuring such balances. Since that time, the emphasis has been placed upon a definition of *retail deposits* which can be applied consistently by banks and building societies, and which centres upon the collection of funds via *branch networks* from personal and smaller business customers. In consequence, M2 was made a sub-set of M4, and hence may be referred to as *retail deposits and cash in M4*.

Since its introduction, M2 has never played a major role in official policy actions, at least publicly. However, recognising the continuing need for the authorities to be able to identify money assets held primarily for transactions purposes, it is quite likely that the recently modified M2 measure will take on a higher profile in future.

The only monetary aggregate which remains to be considered is *M0*. This was introduced in 1984, on the grounds that the then dominant measure of narrow money, M1, was becoming increasingly difficult to interpret. It was argued by the authorities that M0 would provide a better indicator of *monetary conditions* in the economy, and would be more suitable as a basis for the formulation of monetary policy. Also, the political advantages in targeting an aggregate which had been relatively well behaved over a sustained period of time, were probably not irrelevant to the authorities' action.

The M0 measure may be thought of as the odd one out amongst the monetary aggregates, for in itself it is clearly not a measure of the money supply in terms of relating to assets reflecting private sector purchasing power (available either immediately or within a short period of time). Also, the inclusion of banking sector operational deposits at the Bank of England (which are effectively the working balances of the banking sector) is unique to UK measures of the money supply. Nevertheless, between March 1984 and March 1993 M0 was a *target* for monetary controls, and from March 1987 it was the only monetary aggregate for which a target was published. The officially stated reason for the targeting of M0 was that it gave the authorities some control over an important aspect of monetary conditions within the economy. However, economists hold mixed views on the importance of M0 for policy purposes. Some economists would argue that the volume of base money is critical to the determination of the overall volume of liquidity within the economy, and hence that the growth rate of M0 gives a good indication of future monetary trends. Others would argue that M0 merely reflects current transactions, and that the relationship between M0 and the broader measures of purchasing power within the economy is so distant that its policy relevance is minimal. The only conclusion which may be drawn at this stage is that the position of M0 remains somewhat controversial. This fact was effectively recognised by the authorities, in March 1993, when the formal growth target for M0 was replaced by a less rigid *monitoring range*. Deviations from this monitoring range are taken into account by the authorities when setting monetary controls.

1.9   THE REAL VALUE OF MONEY

1.9.1   Price indices

The real value of a unit of money is measured by the *physical quantities of goods and services which it will purchase*. Clearly, the higher is the money price of any particular good, the smaller is the quantity which may be purchased with a given outlay of money; and, conversely, the greater is the amount of money that is required in order to buy a given volume of the good.

The usual approach to measuring changes in the real value of money is to examine changes in the amount of money required to purchase a particular 'basket' of goods at different points in time, and thus to create a price index. For example, a given basket of goods may have the following prices on 30 June of each of the years shown:

1989	£50.00
1990	£54.30
1991	£57.67
1992	£59.80
1993	£61.30

Thus, during the year to 30 June 1990 the amount of money required to purchase the basket of goods rose by £4.30, or 8.6% of the amount required at the beginning of the period. Therefore, in terms of this particular basket of goods, the price level rose by 8.6% during the year, and hence if the price of the basket on the base date of 30 June 1989 is given an index of 100, the price index on 30 June 1990 is 108.6.

In general, price index values are calculated using the formula:

$$\text{Index at time X} = \frac{\text{Price of the basket of goods at time X}}{\text{Price of the basket of goods at base date}} \times 100$$

Thus, in the above example, the price indices on 30 June in each of 1991, 1992 and 1993 are 115.3, 119.6 and 122.6 respectively. These indices are extremely useful as they show directly the percentage increase in the price level between the base date and any selected index date. In consequence individuals and institutions are able to calculate conveniently the real value of changes in incomes, costs and asset prices over time, and hence are able to determine the implications of price changes for living standards and the real value of wealth holdings.

1.9.2 The problems in using price indices

As there are many different baskets of goods and services which may be used as the basis for constructing a price index, there is always a certain amount of *ambiguity* associated with the measurement of the real value of money. Indices may differ both in terms of the actual goods and services included in the basket, and in terms of the weights attached to each item (that is, the amounts of each item included). Therefore, as the prices of individual goods and services need not necessarily move in proportion to each other, the composition of the index basket is vital to the assessment of changes in the real value of money.

In the UK, the authorities publish a number of price indices, constructed so that they reflect the average expenditure patterns of particular groups within society. However, for any given individual, even the most relevant index is likely to provide only an *approximate measure* of changes in real purchasing power over time. The problem is compounded by changes in expenditure patterns over time, both for individuals and for groups in society as a whole. Altering the weights of items within indices or changing their base years only serves to make the calculation of the real value of money that much more complex.

1.9.3 UK price indices

The most commonly quoted price index in the UK is the *general index of retail prices*. This is thought to give a reasonable indication of the rate of inflation in consumer prices for the average household. It is in relation to this index that state benefits, such as pensions and unemployment pay, are fixed, and an important element in many wage negotiations would appear to be movements in this index.

The rate of inflation as indicated by the index of retail prices is often referred to as the *headline rate of inflation*. The *underlying rate of inflation* is calculated by removing the effect of changes in mortgage interest payments from the headline rate. It is in relation to this adjusted index of retail prices that, since October 1992, the Government has set a *target range for inflation* as a key aspect of its economic policy. A problem for the Government in using the unadjusted index of retail prices is that a tightening of monetary policy, designed to reduce inflation (by raising interest rates and hence damping down consumer demand), may, in fact, lead to an increase in the recorded rate of inflation in the short term, due to higher mortgage interest payments. The Government's preferred measure of underlying inflation avoids the undesirable impact which this occurrence may otherwise have on inflationary expectations within the economy. Of course, it has to be recognised that expenditure on housing services forms a significant part of total household spending, and so merely ignoring changes in mortgage interest payments is itself likely to distort the measurement of the purchasing power of money. This point emphasises the importance of considering a range of measures of inflation, noting the inherent weaknesses of all price indices. Indeed, recognising the problems associated with mortgage interest payments, the Bank of England has constructed a *housing-adjusted retail price index* (or HARP index), which replaces mortgage interest payments with an alternative measure of owner-occupied housing costs.

The authorities also publish a range of other measures of inflation, including *producer price indices*, relating to the costs of materials and fuels purchased by manufacturing industry and the prices of manufactured output, and *pensioner price indices* for both one- and two-person households. In addition, there is the *implied deflator for gross domestic product* (GDP), which may be used as an index for measuring overall price changes for goods and services produced in the UK economy. The implied deflator for GDP is calculated by dividing the value of GDP at current prices by GDP measured at constant (base year) prices.

Table 1.2 shows a selection of price indices for the period 1980 to 1992. It is interesting to note the significant differences in index movements which may arise in the shorter term; although history has shown that over longer periods of time the general trends of most recognised prices indices have been very similar.

Table 1.2   **Selected UK Price Indices, 1980–1992** (Base year 1985 = 100)

	Producer Price Index: Materials and fuel purchased by manufacturers	Pensioner Price Index: Two-person household	General Index of Retail Prices Index	General Index of Retail Prices Percentage increase on year earlier
1980	73.3	71.3	70.7	18.0
1981	80.1	79.5	79.1	11.9
1982	86.0	86.7	85.9	8.6
1983	91.9	90.7	89.8	4.6
1984	99.0	95.3	94.3	5.0
1985	100.0	100.0	100.0	6.1
1986	92.3	103.2	103.4	3.4
1987	95.3	105.8	107.7	4.2
1988	98.4	109.8	113.0	4.9
1989	104.0	115.8	121.8	7.8
1990	103.8	124.5	133.3	9.5
1991	102.6	133.5	141.1	5.9
1992	103.1	138.7	146.4	3.7

Source: *Economic Trends*, Central Statistical Office, various issues.

1.9.4   Index-linking of financial assets

The existence of *price inflation,* and hence the erosion of the real value of money over time, undermines the *store of value* property of money and calls into question the desirability of holding financial assets denominated in money terms. Where a financial asset pays no interest, for example an ordinary current account with a bank, the problem is obvious. However, where interest is paid, some *compensation* for the loss of real capital value caused by inflation is obtained, and so long as the rate of interest remains above the rate of inflation, the asset provides a reasonably good store of value. Although as higher rates of interest tend to be paid on the less liquid financial assets, it is possible that the wealth holder may have to choose between holding a good store of value and holding 'immediate' purchasing power.

If inflation rates could be predicted accurately, it might be possible for a lender to seek an interest rate which provides adequate compensation for inflation over the life of the asset created when lending takes place. Unfortunately, accurate prediction of inflation rates is difficult to achieve, particularly into the longer term, and this introduces an additional element of *risk* into all borrowing/lending transactions. One method of overcoming this risk is to index-link the principal sum lent and the interest payments, as a means of protecting their real value.

Index-linking means that the borrower agrees to repay a sum of money at a future date which has the same purchasing power as the money initially borrowed, and in addition there will normally be a fixed percentage rate of interest payable on the index-linked nominal value of the principal. Thus, for example, if £1,000 is borrowed for a period of one year at an interest rate of 8%, the borrower will be expected to repay £1,080 at the end of the year, where there is no indexation. However, if the principal sum is linked to an appropriate price index, and this shows an inflation rate of 10% during the year for which the loan is outstanding, the borrower will have to repay an index-linked principal of £1,100, as well as a further 8% of this amount to cover the interest payment. Thus, in total, the borrower will repay £1,188, which represents a real return of 8% for the lender. (In practice, the existence of index-linking would probaby result in the lender being willing to reduce the rate of interest required on the loan.)

The use of indexation shifts the risk for the lender from the *real return* to be earned on the loan to the *nominal return.* In other words, the lender will not know in advance what amount of cash is to be received when the loan matures. By the same token the borrower has to make an *open-ended commitment* to repay whatever amount of cash is required to protect the real value of the loan and the associated interest payment. This is probably the main reason for the *unpopularity* of index-linked instruments amongst private sector borrowers. The fact that governments can always fall back on taxation or borrowing from their central bank should they experience cash flow problems as a result of index-linked commitments, is perhaps the reason why most index-linked debt in the UK is found to originate with the public sector. Since 1975 index-linked National Savings Certificates have been available, and in 1981 the Government introduced index-linked gilt-edged securities.

Finally, it should be recognised that the concept of indexation may be applied well beyond financial instruments. Potentially, any form of money-denominated transaction over time may be index-linked. Thus, salary and wage agreements, contracts for the delivery of goods in the future, and the calculation of the costs associated with business activities may all be related to selected price indices as a means of protecting the real financial positions of the parties involved. However, it should also be noted that in itself indexation is aimed at dealing with the *symptoms* of inflation, and does little to cure the problem itself, except, perhaps, through the *encouragement of saving*. Indeed, some economists would argue that widespread indexation may actually encourage *inflationary pressures* by reducing the fear of its effects on real living standards, and by *institutionalising regular price and/or wage rises*.

1.10 THE DETERMINATION OF THE VALUE OF MONEY

It was stated above that the real value of money depends upon the level of prices within the economy. However, it is also generally accepted that the amount of money available within the economy is itself an important determinant of the rate of price inflation. The arguments on the relationship between the money supply and the rate of inflation have continued unabated for most of the past half century, and there is still much *controversy* in respect of this issue. Nevertheless, it is possible to consider the broad economic principles involved in the relationship without becoming enmeshed in complex technical analysis. Indeed, an understanding of the basic mechanisms underlying the determination of the inflation rate within the economy is vital to an appreciation of the relevance of official monetary policy and control.

1.10.1 The quantity theory of money

A useful starting point for the analysis of the relationship between the money supply and the price level is the *Fisher formula* (sometimes referred to as the equation of exchange). This may be stated as:

$$MV = PT$$

where M = money supply;
       V = velocity of circulation of money (i.e. the number of times per period that the average unit of money changes hands);

P = average price level of all transactions;
T = number of transactions per period.

As MV gives the total value of all expenditures per period of time, and PT gives the total value of all sales per period of time, and as, by definition, for every sale there must be an expenditure of equal value, the Fisher formula is no more than a statement of fact; i.e. MV must be *identical* to PT by definition. The Fisher formula only becomes a theory of the price level when certain *assumptions* are made about the values of V and T.

Specifically, if it is assumed that V is effectively constant for significant periods of time (this being justified on the grounds that payments methods change only slowly) and that T is at or close to its full employment level (which is justified on the grounds that the price mechanism will adjust to ensure that unemployed resources are directed into employment), then the Fisher formula may be rewritten as:

$$P = \frac{MV}{T}$$

Thus, as V and T are taken to be constants, this equation effectively states that *the price level is proportional to the money supply* in the economy. The underlying rationale for this result is based on the assertion that people hold money only as a *medium of exchange;* they do not want money for itself, but rather for the goods, services and assets which it can purchase. Thus, it is argued that if people find that they are holding more money than they require to cover their desired transactions needs, they will tend to spend these excess balances on all forms of goods, services and assets. But as it is assumed that the economy is working at or near to full employment output, the result is that the excess money balances chase a relatively fixed supply of goods, services and assets, and hence prices are pushed upwards. The price level will continue to rise until all the available supply of money is required to cover the resulting higher nominal value of day-to-day expenditures.

The quantity theory of money is part of the *classical theory* of economics, and within this framework the level of output is determined by *real forces*, such as the productivity of labour and capital, the availability of labour, raw materials and capital, and the nature of technical innovation. As explained above, within this system money is neutral, in the sense that it determines only absolute prices, and does not affect the structure of relative prices and hence decisions on resource distribution. Also, it should be recognised that the quantity theory depends crucially upon assumptions which real world experience would tend to call into question. However, whilst the theory may be criticised on a number of counts, it may nevertheless be regarded as an important starting point for somewhat more sophisticated analysis which has drawn considerable support in recent years. In particular the classical view on money forms the basis of modern monetarism, which has had a very significant influence on official monetary policies since the mid-1970s.

1.10.2 Modern monetarism

The monetarist approach to the analysis of the effects of money on the economy may be thought of as being a more realistic version of the classical view on money. That is, although monetarists base their arguments on the Fisher formula, they take a more pragmatic position on the operation of the economy, and they acknowledge the real world evidence which serves to undermine the simple classical views. Thus, monetarists believe that V is *predictable*, and whilst it is recognised that its value might move about over time, it is suggested that its long-term trend value is fairly stable. They also recognise that in the short-term the market system may not adjust smoothly, and unemployed resources may be available; but they would argue that in the long term *market forces* will dominate activities, and hence that T does have a naturally determined long-term value. In addition, they argue that whilst individuals may be willing to hold any extra money balances which come into their possession, they will only do so if they believe that the benefit to be gained from the convenience of holding additional liquidity is greater than the benefit to be gained from the goods, services and assets which may be purchased with the funds. Thus, taking the economy as a whole it is likely that an increase in the money supply will lead to some additional expenditures on the whole range of goods, services and assets available within the economy.

According to monetarist thinking, an increase in the money supply may, in the short term, lead to an increase in output and employment in the economy, so long as unemployed resources are available. There may also be some reduction in interest rates if some of the new money is used to purchase interest-bearing financial assets (i.e. is made available for lending). However, monetarists go on to argue that as the economy will approach its full employment position naturally, given time, and as the velocity of circulation of money follows a stable and predictable trend, then the only permanent impact of the higher money supply is to *raise the price level* above what it otherwise would have been. In other words, the monetarists come to the same conclusion as the classical school of thought; namely that changes in the money supply primarily determine the rate of inflation, and have little effect on real output. The only fundamental difference is that monetarists see this result as occurring in the *long run*, whereas the classical school appears to imply that adjustments within the economy occur relatively quickly.

As monetarists believe that changes in the money supply have a direct and powerful effect on the economy, it might be thought that they would argue

continued on next page

in favour of using monetary policy as a means of managing the economy, perhaps influencing the rate of economic growth or the balance of payments position. However, this is not the case; for monetarists believe that the effects · of changes in the money supply are not only powerful, but also are unpredictable in their timing and precise magnitude. Thus, they argue that it is dangerous to manipulate the money supply with the view to managing the economy, as the effects of discretionary changes in the money supply might bite at the wrong time, and hence make matters worse, rather than better. Consequently, and in the light of the inflationary effects which it is argued will always occur when the money supply is allowed to grow excessively, monetarists favour strict *money supply growth rules*. They argue that if the supply of money in the economy is allowed to grow steadily and predictably over time, in line with the trend growth in real output in the economy, this will instil in the private sector a confidence in the monetary stability of the economy. To the extent that the money supply is allowed to grow at a faster rate than the growth in real output, then inflationary pressures will be generated.

1.10.3 Practical aspects of monetarism

During the late 1970s the UK government leaned increasingly towards monetarist principles in relation to the operation of monetary policy. With the return of a Conservative government in 1979, monetarism became the guiding light for policy formulation. The major issues relating to the implementation and operation of monetary policy in the UK since the early 1980s will be examined in Chapter 8. However, for the moment, it should be recognised that the simple interpretation of monetarism, as outlined above, has proven to be somewhat optimistic, at least on the experience of the 1980s. In particular, the UK monetary authorities have had only very limited success in achieving their money supply growth targets, but nevertheless the UK's inflation rate fell markedly during the first half of the 1980s. It would also appear that during more recent years there has been little discernible direct relationship between the growth of the money supply according to the measures which have featured in the official policy position and the rate of inflation.

One explanation which has been put forward for the apparent contradictions in the relationship between monetary conditions and the course of inflation relates to the effects of *financial innovation*. Specifically, it has been argued that as new types of financial instruments have been introduced, and as the characteristics of existing financial assets have altered, not only has the substitutability between financial assets increased, but also a wider range of assets have become attractive for their store of value properties. Therefore,

continued on next page

serious doubts have been raised about the appropriateness of the monetary aggregates which have been selected for policy purposes. In other words, supporters of the monetarist view have been made very much aware of the problems involved in defining money (and hence purchasing power) within the modern economy. They have also been faced with the fact that the willingness of individuals and organisations to hold money balances may alter over time as the characteristics of money assets alter, and as general economic conditions evolve. Consequently, confidence has been undermined in the application of simple mechanistic policy rules as propounded by the monetarists. Indeed, an alternative approach to the analysis of economic activity, known as the *Keynesian* school of thought, argues very strongly that the ability of the financial system to respond to pressures for the creation of credit and for the provision of new means of making payments will undermine attempts to reduce inflation via control of the money supply, at least in the short to medium term. Hence, Keynesians argue in favour of somewhat more direct controls on prices and incomes, and on the level of demand within the economy, as a means of easing inflationary pressures.

Nevertheless, there is still a general belief held by most economists that a faster rate of money supply growth, especially if this is reflected across a wide range of money supply measures, will ultimately cause the rate of inflation to be higher than it otherwise would have been. It is this belief which continues to drive economists to seek better explanations of the effects of changes in the money supply on the rate of inflation.

1.10.4 The problems caused by inflation

In order to understand the importance attached by governments to the defeat of inflation, and hence in order to understand the fundamental relevance of the controversy over the effects of money supply growth on inflation, it is necessary to appreciate the serious problems which may be caused by the occurrence of inflation.

It is, perhaps, appropriate to begin by recognising the impact of inflation upon the functions of money itself. The key *medium of exchange* function of money is unlikely to be affected significantly until inflation reaches very high levels. However, once so-called *'hyper-inflation'* is reached, the loss of value of conventional money becomes so rapid that, despite its benefits for transactions purposes, it may be abandoned in favour of real commodity money or barter trade. Moreover, once *general confidence* has been lost in the value of a country's money supply, it is extremely difficult for the authorities to re-establish monetary stability. The only viable solution in this case is likely to be the introduction of a completely new currency, with the possible adoption of a strong overseas currency as the valuation base for domestic transactions.

In the Western world hyper-inflation is extremely rare. The more common problem is that of a moderate level of inflation gradually undermining the other functions of money. For example, even relatively low rates of inflation tend to distort the comparison of money values over time, thus calling into question its use as a *unit of account*. A more realistic comparison of values over time may be obtained by using current (as opposed to historic) cost accounting methods, although accountants are divided on the accuracy and interpretation of current cost valuations. There is also difficulty in coping with the impact of inflation on the credit function of money. Quite simply, the *standard for deferred payment* is eroded, and unless interest payments are made on borrowed funds which more than compensate for the effect of inflation, borrowers gain at the expense of lenders. Charging an appropriate rate of interest for credit is crucial, but the financial uncertainty engendered by inflation makes this difficult. As mentioned earlier, indexation of debt may be the only way to protect the lenders' real return. A similar problem exists in respect of the *store of value* function of money. The relationship between the rate of interest paid on money assets and the rate of inflation is the vital factor, and indexation of capital values, or the holding of real (physical) assets may be the only solutions for the protection of the real value of wealth holdings. The possibility of inflation causing unanticipated transfers of wealth from lenders to borrowers may provide a reason for individuals reducing their *rate of saving* during periods of inflation, and instead increasing their spending either on consumption or on real assets. Such tendencies would only serve to exacerbate the inflationary pressures within the economy. Although, in fact, there is some evidence to suggest that some people react to higher rates of inflation (and the associated economic uncertainty) by raising their rates of saving, as a means of making good the effects of inflation on the real value of their financial wealth holdings.

The difficulty involved in predicting accurately the rate of inflation, and hence in setting interest rates which give a fair real return to lenders of funds, may cause serious problems for the operation of businesses. In general, evidence has tended to show that the higher the actual rate of inflation, the less predictable are future rates. Thus, higher rates of inflation tend to *undermine business confidence*, and may restrict the rate of economic growth. Clearly, the higher interest rates sought by lenders as a means of protecting the capital value of their funds are likely to dissuade businesses from borrowing, unless they can be sure that they can pass on the higher costs to their customers, which, if they are successful, will tend to push up inflation still further. Indeed, during inflationary periods the whole issue of predicting future costs and revenues, which is crucial to rational decision-making, becomes problematic.

Individuals in receipt of incomes which are *fixed in money terms*, or which are reviewed only periodically, are particularly vulnerable to the effects of inflation on their living standards. People who depend upon earnings from fixed interest investments, especially where interest rates were set when the rate of inflation was low and was expected to remain low, and those who have little influence on the setting of their incomes, such as people receiving unemployment pay, are likely to be badly hit by higher levels of inflation. In addition, even where incomes and interest payments are adjusted to compensate for the effects of inflation, recipients may still find themselves worse off in real terms due to tax payments which may have to be made on the extra earnings.

The effects of inflation on the operations of *financial institutions*, at least in the short term, are likely to be mixed. So long as intermediaries are able to establish a margin between the interest rate which they pay for deposits and the rate which they charge on loans, which is more than sufficient to cover rising operating costs, profitability on intermediation activities should be maintained. However, banks may suffer from the effects on business confidence mentioned above, and all lending institutions may experience an increasing tendency for customers to get into financial difficulties and be unable to meet their debt servicing commitments. Also institutions which are committed to providing income-related pensions and insurance payments into the longer term may be placed under pressure as they seek to improve their own investment performance. This, in turn, may cause them to purchase somewhat riskier assets which tend to offer the prospect of higher returns.

For the economy as a whole, the existence of inflation rates which are above those being experienced by major overseas trading partners may lead to *balance of payments problems*. Thus, for example, if the UK's inflation rate is persistently above the rate experienced by the USA, then, other things being equal, UK exports will become increasingly expensive in the USA, relative to United States domestic produce, and United States imports into the UK will become cheaper relative to UK domestic produce. If elasticities of demand for internationally-traded goods and services are sufficiently high, the UK's balance of payments current account will deteriorate, and serious economic and financial problems are likely to ensue. (These important issues are discussed in detail in Chapters 9 and 10.) It is only if there is a compensating reduction in the exchange value of sterling for dollars that the dollar price of UK exports and the sterling price of imports from the USA will maintain their initial values relative to the prices of domestic produce. But even here, the uncertainty created by possible exchange rate movements can only serve to damage international trading relations, and hence diminish the benefits to be gained from international trade and specialisation.

Without doubt the economic effects of inflation may be severe, and the living standards of the whole nation may be threatened by its existence. Clearly, the greater the rate of inflation, the more serious the problems are likely to be. However, it should be remembered that even with inflation as low as 5% per annum, money loses around one-third of its purchasing power over a seven-year period.

1.11   EXAMINATION PRACTICE

1.11.1   Questions

The following questions are taken from past examination papers, and are intended to give students an indication of the type of questions which they are likely to face within the topic area of Money and Inflation. Students may care to map out answers to these questions before consulting the guidance notes in 1.11.2. Each question carries 25 marks.

(1) (a)   Briefly describe the FOUR main functions of money.   (8)
    (b)   To what extent is each function affected by inflation, and how, in each case, can the problems which arise from inflation be overcome?   (17)

(May 1992)

(2) (a)   What factors lay behind the Bank of England's decision in June 1989 to discontinue the M1 and M3 money supply measures?   (7)
    (b)   Why is it considered necessary to monitor and target money supply growth?   (10)
    (c)   State whether the following are included in measures of money. In each case, indicate whether it is in the broad or narrow measure and give reasons for its appearance in, or exclusion from, the money supply:
    (i)   Treasury bills;
    (ii)   equity shares in a company;
    (iii)   gilt-edged securities.   (8)

(May 1990)

(3) (a)   Why do central banks in developed countries find it necessary to monitor a *range* of monetary aggregates rather than a single definition?   (9)
    ‡(b)   Define the monetary aggregate known as M0 in the UK, and discuss its role in current UK monetary policy.   (10)
    (c)   What is the current role of broad monetary aggregates in UK policy?   (6)

(October 1990)

(4) (a)   How do the authorities of a country measure the rate of inflation?   (8)
    (b)   Describe the relationship between the money supply and the rate of inflation.   (5)

29

    (c)   What problems are created by inflation?   (12)

(October 1991)

(5)   (a)   What is meant by index-linking of financial assets? Include some examples of index-linked assets in your answer.   (9)

    ‡(b)   To what extent is index-linking likely to succeed in curbing inflation? How also might governments attempt to deal with the problem?   (16)

(April 1986)

1.11.2 Guidance notes

(1) (i) The answer to part (a) of this question merely requires a brief outline of the *medium of exchange, store of value, unit of account,* and *standard for deferred payment* functions of money.

(ii) Part (b) involves discussion of the *impact of inflation* on the ability of money to perform its functions, recognising the relevance of the *level* of inflation to the answer.

(iii) Part (b) also requires discussion of how the *problems* caused for the functions of money by inflation may be *overcome.*

(iv) There is no need for consideration of the causes of inflation, the means for reducing the rate of inflation or the current Government policy on inflation.

Source of relevant material:

Part (a) 1.5.
Part (b) 1.5 and 1.10.4 (paragraphs 2 and 3).

(2) (i) The answer to this question must focus upon the *specific issues* raised, and should not degenerate into a general discussion of money supply measures in the UK.

(ii) The key to part (a) is the recognition of the *institutional developments* which have made money supply measures based exclusively on bank liabilities increasingly unacceptable. The relevance of the Abbey National conversion to retail bank status should be noted.

(iii) Part (b) requires a straightforward and concise summary of the importance of the money supply for the *operation of the economy,* and hence an explanation of why the authorities may desire to *monitor* and *target* money supply growth. Detailed discussion of the underlying theory is not necessary, and neither are comments on the UK's monetary policy successes and failures.

(iv) Part (c) relates to the *currently used official money supply measures.* It is not enough merely to make a vague statement on whether or not the assets listed are included in money supply measures. It is necessary to state explicitly whether each asset is included in broad or narrow money, and to *explain* why it is included in or excluded from the measures.

Source of relevant material:

Part (a) 1.8.3 (paragraphs 1 to 4 and 6).
Part (b) 1.7.4 (paragraphs 1 and 2).
Part (c) 1.6 (paragraph 3(c), (d) and (g)), 1.7.3, 1.8 and 1.8.1.

(3) (i) The answer to part (a) requires a discussion of the difficulty faced in *identifying money* in a modern economy, recognising the availability of a *wide range of financial assets* and, in particular, the problem in separating *money assets* from *other liquid assets*. The *uncertainty* in respect of the precise influence on the economy of different groups of money assets must also be noted.

(ii) Discussion of the mechanisms by which money affects the economy or of the methods which may be used to control the money supply is not required.

(iii) A *clear and full definition of M0* must be given in part (b), and the use of a *monitoring range* for M0 must be explained. It should be recognised that M0 was often criticised as a policy target, and that it represents only one aspect of monetary conditions.

(iv) Part (c) requires comments on the *current policy role* of the broad monetary aggregates (M4 and M3H). Discussion of the aggregates used in the past is not relevant, and there is no need to mention the recorded growth rates of the aggregates or their determinants. The difficulty experienced in interpreting the behaviour of broad aggregates, due to *financial innovation*, should be noted, as this is crucial in explaining the absence of formal targets for their growth rates.

(v) Care should be taken not to confuse targeting with monitoring in respect of monetary aggregates.

Source of relevant material:

Part (a) 1.7.3 and 1.7.4.
‡Part (b) 1.8, 1.8.3 (paragraphs 9 and 10) and Chapter 8, Table 8.2.
Part (c) 1.8.1 and 1.8.3 (paragraphs 2 to 5).

(4) (i) Part (a) of this question requires a brief discussion of the use of *price indices* to measure the rate of inflation, noting their inherent defects. Mention should be made of the UK retail price index (both headline rate and underlying rate versions), and examples of other indices should be quoted.

(ii) An outline of the *theoretical impact of changes in the money supply* on the general price level must be given in part (b). The *Fisher formula* should be used as the basis for the answer. Comments may be made on the *evidence* on the relationship between the money supply and inflation in recent years in the UK. The possible impact of inflation on borrowing, and hence on money supply growth, may also be mentioned.

(iii) Discussion of the general causes of inflation or the policies which may be implemented in order to deal with inflation is not required.

(iv) The answer to part (c) should include an outline of the *possible effects of inflation* on the main functions of money, the distribution of income and wealth, business confidence and the current account of the balance of payments. It should be noted that the nature of the problems will depend upon the *actual rate* of inflation experienced.

Source of relevant material:

Part (a)   1.9.1, 1.9.2 and 1.9.3.
Part (b)   1.10.1, 1.10.2 and 1.10.3.
Part (c)   1.10.4.

(5) (i)   Part (a) requires a straightforward explanation of the process of *indexation of financial assets*. It is useful to illustrate the answer with a simple numerical example of indexation. It is not necessary to discuss either the formulation of price indices or the problems associated with their interpretation.

(ii) Examples of index-linked assets such as National Savings Certificates and certain gilt-edged securities should be given in part (a). There is no need to give examples of the wider application of indexation.

(iii) Part (b) relates to *indexation in general*. Therefore, it is necessary to comment upon the possible effects on expenditure and saving decisions of the existence of index-linking in its broader context. In particular, remember that index-linking is aimed primarily at dealing with certain symptoms of inflation, and that consequently it may undermine attempts to curb inflation.

(iv) The second half of part (b) requires a concise summary of the *types of policies* which might be introduced to deal with inflation. Whilst monetary policy is of great significance, it should not be forgotten that fiscal, prices and incomes and exchange rate policies might also be used by the government.

Source of relevant material:

Part (a)   1.9.4 (paragraphs 1 to 4).
‡Part (b)   1.9.4 (paragraph 5) and Chapter 8, at 8.1.2 and 8.3.1.

1.12   FURTHER STUDY

The basic concept of money, its functions and importance within the modern economy are established in the literature. However, experience has shown that the official measures of the money supply and their position in respect of policy formulation have tended to alter over time. Therefore, students are advised to watch out for policy statements from the Government and the Bank of England in respect of these issues. The best source of relevant information is undoubtedly the *Bank of England Quarterly Bulletin,* although *The Economist* and the financial pages of the quality press are also extremely useful in this respect. It should also be recognised that the theoretical debate on the nature of money and its relationship to the rate of inflation continues to evolve.

Students should note that for examination purposes it is the broad concepts and principles which matter, rather than detailed knowledge of the sizes of components of monetary aggregates or their growth rates during given periods of time. Nevertheless, students should remain aware of recent developments in respect of the growth rates of the major monetary aggregates (especially M0 and M4) and the rate of inflation in the UK. (Both of these issues will be discussed in Chapter 8.)

2 CORPORATE SECTOR FINANCES

2.1 INTRODUCTION

A very important function of the financial system is to meet the financing requirements of the corporate sector. Companies in the UK have amassed huge debts to the banking sector, as well as being important customers for other banking services. They are also the source of equity and debt securities, the issue and trading of which dominate capital market activities; and a significant proportion of the turnover of the money markets relates to short-term corporate financing. Therefore, trends in the financing operations of the corporate sector have crucial implications for the prosperity and development of financial institutions and markets, and hence it is useful to consider the nature of corporate sector finances at an early stage of this book.

In order to emphasise the importance of corporate sector finances within the UK financial system, this chapter will begin by examining briefly the corporate sector's aggregate financial position, balance sheet and sources and uses of funds in recent years. This analysis provides an insight into the broad patterns of corporate sector financing, and sheds light on its relevance for the activities of financial institutions and markets.

Companies may meet their financing needs via the generation and retention of profits and the sale of assets, which are referred to as *internal funding*, and through borrowing and the issue of various types of equity shares, which are referred to as *external funding*. Traditionally, an important source of external funding for UK corporates has been borrowing from banks. However, during the early 1990s there was an unprecedented shift away from such funding, generating an overall net repayment of debt to banks. The substantial reduction in the use of external funds and the relatively greater reliance on equity-based finance has important implications for the operations of financial institutions and markets. The extent and speed of any reversal in this recent trend is likely to be dependent upon the strength of the recovery from economic recession, and market expectations of business prospects in general. Also, the ability of the banking sector to provide the borrowing facilities required by companies at competitive interest rates will be a crucial factor in determining whether or not the banks are able to regain the share of the corporate financing market which they previously held.

Even before the recent recession, there was a clear trend towards the increasing use of *marketable securities* by companies for the raising of finance. This activity, often referred to as *disintermediation* (see Chapter 4,

35

at 4.2.5 for detail), has added to the competitive pressures faced by banks in respect of their lending activities, and may have been partly responsible for the shift towards *transaction banking*, during the 1980s, whereby larger corporates tended to select specific banking products and services on the basis of their price from a range of banks, rather than maintaining a *full banking relationship* with a single bank or group of banks. The weakening of the financial position of many corporates, and the increased attention being paid to the quality of borrowers by banks, in the aftermath of the recession, may have reversed this trend to some extent. In any event, many banks today are active in the management of securities issues by corporate customers, and some are involved with the trading of such instruments. By doing this, banks are able to earn fees and commissions, whilst avoiding the impact on their balance sheets that normal on-lending would involve. Banks have also become increasingly active in assisting their corporate customers to *manage the financial risks* which have become more apparent in recent years. In particular, the widespread use of market-related (floating) rates of interest on corporate debt, and of instruments denominated in foreign currencies, against the background of periodic volatility of interest rates and exchange rates, has led to a major growth in the use of hedging techniques, involving forward exchange transactions, swaps, options, and so on. An introduction to these techniques, which may be regarded as complementary to the standard corporate finance facilities offered by banks, is given in 2.8 below.

2.2   THE CORPORATE SECTOR WITHIN THE UK ECONOMY

For official accounting purposes the UK corporate sector (technically referred to as *industrial and commercial companies*) comprises all private sector companies which are not classified as banks or other financial institutions. Subsidiaries and branches of overseas companies operating in the UK are included, but subsidiaries and branches of UK companies operating overseas are excluded. As is shown in Table 2.1, the corporate sector in aggregate has generated *substantial financial deficits* in recent years, with a record deficit of £22.7b being recorded in 1989.

Table 2.1   UK corporate sector, aggregate financial balance, 1988 to 1992 (£b)

	1988	1989	1990	1991	1992
Corporate sector deficit	7.7	22.7	19.9	11.1	10.5

Source: *Financial Statistics*, Central Statistical Office, May 1993.

The continual increase in the net indebtedness of the corporate sector, over the years 1988 to 1992, was in sharp contrast to the position between

1981 and 1987 when the sector was a substantial net provider of funds to other sectors of the economy. The financial position of the sector during 1989/90 was not felt to be sustainable, and at the time many commentators argued that the stability of the sector would be threatened unless action was taken to limit the sector's debt burden. As things turned out, the onset of the *recession* in the UK in 1990 caused *marked adjustments* to occur in the financial behaviour of UK companies in aggregate, although the scale and speed of adjustment proved to be much slower than that experienced by the personal sector, which had also lurched into a substantial financial deficit at the end of the 1980s (as will be explained in Chapter 3, at 3.2). During 1992 the corporate sector's deficit was £10.5b, the lowest for four years, but still high by historical standards. However, within this trend, it is interesting to note that the amount of *borrowing from banks fell very sharply*. Indeed, in both 1991 and 1992 the corporate sector made net repayments of debt to the banking sector. In general, other financial institutions were less badly hit by the corporate sector's reduced financing requirements, although during the period of recession there was a broadly based downturn in corporate sector financial activities, with purchases of investments in other UK companies and overseas markedly reduced.

2.3 THE CORPORATE SECTOR BALANCE SHEET

The UK corporate sector's aggregate balance sheet for the years 1987 to 1992 is shown in Table 2.2. The key aspects of this balance sheet may be summarised as follows:

(a) *Financial assets*
   (i) *Notes and coin* form only a tiny fraction of total financial assets held. This is as would be expected given the sophistication of financial facilities available to companies, the security problems in holding large volumes of cash, and the zero return which it generates. The bulk of cash held is for day-to-day transactions purposes in respect of retail distribution outlets.
   (ii) *Public sector debt instruments* include a range of Treasury bills, gilt-edged securities, and National Savings and tax instruments.
   (iii) *Bank deposits* are an important item on the balance sheet, and have grown steadily in recent years. At the end of 1992, they formed about 16% of total financial assets held by companies. Time deposits dominate these funds. Interestingly, whilst company deposits with banks in total grew by 41% between the end of 1987 and the end of 1992, *company deposits with building societies* grew by 170% over the same period. This illustrates the extent to which the building societies are now able to compete with banks across a wide range of banking activities.

Table 2.2   UK corporate sector, aggregate balance sheet, 1987 to 1992 (end year figures), £b

	1987	1988	1989	1990	1991	1992
Financial Assets						
Notes and coin	1.2	1.3	1.4	1.4	1.4	1.5
Public sector debt instruments	4.7	4.1	4.0	5.2	5.7	4.6
Bank deposits: sterling	44.7	49.9	57.5	59.6	63.9	62.9
: foreign currency	9.3	9.6	12.7	14.7	12.4	13.1
Building society deposits	1.9	1.5	1.9	3.7	5.4	5.1
Credit extended by retailers	2.2	2.4	2.4	2.4	2.5	2.7
Trade credit	79.8	83.9	88.1	92.7	92.5	92.9
Company securities: UK	50.7	58.4	71.7	68.2	79.6	83.3
: overseas	2.0	2.6	2.7	2.1	2.5	3.3
Direct and other investment overseas	72.2	91.5	107.3	101.4	115.5	144.9
Miscellaneous and adjustments	33.7	37.3	48.6	50.8	54.9	64.1
Total financial assets	302.4	342.5	398.3	402.2	436.3	478.4
Financial Liabilities						
Public sector lending	4.6	5.4	5.6	4.0	5.1	7.2
Bank lending: sterling	67.2	89.8	118.5	134.9	131.3	126.3
: foreign currency	17.6	26.0	37.6	34.9	33.5	36.9
Other financial institution lending	10.4	12.4	16.3	19.0	18.7	18.0
Trade credit	81.4	86.7	90.6	93.0	95.1	96.6
UK company securities	382.2	421.6	539.3	495.6	594.1	632.7
Overseas direct and other investment in the UK	48.1	54.2	77.3	89.9	102.0	115.8
Miscellaneous and adjustments	37.7	45.9	55.3	58.9	70.2	83.8
Total financial liabilities	649.2	742.0	940.5	930.2	1050.0	1117.3
Net financial assets	−346.8	−399.5	−542.2	−528.0	−613.7	−638.9
Tangible assets	443.5	491.9	582.8	645.8	668.0	n/a
Total net assets	96.7	92.4	40.6	117.8	54.3	n/a

Source: *Financial Statistics*, Central Statistical Office, May 1993.
National Income and Expenditure, 1992, Central Statistical Office.

(iv)   The largest items effectively relate to *claims on other businesses*, both in the UK and overseas. The amount of trade credit outstanding, which accounted for 19.4% of total financial assets at the end of 1992, was relatively stable during the early 1990s. This probably reflects the depressed state of the UK economy during these years. By contrast there has been a steady increase in the value of both *UK and overseas company securities* held. In respect of the interpretation of changes in the value of company share holdings, it must be remembered that share prices are determined by *market forces*. Hence, the general upwards movement of share prices during the years following the stock market collapse of October 1987, raised the value of share holdings over and above that occurring due to the purchase of additional shares by companies.

(v) The importance of overseas asset holdings is shown by the value of UK companies' *direct and other investment overseas*. This balance sheet item has grown strongly since 1990, although its more recent increase is likely to have been due, at least in part, to the significant depreciation of sterling following its withdrawal from the EC's Exchange Rate Mechanism in September 1992. (See Chapter 8, at 8.7.3.) The lower exchange value for sterling means that the sterling equivalent of foreign currency denominated claims is inflated.

(vi) At the end of 1992, the total value of financial assets held by UK companies amounted to £478b, which was some 58% higher than the corresponding value five years earlier. During this period, the retail price index rose by 36%, thus implying a steady increase in the real value of financial assets held, although, as suggested above some of this increase was probably due to exchange rate movements and stock market conditions, rather than the acquisition of additional assets.

(b) *Financial liabilities*

(i) A large proportion of *public sector lending* to the corporate sector is in the form of purchases of commercial bills by the Bank of England. This action by the Bank is primarily related to bank liquidity and monetary control objectives (as will be explained in Chapter 5, at 5.3.3), but nevertheless the process effectively provides short term funds to the corporate sector.

(ii) The importance of banks as lenders to the corporate sector is clear. The total amount of *bank debt* almost doubled during the period covered by Table 2.2, representing a significant real (inflation adjusted) increase. At the end of 1992, the £163b owed to the banking sector accounted for about 60% of what might be thought of as corporate sector debt (as opposed to equity-based and investment liabilities).

(iii) As would be expected from the comments made above in respect of *trade credit* as an asset of the corporate sector, trade credit also forms an important part of companies' financial liabilities. The differences between the asset and liability values for trade credit are due to credit taken and given in respect of other sectors and accounting errors.

(iv) The largest item of financial liabilities by far relates to the *securities issued by the corporate sector*. A large proportion of these securities is in the form of equity shares which can only be redeemed in very special circumstances, and hence the item should not be viewed as a liability in the same sense as bank loans, which entail a legally-binding servicing commitment. Also, as the value of company shares depends upon stock market conditions, the corporate sector in aggregate could find that improved business performance, leading to a rising trend in share prices, actually reduces the value of the sector's net assets, by raising the market value of its financial liabilities. Indeed, examination of the data shows that if UK company securities were to be excluded from the liabilities side of the balance sheet, the financial position of the sector would have been almost in balance in recent years.

(v) *Overseas direct and other investment* in UK-based companies has grown significantly in recent years. This trend is likely to have been influenced by the UK's relatively high rate of economic growth during the late 1980s, by its position within the EC, and by the low labour costs (relative to other major European nations) in certain sectors of industry.

Considering the balance sheet overall, it may be observed that the corporate sector in recent years has had *substantial net financial liabilities*, which have tended to grow in real terms. However, as mentioned above, the special position of equity claims on companies must be recognised, as must the fact that in a capitalist economic system private individuals ultimately own a large proportion of all national wealth, either directly or indirectly (via claims on financial institutions). In addition, it should be noted that the corporate sector holds substantial amounts of *tangible assets*, such as buildings, plant and equipment, stocks of raw materials, finished goods and work-in-progress. When these items are taken into account, the net asset value of the sector is normally positive, and stood at £54.3b at the end of 1991. Although there are serious problems in respect of the valuation of real assets, the numbers quoted in the balance sheet give a crude measure of the corporate sector's real wealth and productive capital base.

The importance of financial institutions for the financial operations of the corporate sector is clearly illustrated by the balance sheet structure. The role of the banks is crucial to corporate sector finances, and so too are the institutions (including banks) which provide capital market services in respect of corporate equity and debt issues and trading. The specific functions of the financial institutions and the markets within which many of the relevant transactions are undertaken are examined in detail in Chapters 4 and 5.

2.4 CORPORATE SECTOR SOURCES AND USES OF FUNDS

The balance sheet analysis undertaken in the previous section is useful for determining the relative importance of various assets and liabilities held by the corporate sector at specific points in time, but without access to additional data it is not possible to draw precise conclusions on the flows of finance over periods of time. For example, an increase in overseas asset holdings may be due to the use of funds for the purchase of additional overseas assets, but it might equally be caused by favourable exchange rate movements or increases in the prices of marketable securities. Therefore, in order to shed light on the corporate sector's flows of finance in recent years, it is necessary to examine the sector's sources and uses of funds. Table 2.3 provides this information for the UK corporate sector for the years 1988 to 1992.

(a) *Sources of funds*

The sources of funds for a company may be divided into *internal* and *external* sources. Internal funds relate basically to the *net income generated* by a company which has been *retained* rather than distributed to shareholders. It is interesting to note that whilst there was a relatively modest downturn in internal funds flows for the UK corporate sector after 1989, as the recession began to take hold, the importance of these funds for the financing of companies grew significantly during the early 1990s. In 1989, internally-generated funds accounted for only 32.8% of total funds used by the corporate sector; in 1992 this proportion was 61.3%. Underlying this trend was a *massive reduction in the amount of bank borrowing* undertaken. In 1989, £34b was raised from banks (with a further £9.1b coming from loans from other sources); in 1992, the corporate sector made net repayments of bank debt amounting to £1.9b.

Throughout the period 1988 to 1992, *share and other capital issues* by the corporate sector were *substantial*, but rather *variable*, with the peak value in total being £20.7b raised in 1991. Consequently, it would appear that during a period of *increasing economic uncertainty*, the corporate sector as a whole attempted to *reduce its dependence on borrowed funds*, requiring regular servicing, and to shift the balance of external funding towards ordinary shares and other capital market instruments. As dividends on share capital may be waived if a company faces poor trading conditions, this trend in financing helps companies to *manage their cash flows*. Also, there is some evidence that during the period of recession at the beginning of the 1990s, *many banks widened their operating margins* (that is, the spread

41

between the rate of interest paid on deposits and that charged on loans) and became somewhat more demanding in the *conditions attached to loans*. These factors can only have made bank loans less attractive relative to other sources of funds for companies.

In recent years *overseas sources* have made important contributions to the total external funding used by UK companies. In addition to the explicitly recognised '*other overseas investment*' element in Table 2.3, it should be noted that the overseas sector has been active in *purchasing UK*

Table 2.3 UK corporate sector, sources and uses of funds, 1988 to 1992, £b					
	1988	*1989*	*1990*	*1991*	*1992*
Sources of funds					
Internal funds	39.9	34.6	33.8	32.7	32.2
External funds:					
Bank borrowing	31.5	34.0	19.9	−0.9	−1.9
Other loans	5.8	9.1	8.0	3.6	2.5
Ordinary share issues	4.3	1.9	2.9	9.7	5.1
Debentures and preference share					
issues	4.4	6.4	3.6	5.5	1.6
Other capital issues	2.5	7.5	7.5	5.5	6.3
Other overseas investment	8.0	11.2	11.7	10.3	6.5
Other external funding	1.5	0.8	1.4	0.6	0.2
Total identified sources	97.9	105.5	88.8	67.0	52.5
Uses of funds					
Liquid assets:					
Bank deposits, notes and coin	5.6	10.5	5.0	3.6	−1.7
UK government securities	−0.4	−0.1	0.9	0.5	−0.8
Other liquid assets	−0.8	1.2	2.3	1.6	−0.1
Other financial assets	2.0	4.6	8.6	1.7	−0.2
Gross domestic fixed capital formation	43.5	52.3	54.9	49.9	48.4
Increase in book value of stocks	9.8	9.2	4.1	−2.7	0.3
Investment in UK company securities	14.5	17.9	2.3	5.1	1.6
Investment overseas	12.7	10.4	0.5	4.3	2.5
Other uses of funds	1.7	0.5	2.5	0.7	0.5
Total identified uses	88.6	106.5	81.1	64.7	50.5
Balancing item	9.3	−1.0	7.7	2.3	2.0

Source: *Financial Statistics*, Central Statistical Office, May 1993.

company securities, and *overseas banks* have lent large amounts of funds in the UK. It was only during the later stages of the UK recession, in 1992, and at a time when many major overseas economies were themselves slipping into recession, that the inflow of funds from overseas began to diminish.

(b) *Uses of funds*

Table 2.3 shows the steep downwards trend in the total amounts of funds utilised by UK companies between 1989 and 1992. A major factor explaining this trend was the deteriorating state of business prospects over this period, and hence the reduced desire for participation in activities which required companies to raise additional funds. The aspects of corporate financial activities which bore the brunt of the economic downturn are clear from the uses of funds section of Table 2.3.

It is interesting to note that between 1989 and 1992 the corporate sector continued to build up its holdings of *liquid assets*, and especially *bank deposits*. The high level of competition for funds between banks and other financial intermediaries, and hence the relatively *attractive returns* available on deposits, may partly explain this trend; so too might the desire of companies to build up liquid reserves to cover *unforeseen contingencies* at a time of economic uncertainty. This trend is not inconsistent with the corporate sector also increasing the total value of outstanding bank loans, as there may simply be two distinct sets of companies with differing financial positions. In addition, sometimes companies with operations in a number of countries may gain tax or risk management advantages by holding funds in specific locations; and the pre-funding (that is, borrowing in advance of needs) of acquisitions may also occur. It was only during the final full year of the recession (in 1992) that liquid asset holdings were reduced. This may reflect a stabilisation of economic conditions for many companies, or perhaps an outcome of competition through price discounting in many of the depressed markets for final outputs.

In money terms, *gross domestic fixed capital formation* (which is basically the gross investment in real capital and equipment by companies) was affected only marginally by the adverse economic conditions during the early 1990s. This may be somewhat surprising, given the picture painted in the media of UK industry slashing its capital investment in response to high interest rates. Of course, the impact of inflation really needs to be taken into account in order to determine the true scale of the reduced level of capital investment.

A significant reduction in the usage of funds occurred in respect of *stock building*. In 1988, the book value of stocks was raised by almost £10b; during 1991 and 1992 taken together, there was a net reduction in the value of stocks amounting to £2.4b. The other major reduction in the usage of funds, during the period covered by Table 2.3, was in respect of *investment in UK company securities* and *investment overseas*. Quite simply, the deteriorating state of the world economy in general, and the UK economy in particular, at the beginning of the 1990s, made investments in both UK and overseas companies rather unattractive and fairly risky. Instead, in order to protect their core businesses, some UK companies rationalised their operations, either disposing of or closing down entirely peripheral aspects of their businesses. In 1989, the total funds used for purposes of increasing stocks, investing in UK company securities and investing overseas amounted to £37b; in 1992 the corresponding value was £4.4b. This trend, taken with the run-down in liquid asset holdings during 1992, largely explains the substantially reduced requirement for funds by the corporate sector.

It may be concluded that there have been some fundamental changes in the patterns of UK corporate sector finances in recent years. These changes have had important effects on the corporate financing facilities provided by both banks and other financial institutions. As the UK economy moves into a period of economic recovery, it is likely that the financing needs of UK companies will expand once again, but there is no guarantee that the distribution of financing methods will revert to its former pattern. The nature of *competition* between financial institutions for corporate business, and the *continuing evolution* of the financial markets will be critical factors in determining the future pattern of corporate financing.

2.5 SHORT-TERM DEBT FINANCE

2.5.1 Overdraft facilities

Most clearing banks are willing to allow their corporate customers to *overdraw* their current accounts *up to an agreed maximum sum*. An agreed facility is likely to be reviewed periodically, in the light of the customer's performance in servicing the debt and the bank's lending policies. Strictly, overdrafts are *repayable on demand*, although in the interests of maintaining good relationships with their customers, banks are normally loath to call for repayment without notice.

From the point of view of the borrower, an overdraft is an *extremely flexible* financing instrument, being ideal for *day-to-day financing requirements*, and not being tied to specific underlying commercial transactions (unlike commercial bills). Overdraft facilities are easy to arrange and involve a minimal amount of documentation, especially where the funds drawn are unsecured. However, when the borrower is willing to offer security (perhaps a charge on the fixed assets of the company), the interest charges on the overdraft are likely to be lower than for unsecured funds. A further attraction of overdraft facilities is that *interest is charged on daily debit balances*, and hence the borrower only has to pay interest on the *actual amounts borrowed* on any given day. Furthermore, where a number of companies within a single group hold accounts with the same bank, it is possible for the group to negotiate a *net overdraft facility*, whereby the daily credit and debit balances on the individual companies' accounts are aggregated to give a net overdraft position for the group, upon which the bank will charge interest. Clearly, this facility helps to reduce the group's interest charges, by ensuring the efficient utilisation of funds held within the group.

An important drawback of an overdraft facility for the borrower is that the funds could be *recalled without notice*. Hence, however unlikely it is in practice that the bank granting the facility will take such action, the borrower must be willing to accept a certain degree of risk in this respect. Also, the interest charged on overdrafts is *linked to base rate*, and so the borrower is exposed to interest rate movements; although base rate does not experience such volatile movements as money market rates. However, it should also be recognised that base rate tends to be somewhat higher than LIBOR, which may be used as the basis for charging interest on alternative forms of short-term loans. (Base rate and LIBOR are discussed in Chapter 7, at 7.7).

2.5.2 Short-term bank (money market) loans

A bank may be willing to grant a corporate customer a *LIBOR-linked loan facility*, for an agreed period of time, denominated either in sterling or in a major foreign currency. Within the limit set by the bank's commitment, the customer may *withdraw blocks of funds* of various maturities normally of between one and three months. This form of facility is usually made available only for amounts of £250,000 and above, and the minimum individual loan within the facility is usually £100,000.

A major advantage of this type of funding for the borrower is that the bank gives a *firm commitment* to provide finance up to a *specified maximum amount* (although in certain circumstances the bank may insist at the outset upon an 'on demand' clause, whereby the facility may be withdrawn without notice). Also, as with overdraft facilities, arrangement and documentation are relatively simple, and there is no need for the loan to be the counterpart to a specific commercial transaction. However, being linked to LIBOR, the interest charges tend to be lower than those which would be made on an overdraft of comparable size. Indeed, the degree of competition between banks for good quality corporate borrowers, especially where they are willing to offer security for loans, means that the margins charged over LIBOR may be very fine.

Disadvantages of short-term bank loans for the borrower, relative to the use of overdraft facilities, are that a *commitment fee* is normally required by the bank to set up the facility, and *fees are payable on unutilised parts of the facilities granted*. Therefore, these loans are more appropriate where the borrower has a *fairly certain financing requirement*.

Where there is uncertainty in respect of financing needs, the use of an overdraft may be preferable despite a possibly higher rate of interest on the funds actually drawn. There is also the exposure to interest rate movements which must be borne in mind. LIBOR fluctuates more than base rate, and so the risk faced by the borrower, where loans have to be renewed within the facility, is likely to be greater than that faced in relation to an overdraft.

Finally, it should be recognised that major public limited companies possessing *sufficient creditworthiness* may enter the *inter-bank market* directly for the purpose of raising short-term funds. By avoiding the use of a banking intermediary, the borrower is often able to achieve a narrower margin over LIBOR than would be available from a bank. Also, the borrower has no commitment fee to pay. However, the minimum facility via direct borrowing is normally £1m, and it must be emphasised that only the top calibre companies may engage in such borrowing.

2.5.3 Acceptance credits

A company may raise short-term finance via the drawing of *bills of exchange* as the *counterpart to commercial transactions*. Quite simply, a company may sell goods on credit, but may be in need of funds before payment is due. Therefore, it may draw a bill of exchange (which is effectively a claim to the amount owed by the purchaser of the goods), which is then *accepted* by a bank for a fee. This means that the bank *guarantees payment* against the bill to whomsoever holds the bill at maturity. Consequently, the drawer is then much more likely to find a third party willing to discount the bill, i.e. to purchase the bill for an amount below its value upon maturity. (Indeed, the accepting bank may itself be willing to discount the bill for its customer.) The difference between the maturity value of the bill and its discounted value measures the implicit interest payment on the funds locked away in the underlying debt; the greater is the discount which the drawer has to accept, the lower is the price obtained for the bill, and hence the greater is the effective interest rate which has to be paid in order to obtain the funds before the bill's maturity.

Whilst it is possible for a company to draw bills and to have them discounted without bank acceptance, the discounting process is made easier, and the rate of discount reduced, if the bills have been accepted by a bank. Once this has occurred, the ordinary commercial bill becomes known as a *commercial bank bill*. If the bank happens to be an eligible bank, the bill becomes an *eligible bank bill*. As eligibility status is only endowed upon banks which meet minimum criteria laid down by the Bank of England (in respect of the quality of their acceptance business, their market standing, and, for foreign banks, the treatment of UK banks in the relevant overseas market), eligible bank bills command very fine rates of discount. This position is enhanced by the fact that eligible bank bills are rediscountable at the Bank of England (see Chapter 5, at 5.3.1).

Depending upon the fees involved, bill finance may be cheaper than funds raised via short-term bank loans; with the discount rate on eligible bank bills normally being below LIBOR. However, by definition, bill finance must be related to *specific identifiable commercial transactions*, so that the bill is effectively a *self-liquidating instrument*. In addition, as the discounter of a bill may subsequently sell (rediscount) the bill to another party, the drawer's name and an indication of the nature of the underlying transaction (which must be specified on the bill) could become public knowledge, with obvious implications for the drawer's commercial position.

It is common for a company drawing bills to arrange an *acceptance facility* with its bank, which will allow it to have bills automatically accepted, without further negotiations, up to the limit of the facility. The minimum total facility is usually around £500,000, with the minimum denomination for any single bill usually being £50,000. As the facility is arranged on a committed basis, the customer is assured of being able to raise funds against the value of its debtors. For this privilege, the customer has to pay a *commitment fee*, in addition to the acceptance commission on each bill accepted. As these payments are known in advance, and as the discount rate is fixed when the bill is sold, the company drawing the bill knows precisely what the total cost of the funds will be when they are obtained, and hence financial management is facilitated. In addition, bills may be drawn for any maturity up to 187 days, thus giving added flexibility to the instrument.

2.5.4 Commercial paper

Commercial paper relates to *short-term, marketable, unsecured promissory notes issued by companies and purchased directly by investors*. The notes are issued at a discount to their face value, and the discount rate is usually linked to the London Inter-bank Bid Rate (LIBID). This form of corporate borrowing by-passes normal bank intermediation facilities, and where borrowers have sufficiently high credit ratings, it is possible for them to borrow more cheaply than via the raising of bank loans, whilst investors may earn a higher return on their funds than is available on bank deposits. This is despite the fact that the borrower will have to cover the expenses associated with the management of the issue of paper, which is often undertaken by a bank. The sterling commercial paper (SCP) market, which is examined in detail in Chapter 5, at 5.4.7, is one of the three main commercial paper markets. The other two are the United States dollar commercial paper (USCP) market and the euro-commercial paper (ECP) market.

A major advantage of commercial paper over bill finance is that it *does not have to be issued as the counterpart to a specific commercial transaction*, thus giving the issuer *flexibility* in respect of short-term financing. However, the *minimum denominations* for paper are high relative to those for bill issues (£100,000 for SCP relative to £50,000 for commercial bills), and it is necessary for fairly regular issues of paper to be made in order for the borrower to maintain a high market profile, and hence a wide interest amongst investors. Also, it is expensive to set up a commercial paper programme, and companies using this channel to raise short-term funds are unable to hide the fact that they are borrowing, and hence the market's evaluation of the company's prospects may be influenced, especially if large sums are involved. Further limitations on the use of commercial paper are that the *documentation requirements may be demanding*, and there is no guarantee that an issue will be taken up by investors at a discount rate which is acceptable to the issuer. Consequently, whilst the setting of the discount rate at the outset avoids the company being exposed to the risk of interest rate movements over the period of the debt, it may still have to hedge its position by arranging *stand-by funding*, perhaps from a bank, in order to cover the possibility of an issue of paper being undersubscribed. The minimum requirement for the net assets of companies issuing commercial paper (£25m in the case of SCP), also precludes smaller companies from the market, and issuing companies or their guarantors must be listed on a major stock exchange. It should also be noted that since the enactment of the Companies Act 1989, it has been possible for companies to issue SCP with original maturities of up to five years. Issues with original maturities in excess of one year are normally referred to as *medium-term notes* (MTNs).

If a company wishes to issue paper on the USCP market it must first obtain a *credit rating* from one of the major rating agencies, such as Moodys or Standard and Poor. These ratings are expensive to obtain, and hence set an initial fixed cost of entry into the market. Also, there is no guarantee that the company will obtain the rating it was hoping for, and hence it may not be able to obtain the best discount rates available. However, a good rating is likely to make it easier to attract investors and will almost certainly allow funds to be raised at an attractive cost. Whilst such ratings are not compulsory on the SCP or ECP markets, in the present economic climate it is virtually impossible to make an issue without a rating, unless a bank guarantee has been arranged.

2.6 LONG-TERM DEBT FINANCE

2.6.1 Bank loans

Given the high level of competition between banks in respect of the corporate finance market, it is hardly surprising that there is a *tremendous variety of bank loans available to the corporate customer.* Indeed, today, many banks are willing to put together unique facilities to meet the precise requirements of individual customers. Consequently, broad generalisations on the nature of longer-term bank loans are of only limited relevance. Nevertheless, it is possible to identify the *key characteristics* of longer-term loans, and hence to appreciate the range of lending packages which may be assembled by banks:

(a) *Term to maturity.* Whilst many loans to corporate customers fall within the maturity range of one to 10 years, it is no longer rare for banks to advance funds for periods of up to 30 years. Repayment of capital may be made over the whole life of the facility, but some banks are willing to allow deferral of capital repayment for a fixed period from the start of the loan. In some circumstances interest payments may also be deferred for a fixed period. In addition, the borrower may be given the option to repay some or all of the facility before its scheduled repayment date, although a fee may be required by the bank if this option is taken up.

(b) *Interest charges.* These may be set at fixed or variable rates, and in some cases there is the option for the borrower to switch between different rates at pre-determined points in time. Thus, for example, a borrower may initially agree to a fixed rate loan, but if market rates of interest fall below what was expected at the time that the loan was taken out, the borrower may decide to switch to a market related (floating) rate. Clearly, expectations of future interest rate movements will determine the willingness of banks to offer fixed rate loans (recognising that most of their funds are raised at floating rates), and the customer's preference between fixed and floating rate debt. However, irrespective of the type of rate selected, both parties face the risk of their expectations being unfounded, and of losses being incurred (as will be explained in 2.8 below). The interest rate position is made even more problematic by banks being willing to link lending rates to base rate or to LIBOR, perhaps with the possibility of the borrower being able to switch between rates on specified dates.

(c) *Lending conditions.* The majority of long-term sterling bank loans have to be secured against specified assets owned by the corporate borrower, or against the company's assets in general. Where the borrowed funds are to be used for the purchase of real estate, the loan may be secured against a mortgage on the property. Alternatively, capital equipment and machinery may be used to secure the loan. Where security is pledged, failure to service the debt within the terms of the loan agreement puts at risk assets of the company, and hence may threaten its long-term survival.

(d) *Fees.* The majority of banks charge arrangement fees for the setting up of lending facilities. Also, where the borrower is allowed to draw down a facility in blocks, there may be charges made on the unutilised portion of the facility.

(e) *Size of loans.* Most banks are willing to make longer-term loans to corporate customers for almost any amount, ranging from a few thousand pounds upwards. However, where very large amounts of funds are required, the borrower may have to raise the loan via a *syndicate.* In this case, a group of banks will come together in order to provide loans which are far greater than any individual member of the group would be willing and able to make available on its own. Thus, banks are able to obtain business which would otherwise not be available, and are able to spread the risk associated with a specific borrower. In consequence the borrower may be able to obtain a large scale loan from a single source on relatively attractive terms. The lead member of the syndicate will normally undertake the negotiations with the borrower, and will be responsible for ensuring that appropriate security is taken against the loan. It is likely that transactions costs for the borrower will be considerably lower than they would have been had the funds been raised via a number of separate loans for smaller amounts.

2.6.2 Sterling debentures

Sterling debentures (sometimes referred to as sterling bonds) are *transferable registered stock*, which may be issued by way of an *offer for sale to the general public*, or via a *private placing with investors* lined up by the intermediary responsible for managing the issue. The debentures of public listed companies are quoted on the London Stock Exchange.

The nature of debentures means that they are only suitable for the raising of *large amounts of funds*, with the typical issue size being in the range of £30m to £100m. They also have *fixed maturity dates*, with a minimum maturity of five years. Many issues have had maturities of five to seven years, although there has been a trend in recent years for longer maturities to be selected, often in the range of 15 to 25 years. When debentures are issued, a trustee is appointed to act in the interests of the investor, within the terms of the trust deed under which the debentures must be issued.

The interest payments on debentures are *fixed* at the time of issue, and hence there is *a known debt servicing commitment* for the borrower for the period of issue. However, the borrower is usually empowered to *repurchase* its debentures from the market should it wish to do so, and hence if the borrower expects that market rates of interest are going to fall appreciably, it may be worthwhile for it to reduce its outstanding debt, and refinance its requirements at a lower rate.

An advantage of raising capital funds via debentures, as opposed to the issue of equity shares, is that the interest payments on the debentures are *tax deductible* (as an expense of the company), whereas dividend payments on equity shares are charged against after-tax profits. In addition, debenture holders are creditors of the company, having no rights to interfere with its running. Shareholders are effectively the owners of the company, and may influence its business policies. A relative disadvantage of debentures is that the interest payments on them must be made irrespective of the company's profitability or cash flow position, and as debentures are likely to be secured against assets of the company, failure to adhere to the agreed terms of the debt may place at risk the continuation of the company.

In order to enhance the attractiveness of an issue of debentures, without having to offer excessively high rates of interest, a company may attach to them an option for the holder to *convert* the debentures into ordinary equity shares. Where this occurs, it is normal for the company to stipulate the precise terms of conversion and the dates upon which the option can be exercised. Nevertheless, convertible debentures give the holder the same security as normal debentures, but also the ability to participate in the company's ownership should its performance prove to be sufficiently good.

2.6.3 Eurobonds

Eurobonds are *foreign currency denominated bearer securities*, which may be issued by way of an *offer for sale to the general public* or via a *private placing with investors*. Public issues are normally made through a syndicate of banks, which underwrites the bonds and distributes them to investors. These issues are normally listed on one or more of the world's major stock exchanges. Private placements tend to result in a narrower ownership for the bonds, and the issues are rarely announced publicly or listed on major stock exchanges.

Eurobond issues are only suitable where *large amounts of funds* have to be raised, with the minimum acceptable issue being in the region of US$75m or its equivalent. Thus only large companies are attracted to the market. Also, in order to gain the best rates on the bonds, it is necessary for the issuer to have a *high credit rating* and, preferably, an *international presence* and a *widely-recognised name*. Nevertheless, eurobonds provide a flexible form of finance, and issues do not have to be secured against the assets of the issuing company (which is useful in helping it to maintain its credibility with other providers of finance who may seek appropriate security).

Eurobonds may be issued with either *fixed or floating* rates of interest. A floating rate may be linked to LIBOR or to some other internationally-recognised market rate. Eurobonds normally have a *fixed maturity date*, which is rarely more than 15 years from the date of issue, and often in the range of five to seven years. The issuer may include a clause allowing for their repurchase in the market, which helps to counteract the risks flowing from significant movements in market rates of interest after the issue has been made. However, this form of protection for the issues will tend to push up the rate of interest which has to be paid for funds relative to what it would otherwise have been. As with debentures, eurobonds may be issued with the *option to convert* into ordinary equity shares at a price set at the time of issue. Alternatively, bonds may be issued with *warrants* attached, which effectively give the holder a right to purchase ordinary equity shares or subscribe to further debt issues of the bond issuer at a pre-determined price. A further variant is the *zero coupon bond*, which attracts no interest, but which is issued at a heavy discount and redeemed at par value upon maturity. This form of bond may be attractive from a taxation point of view, as the return is all in the form of capital gain (rather than income). If the holder wishes to realise some of the accrued capital gain before maturity, it is merely necessary to sell some of the bonds on the open market.

From the point of view of the issuer, eurobonds provide a convenient means of raising large amounts of foreign currency denominated funds, without having to enter overseas financial markets. Also, as interest rates within euromarkets tend to reflect the rates ruling within the domestic market from which the relevant currency originated, it may be possible to raise funds at a lower rate of interest than is available on domestic currency funds. However, if the borrower intends to use the funds raised for investments which will generate incomes denominated in currencies other than one in which the eurobond is denominated, there is the risk that exchange rates will move adversely, and hence that the real rate of interest may prove to be much higher than the nominal rate payable on the bonds. For example, if a British company issues eurobonds denominated in United States dollars, the interest payments and repayment of principal will also be denominated in dollars. If the company's income is denominated solely in sterling, then a subsequent depreciation in the value of sterling relative to the dollar will result in increasing amounts of sterling being required to service the debt. The end result will be a much higher cost of borrowed funds than is apparent from the dollar rate of interest payable on the bonds. (Ways in which a company may deal with this form of exchange rate risk will be examined below at 2.8.)

2.7 EQUITY FINANCE AND CAPITAL STRUCTURE

2.7.1 Equity shares

Companies may raise long-term finance via the issue of various forms of equity shares. Investors purchase shares in the hope of earning *dividends* (effectively the distributed profits of companies) and possibly making *capital gains*, should they subsequently choose to sell the shares on the capital market. The shareholders are the *owners* of a company, and have rights and privileges according to the type of shares held. The most common form of share is the *ordinary share*, which gives the holder a claim to the residual profits of the company after all other claims have been met. Ordinary shareholders normally have voting rights at the general meetings of the company, and may vote to dismiss the company's directors should they choose to do so. However, should the company be liquidated, they are at the end of the queue in terms of receiving any payment from the company's assets. Thus, ordinary shares are the *most risky* investments in a company, but are potentially the most profitable.

From the point of view of the company itself, the major advantage of issuing ordinary shares is that long-term capital is committed to the business which does not have to be serviced if trading conditions prove to be unfavourable. In other words, *dividends may be waived* if profits are depressed, and hence the company will not be forced into liquidation for the sake of having to meet charges on its share capital. However, recognising that shareholders are unlikely to be pleased by the cutting of dividends, the directors will normally only recommend such action if it is absolutely necessary. Indeed, the *decison-making power* which has to be surrendered to ordinary shareholders provides a good reason for companies limiting issues of ordinary shares; although even rights issues (where additional shares are offered to existing shareholders on favour-able terms) may find their way onto the open market, thus diluting the control of the original owners of the company. Furthermore, as was mentioned above, dividend payments are *not tax deductible* expenses for a company, and this adds to the effective cost of equity finance relative to debt finance.

Companies may also raise finance through the issue of *preference shares*, which, in normal circumstances, have no voting rights attached, but which represent *prior claims* over ordinary shareholders on the company's income and capital. These shares usually offer *fixed dividend payments*, which are likely to be higher than the fixed interest payments on comparable debt instruments. This is because of the greater risk incurred by the preference shareholders, in the sense that the company has no legal commitment to pay dividends during any particular time period; whereas interest payments on debt must be made regularly. Also, in the event of liquidation of the company, the debt holders have a prior claim over all classes of shareholders. However, preference shares may be of the *cumulative* variety, which involve a facility for dividends to be carried forward into future periods, if the company is unable to pay dividends in the current period. The fixed return on such shares is likely to be marginally lower than that payable on normal preference shares in the light of the reduced risk for the shareholder.

Most equity shares are *irredeemable*, in the sense that they represent the permanent capital of a company, which cannot be withdrawn except by the company going through a lengthy legal process, involving an application to the courts for permission to reduce its capital base. The reason for this is largely the protection of the creditors of the company, who have an obvious interest in the company maintaining sufficient capital to allow it to cover losses on its assets. However, it is possible for companies to issue a certain amount of *redeemable* equity (determined by the size of its irredeemable equity base). Redeemable preference shares, which will be repurchased by the issuing company on or after a specified date, are very little different from debentures, other than in the company's ability to waive dividends when trading results are poor.

It is important to emphasise that a company may build up its capital base by *retaining profits*. This forms an internal source of financing for the company, and adds to the total of shareholders' funds locked away within the business. This form of financing is not without cost for the company, as the funds which are retained could have been used to purchase, for example, interest-bearing assets. Hence, effectively, the shareholders are forgoing the opportunity to increase their income from other sources by agreeing to the retention of profits. This must imply a belief that the company will be able to produce a better return on those funds than could be obtained from other investments of comparable risk.

2.7.2 The importance of the capital structure

In relation to companies which are not financial institutions, the term 'capital' is normally defined as the sum of their long-term finance, including shareholders' funds, debentures outstanding, long-term bank loans, and so on. (Care should be taken not to confuse this definition of capital with that which is relevant for the operations of financial institutions, as is specified in Chapter 4, at 4.4.5(b).) It is important that a company obtains a sufficiently large proportion of its finance from *long-term sources*, and hence does not become overburdened with short-term debt commitments. This is because the pressures created by the need to repay short-term debt may cause the company to pursue policies which emphasise short-term cash returns rather than long-term profitability. In addition, it is vital to the *long-term prosperity* and *stability* of the company that it maintains a suitable balance of equity and debt financing within its capital structure.

As explained above, the different forms of financing available to a company involve differing after-tax costs and differing legal commitments. Thus, in general, whilst interest-bearing debt is often much cheaper to raise than

continued on next page

---

equity finance (particularly as interest payments are tax deductible whilst dividend payments are not), it does involve a legal commitment to regular interest payments. These payments must be made irrespective of the level of profits generated or the state of the company's cash flows, and hence a large debt burden could lead to the company's downfall, if flows of funds proved to be insufficient to cover the debt interest payments. Indeed, not only does an increasing ratio of debt to equity (often referred to as the *capital gearing ratio*) raise the overall financial riskiness of the company, it is also likely that the unit cost of debt will be pushed upwards, as prospective lenders seek a greater return to cover the perceived greater risk associated with lending to the company. It is for these reasons that a bank manager will always look to the financial commitment of the owners of a business before deciding whether or not funds will be advanced. The size of the prospective borrower's gearing ratio is also likely to influence the margin charged over base rate or LIBOR when funds are advanced.

It is not only those who lend funds to a company who may be perturbed by a high gearing ratio, the shareholders may also be concerned about the situation. Thus, whilst shareholders may be quite content to allow their company to raise its gearing, in the hope of it benefitting from the use of relatively low cost debt funds, there are likely to be limits beyond which the increased risks associated with the higher gearing will cause the shareholders to lose confidence in the company. In practice this may result in the company's share price being depressed, as shareholders seek to reduce their exposure to the now riskier shares, which in turn will make it both harder and more expensive for the company to raise equity finance in the future. Therefore, as the gearing ratio is raised, a point will be reached where the overall cost of capital funds begins to rise and the availability of such funds is called into question. In other words, for any given company there is likely to be a particular combination of debt and equity finance which will *minimise the cost of capital*, and hence which will be optimal in respect of the company's profitability. The optimal gearing ratio will differ between companies, depending especially upon the stability of profits and cash flows. The more stable are profits and cash flows, the higher the gearing ratio may be raised before the risk of the company being unable to service its debts becomes excessive. However, it must be emphasised that companies will only raise their borrowing if they believe that the additional funds obtained may be used profitably. It does not make sense to borrow funds where the return to be earned by the company does not cover the interest charges incurred.

2.8   RISK MANAGEMENT

2.8.1   The nature of financial risks

Companies may borrow funds at either fixed or floating rates of interest. Notwithstanding the possibilities which may exist for switching between fixed and floating rates during the life of a loan, it is normal for there to be some form of commitment to one type of interest payment or the other for a fixed period of time. Consequently, expectations of future interest rate movements, the margin which has to be paid over a floating market rate, and the level of fixed interest rates are critical variables in determining whether to borrow at a floating rate or a fixed rate, assuming that a choice is available to the borrower. However, irrespective of whether a fixed or floating rate commitment is made, *the borrower faces risk*. In the case of a floating rate, there is the risk that the market rate of interest will rise beyond the level which was initially expected, leading to *cash flow problems* due to unexpectedly high debt servicing charges. There is also the problem that competing companies may have chosen to borrow via fixed rate debt, and hence the company's overall *competitive position* in the market for its final product may be undermined. This financial risk is, of course, in addition to the business risk faced by companies as a result of higher interest rates depressing the demand for their products. In the case of a fixed rate commitment, there is no risk in relation to the cash flows associated with the servicing of the debt, which are obviously fixed by the loan agreement; rather, the problem is that market rates of interest may fall below the level which was initially expected, and hence the borrower may become *uncompetitive* relative to other companies which have borrowed via floating rate debt.

It should be recognised that *lenders face opposite risks* to those incurred by borrowers. Thus, when funds are lent at a floating rate, the lender loses out if market rates of interest fall below the level which was initially expected. Where fixed rate loans are made, there is no opportunity to earn higher interest rates even if the market rates rise. Financial intermediaries run particularly severe risks should they borrow short-term funds at floating rates and yet on-lend long-term at fixed rates. An unexpected rise in market rates of interest could drive them into insolvency. Lending long-term at floating rates and borrowing long-term at fixed rates could have a similar effect if market rates were to fall unexpectedly. Clearly, from the point of view of risk limitation, it is sensible for the intermediary both to borrow and to lend at market related rates, or to restrict both borrowing and lending to fixed rates using instruments of similar maturities.

A further risk faced by borrowers and lenders is that relating to *unexpected exchange rate movements* when transactions are denominated in foreign currencies. Thus, for example, if a UK company borrows United States dollars at a fixed rate of interest and immediately switches these into sterling, a subsequent depreciation in the value of sterling relative to the United States dollar will not only raise the amount of sterling required to cover interest payments, but also the sterling value of the principal at repayment will increase. The ultimate effect may be a real rate of interest on the dollar funds which is far in excess of what was initially anticipated. Of course, the risks associated with unexpected exchange rate movements go well beyond those related to borrowing and lending. All forms of business activity involving the use of foreign currencies may be threatened by such movements. For example, a major fear for exporters is that having set the prices of their goods in foreign currency terms, there will then be an appreciation in the value of the domestic currency relative to the relevant foreign currency. This will result in domestic currency earnings falling below the level which was initially anticipated. By contrast, an importer fears a depreciating domestic currency, as this will push upwards the domestic price of imported goods invoiced in foreign currency terms.

Despite careful financial planning most companies are *unavoidably exposed to risks* emanating from *unexpected interest rate movements*. An increasingly large proportion of companies is also at risk from *unexpected exchange rate movements*. Given the observed volatility of interest rates in most Western countries in recent years, as well as the apparent instability of exchange rates between major currencies, it is hardly surprising that financial institutions and markets have produced a wide range of *instruments and techniques* designed to help companies *cope with the financial risks* which they face. However, as none of these instruments and techniques for hedging risks is without cost to the user, a company may still decide to leave its risks unhedged, or may choose to cover only the potentially most damaging risks.

2.8.2 The hedging of interest rate risks

There are many different approaches to the management of interest rate risk. For example, a company may seek to reduce its exposure to interest-bearing debt by shifting the balance of its financing towards equity capital, and hence *reducing its capital gearing ratio*. Using *fixed interest rate debt* removes the cash flow risk associated with floating rate debt, but still leaves the company exposed to the competitive threat from other companies using floating rate debt when interest rates decline. Therefore, the company may reduce its dependence on short-term bank loans by using *factoring services* to turn its outstanding debtors into cash. Factoring is the process whereby a bank or other financial institution buys from a company claims against debtors at a discount to their face value. Unfortunately, this may provide only a short-term solution, as the discount rate on subsequent batches of debtors is likely to vary with market rates of interest. As a longer-term solution, the need to borrow funds in the first place may be reduced via the *leasing* of capital equipment as opposed to its outright purchase. Again banks play an important role in the provision of leasing facilities. However, most attention tends to be focussed upon the so-called *external approaches* to the hedging of interest rate risk, which may be summarised as follows:

(a) *Forward rate agreements (FRAs)*

FRAs relate to the *fixing of an interest rate for a specified period of time in advance and independently of the principal sum borrowed.* For example, a company may have a long-term bank loan outstanding which attracts a floating rate of interest. Fearing an excessive increase in the market rate of interest, the company may wish to limit the rate that it has to pay over a future period. It may be able to do this by negotiating an FRA with a bank (not necessarily the bank from which the loan has been taken), which will effectively fix the rate of interest at, say, 15% p.a. for a specified term. If the floating rate goes above 15%, the bank entering into the FRA will cover the excess interest payments on behalf of the borrower; if the floating rate is below 15%, the borrower will pay the difference to that bank. Thus, the borrower removes the risk of the rate of interest exceeding 15%, but at a cost of not being able to benefit from a floating rate below this value. If the floating rate remains below 15% for the whole of the period of the FRA, the borrower would obviously have been better off not entering into the agreement.

Major limitations on the use of FRAs are that they are normally available only on amounts of £100,000 and above, and they are difficult to obtain for periods in excess of one year. Nevertheless, within these constraints, they can be tailor-made to fit the requirements of the borrower.

(b) *Financial futures*

A financial futures contract is an agreement to buy or sell a standard quantity of a specific financial instrument, at a future date, at an agreed price. Futures contracts are established via organised exchanges, for example the London International Financial Futures and Options Exchange (LIFFE). A borrower wishing to hedge against a rise in interest rates will sell futures contracts; a lender wishing to hedge against a fall in interest rates will buy futures contracts. Once contracts have been set up, any subsequent changes in interest rates will be reflected in changes in the value of the futures contracts, which will be just sufficient to cover losses incurred by the borrower or the lender (depending upon which way interest rates move).

When a futures contract is taken out, only a small proportion of its face value (known as the margin) has to be deposited with the relevant exchange, by both the buyer and seller. If interest rates move from the level agreed within the contract, the amount of margin will be adjusted accordingly. Thus, on LIFFE, the sterling interest rate contract has a nominal value of £250,000 with an associated margin of £1,500. If a borrower wishes to ensure an interest rate of, say, 12% p.a. on a floating rate loan of £500,000 for three months, then two 12% contracts will be sold, and £3,000 of margin will be deposited. The buyer of these contracts also deposits £3,000. If, during the life of the contracts the interest rate rises to 14%, the value of the contracts will fall by 2%, the seller's account is credited with £2,500 (i.e. £500,000 x 2% p.a. x 3 months), and the buyer's account is debited by £2,500. If the futures contracts are then 'closed out' (without the underlying funds to which they relate changing hands), the borrower will receive back the original margin of £3,000, together with an additional £2,500, which covers exactly the extra interest which has to be paid on the loan as a result of the interest rate rising by 2%. The buyer of the contracts will lose £2,500 (recouping only a net £500 of the original margin), but this is exactly equal to the extra interest earned on the funds lent as a result of the interest rate rising by 2%. Thus, both borrower and lender have fixed their effective rates of interest at 12%. Had market rates of interest fallen during the period of the contracts, there would have been a net transfer of funds to the buyer of the futures contracts, to compensate for the lost interest earnings on the loan made. The borrower, having gained from the lower rate of interest, covers this compensation payment.

Once the contracts have been entered into neither party is able to gain from favourable movements in market rates of interest. In addition, it should be recognised that as transactions expenses are involved in dealing in futures contracts, the effective cancelling out of risks between borrowers and lenders is not without a net cost. Also, the parties involved will be required to top up their margin payments when the funds in their accounts fall below their initial value. However, a more important weakness of futures is their inflexibility in respect of the standard characteristics of contracts traded, with their values, maturity periods, and currencies of denomination being strictly limited. Nevertheless, interest rate futures are frequently used by financial institutions wishing to cover open positions arising due to a mismatch of assets and liabilities. They are also an attractive means of financial speculation, as there is no requirement that the buyers and sellers should actually be lenders and borrowers respectively of amounts equal to the nominal value of the contracts. Thus, a relatively small outlay for margin may lead to a substantial gain if interest rates move favourably. The losses following adverse interest rate movements may be equally substantial. This speculative potential of the futures serves a useful purpose by attracting a wide range of participants to the market, thus helping to ensure its viability.

(c) *Interest rate options, caps, floors and collars*

An interest rate option is a right to borrow or to lend a specified sum at a guaranteed rate of interest. The buyer of the option pays a premium (normally a very small fraction of the sum involved) to the seller at the time that the option is sold. On the day that the option expires, the buyer must decide whether or not to exercise the right to borrow or to lend. In the case of an option to borrow, the option will be allowed to lapse if the market rate of interest is below the rate agreed on the option, (it would not make sense to borrow at 10% as per an option agreement, if funds could be raised at 9% on the open market). The buyer's maximum loss is, therefore, limited to the premium payment. For this charge the risk of upwards movements in rates is removed. If the market rate of interest rises above the agreed rate, the option will be exercised. The seller of the option has a commitment to lend funds at the agreed rate, and hence may face substantial losses if these have to be raised at a significantly higher market rate, although the premium will, to some extent, offset these losses. Interest rate options are widely used by corporate treasurers, largely due to their simplicity and flexibility. Most major banks are willing to sell options with characteristics tailor-made for their customers' requirements, in terms of value, period of maturity, currency of denomination and agreed rate of interest.

In addition to normal interest rate options, there are instruments which are sometimes referred to as *synthetic options*, namely *caps, floors and collars*. Basically, a *cap* may be purchased from a bank in order to protect the holder of an existing floating rate loan from the interest rate moving upwards beyond the level specified by the cap contract. The borrower is still able to benefit if interest rates fall, but may claim any excess interest charge over the cap level from the seller of the cap. A *floor* has the same characteristics as a cap, except that it protects an investor or depositor against a floating rate of interest falling below the specified floor level. The seller of the floor will pay the purchaser any interest losses below the floor rate. The purchaser is still able to benefit from increases in interest rates. A *collar* is effectively a combination of a cap and a floor, and may be purchased by a company wishing to protect itself against the interest rate on outstanding debt going beyond a capped level, but prepared to forgo the gain from the interest rate falling below a lower specified level in exchange for a lower premium on the cap. (In effect the company sells a floor to the bank in exchange for a reduced premium on a cap.) This device may be particularly attractive when markets are volatile, and hence premiums on caps are expensive. Caps, floors and collars normally cover periods of less than five years.

(d)   *Interest rate swaps*

An interest rate swap occurs when *borrowers raise funds independently and then swap the associated debt servicing commitments on equal sums.* Borrowers may engage in swap transactions merely because their *expectations differ* as to future interest rate movements. For example, a borrower with outstanding floating rate debt may believe that interest rates are set to rise substantially, and hence may seek a counterparty with fixed rate debt outstanding who is willing to swap commitments. For a swap to be agreed, the counterparty must believe that the floating rate commitment is more attractive than the fixed rate. This need not mean that the total interest payments to be made are expected to be less than those arising under the fixed rate commitment; rather it may be that the pattern of interest payments under floating rates is expected to be better suited to the counterparty's financial requirements. Swaps may take place between *fixed and floating rates*, and between *different floating rates* (for example, six-month LIBOR and base rate). Financial institutions may engage in swap transactions as a means of improving the match between the financing flows attached to their assets and those attached to their liabilities. Maturities for swaps can exceed 10 years, and they are commonly transacted for sums in excess of US$100m.

It is important to appreciate that the parties to a swap transaction *maintain their original responsibilities* to the lenders of the funds. Therefore, whilst the parties may have hedged certain interest rate risks, they must be willing to accept *counterparty risk*, in the sense that if a counterparty defaults on a commitment to make interest payments, the original borrower is still liable for the debt servicing. Consequently, *complex legal problems* may arise in respect of swap transactions which may deter borrowers from becoming involved. However, increasingly banks have become involved in the '*warehousing*' of swaps, whereby they themselves become counterparties to swap transactions until suitable third parties can be found to take up the commitment. This development has facilitated the growth of the swaps market, but clearly it has important implications for banks' own risk exposure.

Swap transactions may be lined up between counterparties even before the underlying borrowing has taken place. This may be motivated by *imperfections in the markets*, which give certain borrowers access to particular financial facilities which are not available to other borrowers. A good example in this context is the ease of access to the sterling bond market for large well-known UK companies. These borrowers are able to raise large amounts of fixed-rate funds on relatively attractive terms. Smaller companies may prefer fixed rate funds but may only be able to raise funds at floating rates. Thus a smaller company may arrange to swap its floating rate commitment for a fixed rate commitment, and may pay the larger company a swap fee for the privilege. The larger company benefits, by obtaining an effectively subsidised floating rate (when the fee is taken into account), and the smaller company obtains the fixed rate commitment it desires. Given that the size of financing requirements is likely to differ between the counterparties, brokers may be used to arrange transactions involving several counterparties.

Finally, it should be recognised that the *external mechanisms* for the management of interest rate risk may be divided into two groups:

(i)   Those which *deny the user the opportunity to benefit from favourable interest rate movements* and/or *create an additional exposure to risk* if the underlying borrowing is paid off early or is not required — borrowing at fixed interest rates, financial futures, interest rate swaps, collars and forward rate agreements fall into this category; and

(ii) those which *allow the user to benefit from favourable interest rate movements* with an initial premium payment effectively buying *insurance* against risk. Options, caps and floors fall into this category.

2.8.3   The hedging of exchange rate risks

Companies may be exposed to risks from currency exchange rate movements in a number of different ways:

(a)   *Transaction exposure* arises from normal international trading activities, when the prices of exports are fixed in foreign currency terms or imports are invoiced in foreign currency terms. This form of exposure to risk has already been explained above.

(b)   *Translation exposure* arises when there is a mismatch between the currencies of denomination of assets and liabilities. For example, if a company has one-half of its liabilities denominated in United States dollars and one-half in sterling, but has only one-quarter of its assets denominated in United States dollars and three-quarters in sterling, then a depreciation in the value of sterling relative to the United States dollar will raise the value of liabilities relative to assets, and upon translation into sterling, the net worth of the balance sheet will fall. Therefore, exchange rate movements may affect the attitude of investors and lenders to a company's financial strength, and hence may influence its ability to raise additional finance on favourable terms.

(c)   *Economic exposure* relates to the effects on the overall international competitiveness of a company resulting from exchange rate movements. For example, a UK company relying upon imports of raw materials invoiced in dollars, whilst exporting most of its output to other EC countries, would have its competitiveness threatened if sterling was to depreciate against the dollar and/or appreciate against other EC currencies.

In principle, the avoidance of translation exposure is simple. A company merely needs to ensure that its assets and liabilities are *balanced* in terms of their *currencies of denomination*. If an imbalance emerges, the company may consider, for example, switching between holdings of marketable securities denominated in different currencies, although this may generate other forms of risk in relation to capital losses on trading and interest rate exposure.

Economic exposure is somewhat more difficult to deal with, as it relates to the *overall performance* of a company relative to foreign competitors. However, the company may minimise its vulnerability by ensuring that its operations are undertaken as efficiently as possible, and that profitability is maintained at a high level. This will allow the company to be more able to absorb adverse cost and price changes arising from exchange rate movements. In addition, it may be in the company's interests to *diversify its base of suppliers and customers* over a range of different countries, thus reducing its exposure to shifts in individual currency exchange rates.

Companies may seek to reduce their transactions risk by way of appropriate management of those aspects of their business which generate such exposure. These *internal risk management devices* include the use of *foreign currency bank accounts*, into which a company deposits foreign currency receipts in readiness to cover anticipated foreign currency expenditures. This mechanism not only *avoids the risks of exchange rate movements* between the time of receipt of the foreign currency funds and the time of expenditure, but also *avoids the payment of commissions and fees* which would otherwise be incurred if the funds were to be switched into, and then subsequently out of, the domestic currency. Of course, this approach is only feasible where payments and receipts are denominated in the *same* foreign currency, and some exposure to risk still remains if there is *uncertainty* in respect of the *magnitude* of the future foreign currency payments. A similar device, which may be used by a large group of companies with a centralised treasury function, is known as *multilateral netting*. Here, the central treasury acts as a clearing house for foreign currency receipts and payments, and takes responsibility for hedging the *net risk exposure* of the group, perhaps using one or more of the external risk management instruments listed below. Whilst netting is a relatively simple concept, the *information systems* required to support its efficient operation may be expensive. In the longer term, it may be appropriate for a large company selling output overseas to *move* some of its *production activities* to countries where its products are purchased, as a means of aligning more closely its revenues and costs in terms of currency of denomination.

Companies may also consider the use of various forms of *external hedging instruments*. This form of risk management is especially relevant for transaction exposure where specific financial commitments have to be honoured at dates which are more or less known in advance. Some of the instruments used to manage currency risk are similar in form to those outlined above in respect of the management of interest rate risk. The most widely used instruments are as follows:

(a) *Forward exchange contracts*

A forward exchange contract is *a firm and binding contract for the sale or purchase of a fixed amount of currency at a future date, at a rate of exchange which is agreed when the contract is made.* Banks are normally willing to enter into forward contracts for most currencies for up to one year in advance, and for major currencies such as the United States dollar, yen, sterling, and deutschmark, contracts for up to five years in advance are available. There are two forms of forward contract:

(i) a *fixed forward contract* relates to a specified maturity date when the currencies in question will be traded;

(ii) an *option forward contract* gives the bank's customer the right to complete the contract on any day of the customer's choosing within the period specified by the contract.

It is important to recognise that forward contracts can only be completed by the currencies to which they relate actually changing hands. Thus, once a contract has been agreed, it is not possible for the bank's customer to take advantage of favourable movements in the spot rate for the currencies involved. For example, if a company contracts to purchase an amount of United States dollars in exchange for sterling at a rate of £1 to $1.50, the purchase must go ahead even if the value of sterling appreciates on the spot market to more than $1.50 for £1.

The *premium or discount* which has to be paid on forward transactions relative to spot transactions, is determined by the *differential between interest rates* available on money market deposits denominated in the currencies concerned (see Chapter 7, at 7.9.2 for details). Where an option forward contract is entered into, the customer is likely to be quoted rates which are somewhat less favourable than on fixed forward contracts, for the obvious reason that the bank must carry additional risk in respect of its own portfolio management, with the date at which the contract is to be completed being at the discretion of the customer within the agreed period. In addition, the customer will also have to pay various administration charges for the setting up of the forward contract. Nevertheless, such contracts guarantee the domestic currency value of foreign currency earnings, or the domestic currency costs of foreign currency expenditures, and hence remove the customer's exposure to exchange rate risk where foreign currency values are known in advance. Where a company is unable to determine the amounts of foreign currency likely to be involved in future transactions, other forms of hedging, for example currency options, may be more suitable.

(b) *Currency options*

A currency option gives the purchaser a right to buy (a call option) or sell (a put option) a specified amount of currency at an agreed exchange rate at a future date. Currency options purchased in Europe may only be exercised on the expiry date, but options purchased in the United States may be exercised in whole or in part at any time up to the expiry date. Most major banks are willing to sell options on a tailor-made basis to meet their customers' specific requirements.

A company buying a currency option is assured of a specific exchange rate when a future expected foreign currency transaction occurs. However, if, by the expiry date for the option, the relevant spot exchange rate has moved in favour of the company, such that the required currency may be purchased cheaper on the spot market than via the exercise of the option, then the option will be allowed to lapse. For example, a UK company may buy a call option to purchase United States dollars for sterling at a rate of £1 to $1.80. At the expiry date the spot rate may be £1 to $1.84, which means that the dollars could be purchased for less sterling on the spot market. Had the company known that the exchange rate was going to move in this manner, clearly the cost of the option could have been avoided. Thus, in practice the option sets the maximum price for the purchase of a currency, but leaves the holder free to take advantage of lower prices on the open market.

If the spot exchange rate moves against the purchaser of an option, then it will either be exercised or sold back to the bank which provided it. Thus, extending the above example, if the spot rate at the expiry date is less than $1.80 for £1, the exercise of the option gives the purchaser access to dollars at a sterling price below that ruling on the spot market. Therefore, even if the expected transaction for which dollars were required does not materialise, the dollars will still be purchased, as they may then be resold at a profit on the spot market. Consequently, the bank which sold the option may be willing to repurchase it at the expiry date, thus allowing both parties to benefit from the avoidance of the transactions costs which would be incurred if the option was to be exercised and the currency resold on the spot market.

A disadvantage in using options is that for a given amount of exchange rate cover, they tend to be more expensive than forward exchange contracts. This is to be expected given the additional risk which the bank has either to carry or to offset through further risk management transactions of its own.

(c) Currency futures

Currency futures operate on precisely the same basis as interest rate futures. The value of currency futures alters to offset the gains or losses experienced by the buyers or sellers as a result of the spot exchange rate deviating from the rate specified by the futures contract. Thus, neither buyer nor seller is able to gain any benefit from 'favourable' movements in the spot exchange rate. This, of course, assumes that the buyers and sellers of futures contracts do in fact have actual foreign-currency exchange commitments which will be affected by movements in the spot rate. In practice, futures contracts may be entered into for purely speculative purposes, where there is no actual underlying transaction to be covered. Where this occurs, the potential returns may be great, but so too is the risk.

Currency futures are bought and sold on established exchanges such as the Chicago International Money Market, but are no longer available on the LIFFE.

(d) *Currency swaps*

A currency swap arises when two counterparties agree to *exchange equivalent borrowed sums of two different currencies*, together with the *associated interest commitments* on those sums. For example, a UK company may raise a loan denominated in deutschmarks, with interest payments and the ultimate repayment of principal to be made in deutschmarks. A German company may raise a loan denominated in sterling, with associated servicing payments to be made in sterling. The two companies may then swap the principal sums, with the UK company taking on responsibility for servicing the sterling debt, whilst the German company will be responsible for servicing the deutschmark debt. The swap transaction may be motivated by *market imperfections* which allow the UK company to raise funds denominated in deutschmarks at a lower rate of interest than the German company would be charged for deutschmarks, and the German company to raise sterling loans more cheaply than could the UK company. In this instance the swap is to the companies' mutual benefit in terms of reduced interest payments alone. However, by swapping, the companies are also able to avoid the exchange rate risk which would occur had they borrowed funds and then switched into the desired currency via the foreign exchange market. The swap gives the German company access to deutschmarks and a commitment to service its debt in deutschmarks. If this company's revenues are also denominated primarily in deutschmarks, movements in the exchange rate are irrelevant in relation to its debt servicing burden. Similarly, the UK company generating sterling revenues faces no exchange rate risk in respect of its debt servicing.

The obvious benefits of currency swaps, from the point of view of managing exchange rate risks, may motivate their use even when there are no immediate interest rate gains to be made. Swaps enable companies to obtain a *better balance of currency denominations within their asset and liability portfolios*. They may also allow the simultaneous switching between fixed and floating interest rates, or between different forms of floating rates. However, the arrangement of swap agreements is not without cost, and banks often earn large fees in this respect. It must also be remembered that each *counterparty remains liable for its original debts and the related servicing*, and hence there is always the risk that one counterparty may suddenly find itself exposed to exchange rate risk if the other should default on its commitment. For an additional fee, the intermediary bank may be willing to guarantee the counterparties' payments, thus allowing them to buy-out this residual risk associated with the swap transaction. Banks may also *'warehouse'* currency swaps, in the same way as explained above in respect of interest rate swaps.

(e) *Currency borrowing for exporters and currency deposits for importers*

A UK company *expecting to receive a foreign currency payment* at a future date may *borrow* that amount of foreign currency immediately and *convert* it into sterling at the *current spot rate*, thus fixing the exchange rate on the transaction. When the foreign currency payment arrives it will be used to pay off the foreign currency loan. Some adjustment to the amount borrowed will be required in order to take account of the interest to be paid on the loan, and, of course, the company takes the risk that the foreign currency payment will not materialise, and hence that it will be left holding a foreign currency debt requiring servicing.

A similar device may be used by a company *expecting to make a foreign currency payment* at a future date. In this case a UK company would *purchase foreign currency at the current spot rate*, and would then *deposit* the funds into an *interest-bearing account* in readiness to make the future foreign currency payment. The risk here is that the expected future transaction will not occur, and that the foreign currency funds will not be required, thus leaving the company holding foreign currency funds that have to be converted to sterling at the ruling spot rate.

Finally, it should be recognised that most of the *external instruments* used for the management of exchange rate risk may create *further exposure to risk* if the expected underlying transaction does not occur, or, in the case of a swap, if the counterparty defaults. It is only with the use of *options*, where an initial premium payment effectively *buys an insurance* against risk, that no further exposure is incurred by the user.

2.9 EXAMINATION PRACTICE
2.9.1 Questions

The following questions are intended to give students an indication of the type of questions which they are liable to face within the topic area of Corporate Sector Finances. As most of the subject matter of this topic area has only been examined within The Monetary and Financial System syllabus since 1991, only questions (2), (4) and (5) are drawn from past examination papers. Students may care to map out answers to these questions before consulting the guidance notes at 2.9.2. Each question carries 25 marks.

(1) (a) Within the context of corporate finance, what is meant by the terms 'internal funding' and 'external funding'? (7)

      (b) Outline the main types of external funding available to a large company. (18)

(2) The finance director of a large manufacturing business informs you that his company is likely to require short-term finance.

      (a) Outline the main methods available to the company to meet its short-term financing requirements. (13)

      (b) Discuss the advantages to the company of any THREE of the methods you have identified in (a). (12)

(October 1991)

(3) (a) For many UK companies, borrowing from banks provides a major source of funds. Identify the main types of financing which are available from banks for corporate customers. (10)

      (b) Companies may raise funds via the issue of sterling debentures and eurobonds. Describe these instruments, and explain the circumstances in which they are likely to be appropriate for the raising of funds by a company. (15)

(4) (a) What risks might an industrial company face as a result of interest rate movements? (12)

      (b) Explain the main financial instruments which a company can use to reduce these risks. (13)

(October 1992)

(5) The Finance Director of a small manufacturing company is concerned about the financial risks the company faces as it expands its business at home and abroad. He approaches you for advice. Explain to him:

(a)   the main interest and exchange rate risks facing a company; (9)
(b)   how a company can protect itself against the risks you have
      discussed in (a).   (16)

(May 1991)

2.9.2   Guidance notes

(1)   (i)   This question requires a broad understanding of the nature of
             corporate finance.
      (ii)   The answer to part (a) of the question should differentiate
             clearly between funds which are raised from *the generation of
             profits and the sale of assets* (internal funding) and those which
             are raised from other sources, involving *borrowing and the
             issuing of equity shares* (external funding).
      (iii) Part (b) of the question requires an outline of the main means
             via which a company may *borrow funds*, including the use of the
             euromarkets. Mention must also be made of the raising of funds
             via the *issue of equity shares*.
      (iv)   Detailed discussion of specific instruments used by companies
             to raise funds is not required.

Source of relevant material:

Part (a)   2.1 (paragraph 3).
Part (b)   2.4(a) and 2.5.1 to 2.7.1 (first paragraphs of each section).

(2)   (i)   This question relates to a *large company*, and hence the *full
             range* of *short-term financing instruments* is potentially avail-
             able.
      (ii)   The answer to part (a) requires a *brief description* of the main
             short-term financing methods available to a large company;
             namely, bank overdrafts, bank (money market) loans, accept-
             ance credits and commercial paper. It is not enough merely to
             list the instruments. Other forms of short-term financing such
             as direct borrowing from the inter-bank market and factoring
             may be mentioned.
      (iii) Part (b) requires a discussion of the *advantages* to the company
             of *any THREE* of the methods outlined in part (a). Discussion
             of the disadvantages of the instruments is not required.

Source of relevant material:

Part (a)   2.5.1, 2.5.2, 2.5.3 and 2.5.4.
Part (b)   2.5.1, 2.5.2, 2.5.3 and 2.5.4.

(3) (i) Part (a) of this question focuses upon the provision of funds by banks to corporate customers. The answer requires a listing of the *different types of bank finance available,* including *overdraft facilities, short-term (money market) loans* and *long-term loans.* It is not necessary to examine in detail the various characteristics of bank loans, but comments should be made on the wide variety of facilities which are available from banks.

(ii) It should be noted that banks may provide finance to corporate customers via the *purchase of marketable securities.*

(iii) The answer to part (b) should begin with a clear description of *sterling debentures* and *eurobonds.* Then, recognising the *minimum size of issues* of these instruments, together with their *currency of denomination,* comments should be made on when their use is likely to be appropriate.

(iv) It is not necessary to discuss the fine technical details relating to the issue and trading of debentures or eurobonds.

Source of relevant material:

Part (a) 2.5.1, 2.5.2 and 2.6.1, and (as background) 2.5.3, 2.5.4, 2.6.2, and 2.6.3.

Part (b) 2.6.2 (paragraphs 1 to 3) and 2.6.3 (especially paragraphs 1 and 2).

(4) (i) Part (a) of this question requires a *description of the risks* faced by a company in terms of the impact upon its *interest commitments* and *competitive position* if it has either *floating* or *fixed* rate debt outstanding. The impact of interest rate movements upon *fixed/floating rate assets* should be noted, as should the possible effect on *demand for the company's output.*

(ii) The answer to part (b) should include a *brief explanation* of the *instruments* which may be used to manage interest rate risk. Recognition should be given to interest rate options, caps, floors and collars, use of fixed rate loans/deposits, forward rate agreements, financial futures and swaps. Simply listing the instruments is not enough.

(iii) There is no need to discuss actual experience of interest rate movements or risk management in the UK or in any other country.

Source of relevant material:

Part (a) 2.8.1 (especially paragraphs 1 and 2).
Part (b) 2.8.2.

(5) (i)   Part (a) of this question requires a brief outline of the nature of both *interest rate risks* and *exchange rate risks*, which may be faced by a company. In respect of interest rate risks, the possible impact on *cash flows* and *competitive position* should be noted. In respect of exchange rate risks, it is necessary to mention *transaction, translation* and *economic exposures*.

      (ii)   Notwithstanding the fact that certain risk management instruments are likely to be inappropriate for a small company, the *full range* of interest rate and exchange rate risk management methods should be outlined in the answer to part (b). Recognising the scope of this question, the answer must be *concise*. Detailed examination of the risk management methods is not required.

    (iii)   There is no need to discuss the causes of fluctuations in interest rates or exchange rates.

Source of relevant material:

Part (a)   2.8.1 and 2.8.3 (paragraph 1).
Part (b)   2.8.2 and 2.8.3.

2.10   FURTHER STUDY

The examination syllabus requires that students should possess a basic knowledge of the corporate sector's balance sheet and sources and uses of funds, and of certain aspects of corporate finance and risk management, with a breadth and depth as indicated by the foregoing sections of this chapter. When undertaking further study, students should bear in mind that the complex technical details to be found in most textbooks dealing with these topics go well beyond examination requirements.

The basic instruments associated with corporate finance and risk management are well established, and comprehensive treatment of their characteristics is given in the standard textbooks on the subject areas; for example *An Introduction to Corporate Finance* by P. Davies (ed.), (1990), and *Treasury Management* by A. Watson and R. Altringham (1986), (both published by The Chartered Institute of Bankers). However, students wishing to keep up-to-date with the rapidly evolving array of variants on the basic instruments should consult one of the periodicals aimed at practitioners in the field; for example, *The Treasurer* or *Euromoney*. The Companies and Markets section of the *Financial Times* also provides a wealth of useful background information.

Coming somewhat closer to home, students should remember that all major clearing banks operate corporate finance departments, and most are quite willing to provide copies of brochures detailing the facilities which they offer to corporate customers. This sort of publication is useful for providing practical examples of facilities which are dealt with only in general terms in textbooks; although it must not be forgotten that such material is produced with the aim of attracting corporate customers, and hence is unlikely to give a totally objective analysis of the relative merits of different forms of financing instruments.

On the broader background of corporate finance and risk management, the *Bank of England Quarterly Bulletin* provides a useful annual survey on UK company financing, as well as occasional articles on specific relevant topics, such as recent developments in financial instruments and markets. *The Economist* and the financial pages of the quality press are also useful in this respect.

Finally, students should recognise that the instruments of corporate finance and risk management normally involve the participation of financial institutions and/or the facilities offered by financial markets. Hence students should remain alert for possible examination questions linking the material covered in the present chapter to that included in Chapters 4 and 5. In particular, corporate financing is an important activity for most major banks, and is crucial to the operation of the capital market.

3 PERSONAL SECTOR FINANCES AND THE HOUSING MARKET

3.1 INTRODUCTION

Personal sector financial requirements are of crucial importance to the operation of the UK financial system. A large proportion of the activities of the retail banks, and almost all of the activities of the building societies, are directed towards satisfying the demands of personal sector customers, and they also dominate the work of pension funds and many insurance companies, unit trusts and investment trust companies. In recent years, with the exception of a short period at the end of the 1980s, the personal sector has been *a major net provider of funds* to the other sectors of the economy, and hence much attention has been paid by financial intermediaries to *attracting personal sector savings*. Whilst a significant proportion of these funds has been channelled back to the personal sector, in the form of mortgage loans and consumer credit, substantial volumes of funds have been used to make loans to industry and commerce, and to purchase securities issued by both private sector companies and the public sector. The importance of such flows of funds for the *efficient operation of the economy* cannot be over-emphasised, and hence a useful starting point for the present chapter is an examination of the personal sector's aggregate financial position, and the recent trends in its balance sheet and sources and uses of funds. This analysis provides a useful insight into the interaction of the personal sector with the major groups of financial institutions, and underlines the importance of the sector for their ongoing development.

For many people, the ownership of residential property represents their single most important investment (excluding their pension arrangements), and the purchase of such property is probably the largest single expenditure that most people will ever make in their personal capacity. However, as most people entering the housing market for the first time or trading up to more expensive property need to borrow funds in order to do so, the *provision of housing finance* is an extremely important aspect of personal sector finances. In the second half of this chapter, housing finance is examined from the perspective of the borrower (the relevant operations of the major providers of such finance, that is the building societies and the retail banks, are considered in Chapter 4, within the more appropriate context of their business activities as a whole). The final section of this chapter is devoted to an analysis of the *determination of house prices* in theory and practice. As will be explained, movements in house prices are not only of crucial significance to the operation of the housing market and its related financing needs, but also have major implications for the welfare of the personal sector and the development of the economy as a whole. (It should be noted that throughout this chapter the terms 'residential property' and 'houses' will be used inter-changeably, although the former is a more accurate description of the relevant concept.)

3.2 THE PERSONAL SECTOR WITHIN THE UK ECONOMY

For official accounting purposes the UK personal sector is defined as all individuals resident in the UK, unincorporated businesses, and non-profit-making institutions (such as registered charities, friendly societies and trade unions).

Table 3.1 shows that between 1988 and 1992 the overall financial position of the personal sector changed markedly. In 1988 a *record financial deficit* was generated by the personal sector. The amount spent by the sector on consumption and investment in real capital assets exceeded personal disposable income by £13.5b, and hence this amount of funds had to be borrowed in net terms from other sectors. A large part of this net borrowing was from *building societies* and *retail banks*, and was in the form of mortgage loans, as will be detailed below. However, by 1990 the personal sector had returned to an overall *financial surplus*, as had been the case during the decade prior to 1988. This surplus grew rapidly between 1990 and 1992, most probably influenced by the impact of the UK's *recession* on *consumer confidence*, undermining the desire of members of the personal sector to take on further debt, and especially affecting conditions in the *housing market*. Significant reductions in the rate of borrowing for house purchases were recorded during the early 1990s, and many members of the personal sector reduced their outstanding exposure to debt. In 1992, the personal sector generated a record financial surplus of £30.8b, emphasising its importance as a *net provider of borrowed funds* within the UK financial system.

Table 3.1 UK personal sector, aggregate financial balance, 1988 to 1992, £b					
	1988	*1989*	*1990*	*1991*	*1992*
Personal sector deficit/surplus	− 13.5	− 6.5	4.0	17.4	30.8
Source: *Financial Statistics,* Central Statistical Office, May 1993					

It is interesting to note that the strengthening of the personal sector's overall financial position since the late 1980s has been mirrored by an equally rapid deterioration in the public sector's financial position. Unusually this sector produced financial surpluses during 1988 and 1989, and was able to make net repayments of its debt to other sectors. In 1990, the public sector returned to a financial deficit position, which subsequently expanded to unprecedented levels. In 1992 the sector's financial deficit was almost £38b, amounting to more than the combined surpluses of the personal sector and the financial institutions sector. Consequently, had it not been for the marked improvement in the personal sector's financial position, the total financial deficit of the domestic economy would have been worse than the £13.8b recorded in 1992, and the requirements for overseas funding would have been correspondingly higher.

3.3 THE PERSONAL SECTOR BALANCE SHEET

At the outset it must be recognised that some elements of data reported in respect of personal sector financial behaviour may be of questionable accuracy. The very nature of many personal sector financial transactions means that data must be collected indirectly from the records of transactions with members of other sectors, and via residual balances once other sectors have been accounted for. Nevertheless, certain elements relating to transactions with the major financial intermediaries are very reliable, and the broad trends in these items of data are probably the most important in relation to the analysis of personal sector finances. With this warning in mind, the UK personal sector's aggregate balance sheet for the years 1987 to 1992 is shown in Table 3.2. The main aspects of the balance sheet may be summarised as follows:

(a) *Financial assets*
  (i) The amount of *notes and coin* held by the personal sector is substantial, and has tended to grow steadily over time. However, it forms only a small proportion of the total financial assets held by the sector, and its relative importance has gradually diminished. This is largely as would be expected given the *increasing financial sophistication* of the personal sector and the wide range of *alternative payments facilities* available.
  (ii) Personal sector holdings of *UK government securities* and *National Savings instruments* broadly reflect the state of the UK public sector's finances. As will be explained in Chapter 6 (at 6.5), it is advantageous for monetary control purposes if public sector budget deficits can be financed by sales of gilt-edged securities and National Savings instruments to the non-bank, non-building society private sector. Therefore, as the public sector's borrowing requirement grows, the effort put into selling such debt instruments to the personal sector is likely to

intensify. During the period of public sector financial surpluses in 1988 and 1989, personal sector holdings of UK government securities and National Savings instruments fell. Since that time holdings have risen steadily, although by 1992 their combined value amounted to only 4.4% of total financial assets held, compared to 6.3% in 1988.

(iii) *Bank and building society deposits* form an *extremely important* part of the personal sector's financial assets portfolio. At the end of 1992 their combined value was £353b (25% of total financial assets). It should be noted that the conversion of the Abbey National Building Society to retail bank status in 1989 caused a substantial shift of assets from the building societies sector to the retail banks sector, thus exaggerating the growth trend of bank deposits during the late 1980s, whilst retarding the growth of deposits with the building societies. During the early 1990s, deposits in aggregate continued to grow, but at a somewhat slower rate.

(iv) The *trade credit* element of the balance sheet represents the credit granted by the unincorporated businesses included within the personal sector. The bulk of the credit extended relates to the normal terms of trade with other businesses. Significantly, the amount of trade credit has grown steadily in recent years, despite the poor trading conditions experienced during the early 1990s.

(v) Direct holdings of *company securities* form a significant element of total financial assets (15.4% at the end of 1992). However, of much greater importance are the indirect holdings of company securities via investments in *life assurance, pension funds* and *unit trusts*. Whilst the total value of claims on these financial intermediaries does not relate exclusively to company securities (as they also hold public sector debt instruments, bank deposits and real property), around 70% of their assets are represented by such instruments. Therefore, in total, almost a half of the personal sector's financial asset holdings relate ultimately to company securities, although about three-quarters of these are effectively locked away in life assurance policies and pension funds, and hence cannot be realised at will (except for certain life assurance policies, but even here substantial capital losses may be sustained upon surrender). As explained in Chapter 2, the importance of personal sector claims on the corporate sector is to be expected within a capitalist free market economy. Also, it must be remembered that the value of these claims is at the mercy of market forces. Thus, given the significance of such claims for the personal sector, a collapse of

Table 3.2   UK personal sector, aggregate balance sheet, 1987 to 1992 (end year figures), (£b)

	1987	1988	1989	1990	1991	1992
Financial Assets						
Notes and coin	11.5	12.4	13.1	13.0	13.4	14.4
UK government securities	18.9	13.0	9.7	10.6	12.0	18.8
National Savings	34.9	36.3	34.8	35.6	37.7	42.7
Other public sector debt	1.2	1.0	0.9	0.8	0.7	0.6
Bank deposits: sterling	78.1	94.5	141.8	157.2	162.2	166.5
: foreign currency	2.2	2.5	4.2	3.3	2.9	3.3
Building society deposits	129.3	149.6	140.6	158.5	175.9	186.3
Domestic trade credit	29.1	32.7	35.1	36.1	41.1	44.0
Unit trust units	17.1	18.5	26.5	19.0	20.4	23.2
Company securities: UK	113.6	117.8	144.3	123.7	137.2	131.3
: overseas	9.9	11.4	12.4	9.0	10.5	11.9
Life assurance and pension funds	390.2	458.7	578.9	586.9	610.9	713.3
Direct and other investment abroad	0.5	0.5	0.6	0.6	0.6	0.8
Miscellaneous and adjustments	22.7	26.3	33.5	37.3	40.9	43.7
Total financial assets	859.2	975.2	1176.4	1191.6	1266.4	1400.8
Financial liabilities						
Public sector lending	0.2	0.3	0.4	0.3	0.4	0.4
Bank lending: sterling	51.9	64.4	77.5	84.8	85.1	82.0
: foreign currency	1.0	1.3	1.8	1.9	1.6	1.1
Credit extended by retailers	2.2	2.4	2.4	2.4	2.5	2.7
Domestic trade credit	25.2	26.6	28.5	30.5	32.5	34.0
Loans for house purchase: building societies	131.6	155.3	152.5	176.7	197.6	211.5
: other	52.1	68.5	105.4	117.8	123.9	128.2
Overseas investment in the UK	3.7	5.3	6.3	7.2	7.7	6.9
Miscellaneous and adjustments	14.5	16.2	18.4	20.5	21.1	21.5
Total financial liabilities	282.4	340.3	393.2	442.1	472.4	488.3
Net financial assets	576.8	634.9	783.2	749.5	794.0	912.5
Tangible assets	851.8	1134.9	1235.3	1245.0	n/a	n/a
Total net assets	1428.6	1769.8	2018.5	1994.5	n/a	n/a

Source: *Financial Statistics*, Central Statistical Office, May 1993.
National Income and Expenditure, 1992, Central Statistical Office.

equity prices, as occurred in October 1987, can have a substantial adverse impact on the value of the personal sector's total wealth.

(vi) At the end of 1992, *total financial asset holdings* of the UK personal sector amounted to £1,400b, which was 63% higher than the corresponding figure five years earlier. During this period, the retail price index rose by 36%, thus implying that the real value of financial asset holdings rose significantly. As around 40% of the personal sector's financial assets could be redistributed within portfolios relatively quickly (notwithstanding periods of notice attached to deposits and associated transactions costs), the efforts that financial intermediaries put into the marketing of financial products to the personal sector is easy to understand.

(b) *Financial liabilities*

(i) *Bank lending* to the personal sector, for purposes other than the purchase of residential property, has accounted for around 20% of the sector's total outstanding financial liabilities in recent years. However, the rate of new bank lending to the personal sector fell markedly during the early 1990s. Whilst net lending still took place in all years covered by Table 3.2, the total outstanding bank debt actually fell in 1992. This phenomenon was caused by the writing-off of bad debts to the personal sector, with both unincorporated businesses and individual borrowers being badly affected by the recession.

(ii) The largest category of financial liabilities of the personal sector relates to *loans for the purchase of residential property*. At the end of 1992, such debt amounted to £340b (almost 70% of total financial liabilities), having continued to increase throughout the period of recession, albeit at a slower rate than during the later years of the 1980s. At the end of 1992, the amount of housing finance related debt outstanding was about 84% higher than five years earlier, which represents a significant increase in real value. The dominant provider of this finance was the *building societies sector*, although the *retail banks* made significant contributions to the total of funds lent. The importance of mortgage loans within the personal sector's liabilities portfolio explains both the political sensitivity and the potentially large economic impact of changes in mortgage loan interest rates.

(iii) *Domestic trade credit* has maintained its importance as a financial liability of unincorporated businesses within the personal sector, although its growth has been slow in recent years.

The total financial liabilities of the personal sector grew somewhat more rapidly than the sector's financial assets during the period 1988 to 1992, although a *healthy balance of net financial assets was maintained throughout*. Only in 1990 was a reduction in net financial assets recorded, and this coincided with a reduction in the value of company securities and unit trust holdings, which may be partly explained by depressed stock market conditions, and partly by net withdrawals of funds from company security investments (as will be explained at 3.4 below). At the end of 1992, total net financial assets of the personal sector amounted to £913b, a large proportion of which is accounted for by claims against the corporate sector. In addition, it should be noted that the personal sector owns substantial amounts of *tangible assets*, the value of which has persistently exceeded the value of net financial asset holdings. By far the most important element of tangible assets relates to *ownership of residential property*. At the end of 1990 (the most recent date for which official data are available as at summer 1993), the value of personal sector holdings of residential property amounted to £1,119b, or 90% of all tangible assets held. These figures show graphically the importance of house price movements for the total value of personal sector wealth. To the extent that *consumer behaviour* is influenced by perceptions of personal wealth, changes in house prices may, therefore, have a significant impact on broader economic trends.

The importance of the activities of *financial institutions* for personal sector finances is clearly illustrated by the balance sheet structure. The crucial role of the banks and the building societies on both sides of the balance sheet is without question, particularly in respect of the taking of sterling deposits and the making of mortgage loans. However, *non-bank financial intermediaries dominate the assets side*, with life assurance companies, pension funds and unit trusts playing a key role in personal investment activities. A range of other institutions, offering broking and financial advice, are also used in respect of securities transactions.

3.4   PERSONAL SECTOR SOURCES AND USES OF FUNDS

Table 3.3 provides a summary of the personal sector's sources and uses of funds for the period 1988 to 1992. These data help to clarify the recent trends in personal sector financial activities, effectively by-passing the impact on financial asset and liability holdings caused by changes in the market prices of securities and decisions by lenders (primarily financial intermediaries) to write off outstanding debt.

(a)   *Sources of funds*

The sources of funds used by the personal sector may be divided into *saving* and *borrowing*. Saving relates to the amount of funds remaining after consumption expenditure has been deducted from personal disposable income. Since 1988 there has been a *rapid growth* in the rate of *personal sector saving*. In 1988 the ratio of saving to personal disposable income was 5.6%, an extremely low value by historic standards for the UK. By 1992 this ratio had risen to 11.6%, against the background of deteriorating economic conditions. Furthermore, the general uncertainty in respect of the UK's future economic prospects during the early years of the 1990s was probably responsible for a *massive reduction* in the personal sector's demands for *borrowed funds*. These two marked trends altered fundamentally the balance of personal sector funding. In 1988 saving accounted for only 25% of the sector's sources of funds; in 1992 the proportion was 74%. Within the borrowed funds category, the amount of *net borrowing from banks* for purposes other than the purchase of residential property *largely collapsed* over the period, with only £400m net borrowing taking place in 1992, as opposed to £13.5b in 1989. Borrowing for the purchase of residential property also declined, but less rapidly, falling from £40.1b in 1988 to £17.8b in 1992. Interestingly, both banks and building societies managed to increase their share of the mortgage loan market during this period as the specialist and public sector providers of funds limited their exposure to the mortgage loan market. The reduced rate of mortgage lending was due to a cumulation of factors affecting both borrowers' demands (especially rising unemployment and generally adverse economic conditions) and lenders' supply (with lending criteria being tightened in the face of a rising level of mortgage loan servicing problems and falling house prices affecting security values).

The fundamental shift in the balance of saving and borrowing has had a *major impact on the importance of both banks and building societies* as a source of personal sector funds. In 1988 banks accounted for 33.4% of total identified sources of funds, and building societies for 32.7%. In 1992 the corresponding proportions were 9.2% and 20.3% respectively. But looking solely at personal sector borrowing both banks and building societies consolidated their positions during the period noted.

Considering the personal sector's sources of funds relative to those of the corporate sector in recent years, it may be observed that the overall changes in the former have been much more modest than changes in the latter. Whilst both sectors experienced substantial reductions in levels of borrowing, the personal sector adjusted its saving level in a manner which largely compensated for the impact of lower borrowing on its funds flows. The corporate sector has been much slower to adjust its financial position. This is probably as would be expected given the personal sector's ability to alter the balance of its saving and consumption expenditure with relative ease. Adjustments to internal sources of funds are much more difficult to achieve for companies, and the capital market would not be receptive to new issues of equity shares at a time of depressed business conditions.

Table 3.3   UK personal sector, sources and uses of funds, 1988 to 1992, £b

	1988	1989	1990	1991	1992
Sources of funds					
Saving	17.8	23.5	31.7	39.7	50.7
Borrowing:					
Bank borrowing	13.3	13.5	8.5	2.0	0.4
Credit extended by retailers	0.2	—	0.1	0.1	0.1
Loans for house purchase:					
Public sector	−0.2	−0.1	−0.5	−0.9	−0.5
Banks	10.9	7.2	6.4	4.7	5.9
Building societies	23.7	24.0	24.1	20.9	13.9
Other	5.7	3.1	2.4	1.8	−1.5
Other loans and mortgages	0.8	1.4	0.5	−0.4	−1.7
Other sources of funds and adjustments	0.3	−0.7	0.4	0.4	1.3
Total identified sources	72.5	71.9	73.6	68.3	68.6
Uses of funds					
Liquid assets:					
Notes and coin	1.2	0.8	−0.1	0.4	0.8
National Savings	1.4	−1.5	0.8	2.2	5.0
Deposits with banks	16.8	21.5	17.2	6.1	5.9
Deposits with building societies	20.2	17.6	18.0	17.3	10.6
Other	−0.1	0.5	0.1	−0.2	0.5
UK government securities	−1.8	−2.2	−1.0	1.3	3.0
Other public sector debt	−0.5	−0.4	−0.3	0.2	0.4
Company securities	−10.4	−18.9	−9.1	−0.9	4.7
Life assurance and pension funds	20.1	26.5	25.9	24.5	22.2
Investment in fixed assets and stocks	30.1	29.2	27.5	23.6	21.7
Other uses of funds	3.4	3.3	3.3	2.6	2.3
Total identified uses	80.4	76.4	82.3	77.1	77.1
Balancing item	−7.9	−4.5	−8.7	−8.8	−8.5

Source: *Financial Statistics*: Central Statistical Office, May 1993.

(b)   *Uses of funds*

Table 3.3 shows that whilst the overall volume of funds used by the personal sector to purchase financial claims and make capital investments was relatively stable during the period 1988 to 1992, there were, nevertheless, some *very important shifts in the pattern of uses of funds*. The most significant shift related to an increase in the *purchase of securities* and a corresponding reduction in the additions made to *deposits with banks and building societies*. In 1988 total new deposits with banks and building societies amounted to £37b, or approximately 46% of identified uses of funds; in 1992 this flow was down to £16.5b, or about 21% of total uses of funds. This shows clearly that the substantial increase in personal sector savings over this period was not reflected in increased flows of deposits, but rather went into other forms of investment. By contrast, during the late 1980s, when saving was at an historically low level relative to disposable income, the massive increase in bank and building society deposits was matched by the *running down of direct holdings of company securities*, with funds also being *withdrawn from the housing market* as mortgage lending reached record levels. (The latter phenomenon relates to the concept of *equity withdrawal* from housing, and is discussed below at 3.6.7.)

Taking *UK government securities, National Savings and other public sector debt instruments* together, it may be observed that following several years of running down holdings of such claims, the personal sector began to be a net purchaser of public sector debt once again in 1991, reflecting the return to budget deficit for the public sector. In 1992, the personal sector made net purchases of such instruments to the value of £8.4b (or approximately 11% of total personal sector uses of funds). An even greater turnaround in the uses of funds occurred in respect of *company securities*. In 1989 the personal sector withdrew a massive £18.9b from holdings of company securities. Withdrawals on a much smaller scale occurred in the following two years; but in 1992 net purchases with a cash value of £4.7b were made.

Throughout the period covered by Table 3.3, the two main uses of personal sector funds related to *investments in life assurance policies and pension funds* and in *fixed assets and stock* (with the most important element of fixed assets being *residential property*). Over the period 1989 to 1992, the rate of investment in life assurance policies and pension funds decreased slightly, although its total value exceeded that of investment in fixed assets and stocks during 1991 and 1992, following a more rapid reduction in the latter after 1988. Once again, the economic uncertainty prevalent in the UK may be blamed for the reduced commitment of the personal sector to raising its holdings of longer-term investments. Also, the depressed state of the housing market, and more so rising unemployment, undoubtedly undermined the personal sector's willingness to take on debt for the purpose of purchasing residential property and other fixed capital assets (in the case of unincorporated businesses).

Finally, it may be noted that whilst the personal sector continued to build up its total holdings of *liquid assets* during the period 1988 to 1992, the rate of increase slowed markedly. In 1988 flows of funds into liquid asset holdings amounted to £39.5b (49% of total funds); in 1992 the flow was down to £22.8b (30% of total funds). This pattern of flows reflects the *financial pressures* faced by members of the personal sector, especially during the early 1990s, but may also be linked to the *falling levels of returns* available on liquid assets over this period. In the face of falling interest rates, investments in company securities become more attractive, as do fixed coupon gilt-edged securities. An important outcome of these trends was an *intensification of the competition* between retail banks, building societies and other financial intermediaries offering facilities to the personal sector. Of particular note was a growing tendency for intermediaries to offer *fixed interest rates* on deposits (in order to attract depositors fearing further interest rate reductions) and on loans (as a means of attracting borrowers who required certainty in respect of their cash flow commitments, and who believed that interest rates were unlikely to fall much further). Also, many institutions *broadened the range of financial services* made available to their customers. The strong demands for insurance, pension and other longer-term investment facilities not only underpinned the continuing growth of the specialist providers in these areas of activity, but also have encouraged many banks and building societies to expand their own ranges of products either directly or via joint ventures with other institutions.

3.5 PERSONAL SECTOR FINANCIAL RISKS

Members of the personal sector face a number of financial risks which may cause them serious financial problems and threaten their economic welfare. The existence of these risks helps to explain why individuals, unincorporated businesses, and the like tend to hold a range of financial and other assets, and why specific types of financial liabilities are incurred, and why both asset and liability portfolios may be altered in structure over time. The main risks of relevance to the personal sector may be categorised as relating to default, inflation, changes in financial requirements, interest rate movements and changes in government economic policy, although it should be recognised that various aspects of these risks are interrelated.

3.5.1 Default

The most obvious default risk run by the personal sector relates to the granting of trade credit by unincorporated businesses. Quite simply, *debtors may be unable or unwilling to discharge their debt*, and creditors may then be forced to write-off the debt or perhaps initiate expensive legal action. This type of risk is potentially very damaging, especially in areas of business where the granting of substantial amounts of trade credit is regarded as part of the normal terms of trade. The only protection against this risk is for creditors to undertake *careful screening of the creditworthiness of potential debtors* before the credit is granted. If losses on credit become too great, businesses may feel obliged to curtail the provision of credit, perhaps offering a compensating discount for cash sales as a means of maintaining the level of turnover.

The bulk of personal sector financial asset holdings represent claims on financial institutions. In this context, there is always some risk that an *individual institution will fail,* due to inept management or fraud. Depositors or investors with a failed institution may lose the entire value of their deposits or investments, although this type of occurrence has tended to be very rare in the UK. This is because there are often *officially-sponsored depositor/investor protection schemes,* which provide at least some insurance safety net, albeit often limited in scope. The scheme operated in respect of sterling deposits with UK banks provides a good example of the arrangements available in the UK (this is described in Chapter 4, at 4.10.3). In addition the *liquidation value* of a failed institution must be taken into account, as this may allow for some repayment of deposits or investments, although this may take a considerable time to resolve, and may lead to financial hardship in the meantime. The difficulties which may arise in this context were clearly demonstrated by the plight of those individuals dependent upon pension schemes associated with the Maxwell Corporation, which collapsed in 1991.

The *direct ownership of company securities* is *inherently risky,* although certain types of companies are more likely to get into difficulties than others. It is rare for long-established, well-managed 'blue chip' companies to go into liquidation. The more likely occurrence is that such companies may experience a gradual erosion of their trading performances, which will be reflected in their share values. Smaller, and especially unlisted, companies are far more at risk from total failure; and hence investors are wise to hold *diversified portfolios of company securities* in order to spread their risks, and to take *professional advice* before committing funds to such uses.

Government securities issued by major Western nations are effectively *free of default risk,* but if investments in such instruments have to be realised before their maturity dates *capital losses may still be incurred* (if interest rates in general have risen since the instruments were purchased). In practice, the only truly *capital-safe investments* are *National Savings instruments* which may be liquidated for their full nominal values on demand or after a short period of notice; but even here the investor might have to forgo the higher returns on the instruments that would have been available had they been held until their natural maturity date. Also, National Savings instruments are only available in limited quantities for individual investors.

3.5.2 Inflation

As explained in Chapter 1 (at 1.10.4), major problems can arise in respect of financial transactions as a result of the *difficulty in predicting accurately the future rate of inflation*. Consequently, when borrowers and lenders agree on a particular structure of interest rates for borrowed funds, they are taking the risk that the *actual rate of inflation* will turn out to be *significantly different from the rate expected*. For example, if the rate of inflation proves to be higher than expected, then a borrower with a fixed interest rate commitment will gain at the expense of the lender (as the real value of the interest payments is eroded by inflation, and the payments may even prove to be insufficient to maintain the real value of the sum borrowed, let alone provide a real return on the investment). *Linking interest payments to market rates of interest* (which may be expected to move broadly in line with the trend of inflation) or to a suitable *price index* may help to alleviate this problem of *unanticipated transfers of wealth* between borrowers and lenders (see Chapter 1, at 1.9.4), but these approaches still leave the parties uncertain as to the actual cash payments which will have to be made, and this may cause serious budgetary problems.

In order to avoid the problems which interest-bearing debt may entail during periods of inflation, personal sector savers (investors) may *purchase company equity shares*, the capital values of which, and the income from which, tend to rise with inflation. Of course, the selection of a suitable portfolio of equities is itself risky, and investments in individual companies may prove to be disastrous even when the stock market as a whole is performing well.

A further possible hedge against inflation is *residential property*. But as recent experience has shown, house prices can fall as well as rise, and even over sustained periods of time the investment value of houses may be in doubt.

Personal sector financial behaviour may be affected by inflation in a more general way via its impact on the *broad balance between consumption and saving*. It might be thought that the expectation of inflation would encourage individuals to *reduce their rate of saving*, and *bring forward purchases of goods, services and real assets* before their prices are pushed upwards. However, the evidence would suggest that often the opposite reaction occurs. That is, the increased economic uncertainty generated by inflation, including the fear of future unemployment (perhaps in expectation of deflationary policies to combat inflation), *causes saving to rise* as a means of providing *added financial security*. There is also the view that some people may raise their rates of saving in order to *preserve the real value of their wealth holdings*, which would otherwise be eroded by the effects of inflation.

3.5.3 Changes in financial requirements

Against a background of *economic uncertainty*, it is difficult for both individuals and businesses to *predict their future financial needs*, especially several years in advance. Consequently, decisions over the deployment of financial asset holdings may entail significant risk arising as a result of *unanticipated changes in financial circumstances*. As liquid assets which can be turned into spending power quickly without loss tend to offer lower yields than longer-term investments, an investor faces the *choice between easier access to funds or higher returns*. Once an investment portfolio has been selected, an unanticipated change in financial circumstances may necessitate the *forced sale of securities*, with the associated risk of capital loss, or the *premature withdrawal of deposits* from financial institutions, which may incur interest penalties. Indeed, where access to funds is either not possible or would involve excessive costs, the investor may be in the invidious position of having to borrow funds at rates of interest higher than the returns being earned on the investments held. This possibility provides a powerful incentive for investors to hold *a range of financial assets of differing maturities and characteristics*; although for many individuals the freedom of choice of portfolio is limited by their pension and life assurance needs and their outstanding debt commitments.

Unanticipated changes in financial circumstances may have particularly serious implications for individuals who are *net debtors*. For example, where there is a large mortgage loan outstanding, the plans for its servicing may be thrown into confusion by the loss of a job, illness, the separation from a partner, and so on. Various forms of *insurance* may be taken out in respect of some such eventualities, but these always entail costs and so may not be taken up. In any event full insurance cover may not be available against some risks, or may only be available at a prohibitive cost. In practice, it is probably impossible to protect fully against the effects of unanticipated changes in financial circumstances, and the minimisation of the associated risks can only occur against the background of *prudent financial decision-making* which avoids all unnecessary financial commitments, and leaves flexibility to alter asset portfolio compositions as events unfold.

3.5.4 Interest rate movements

The interest rate risks faced by members of the personal sector are basically the same as those faced by companies (explained in Chapter 2, at 2.8.1). Briefly, individuals holding *variable rate deposits* will find that their interest income declines as market rates of interest fall, and this may cause difficulties for those people with only limited alternative sources of income, such as pensioners. By contrast, individuals holding *fixed rate instruments* will be protected against the cash flow implications of movements in interest rates, but they will not benefit from a general increase in the level of interest rates, which may be serious if the increase occurs in response to a rising level of inflation. The implications of interest rate movements for borrowers are the opposite of those for the lenders of funds. Thus, borrowers with variable rate debt benefit when interest rates fall, but miss the opportunity for reduced servicing costs if fixed rate debt is held. An increase in interest rates may create difficulties where substantial amounts of variable rate debt are held; for example, in respect of a large mortgage loan.

The *market valuation of securities holdings* may be affected by interest rate movements. When market interest rates rise (fall), fixed interest marketable securities may incur capital losses (gains) if they are sold prior to their maturity date. The *market value of company shares* may also be affected depending upon the perceived impact of the interest rate changes on corporate cash flows and future profitability. (For further discussion of the possible indirect effects on financial decisions of interest rate movements, see Chapter 7, at 7.10.)

Other than not holding interest-bearing claims and not borrowing funds, there is little that members of the personal sector can do to avoid interest rate risk entirely. It would appear that for savers, the only sensible course of action is for asset portfolios to be *diversified*, including various types of interest-bearing instruments, as well as equity-based claims and real property. Notwithstanding possible unforeseen changes in circumstances, borrowers should ensure that they are able to cope with the cash flow implications if interest rates were to rise to the *maximum level* which would appear realistic within the ruling political and social environment.

3.5.5 Government economic policy changes

The operation of government economic policy, and especially *sudden changes* in the direction of policy, may have adverse effects on personal sector finances, via both asset and liability holdings. An obvious example of the type of difficulties which may arise is in respect of the impact which *monetary policy* may have on *interest rates*. As outlined above, significant movements in interest rates may have serious implications for both asset holders and borrowers, depending upon whether rates fall or rise. In addition, attempts *to control money supply growth* may require constraints to be placed on *bank and building society lending*, thus making it harder for the personal sector to finance its desired activities. The policy may also affect financial decisions via its impact on *general economic developments*, and hence the desire to consume or save and attitudes towards the deployment of assets and borrowing.

Changes in *fiscal policy* may impact directly on personal sector financial decisions by altering the *tax regime* in respect of interest earnings or payments or capital gains. Privileged tax positions for investments in pension schemes, National Savings instruments and personal equity plans, and the tax relief currently available on mortgage interest payments could all be affected by policy changes, with potentially massive effects on personal sector finances given the importance of such instruments within the sector's balance sheet. *The public sector's expenditure plans and overall budgetary position* are also of relevance. In particular, the need for the Government to finance large borrowing requirements may necessitate the improvement of returns on public sector debt instruments, which may have repercussions in the markets for other financial instruments. General upwards pressure on interest rates may affect the personal sector as indicated above at 3.5.4. Of course, if the public sector borrowing requirement is believed to be excessively large, then *business confidence may be undermined and economic growth threatened*, thus adding further *uncertainty* to the financial environment. In practice, the implications of fiscal policy for personal sector finances are usually complex, and often wide-ranging. In addition to its direct effects, it is also necessary to take account of its *broader economic implications* as they relate to aggregate demand, output, employment, inflation and business expectations. As suggested above these factors may be extremely important in the determination of personal sector financial decisions.

Whilst monetary policy and fiscal policy are perhaps the most relevant aspects of government economic policy for personal sector financial decision-making, it must be recognised that changes in *any aspect of government policy* may have some influence on personal sector finances. A good example in this context was the UK Government's decision to withdraw sterling from the EC's Exchange Rate Mechanism in September 1992. This event precipitated a substantial reduction in interest rates in the UK and led to a marked depreciation in the exchange value of sterling. The possibility of these developments had largely been rejected by many investors and borrowers during the months preceeding the Government's change of policy. Consequently, it is probable that many people found themselves holding portfolios of financial assets and liabilities which they would not have chosen had they known the changes in circumstances which were going to occur. Moreover, the Government's willingness to abandon its high interest rate and stable exchange rate policy introduced a significant additional risk factor into all financial calculations, and altered the relative attractiveness of various types of financial assets from the viewpoint of both lenders and borrowers.

3.6 HOUSING FINANCE IN THE UK

3.6.1 Background

The purchase of residential property is the largest single expenditure that most individuals are ever likely to make in their personal capacity, and, as Table 3.4 clearly demonstrates, the popularity of owner-occupation of dwellings has grown significantly in recent years. In fact, the UK has one of the highest proportions of owner-occupation in the world, amounting to two-thirds of all tenures at the end of 1992. The absolute amount of rented accommodation available in the UK has diminished steadily since the early 1980s, although a significant part of this reduction is accounted for by the purchase of local authority houses by their tenants under the Government's policy to stimulate home ownership.

A large proportion of purchases of residential property are financed, at least in part, by *mortgage loans*. As explained above, for the UK personal sector in aggregate, such loans dominate total financial liabilities. In 1980, the proportion of personal sector financial liabilities in the form of mortgage loans was 57%; by the beginning of 1993 this proportion had risen to almost 70% (amounting to approximately £340b). The importance of housing finance to the personal sector cannot be denied, and it may be argued that the flow of mortgage interest payments provides an important channel for the implementation of government monetary policies. For example, higher rates of interest reduce the spending power (net of interest commitments) available to people with outstanding variable rate mortgage loans. As such people often tend to consume a large proportion of their income, whilst those in receipt of interest earnings on variable rate deposits are perhaps less likely to alter their spending patterns as interest rates rise, the aggregate effect on consumer spending may be substantial.

Some economists would argue that changes in the *real value of residential property* may also affect *personal sector expenditure decisions* in aggregate. Thus, during periods when house prices rise faster than the general rate of inflation, it is argued that people feel better off and hence are willing to spend a higher proportion of their disposable income. This, of course, will tend to underpin economic growth, support both consumer and borrower confidence, and hence create an economic climate within which people feel more willing either to enter the housing market for the first time or to move to more expensive properties. The outcome is that *house prices* may be pushed up still further, reinforcing what might be seen as a virtuous cycle, with residential property becoming an increasingly attractive *investment medium*. In many respects this was the type of situation which existed in the UK during the late 1980s. Unfortunately, if the underlying economic conditions alter, the *accumulated mortgage debt* may become a serious obstacle to future progress. For example, if the pace of economic growth

Table 3.4   UK housing tenure, 1980 to 1992 (end year figures)

Year	Owner occupied		Public sector rented		Private sector rented		Housing association rented		Total dwellings
	m	%	m	%	m	%	m	%	m
1980	11.6	55.5	6.5	31.1	2.8	13.4	—	—	20.9
1981	12.0	55.8	6.6	31.0	2.4	11.1	0.5	2.2	21.5
1982	12.6	58.1	6.4	29.3	2.2	10.3	0.5	2.3	21.7
1983	13.0	59.4	6.2	28.5	2.2	9.8	0.5	2.3	21.9
1984	13.4	60.6	6.1	27.7	2.1	9.4	0.5	2.4	22.1
1985	13.8	61.6	6.0	27.0	2.0	8.9	0.5	2.5	27.3
1986	14.1	62.7	6.0	26.4	1.9	8.5	0.6	2.5	22.6
1987	14.5	63.8	5.8	25.6	1.8	8.1	0.6	2.6	22.7
1988	15.0	65.0	5.7	24.6	1.8	7.8	0.6	2.6	23.1
1989	15.4	66.3	5.4	23.4	1.8	7.6	0.6	2.8	23.2
1990	15.7	67.1	5.3	22.5	1.7	7.5	0.7	3.0	23.4
1991	16.0	67.7	5.2	21.9	1.7	7.3	0.7	3.1	23.6
1992	16.1	67.7	5.1	21.4	1.8	7.5	0.8	3.4	23.8

Source: *Housing and Construction Statistics*, Department of the Environment, various issues.

Note: The 1980 figures for 'housing association rented' tenure are included within the 'private sector rented' category.

starts to decline, and more so if unemployment rises, *consumer confidence* may be dented, potential entrants to the housing market may be deterred and trading up to more expensive properties becomes less attractive. If a substantial rise in interest rates accompanies, or perhaps precipitates, these changes in economic conditions, then a downwards spiral of economic decline centred on the housing market may be established. Quite simply, high mortgage loan interest rates do not only *drain spending power* away from groups in society with high propensities to spend, but also may cause debts to become unmanageable for individuals who have become *over-committed* during the boom years, or who find themselves unemployed. As house prices stagnate, and in some instances fall, due to a decline in new demand coupled with forced sales required to clear mortgage and other debts, people in general feel worse off, and confidence in economic prospects declines, thus intensifying the recessionary conditions. During the early 1990s the UK experienced this phenomenon. Whilst other factors, including a downturn in many of the UK's overseas markets, contributed to the economic stagnation, there is little dissent from the view that the nature of the UK's housing market and housing finance system played an extremely important part in the events observed.

Future trends in the demand for housing finance are difficult to predict, and the recent slump in the housing market may have altered the personal sector's perception as to the benefits of owner-occupation. Of continuing relevance will be demographic factors, such as changes in population growth, age profiles and family size. The Government's policies relating to support for the housing market and local authority house sales, and any changes to the tax regime are also likely to be significant. However, perhaps the most important factor is the *confidence* which the personal sector has in the *medium-term prospects for the UK economy*. Uncertainty in respect of future employment patterns and the general trends in economic growth places a major constraint on the willingness of potential first-time buyers to commit to house purchases, and the whole of the housing market is then depressed.

3.6.2 Government regulation of housing finance

A fundamental concept relating to the provision of housing finance is the *mortgage*. Legally, a mortgage is a *charge over property*, conferred by the owner of the property (the borrower) on a lender, in order to *secure the loan*. If the borrower defaults on loan repayments or fails to meet the terms of the loan in some other way, the lender may apply to court for *possession* of the property, and may then dispose of the property in order to discharge the debt. The law obliges the lender to seek the *best price available* for a property taken into possession, and any surplus remaining after the debt has been discharged must be used either to repay any other lender with mortgage claims over the property, or be returned to the borrower. In addition, the law requires that, at all times, *the borrower must be treated fairly* by the lender holding a mortgage claim; and this helps to ensure various rights for the borrower, including being able to repay the mortgage loan at any time before its maturity, should he or she wish to do so.

The major piece of UK legislation relating to the granting of credit to members of the personal sector is the *Consumer Credit Act 1974*. However, both banks and building societies are exempt from the main provisions of this Act in respect of loans made for house purchases and secured against a first mortgage. The relevance of the Act for mortgage lenders relates to the *Advertisements and Quotations Regulations* made under the Act. Basically these regulations specify the information which must be made available to a potential borrower in respect of the annual percentage rate of interest to be paid, the total amounts of interest payments and any life assurance requirements associated with the loan. The objective here is that borrowers should be made fully aware of the commitments that they are taking on before any contract is finalised.

The major influence which official regulation has on the housing finance market flows via legislation relating to the operations of the main mortgage lenders. Of particular importance are the *Building Societies Act 1986*, which delegates supervisory powers over building society activities to the Building Societies Commission, and the *Banking Act 1987*, which gives equally wide-ranging supervisory powers to the Bank of England in respect of banks' operations. The overall aims of these pieces of legislation are to ensure that the operations undertaken by building societies and banks adhere to the generally accepted principles of good business practice; to limit the risk of building society and bank customers being disadvantaged by fraudulent or incompetent transactions; and to protect the integrity of the financial system as a whole. (The supervisory frameworks for bank and building societies are examined in detail in Chapter 4, at 4.6.2, 4.10 and 4.12.)

Despite the steep increase in the number of borrowers who experienced difficulties with mortgage loan repayments during the early 1990s, and the record number of possessions which were undertaken by lenders at this time, it is still true that mortgage lending is seen as being one of the lowest risk activities for financial intermediaries. It is also viewed as being one of the least controversial areas of intermediation activity, commanding a reasonably high degree of esteem from the population in general. This is due largely to the quality of the institutions which dominate the housing finance market, and the regulatory frameworks within which they operate.

3.6.3 Government support for the housing market

The main source of support given to owner-occupation by the Government is the *tax relief on mortgage interest payments*. Tax relief may be claimed on the interest payments associated with the first £30,000 of a mortgage loan for a single property. As from April 1994 this relief will be limited to the reduced rate tax of 20% for all tax payers; prior to that time relief is available to both basic rate and higher rate tax payers at the 25% basic rate of tax. This tax relief is normally given through the MIRAS (mortgage interest relief at source) arrangement, whereby the borrower pays interest net of tax relief to the lender, and then the lender collects an amount equal to the tax saving from the Inland Revenue. Thus, for example, if the mortgage interest rate is 8%, the borrower pays only 6.4% to the lender (assuming a 20% tax relief), and the lender collects the other 1.6% from the Inland Revenue.

Tax relief on mortgage interest payments has periodically attracted critical comment, especially in respect of it appearing as a *public sector subsidy* to people who are often thought to be amongst the better-off in society. It is also argued that by bolstering the demand for residential property, house prices have been *inflated*, making it harder for the less well off first-time buyers to enter the market, but benefitting builders and landowners. Also, mortgage lenders have been able to grow by offering higher returns to depositors than would have been the case in the absence of the tax relief to borrowers (effectively implying that lenders have been able to charge a higher gross rate of interest on mortgage loans than would otherwise have been possible). In fact, in recent years, the Government has acted to *limit the tax relief* in two ways: firstly, in 1988, by *removing multiple tax relief* from joint purchasers of a property (that is, by limiting to £30,000 the total amount of a loan, relating to a single property, for which relief may be claimed); and secondly, in 1991, by *restricting claims* to the 25% (and from April 1994 to the 20%) tax rate. With pressure for further reform coming from many quarters, including some major mortgage loan providers, and with the predicted continuing weakness of public sector finances, it would not be surprising if the tax regime in respect of housing finance was to be altered in the foreseeable future. The main constraint on Government action, as at summer 1993, is probably the weak state of the UK housing market, and the Government's wish not to do anything which might slow down the recovery of consumer and business confidence. There are also political reasons for not antagonising an important group of voters.

At the very least there is a good social argument for *concentrating tax relief* on mortgage interest payments on lower income groups and/or first-time buyers entering the cheaper end of the housing market. A more radical solution would be to *abolish the tax relief*, and to use the funds released to provide *improved housing benefits* for all those people having disposable income below a certain level. It may be noted that limited state support is already available towards mortgage interest payments for people who find themselves unemployed after taking out a mortgage loan. If the Government wished to avoid distorting the free market mechanism and consumer choice, the earmarking of state support for housing would be removed entirely. Instead, the *income tax burden* on the lowest earners could be reduced, and improvements could be made in the level of state benefits for the unemployed.

If tax relief on mortgage interest payments was to be abolished, the overall impact on the housing market would depend upon the use made by the Government of the massive savings (estimated at £4.3b in 1993/94) to the Inland Revenue. However, it would seem reasonable to suggest that as the effective cost of borrowed funds would rise, the *level of demand* for residential property would fall, thus causing *house prices* to be lower than they otherwise would have been. Consequently, *house builders' profits* would be adversely affected by both the lower level of demand and by the lower value of completed houses relative to building costs. *Landowners* would also suffer as the demand for building land fell, and the *investment value* of residential property would be undermined. Of course, it must be remembered that many people purchase residential property, in whole or in part, using the proceeds of liquidated investments (savings), and hence the impact on the housing market is likely to be less severe than the impact on the housing finance market. The *reduced demand for mortgage loans* would hit the building societies badly, and the retail banks would also be affected. One outcome would probably be *intensified competition* between the providers of mortgage loans, possibly leading to *reduced mortgage interest rates*, and possible downwards pressure on the interest rates which institutions felt able to offer to depositors.

If owner-occupation was to be made less attractive by the abolition of tax relief, the *rented housing sector* might be given a boost. There would be less incentive for local authority tenants to buy their homes, and more people would wish to take rented accommodation in preference to owner-occupation. This could put upwards pressure on the level of rents, and might stimulate increased private sector provision of rented properties, with positive implications for the construction sector. The Government's attitude to an expansion of public sector housing would be crucial in determining the response of this sector.

As suggested above, the overall impact of abolition of tax relief would depend upon what the Government did with the funds saved. One option would simply be to *reduce the public sector borrowing requirement*, which might contribute towards underpinning confidence in public sector finances and hence the stability of the economy as a whole. Alternatively, the Government could take a more *interventionist approach*, diverting funds towards the support of industrial investment, research and development in industry, and training and education of the workforce. The longer-term growth of the economy would probably be enhanced by such policies, particularly if personal sector savers diverted a larger proportion of their wealth towards investment in industry, as opposed to investment in residential property. To the extent that this led to an improved economic outlook for members of the personal sector, the housing market itself might benefit, perhaps counteracting, at least to some extent, the negative impact that the abolition of tax relief might entail. However, the economic relationships involved in determining the final outcome are so complex that it is impossible to be certain what ultimately would happen to the housing market if tax relief on mortgage interest was not available.

3.6.4 Types of mortgage loans and interest arrangements

There are basically three types of mortgage loans, all of which commit the borrower to make regular payments to the lender, usually for a period of between 20 and 25 years:

(i) The *annuity mortgage* involves the *repayment of the loan plus interest by equal instalments* (assuming that the mortgage interest rate does not alter) over the life of the loan. During the early years of the loan, a large proportion of each instalment is consumed by the interest element, and only a small amount of the principal is repaid. As the loan moves towards maturity, the interest element diminishes (as the outstanding principal falls), and an increasing proportion of each instalment is used to pay back the loan. Prior to 1983, this type of loan was the dominant form in the UK. During the second half of 1992, only 17% of new loans were of this type.

(ii) The *endowment mortgage* links the loan to an *endowment assurance plan*. In this case the borrower *pays interest only* to the mortgage lender during the term of the loan, but at the same time pays a *regular premium* to an *insurance company*. If the premium has been calculated correctly, and if the insurance company's investments have performed as expected, the proceeds from the plan at maturity, which is timed to coincide with the maturity of the loan, should be sufficient to pay off the loan and to leave a surplus to be received by the borrower. The endowment plan will also include an element of life assurance, which will be used to discharge the mortgage loan if the borrower dies before the loan matures.

In recent years, endowment mortgages have become increasingly common. During the second half of 1992, such loans accounted for 70% of all new mortgage loans made. However, whilst these loans have certain attractions when the stock market is performing well and house prices are rising steadily, the repayment arrangements are relatively *inflexible*. Also, there has been certain media criticism that borrowers have often been pressured into taking out this type of mortgage loan by lenders eager to earn the *substantial commissions* which are generated by the sale of the related endowment (insurance) policies. Particular problems may arise where the stock market is performing poorly, and the housing market is stagnant. In these circumstances, a borrower wishing to sell a house during the early years of a loan may find that the sale price of the house is insufficient to cover the loan, and that the surrender value of the endowment policy is meagre (due to the heavy front-end loading of most insurance policy commission arrangements).

A variant of the endowment mortgage is the *pension mortgage*. This involves the borrower paying *interest only* to the lender during the term of the loan, whilst also *contributing to a pension scheme*. On retirement part of the lump-sum pension payment is used to discharge the mortgage loan. The advantage to the borrower is that the pension contributions attract *income tax relief* along with the interest payments. For the lender a pension mortgage is more risky than an endowment mortgage, as a pension scheme cannot be assigned in the same way as an insurance policy can. These loans are not very popular. During the second half of 1992, only 2% of new mortgage loans were of this form.

(iii) *Interest only mortgage loans*, as the name implies, involve a commitment only to pay interest for the term of the loan. The borrower must make *separate arrangements* for the *ultimate repayment* of the debt. This might involve some form of savings plan with a financial institution, or it may involve the borrower ultimately disposing of the property and perhaps trading down to a cheaper property or moving into rented accommodation; alternatively, a new mortgage loan may be negotiated. This form of loan accounted for 11% of new mortgage loans during the second half of 1992.

In the UK, the vast majority of mortgage loans are associated with *variable rates of interest*, although some lenders are willing to *fix rates* for a period of time, say two or three years, and a very few have recently fixed rates for the whole term of some loans. (In many other countries, mortgage interest rates fixed at the outset for the full term of loans are common.) For variable rate loans, in the UK, there are no legal constraints on lenders altering interest rates at any time during the term of their loans. In practice a period of notice is usually given of impending changes in rates, and many lenders now only alter the actual flow of payments once a year for existing borrowers, irrespective of the number of rate changes announced during the year. The obvious *disadvantage* of variable rate loans to the borrower is the *uncertainty* attached to the *total cash outlay* required to service the debt. The main *advantage* accrues when *interest rates fall*. Also variable rate loans mean that all borrowers can be treated on the *same basis*. If this was not so then borrowers who had taken out mortgage loans during periods of high interest rates would be foolish not to repay those loans prematurely if interest rates fell, and to take out new loans at the lower rates of interest. If this happened it could cause serious problems for lenders, as they may have raised longer-term fixed rate funds, in order to hedge their own interest rate exposure, at rates which subsequently prove to be uneconomic. With variable rate loans, lenders are able to raise *short-term funds to back long-term mortgage loans* without the fear that short term interest rates will rise and leave them with inadequate cover for their costs. This improves the stability of the mortgage loan market, and ultimately benefits the borrower by allowing generally cheaper shorter-term funds to be used to create (cheaper) mortgage loans.

The variable rate mortgage loan arrangement may also have broader implications for the management of the economy, as it is likely to *dampen the impact of interest rate changes* on the housing market and house prices. Borrowers know that if they take out mortgage loans at a time when interest rates are relatively high, in all probability rates will fall to more normal levels during the term of their loans. Similarly, borrowers should be aware that it is most unlikely that unusually low mortgage interest rates will persist indefinitely. Therefore, the effects on the demand for houses, and hence on house prices, of all but the most extreme movements in interest rates are likely to be muted, and this should provide some reassurance to lenders in respect of the value of their security. This fact, of course, blunts the impact of monetary policies, and may require the authorities to initiate more extreme shifts in interest rates than would otherwise have been required. The authorities would also have to convince the personal sector of their determination to maintain interest rates at the altered level for as long as is required by the policy's objectives.

The economic conditions experienced during the early 1990s in the UK were most unusual, in that rising unemployment and high real interest rates followed a period of rapid house price rises and increasing personal sector debt. The *collapse of consumer confidence* precipitated an *unprecedented stagnation in the housing market* with exceptional effects on house prices in some parts of the UK (see 3.7.2 below). However, it might be argued that without the variable interest rate arrangement, the outcome would have been much more severe for both borrowers and lenders.

Finally, it should be noted that in certain circumstances mortgage lenders may be willing to formulate special loan/interest schemes in order to help lower income house buyers who would otherwise not be able to enter into owner occupation. These types of schemes are sometimes referred to as *'low start' mortgage loans*, and generally involve a mechanism whereby servicing costs are reduced during the early years of the loan, with compensating increases being built into the repayment schedule in later years. These schemes do not reduce the overall costs of buying residential property, but rather *redistribute interest and repayments of principal* in a way which should help the borrower. The *disadvantages* of these schemes are that servicing costs may begin to rise at a time when household budgets become strained because of the expenses related to bringing up children, and that if the borrower's income does not rise over time as expected, the growing servicing costs may become unmanageable. A variant of the low start mortgage scheme is that of *joint ownership of property*, whereby a mortgage lender funds the purchase of property owned partly by a housing association or a local authority and partly by the occupier. The occupier covers an agreed portion of the mortgage loan interest and repayments, and pays a rent to the housing association or local authority in respect of their part ownership. Over time the owner/tenant may buy out some or all of the joint owner's share of the property, and ultimately become the sole owner. Such schemes require detailed arrangements to be made at the outset in respect of the rights and responsibilities of the parties involved (issues relating to maintenance, improvements, insurance and so on must all be resolved). *Shared equity mortgages* work on a similar principle, except that the borrower's interest payments are reduced in return for assigning a claim to a portion of the capital value of the property to the lender. Such arrangements are rare as they tend to be very complex legally, and offer a great deal of scope for dispute over the value of claims and commitments.

3.6.5 Structure of UK housing finance

The *dominant providers* of housing finance in the UK are the *building societies*. They have held this position since the time that the first building societies came into existence in the latter half of the eighteenth century. At the end of 1992, the building societies had mortgage loans outstanding to the value of £212b, which represented 62% of the UK housing finance market. As shown by Table 3.5, at the beginning of the 1980s the dominance of the building societies was even greater, accounting for 80% of the market, with the second most important provider being the *public sector* (largely in the form of local authorities). In line with the Government's policy to reduce public sector involvement in what it believes to be primarily private sector responsibilities, the importance of local authority mortgage finance diminished rapidly during the 1980s.

Table 3.5   Structure of UK housing finance, 1980 to 1992 (end year figures), £b

Year	Building societies	Banks	Insurance companies and pension funds	Public sector	Other financial institutions	Total
1980	42.7	2.9	2.0	4.8	—	52.4
1981	49.0	5.7	2.1	5.5	—	62.3
1982	57.2	10.8	2.1	6.4	—	76.5
1983	68.1	14.8	2.3	6.1	—	91.3
1984	82.6	16.9	2.5	5.9	0.5	108.4
1985	97.2	21.1	2.7	5.4	1.0	127.4
1986	116.6	25.9	3.2	5.0	3.5	154.2
1987	131.6	35.9	4.0	4.6	7.5	183.6
1988	155.3	45.3	4.5	4.4	14.2	223.7
1989	152.5	79.2	4.5	4.3	17.4	257.9
1990	176.7	85.7	4.6	3.9	24.0	294.9
1991	197.6	90.4	4.4	3.0	26.2	321.6
1992	211.5	96.4	4.3	2.5	25.1	339.8

Source: *Financial Statistics*, Central Statistical Office, various issues.

In more recent years the *retail banks* have held second place in the ranks of mortgage lenders. At the end of 1992, approximately £96b was owed to the banks in the form of mortgage loans, accounting for 28% of total mortgage finance outstanding. However, it should be noted that around £40b of this total was owed to Abbey National plc, which was a building society until July 1989. (See Chapter 4, at 4.6.3(c), for a discussion of this institution's change of status.) Nevertheless, this does not detract from the significant inroads made by the banks into the housing finance market since 1980. In that year they provided only 5.5% of total mortgage loans granted; in 1988, the year before Abbey National's conversion, their share of the market was 20% of the total.

Major factors underlying the changes in the pattern of housing finance, since 1980, have been *deregulation within the UK financial system* and the *increasing degree of competition between financial institutions*. A detailed explanation of the relevant institutional changes is given in Chapter 4 (at 4.4.3, 4.6.1 and 4.6.2); for the moment it should be recognised that the *removal of restrictive monetary controls* on banks at the beginning of the 1980s, at a time when conditions in the corporate and international banking markets were not particularly attractive, encouraged banks to enter into mortgage lending on a massive scale. In 1980 the banks made net advances of £500m for the purchase of residential property, and this amounted to about 7% of the flow of new funding. In 1981 the corresponding figures were £2.3b and 24%; and in 1982, £5.1b and 35.9%. During the same period the building societies saw their share of net advances fall from 79% to 58%. After this time the banks continued to build up their mortgage debt portfolio, but at a substantially reduced rate.

Between 1984 and 1991, both banks and building societies found themselves coming under increasing pressure from a number of *specialist mortgage lenders funded entirely from wholesale sources*, and hence able to offer attractive facilities reflecting their low cost bases. In 1990 these specialist institutions provided about 10% of net advances, but since that time the downturn in the housing market and the general reduction in UK rates of interest would appear to have affected them quite badly. Indeed, in 1992, collectively they reduced their exposure to the housing finance market by around £1.5b. This development, taken against the background of a considerably reduced demand for mortgage finance, largely explains the significant upsurge in the market shares of both banks and building societies in 1992.

3.6.6 Competition in the UK housing finance market

As mentioned above, deregulation of the activities of certain UK financial institutions during the 1980s had a significant impact on the housing finance market. In respect of the building societies, the *voluntary removal of barriers to competition*, in particular by way of the *abandonment of interest rate fixing agreements* within the sector, was supported by a number of official actions culminating in the enactment of the *1986 Building Societies Act*. This Act, together with subsequent amendments, opened up to the building societies a wide range of opportunities for the development of their businesses, and placed them in a much stronger position to compete with the retail banks in respect of personal sector financial transactions (see Chapter 4, at 4.6.2).

The clearly visible trend towards increasing competition between institutions providing personal sector financial services has been facilitated by *major advances in technology*, allowing relatively small institutions to offer financial products that were previously the preserve of the largest banks having access to mainframe computers. In addition, since the early 1980s, there would appear to have been a growing willingness amongst members of the personal sector to *seek out the best deals* in respect of both investments and loans, and to move their business between institutions in response to marketing initiatives.

It is generally agreed that the increased competition introduced into the housing finance market during the 1980s has generated *important benefits for both borrowers and lenders*. A major advantage for borrowers is that mortgage loans are now treated very much like any other financial product, whereby so long as certain security criteria are met, the determining factor in obtaining a mortgage loan is the borrower's ability and willingness to pay the market rate of interest. Prior to the early 1980s, building societies tended to hold mortgage loan interest rates *below the market clearing level*, and then *rationed the supply of loans* in the face of *excess demand*. Rationing often involved the requirement that aspirant borrowers should have been savers with the building society from which they wished to borrow for a minimum period of time; and the proportion of the property value covered by the loan would often be strictly limited. Effectively, *mortgage queues* were allowed to form, and the price (interest rate) mechanism was not used for purposes of allocating available funds. The injection of free competition into the housing finance market not only made mortgage queues a thing of the past, but also put *upwards pressure on mortgage interest rates*, at least in the short term, as is the normal market response to excess demand.

A further important aspect of free competition is the pressure placed upon mortgage lenders to *improve their efficiency and reduce their costs*; otherwise they will be unable to attract sufficient savers and borrowers to maintain their market share. Evidence of this phenomenon in the UK was the rapid deceleration in the pace of building society branch expansion during the mid-1980s, followed by a slight contraction in networks at the beginning of the 1990s.

Another outcome of free competition has been the increasing occurrence of *innovation and product differentiation*. As individual institutions are limited in the extent to which they are able to offer lower rates of interest on loans and higher rates of interest on deposits, relative to the ruling market rates, it is natural that they should seek to attract custom via the *characteristics of their products*. Thus, since the mid-1980s, there has been an upsurge in the provision of loans with fixed interest rates for fixed periods of time, special offers for first-time buyers, discounts offered on professional fees or moving costs, and so on. Some institutions have engaged in *backwards integration* of their businesses (for example, the purchase of estate agency chains by building societies), as a means of gaining improved access to potential customers when they are at their most susceptible to sales pressure. Also substantial sums are now spent on *marketing and advertising*, which many senior managers in financial institutions believe are crucial to the establishment of an appropriate market identity.

A further trend during the late 1980s was the increasing provision of mortgage loans equal to *100% of the purchase price of the property*, with many lenders being willing to advance sums equal to *increasingly higher multiples of borrowers' earnings*. These developments, together with the *erosion of profit margins* implied by the competitive market structure, *raised the risk associated with mortgage lending*.

So long as house prices continue to rise, the security for loans is generally sound. But, as was seen in the UK during the early 1990s, a period of recession, pushing up unemployment and causing stagnation in the housing market, can have serious implications for mortgage lenders. If a borrower is unable to maintain repayments, the lender may have no choice but to take the property into possession. If house prices have fallen since the loan was made, and if the loan is in the early years of its term, a forced sale in a stagnant market may result in a *substantial loss* for the lender. Certainly, *insurance* may be taken out to cover such eventualities (and where loans exceed 80% of the purchase price of the property insurance must be taken out), but this involves additional costs which must ultimately be absorbed by either the borrower or the lender, and premiums may become excessive when the housing market is seen to be in a state of sustained decline.

In the UK, the experiences of the early 1990s have led to an obvious *curtailing of the excesses of free market competition*. Most lenders have now reduced both the percentage of a property's purchase price which they are willing to cover and the ratio of amount lent to the earnings of the borrower. It is also likely that the borrower's circumstances will be scrutinised more carefully than they would have been during the late 1980s. Nevertheless, in 1993, against the background of a greater awareness of the risks associated with making mortgage loans, there is still a high level of competition apparent between the major providers of housing finance, with each trying to exploit to the full the generally lower rates of interest ruling in the UK.

3.6.7 Over-financing of the housing market

Since the early 1970s there has been a continual and significant *leakage of funds* from the housing market in the UK, which effectively means that mortgage loans have been used for purposes other than the purchase (or improvement) of residential property. This phenomenon, which may be thought of as a form of *over-financing of the housing market*, and which is often referred to (somewhat inaccurately) as *equity withdrawal*, has caused a certain amount of *controversy*, due to tax relief being available on some mortgage interest payments, but not being deemed to be appropriate in respect of interest payments on other forms of consumer credit. The sums of money involved have been huge, with the estimated over-financing being £21.6b in 1988 (that is, more than a half of the total of net advances made in the form of mortgage loans). More recently, the leakage has subsided, and stood at £3.5b in 1992 (20% of total net mortgage lending).

Concern has been expressed that the market for personal sector finance has been *distorted*, as mortgage loans have provided cheap consumer credit with an unintended state subsidy; although it should be noted that some of the leaked funds have probably been used to cover the transactions costs associated with house purchase. In fact, the situation is not quite as simple as it may first appear, as there are several quite different reasons for funds leaking from the housing market:

(i)   A house which is purchased using a mortgage loan may have been owned by someone who has died. The proceeds from the sale will be paid to the beneficiaries of the dead person's estate, and may be used for consumption or non-housing investment, meaning that the full amount of the mortgage loan leaks from the housing market. In this instance the leakage is inevitable, and *the borrower has genuinely used the funds for house purchase*, and hence the claim for tax relief would appear to be in order. (It might, of course, be argued that the Government should seek to retrieve any tax relief received by the deceased on the house which has now been sold, although this could create tremendous legal problems.)

(ii) An owner-occupier may decide to move house, and may take out a mortgage loan which is larger than the difference between the value of the house being sold (after accounting for any outstanding mortgage debt on this property) and the value of the house being purchased. Effectively, the borrower is *withdrawing equity from the initial property holding*. This leakage could be avoided by the authorities requiring that lenders insist upon all of the net proceeds from the house which is sold being reinvested in the house being purchased. However, in a free market environment, this form of restriction on commercial judgement would not be welcomed by lenders. In addition, it might be argued that, so long as the property being sold was not itself purchased with a 100% mortgage loan, at least some part of the leaked funds merely represent a withdrawal of the borrower's own initial savings.

(iii) A mortgage loan may be taken out with the explicit intention of using the funds for some purpose other than the purchase or improvement of residential property. In this case, the relevant property is effectively being used as security for a personal loan, which is likely to be available on much more attractive terms than other consumer loans. This would appear to be a *genuine withdrawal of equity*, with mortgage loan funds being used to support non-housing expenditure.

The existence of these leakages of funds from the housing market raises questions as to the privileged status of mortgage loans for tax purposes, and the Government's generally benevolent attitude to the operation of the institutions involved in the provision of housing finance. However, unless mortgage interest tax relief was to be abolished, the only alternative would be for the authorities to introduce detailed regulatory requirements and appropriate monitoring in respect of the use of mortgage loans. This development would hardly be attractive to a government which has made deregulation of private sector financial activities a major theme of its economic policies since the early 1980s.

3.7 THE DETERMINATION OF HOUSE PRICES

The price of residential property, just like the price of any other commodity traded in a free market, is determined by the *forces of supply and demand*. However, as the movements in house prices have an important influence on personal sector demands for housing finance, and also affect the value of the security for mortgage loans, it is useful to consider the *special characteristics* of residential property, and how these influence its supply and demand.

3.7.1 Theoretical issues

The key characteristics of the housing market, underpinning the determination of house prices, are as follows:

(i)   Residential property is *extremely durable*; many houses have usable lives well in excess of a hundred years.
(ii)   *The vast majority of the population is housed* at any point in time.
(iii) The time and resources taken to construct new residential property mean that *the total stock can only be increased at a very slow rate* (especially when the demolition of uninhabitable property is taken

into account), and hence even a massive increase in house building would only have a marginal effect on the total number of properties available in the shorter term.

(iv) The bulk of house purchases/sales relate to *second-hand houses*, and so long as these have been adequately maintained their prices are unlikely to be markedly different from those of new houses of comparable size in similar locations.

(v) In general, people entering the housing market for the first time have *considerable discretion over the timing of entry*. Thus, if economic conditions are adverse individuals may defer becoming owner-occupiers, and instead continue to rent or share accommodation or to live with parents or other relatives.

Against this background, the *net supply of homes for sale* on the market is the sum of the following:

(i) *New houses made available*, which depends upon the rate of completions, the stock of previously unsold new houses, and the ability of builders to agree sales before houses have been completed (and in some cases even before work has begun).

(ii) *Houses vacated as a result of the owner's death, emigration or move to rented accommodation.*

(iii) *Houses transferred from rental status*, perhaps due to landlords wishing to extract capital from their property holdings, or because of government pressure on local authorities to dispose of property which they rent out. It must be emphasised that there is only an addition to the net supply of houses when transfers *do not involve sitting tenants*. Thus, if local authority tenants take up the right to buy their homes, this adds both to supply and to demand in equal measure.

The net supply of houses on the market is reduced to the extent that properties are *demolished* for slum clearance or redevelopment purposes. Also, it should be noted that houses placed on the market by *owner-occupiers* wishing to move to other owner-occupied houses have *no impact on the net supply* of houses on the market. The additional supply created is exactly balanced by additional demand, although there may be some short-term timing differences as people may seek to buy houses before they place their existing ones on the market.

The supply of new houses for sale at any point in time is likely to be influenced by factors such as the *general state of the economy*, and *expected trends in unemployment, earnings, inflation and interest rates*. Property developers are more likely to invest in construction of residential property if they are optimistic about being able to sell. Hence supply is likely to rise if real earnings are growing and employment prospects appear good; by contrast rising unemployment and high interest rates are likely to lead to a reduction in supply. Similarly, landlords may be more willing to realise their investments if the housing market as a whole is buoyant, and hence conversion of rented property to owner-occupation is more likely when economic conditions overall are good. A qualification to this pattern is that borrowers with outstanding mortgage debts are more prone to get into financial difficulties as unemployment rises and the economy stagnates, and it is more likely that borrowers facing such difficulties will put their properties on to the market and seek rented accommodation. Indeed, in extreme cases, mortgage lenders may take possession of properties and attempt to sell them in order to clear the associated debts, thus adding to the net supply on the market. (The net supply of houses arising due to the death or emigration of owner-occupiers is unlikely to be markedly affected by shorter-term changes in economic variables.)

Although the Government engages in *little direct intervention* in respect of the supply of owner-occupied housing (except through its influence on local authorities' policies on housing), its *broader economic policies* may be of great importance *indirectly*. *Monetary policy*, affecting the level of interest rates, and *fiscal policy*, affecting the tax regime (and especially income taxes, the tax treatment of mortgage interest payments, and stamp duty on the transfer of properties), may influence attitudes to owner-occupation and the expectations of property developers. The effects of these policies on inflation, employment, economic growth, and so on, may also influence the supply of houses, as indicated above.

The source of the *net demand* for houses is potential purchasers entering the market for the *first time*. Existing owner-occupiers moving between houses have no impact on net demand. The factors which affect the demand from first-time buyers at any point in time are those which have been listed above as the factors which affect supply. In the longer term the number of first-time buyers is affected by *demographic trends* (particularly changes in population and age profiles) and *social conventions* (including the occurrence of single person households and single parent families). The availability of *alternative forms of suitable accommodation* is also of importance, and hence government policies in respect of local authority house building, rent levels and private sector rented property development are of relevance. These longer-term factors are also likely to influence the expectations of future trends in demand held by property developers, and hence will probably also affect the supply side of the market.

It is the interaction of the supply and the demand for owner-occupied houses that determines the level of house prices. Thus, for example, if economic conditions improve, and favourable trends are expected in personal sector earnings and job prospects, it is likely that both demand and supply will be stimulated. But as *demand is able to adjust much more quickly than supply*, there is likely to be *upwards pressure placed on house prices*, at least in the short term. Demand from first-time buyers tends to be concentrated on lower-priced houses, thus if changes in the economic environment were to encourage first-time buyers to enter the market, upwards pressure would be placed on prices at the bottom end of the market, once any surplus of vacant properties had been cleared. A more favourable climate for house sales in the lower price ranges may then stimulate existing owner-occupiers to bring forward plans which they may have to move to more expensive property, thus meeting some of the demand for lower-priced houses and simultaneously creating demand for more expensive property. It is easy to see how a strengthening cycle of adjustments may be initiated in the housing market by a stimulus to net demand from first-time buyers.

The extent of any increases in house prices will depend upon the *speed of adjustment of net supply*, and ultimately the impact on *building costs* and *land prices* as activity in the housing market expands. In fact, a *major constraint* on the ability of the supply of houses to catch up with a rising demand is the *scarcity of suitable building land*. As house prices rise, property developers may bid up the price of building land, with only a marginal impact on the total supply made available. Consequently, supply may never catch up with demand, and prices may thus continue to drift upwards until the trend in demand itself alters. If demand were to fall, perhaps due to the economy moving into a period of recession, the above situation could be reversed with the given supply on the market becoming excessive relative to demand. As property developers do not wish to hold stocks of vacant houses, and as some owner-occupiers with pressing financial problems feel that they have no option but to sell their properties, the pressure on house prices will be downwards. In the first instance sellers may be loath to accept lower prices, particularly if these represent capital losses relative to the original purchase prices. But if demand remains subdued, financial pressures may force prices downwards. The market may then only stabilise once the level of net demand stabilises and the net supply on the market falls to a comparable level.

3.7.2 Trends in UK house prices

For much of the post-war period average house prices in the UK have risen continually. As Table 3.6 shows, between 1980 and 1990, not only was there a *substantial increase in house prices* in nominal terms (174%), but also in real (inflation-adjusted) terms (85%). Indeed, the almost *stable nominal prices* of 1991, and the significant *reduction in nominal prices* in 1992 were *unprecedented* in recent times. However, on a number of occasions there have been sustained periods of time during which there have been *real reductions in house prices*. The early 1980s and the early 1990s provide good examples of this situation. The data also show that the latter half of the 1980s proved to be a boom period in house prices, with annual nominal increases in prices outstripping the concurrent inflation rates by wide margins.

As explained in the previous section, there are many factors which may affect house prices at any given time, and the interaction of these factors is often complex. Nevertheless, it is possible to identify a number of economic developments in the UK in recent years which would appear to be quite compatible with the theory of house price determination. Of major importance were the *favourable economic conditions* experienced in the UK during the second half of the 1980s. With reasonably high rates of economic growth, inflation remaining subdued, unemployment falling steadily (see Chapter 8, at 8.7.4 for details) and average earnings rising moderately in nominal terms and steadily in real terms, there was a *general mood of optimism* in respect of economic prospects. Also, the late 1980s saw a surge in the number of people in the 25 to 29 year old age group, the most common age group for first time buyers. These conditions undoubtedly underpinned the *confidence* of both house buyers and property developers, (the number of houses that were started by builders reached 250,000 in 1988, having stood at 155,000 in 1980). The buoyancy of the housing market was supported by the *newly deregulated retail financial services sector*, eager to compete in the provision of mortgage loans. In 1988 net *mortgage lending reached a record level* of £40.1b; in 1980 the corresponding figure was just £7.3b. Competitive pressures were also probably responsible for the steady increase in the *size of mortgage loans relative to the values of properties purchased*. In 1980 the ratio was 56% for the building societies; by 1988 it was 66%; and it continued to rise until recently, averaging 72% in 1992. In 1988 house prices rose by a massive 23% in nominal terms, and 18% in real terms, the highest rates of increase achieved since the housing boom of 1972/73.

Throughout much of the period covered by Table 3.6, *mortgage interest rates* were *relatively high in nominal terms* (although no account is taken of tax relief in the table), and with the exception of 1980 and 1981 *real rates of interest were significantly positive*, with only a modest degree of fluctuation between 1983 and 1992. There is little obvious correlation between real mortgage rates and house prices (which may be due to a lack of appreciation amongst the personal sector of the true meaning of real interest rates), but high nominal rates do appear to coincide with periods of slow-down in the housing market, which might be explained by the effects of rising rates of interest on confidence within the market. In fact, the *high interest rates* recorded in 1989 and 1990, the *growth in the percentage of house purchase prices covered by mortgage loans*, and the *significant increase in the ratio of house prices to average earnings* during the second half of the 1980s, are likely to have been crucial factors in explaining the *severity of the recession* which hit the UK economy during the early 1990s, and the *rapid reversal of fortunes in the housing market.*

The *inflationary pressures* which began to emerge in 1989 were undoubtedly fed by the consumer-led boom in the UK, which was financed by a *massive increase in personal sector borrowing* and a *reduction in the savings ratio.* A significant proportion of the funds supporting consumption was effectively derived from *leakages from the housing market.* The Government's response to these developments was to *tighten monetary policy*, raising rates of interest, and to place sterling into the *EC's Exchange Rate Mechanism* (see Chapter 8, at 8.7.3), which is generally believed to have rendered UK exports uncompetitive in certain major overseas markets. The depressing effect of these policies on the economy, accentuated by the level of *unemployment* once again beginning to rise from 1990 onwards, had a growing negative impact on confidence in the UK's economic prospects, and *rapidly undermined demand in the housing market.*

In 1990, average house prices in the UK were still rising in nominal terms, but fell slightly in real terms. The real price of houses continued to fall throughout 1991 and 1992, and, as mentioned above, in the latter year there was the unprecedented occurrence of *average house prices falling in nominal terms.* In some parts of the UK, and especially in the southern half of England, downwards movements in nominal house prices had, in fact, started as early as 1988, but it was only in 1992 that the phenomenon became of national significance.

One implication of this trend was that the *quality of the security* for mortgage loans in general was seriously questioned for the first time. The downwards spiral in the housing market was accelerated by the *rapid rise in arrears in mortgage loan servicing*, and ultimately in *possessions by mortgage lenders.* In 1991 the number of possessions reached a record level of 75,540 (or 0.77% of total mortgage loans outstanding). This may not appear to be a large number relative to the size of the market, but the deterioration in conditions becomes clear when it is compared to the 3,480 possessions which took place in 1980 (a mere 0.06% of outstanding mortgage loans), or the 19,300 (0.25%) in 1985. As lenders taking houses into possession are likely to seek the most rapid sale possible, in order to avoid the deterioration of unoccupied property, this trend can only have put further downwards pressure on house prices.

The reduction in house prices in the UK between 1991 and 1993 has had a number of important implications for the economy as a whole, and for the personal sector in particular. For many individuals residential property is their largest single disposable investment, and hence lower house prices may have a significant impact on real wealth holdings, and this may *limit the willingness of consumers to spend.* As explained above (at 3.4) the personal sector has raised its aggregate savings ratio markedly in recent years, and has limited the extent of additional borrowing, although this has

Table 3.6 UK average house prices, average earnings and mortgage loan interest rates, 1980 to 1992

Year	Retail price index %	Average house prices £	Annual change nominal %	real %	Average earnings £	Annual change nominal %	real %	House price: earnings ratio	Mortgage Loan interest rates nominal %	real %
1980	18.0	24307	15.5	−2.5	6725	22.2	4.2	3.61	14.9	−3.1
1981	11.9	24810	2.1	−9.8	7497	11.5	−0.4	3.31	14.0	2.1
1982	8.6	25553	3.0	−5.6	8165	8.9	0.3	3.13	13.3	4.7
1983	4.6	28592	11.9	7.3	8693	6.5	1.9	3.29	11.0	6.4
1984	5.0	30811	7.8	2.8	9447	8.7	3.7	3.26	11.8	6.8
1985	6.1	33187	7.7	1.6	10069	6.6	0.5	3.30	13.2	7.1
1986	3.4	38121	14.9	11.5	10790	7.2	3.8	3.53	11.8	8.4
1987	4.2	44220	16.0	11.8	11648	7.9	3.7	3.80	11.5	7.3
1988	4.9	54280	22.7	17.8	12782	9.7	4.8	4.25	11.0	6.1
1989	7.8	62134	14.5	6.7	14014	9.6	1.8	4.43	13.7	5.9
1990	9.5	66695	7.3	−2.2	15371	9.7	0.2	4.34	15.1	5.6
1991	5.9	66744	0.1	−5.8	16817	9.4	3.5	3.90	12.9	7.0
1992	3.7	63425	−5.0	−8.7	17636	4.9	1.2	3.60	10.3	6.6

Source: *Housing Finance*, Council of Mortgage Lenders, various issues.
Economic Trends, Central Statistical Office, various issues.

Notes: (i) Average house prices are estimated on the basis of house sales for which a mortgage loan is taken out.
(ii) The figures for average annual earnings have been constructed by the Council of Mortgage Lenders using the New Earnings Survey.

been continuing steadily. Technically, even without additional borrowing, a lower real value for wealth holdings *raises the personal sector's capital gearing ratio* (that is, the amount of its outstanding debt relative to its total wealth), which provides a measure of its debt burden.

For a significant number of households with mortgage debt outstanding, the situation has been made even more difficult by the emergence of *negative equity* in respect of their properties. Negative equity arises where the value of the property falls below the outstanding associated mortgage debt, thus meaning that if the property was to be sold, the proceeds would be insufficient to discharge the debt. Its existence has serious implications for such property owners wishing to move house, as this may imply the need to raise a substantial unsecured loan, which may not be easy in a period of unfavourable economic conditions. The *problems for mortgage lenders* are equally serious, as by default they find themselves with mortgage loans outstanding which are partly unsecured. This is particularly awkward for building societies which, in normal circumstances, are limited in the extent to which they are able to make unsecured loans. Recent changes in the official regulations relating to building society lending have sought to alleviate this problem, although this does not reduce the *risk faced by lenders* when borrowers with negative equity find themselves unemployed or otherwise unable to service their debts; and many cases have been reported of borrowers literally walking away from their commitments (and the negative equity!). The impact of negative equity has been felt most strongly in the south of England and East Anglia, where house prices rose most rapidly in the second half of the 1980s, and fell equally rapidly from late 1988 onwards. Owner-occupiers who were most badly hit were first-time buyers who entered the market in the late 1980s, with high loan to property value ratios. Bank of England estimates put the number of negative equity households in the UK at 876,000 at mid-1992, with a total value of negative equity of £6b.

At summer of 1993, the UK housing market is still very subdued, although house prices in general would appear to have stabilised, and a very modest recovery has recently been reported in some regions. Also, the continuing steady increase in average earnings, whilst house prices have been falling, has meant that the *ratio of house prices to average earnings has fallen* from its recent peak in 1989. This implies that *houses have become more affordable* for those in work. *Lower interest rates* are also likely to contribute further support to a recovery in the housing market, as is the recently reported improvement in *economic growth* and slightly *lower level of unemployment*. However, the high levels of outstanding consumer debt, the negative equity problem and continuing uncertainty about the UK's economic prospects will probably ensure that for the foreseeable future there is unlikely to be sufficient pressure in the housing market to generate anything other than relatively modest increases in prices.

3.8   EXAMINATION PRACTICE

3.8.1   Questions

As most of the subject matter of Personal Sector Finances and the Housing Market topic was only introduced into the syllabus for The Monetary and Financial System in 1993, there are no appropriate questions which may be drawn from previous examination papers. Therefore, the following questions have been formulated in order to provide a broad impression of the type of questions which may be set in respect of this topic area. Before consulting the guidance notes at 3.8.2, students may care to map out answers to these questions. As with all sections of the syllabus, the material covered may be examined within questions requiring knowledge drawn from other topic areas. Each question carries 25 marks.

(1)   Discuss the significance of the following for the UK personal sector's finances:

‡(a)   building societies;   (9)
‡(b)   life assurance companies and pension funds;   (8)
‡(c)   company securities.   (8)

(2)   (a)   What are the main types of financial risks faced by a personal sector investor?   (12)
      (b)   Describe the actions which might be taken by a personal sector investor in order to minimise the risks identified in (a).   (13)

(3)   (a)   Outline the main characteristics of the following types of mortgage loans:
            (i)   annuity;
            (ii)   endowment;
            (iii) pension;
            (iv)   interest only.   (12)
      (b)   What are the advantages and disadvantages of the different types of mortgage loans listed in (a) for borrowers and for lenders in the market?   (13)

(4)   Explain the advantages and disadvantages of variable rate and fixed rate mortgage loans for:
      (a)   borrowers;   (12)
      (b)   building societies.   (13)

(5)   (a)   In relation to the housing market, what do you understand by the term 'negative equity'?   (5)
      (b)   What problems might the existence of negative equity entail for:

111

    (i)   an owner-occupier;

    (ii)   a provider of housing finance?   (10)

(c)   Discuss the main factors likely to influence the average price of new houses.   (10)

3.8.2 Guidance notes

(1) (i) The answer to this question must focus upon the significance of the specific financial institutions/instruments listed for personal sector finances. Comments may be made on recent changes in the personal sector's use of these institutions/instruments, but general discussion of their roles and operations as a whole is not required.

(ii) Part (a) of this question requires an examination of the *importance of mortgage loans and building society deposits for the personal sector*. Mention should also be made of the *other services* which building societies provide in respect of personal sector finances.

(iii) The answer to part (b) should emphasise that premium payments to life assurance companies and contributions to pension funds are *a major use of funds* for the personal sector. Investments with these institutions are *a crucial part of the personal sector's assets portfolio*.

(iv) Company securities are held *directly* by the personal sector, but more importantly *via investments with financial intermediaries* (such as pension funds, life assurance companies and unit trusts). The answer to part (c) should *differentiate* between the two types of holdings, and should make clear the importance of *investments based on company securities* in the personal sector's balance sheet. It may be noted that company securities often provide higher yield, but riskier, investments than deposits with financial intermediaries such as banks and building societies.

Source of relevant material:

‡Part (a) 3.3 (especially (a)(iii) and (b)(ii)), 3.4, 3.6.5 and (as background) Chapter 4, at 4.6.2.

‡Part (b) 3.3 (especially (a)(v)), 3.4 and (as background) Chapter 4, at 4.8.1 and 4.8.2.

‡Part (c) 3.3 (especially (a)(v)), 3.4 and (as background) Chapter 4, at 4.8.

(2) (i) This question relates to personal sector investment, hence discussion of the risks associated with personal sector liabilities (debt) is not required.

(ii) The answer to part (a) requires a brief outline of the *possible impact on personal sector financial asset holdings of default, unanticipated inflation, interest rate movements, changes in financial requirements and changes in government economic policy.*

(iii) For each type of risk identified in part (a), it is necessary, in the answer to part (b), to *describe the actions* which a member of the personal sector might take in order to *minimise these risks*. It is important to recognise that the risk management instruments available to the corporate sector are inapplicable to the vast majority of personal sector financial risks.

Source of relevant material:

Part (a)   3.5.
Part (b)   3.5.

(3) (i) The answer to part (a) requires *straightforward descriptions* of the *main characteristics* of the different types of mortgage loan listed. It should be noted that both *variable and fixed interest rate* arrangements may be associated with each of these types of loan.

(ii) It is not necessary to discuss the relative importance of these types of loan in the UK or in any other country.

(iii) Part (b) of this question requires recognition of the positions of both *borrowers and lenders* in the mortgage loan market. The *relative merits* of the different types of loan should be examined for the situation where there are *no repayment problems experienced* by the borrower, and for the situation where the borrower gets into *financial difficulties*.

Source of relevant material:

Part (a)   3.6.4 (i) to (iii).
Part (b)   3.6.4 (i) to (iii).

(4) (i) Whilst there are significant areas of overlap to the answers to the two parts of this question, it is important to ensure that each part is answered separately, with clear cross-references between parts if necessary.

(ii) The answer to part (a) should not only deal with the implications of fixed and variable interest rates for *flows of interest payments*, but also should recognise the possible impact of each regime on the *average level of mortgage interest rates* in the longer term.

(iii) Part (b) of this question requires examination of the implications of fixed and variable rate mortgage loans for building societies' *interest earnings* and their *liability management policies* (that is, the approach taken to raising funds to finance the mortgage loans). The possible impact on the *cost of funds* should be noted. Also, it is important to recognise the *risk aspects* associated with fixed and variable rate loans, both *directly*, in terms of interest flows, and *indirectly*, via the possible effects on the level of defaults by borrowers.

(iv) The question does not require discussion of the broader implications of interest rate movements for either the personal sector or financial institutions.

Source of relevant material:

Part (a)   3.5.4 (as background) and 3.6.4.
Part (b)   3.6.4.

(5) (i) This question relates to general concepts and theoretical possibilities, and hence examination of recent experience in the UK's (or any other country's) housing market is not required.

(ii) Part (a) of this question merely requires a *straightforward definition of 'negative equity'* within the context of the housing market.

(iii) The answer to part (b)(i) should explain that the problems associated with negative equity for the owner-occupier materialise when there is *a desire to sell the property*. For the provider of housing finance, the very existence of negative equity *places in doubt the security of the loan*, and the increase in risk faced by the lender should be explained in part (b)(ii).

(iv) The factors underlying both *the supply of and the demand for new houses* should be examined in the answer to part (c). It should be recognised that existing houses are *very close substitutes* for new houses, and hence that on the supply side of the market it is the total net supply of houses that is of relevance. Also, the demand for new houses is influenced by the price and quality of existing houses on the market.

Source of relevant material:

Part (a)   3.7.2 (paragraph 8).
Part (b)   3.7.2 (paragraph 8).
Part (c)   3.7.1.

3.9 FURTHER STUDY

Recent experience has shown that significant changes in personal sector finances may take place relatively quickly. Therefore, it is important that students keep up-to-date with the *major trends* in this respect, and are aware of the *factors influencing these trends*. The major source of data relating to UK personal sector finances is the Central Statistical Office, through its monthly *Financial Statistics* and its annual *National Income and Expenditure (Blue Book)*. These publications provide a wealth of detail on the personal sector's sources and uses of funds, aggregate balance sheet, and financial relationships with other sectors of the economy. However, it must be emphasised that for examination purposes it is knowledge of the broad trends and relative importance of key variables that matters, rather than statistical details. The annual survey on sector financing in the *Bank of England Quarterly Bulletin* offers a concise analysis of the major trends in UK personal finances. This publication also includes occasional articles on various aspects of personal sector finances and the housing market, which are well worth reading, although some may be rather advanced technically.

Developments in the UK housing market are thoroughly plotted in the statistical annex to *Housing Finance* (published quarterly by the Council of Mortgage Lenders) and by *Housing and Construction Statistics* (published quarterly by the Department of the Environment). *Housing Finance* also provides an extremely useful narrative on recent trends in the UK housing market. The best source of information on recent developments relating to the business aspects of housing finance and on relevant initiatives by specific financial institutions is the monthly *Mortgage Finance Gazette*. *The Economist* also provides relevant background material on the broader trends in personal sector finances and the housing market.

The financial activities of the personal sector are crucial to the operations of a wide range of UK financial institutions. Consequently, students should be prepared for examination questions linking the material included in the present chapter with the topic area of UK Financial Institutions, covered in Chapter 4. Of particular relevance are the operations of the retail banks and building societies. In addition, the importance of interest-bearing debt (and especially mortgage loans) and deposits for personal sector finances means that the linkages with Chapter 7 (on the determination of interest rates) and Chapter 8 (on government economic policy, and monetary policy in particular) should not be ignored.

4 UK FINANCIAL INSTITUTIONS

4.1 INTRODUCTION

UK financial institutions encompass a very broad spread of widely differing organisations, ranging from the financially powerful international banking groups, through to small provincial firms offering little more than financial advice or agency services. However, an extremely important aspect of the operations of a large proportion of these institutions is the provision of financial intermediation services. Indeed, many people refer to these institutions collectively as *financial intermediaries*. Consequently, this chapter will begin by examining the nature of financial intermediation, and its importance within the modern financial system. This provides a useful basis for consideration of the broad types of financial intermediaries which exist within the UK.

Turning to the operations and role of specific financial institutions, it is intended to concentrate attention upon the commercial banks and the building societies, with only relatively brief mention being made of the other major groups of institutions such as the insurance companies, pension funds, unit trusts and investment trust companies. *The emphasis upon the banks and building societies is explained by their central roles within the monetary and payments mechanisms of the economy, and by their importance for the day-to-day financial decision-making of both the personal and business sectors. In addition, recognising their vital importance for the operation of the financial system, the regulatory and supervisory arrangements which relate to UK financial institutions will be examined.*

4.2 FINANCIAL INTERMEDIATION

4.2.1 The nature of financial intermediation

Financial intermediation refers to the activity of *channelling funds* between those people or institutions who wish to *lend* (that is, those who run financial surpluses) and those people or institutions who wish to *borrow* (that is, those who run financial deficits). Some intermediaries specialise in the sectors or groups within the economy which they service. For example, building societies receive deposits from, and channel the bulk of their funds to, the personal sector. A large proportion of this money is intended for the purchase of residential property secured against mortgages. By contrast, other intermediaries, such as the major clearing banks, deal with most sectors of the economy in respect of both the raising and on-lending of funds. Consequently, the channelling of borrowed funds both between sectors of the economy and within sectors is a complex activity, and may often involve transactions between the financial institutions themselves.

It is important to understand that financial intermediaries are not merely agents who 'introduce' borrowers to lenders. Rather, financial intermediaries effectively borrow funds and then on-lend to ultimate borrowers. Therefore, the financial intermediation process leads to the creation of *new financial assets and liabilities* within the economy. The funds lent to an intermediary are transformed into another form of asset which is the liability of the intermediary, until the funds are repaid. In turn, the intermediary on-lends the funds, and hence transforms them into yet another form of asset, which becomes the liability of the ultimate borrower. It should also be recognised that the funds are lent with the view either to generating a monetary reward for the lender (normally in the form of interest or dividend payments) or to obtaining some form of money transmission services (i.e. current account facilities).

An example of the financial intermediation process is where an individual deposits cash into a building society share account. This leads to the creation of interest-bearing building society shares (deposits), which are an asset of the depositor. Some or all of these funds may then be on-lent by the building society to another individual wishing to borrow. Thus, an interest-bearing mortgage loan may be created, which is, of course, an asset of the building society. This operation leads to the creation of additional amounts of two financial assets, matched by equal additional amounts of financial liabilities (that is, the mortgage debt of the ultimate borrower, and the share account debt of the building society).

4.2.2 Financial intermediation as a business activity

Private sector institutions undertake financial intermediation activities in order to make profits. In general, intermediaries pay interest on deposits lodged with them, or they are committed to provide some form of income to the supplier of funds (perhaps in the form of a pension or an insurance endowment). The only exception occurs where deposits are made into non-interest-bearing sight accounts at banks, but even here there are normally costs to be borne in respect of providing money transmission facilities to the depositor. In addition, the intermediaries incur operating costs, such as employees' salaries, rents, property taxes, and telephone and postal charges. If *operating profits* are to be generated, these costs must be more than covered by the sum total of interest earnings on funds on-lent, dividends received on equities held, and realised capital gains on holdings of

continued on next page

marketable assets. In order to calculate *net profits*, it is necessary to deduct from operating profits the amount of profits tax which has to be paid and the value of any provisions made against bad debt.

The calculation of *net profits* may be summarised as follows:

Net profits	=	Gross income from on-lending	−	Cost of funds on-lent	−	Operating costs	−	Taxes on profits	−	Provisions for bad debt

Considering this simple formula, it is tempting to conclude that if the intermediary widens the margin between the rate of interest paid on deposits and the rate charged on funds on-lent, then profits will be raised. However, this need not be the case, as higher rates on loans are likely to depress the demand for loans, whilst lower rates on deposits will probably reduce inflows of new funds. Consequently, turnover may fall, and it is possible that this may swamp the financial advantage to the intermediary of widening the interest rate margin. Also, as certain operating costs are likely to be fixed, at least in the shorter term, unit operating costs may rise as turnover falls.

Finally, it should be recognised that many financial intermediaries also provide *non-intermediation services* for their customers. To the extent that these *fee-earning* activities more than cover their costs, the institution may make an overall profit even if intermediation activities generate losses.

4.2.3 The need for financial intermediaries

The fundamental reason for the existence of financial intermediaries in the modern economy is that the *financial requirements of prospective lenders and borrowers are unlikely to match*. Taking each of the parties in turn:

(a) *The prospective lender.* Having decided to hold financial assets, the lender is likely to consider the following factors before making the final decision to lend:

(i) The *expected return* on the funds lent. This may be a crucial factor in motivating the desire to save in the first place.

(ii) *Risk* of default on funds lent; of capital loss on marketable assets which have to be sold before their maturity date; of unexpectedly high rates of inflation when funds are lent at a fixed nominal rate of interest; and of unanticipated changes in circumstances requiring access to funds.

(iii) The *liquidity* of the asset obtained, in the sense of its convertibility into its full nominal value. Some non-marketable assets are quite illiquid, and funds cannot be retrieved until the date of maturity. For marketable assets, the problem is that of possible capital losses, as mentioned in (ii) above.

(iv) The *transactions costs* involved in obtaining the asset, and in disposing of it at a future date. These costs include brokerage

119

expenses, commissions and fees which must be paid to professional agents and advisers.

(b) *The prospective borrower.* The borrower has to consider the following factors in formulating his or her financial requirements:
   (i) The *amount* of funds desired.
   (ii) The *cost* of the funds.
   (iii) The *period of time* over which the funds are required.
   (iv) *Risk* of the lender being unwilling to extend the term of a fixed period loan, or of having a loan recalled at short notice (where this is allowed within the original loan agreement).
   (v) *Transactions costs* associated with the acquisition of information on the availability and nature of sources of funds, and with the sale of debt instruments.

Given the wide variety of factors influencing the decisions of prospective lenders and borrowers, even on an aggregate level it is most improbable that their financial requirements will match. Thus, for example, other things being equal, the borrower will attempt to minimise interest costs, whilst the lender seeks to obtain the best return on funds. It is also probable that the borrower will seek the most flexible arrangements for the repayment of the debt, at any given interest cost, whilst the lender will wish to maximise the liquidity of funds, and have certainty over the latest date by which the funds will be repaid. In addition, individual borrowers often require more funds than individual lenders have available. The true magnitude of the problem becomes apparent once it is recognised that individual borrowers and lenders may be located in different parts of the country, or even in different parts of the world.

Accommodation of borrowers' and lenders' requirements might come about through adjustment of the interest rate. Thus, for example, a higher rate of interest may cause the prospective lender to offer a larger amount of funds, for a longer time period, on more flexible repayment terms. The prospective borrower may react by cutting back on the volume of funds required, and reducing the minimum period of time for which the funds are to be held. However, it is quite possible that there may be no rate of interest which is mutually acceptable to both borrower and lender, even assuming that the parties are able to get together and agree on all other characteristics of the transaction. Therefore, if borrowers' and lenders' requirements are to be met, there may be no alternative other than the use of the financial intermediation process.

4.2.4 The characteristics of financial intermediation

The major benefits generated by the financial intermediation process may be considered within the context of its key characteristics:

(a) *Maturity transformation of funds*

It is often the case that the assets of a financial intermediary are less liquid than its liabilities. For example, the average maturity of deposits with a retail bank may be just several days, whilst the average maturity of its loans and investments may be a year or more. The bank is able to perform this maturity transformation of funds due to the large number of depositors which it has, and hence its ability to estimate fairly accurately the likely maximum net withdrawal of funds on any given day. Experience shows that for many institutions this maximum net withdrawal is only a relatively small proportion of total deposits, and hence the bulk of funds may be used for long-term lending. Consequently, ultimate borrowers benefit from having access to funds which are likely to be available for *longer periods* than would have been the case had they been obtained directly from ultimate lenders. The latter benefit from the holding of claims against the financial intermediary which are likely to be *more liquid* than had the funds been lent directly to ultimate borrowers.

(b) *Risk spreading*

As financial intermediaries normally lend to a large number of individuals and/or institutions, any defaults on debts or capital losses on marketable instruments may be regarded as losses from their overall asset portfolios. Moreover, these losses are not attributable to any individual ultimate lender, but rather are shared between all lenders supplying funds to the intermediaries. However, as such losses are normally *absorbed* by the intermediaries as costs, they are rarely recognised by ultimate lenders, who merely suffer somewhat lower returns than would otherwise have been the case. Thus, there is a *reduced risk* for the ultimate lenders (as the security of their assets depends upon the solvency of intermediaries themselves). In addition, ultimate borrowers will probably be able to raise funds at a *lower cost* than they would have incurred had direct borrowing been necessary (with the associated higher risk for the lenders).

(c) *Reduction of transactions costs and aggregation of savings*

To the extent that financial intermediaries operate on a large scale, they are able to take advantage of *economies of scale* in the accumulation and interpretation of financial information, to spread the fixed overheads often associated with financial transactions, and to employ specialist personnel capable of assessing the creditworthiness of potential borrowers and the earnings potential of available investments. Also, they are able to advertise their presence, and hence *reduce search costs* for both prospective borrowers and lenders. Indeed, as many lenders often have only relatively small amounts of funds available, financial intermediaries are able to bundle small deposits into amounts which are sufficient to meet the needs of ultimate borrowers.

The operations of financial intermediaries offer clear advantages to both borrowers and lenders, and provide an important means of accommodating their differing financial requirements. In addition, benefits are also likely to be generated for *society as a whole*, through the encouragement of the lending of funds for innovative but risky projects, which might otherwise not be able to elicit the necessary financial support. Thus, the *economic growth* of the nation may be enhanced.

4.2.5 Disintermediation

Whilst financial intermediation provides the mechanism through which the bulk of borrowing and lending takes place within the modern economy, there may be circumstances within which intermediation may not be possible, or when the direct transactions between ultimate borrowers and lenders become relatively more attractive. The term *disintermediation* refers to the situations where ultimate borrowers and lenders come together directly, and thus by-pass the established channels of financial intermediation. The circumstances which motivate disintermediation activity to occur may be divided into two groups:

(a) Where there are *official restrictions* placed upon the free market mechanism (such as the application of monetary controls on bank lending), it is quite possible that creditworthy borrowers will be unable to raise the funds that they require from financial intermediaries. These borrowers may be willing to pay at least the rates of interest that are being charged by the intermediaries, and hence there may be scope for ultimate lenders to earn higher returns than are available from intermediaries, so long as the costs associated with setting up the direct lending transactions are no greater than those which would have been incurred in respect of the intermediaries' operations. The rates earned by the lenders must, of course, be sufficient to persuade them to forgo the benefits which are normally related to the deposit of funds with a financial intermediary, especially in respect of risk.

(b) Where the ultimate borrower possesses a *high credit rating*, it may simply be cheaper for that borrower to raise funds directly from ultimate lenders, perhaps via the issue of marketable securities. Indeed, much of the disintermediation experienced during the 1980s was associated with the trend towards *securitisation* of corporate debt, whereby marketable securities tended to replace normal bank loans for many companies.

(The disintermediation topic is taken up in Chapter 6 (at 6.9), within the context of money supply growth.)

4.2.6 Classification of financial intermediaries

The traditional approach to the classification of the wide array of financial intermediaries to be found within the UK is to divide the institutions into *bank financial intermediaries* (BFIs) and *non-bank financial intermediaries* (NBFIs), and then to sub-divide the NBFIs into *deposit-taking* and *non-deposit taking* institutions. In addition, the activities of all financial intermediaries may be divided into *retail* and *wholesale* transactions.

(a) *Bank and non-bank financial intermediaries*

Until the early 1980s it was normal to regard BFIs as being the only institutions with liabilities which were included in measures of the *money supply*, and the only institutions whose lending activities added to the money supply (as opposed merely to recycling money which had been created elsewhere). However, in the face of significant innovations which took place during the 1980s in the provision of intermediation facilities (especially by the building society sector), and the ensuing controversy associated with the formulation of money supply measures, this approach became increasingly unsatisfactory. Consequently, the classification is now based upon the broad nature of the *business activities* undertaken by financial intermediaries. Quite simply, if an institution offers a sufficiently broad spread of generally-recognised banking facilities, it will be deemed to fall within the BFI group. These facilities include the provision of a range of sight and time accounts, money transmission and payments services, international payments services, advice on investments and taxation, and so on. Unfortunately the continuing diversification of building societies into traditional areas of banking activity is beginning to raise further questions as to the relevance of the existing categorisation of institutions. Nevertheless, and despite the conversion of the Abbey National Building Society to public limited company (bank) status in 1989, the following division is widely accepted:

BFIs

(1) Retail banks:
    (i)   London clearing banks
    (ii)   Scottish clearing banks
    (iii)   Northern Ireland banks

        (iv)   Bank of England Banking Department
        (v)   TSB Bank plc
        (vi)   The Co-operative Bank plc
        (vii)   Yorkshire Bank plc
        (viii)   Girobank plc
        (ix)   Abbey National plc

(2) Wholesale banks:
        (i)   British Merchant banks
        (ii)   other British banks
        (iii)   overseas banks

(3) Discount houses

NBFIs

(1) Building societies
(2) Non-banking sector finance houses
(3) National Savings Bank
(4) Insurance companies
(5) Pension funds
(6) Unit trusts
(7) Investment trust companies
(8) Specialist non-bank intermediaries

(b) *Deposit-taking and non-deposit-taking financial intermediaries*

An alternative approach to the classification of financial intermediaries is to divide them according to whether or not their sources of funds come via *deposits* which may be withdrawn by the depositors at a future date. These deposits, which have a nominal capital value which is normally guaranteed by the deposit-taking institution, may derive from all sectors of the economy, although different institutions tend to place emphasis upon different sectors. For example, building societies have traditionally raised the bulk of their funds from the personal sector in the form of savings deposits, although in more recent years an increasing proportion has been raised in the form of wholesale deposits from other financial institutions. By contrast the retail banks have tended to raise deposits from a much wider range of sources, including domestic personal and corporate sectors, other financial institutions, and the overseas sector.

The deposit-taking institutions include:

    (i)   all BFIs
    (ii)   building societies

continued on next page

(iii) non-banking sector finance houses

(iv) National Savings Bank.

The NBFIs not listed above, and including the insurance companies, pension funds, unit trusts and investment trust companies, form the *non-deposit-taking* financial intermediaries. These intermediaries are the major *long-term savings* institutions in the UK. The common characteristic of their activities is that they collect funds from individual savers and from other institutions wishing to amass financial claims, either through one-off investments or through regular savings commitments. Often investors are unable to liquidate their claims on demand, and certain claims with institutions such as insurance companies and pension funds may not be accessible in any way before specified maturity dates. In addition, whilst certain other claims may be liquidated relatively quickly, the holder risks capital losses as the value of claims is often linked to the market price of securities.

(c) *Retail and wholesale operations*

The operations of financial intermediaries may be divided into retail and wholesale operations. The major difference between retail and wholesale is in respect of the *size of transactions* undertaken. Thus, whilst retail operations relate to the fairly small-scale deposits and loans, wholesale transactions are normally on a relatively large-scale basis. There is no precise dividing line between the two types of operations, although any transaction in excess of £100,000 would normally be included within the wholesale category.

The institutions most readily associated with retail activities are the retail banks and the building societies. Many of these institutions operate through *large branch networks* and depend upon *over-the-counter deposits*, into sight, time or savings accounts, for a significant proportion of their funds. The making of *loans* to *personal customers* and *smaller businesses* is an extremely important aspect of their on-lending activities. In respect of retail banks, such loans are often linked to base rate. In addition, the retail banks and building societies are heavily involved in the provision of *money transmission facilities*, such as cheque book accounts, direct debits, electronic funds transfer, and so on.

Wholesale activities often involve the raising of funds from, and the on-lending of funds to, the *larger corporate customers* of financial institutions. In addition, significant volumes of *inter-institution transactions* take place. Wholesale funds are often channelled through the *money markets* and may involve the *issue of instruments* such as certificates of deposit and commercial paper. These large scale transactions do not require the use of branch networks, and, indeed, some institutions involved in wholesale activities operate from a single location. Interest rates generated on wholesale transactions are more likely to be market-related than those arising from retail transactions, and there is often a finer margin between deposit rates and on-lending rates, due to the *economies of scale* offered by large transactions and the *high levels of competition* found in most wholesale markets.

Finally, it should be recognised that whilst some financial intermediaries, such as merchant banks and discount houses, may engage solely in wholesale transactions, many others are active in both retail and wholesale transactions, to a greater or lesser degree. Thus, for example, whilst the dominant characteristic of retail banks is the raising and on-lending of funds in respect of retail customers, all of them also raise funds and on-lend in wholesale amounts. This division of activities will be taken up later in this chapter, in respect of the individual groups of financial intermediaries.

4.3   THE BANK OF ENGLAND

4.3.1   Background issues

The Bank of England is the UK's *central bank*, and as such has broad responsibilities for the organisation and operation of government monetary and financial policies. Indeed, it has often been argued that the nature of the Bank's functions make it the single most important financial institution in the UK. The Bank was formed in 1694, with the purpose of raising funds for the British Government, but it only came into public ownership in 1946. Nevertheless, since the middle of the nineteenth century the Bank has been undertaking the majority of functions which are normally associated with a central bank, and the Treasury's influence over the Bank's operations has never been seriously questioned. According to the provisions of the *Bank of England Act 1946*, the Bank has a *legal duty* to carry out the wishes of the Treasury in respect of the implementation of the Government's policies on financial, monetary and related matters. However, despite the Bank's legal subordination to the Treasury, the Bank still has a *substantial influence* upon the formulation of official policy and the means of implementation. The accumulated expertise and the reputation of the Bank are such that the Government will normally seek its advice on relevant policy matters before decisions are made. Indeed, given the sensitivity of the financial markets to the official policy position, even relatively minor disagreements between the Bank and the Treasury could be damaging for the stability of the financial system, and might undermine the successful operation of official policy.

Almost every country with a developed financial system has a central bank of some form or other, although their structures and specific functions vary widely. So too does the balance of *public policy functions* and *commercial activities* undertaken. However, the major functions performed by the Bank of England are typical of those performed by central banks throughout the world, although some are much more heavily involved in commercial activities than is the Bank of England.

Whilst the precise functions of the Bank of England are quite varied, and whilst different functions alter in importance over time, as official policies change and as the economic and financial environment evolves, it is nevertheless possible to identify three key areas of operations:

(a) *Banking*, including the issue of banknotes.

(b) *Monetary policy and control*, including the adjustment of banking sector liquidity and the control of money supply growth and short-term interest rates.

(c) *Financial regulation*, including supervisory functions in respect of the banking sector, financial markets and international financial activities.

4.3.2 The Bank of England's banking role

The Bank of England offers a wide range of banking services to its customers; however, the composition of its customer base is markedly different from that of any of the commercial banks. Whilst the Bank operates accounts for a number of personal and non-bank commercial customers, these are of only minor significance. The Bank does not compete with the commercial banks for such custom, and it is sometimes suggested that the Bank only operates these accounts so that it may maintain some direct contact with the day-to-day banking problems faced by the banking sector at large. Of considerably greater importance is the Bank's role in relation to the government and to the banking sector:

(a) *Banker to the Government*

The Bank of England acts as banker to the British central Government, being responsible for the *management of central government finances* and the *provision of advice* to the Government on financial matters. The balances on all central government accounts are brought together at the Bank, and it is responsible for ensuring that any net deficit is financed and that any surplus funds are used to repay outstanding debt (thus minimising the Government's debt servicing costs).

In relation to budget *deficits* (Public Sector Borrowing Requirements, PSBRs), the long-term objective is to cover funding requirements via the issue of gilt-edged securities (to the extent that the Government's borrowing requirement is not financed by net issues of National Savings instruments). The shorter-term financing requirements are covered by

127

issues of Treasury bills (on a weekly competitive tender basis and on tap to official holders). For day-to-day deficits, the Bank will make available to the Government 'ways and means' advances, which are effectively Bank of England overdraft facilities. Where there are *surpluses* on the budget (Public Sector Debt Repayments, PSDRs), the Bank undertakes the necessary net repurchases of debt within the broad framework of the Government's financial policy. These net repurchases may occur 'automatically' via the Bank omitting to fund maturing debt instruments. Alternatively, the Bank may enter the market and repurchase specific categories of debt.

Gilt-edged auctions
During the 1987/88 financial year, the Bank experimented with auctions of gilt-edged securities, as an alternative method of making issues, rather than the traditional tender method. An important characteristic of these auctions was that the Bank did not set a minimum price below which it would not allot stock. Despite some controversy surrounding the operation of the auctions, the Bank subsequently announced that it intended to use such auctions again in the future, although only as a complementary device to the tender method. Indeed, in January 1989, the Bank set up its first 'reverse auction' in gilts, as a means of helping to deal with the large PSDR which had arisen. On that occasion, it invited offers for the repurchase of two short-dated gilts with a value of up to £500m.

Irrespective of whether the authorities face a PSBR or a PSDR, an important function of the Bank of England is to ensure that the financing is undertaken with due regard to the general stability of the financial system and to the monetary policy objectives of the Government. Indeed, it may be argued that this function is really part of the Bank's responsibility to act as *manager of the British national debt*. For not only are there normally large net flows of funds arising from the current budget position to be dealt with, but also there are often large volumes of maturing debt instruments which require funding. By choosing an appropriate mix of debt instruments to offer for sale, or to offer to repurchase, the Bank may attempt to manipulate the characteristics of the outstanding national debt with some particular policy target in view; for example, the smoothing of interest rate movements or the control of the money supply. It should also be recognised that on some occasions, the Bank may find that its responsibilities as banker to the Government conflict with its other duties as controller of the money supply and stabiliser of the financial system. The Government's own policy priorities will then, of course, have to be taken into consideration.

In relation to the administration of the national debt, the Bank of England acts as *registrar* for all holdings of government securities. (It also maintains registers for stocks issued by nationalised industries, some local authorities and other public bodies.) In respect of this role, it is responsible for recording transfers of ownership, paying interest and dividends, and repaying funds upon maturity. In addition, in 1986, the Bank established the Central Gilts Office which provides Gilt-Edged Market Makers and commercial banks dealing in government securities with computerised book-entry transfer facilities and assured payments arrangements.

A further important role of the Bank is as *adviser* to the Government on financial matters. The Bank's accumulated knowledge of the operation of financial markets and monetary systems is invaluable to governmental decision-making. Its wide-ranging contacts with both domestic and overseas financial institutions place it in a unique position to be able to advise the Government on the options open in relation to financial matters, and on the possible implications of pursuing any of those options. The Bank's position in this respect is strengthened by its other roles as *agent* for the Government's foreign exchange market operations (the Bank holds the Treasury's Exchange Equalisation Account, which contains the UK's foreign currency reserves), and as the *official representative* of the UK authorities at various important international bodies such as the Bank for International Settlements and the Basle Committee on international banking supervision.

(b) *Banker to the banks*

Just as ordinary individuals and firms hold accounts with their banks in order to be able to make payments as they fall due, so too the *clearing banks* hold accounts with the Bank of England for a very similar purpose. These accounts contain the banks' *operational balances* which are used in relation to the payments arising from the cheque clearing and electronic funds transfer system. At the end of payments clearing each day, imbalances are likely to exist between the payments made to, and the claims made upon, individual banks. Where a bank experiences a deficit at clearing, its operational balances will be drawn upon in order to meet its commitments to other banks, whereas banks experiencing surpluses will have their accounts at the Bank credited. It is by harnessing the flows of funds through these accounts that the Bank is able to influence monetary conditions in the economy as a whole. For it must be remembered that it is quite possible for the clearing banks in aggregate to experience a deficit upon clearing, and hence pressure may be exerted on market rates of interest as the banks seek to restore their operational balances to the desired level (see Chapter 5, at 5.3.3).

All banks are required to hold *non-operational non-interest bearing deposits* with the Bank of England, currently set for most banks at 0.35% of their eligible liabilities (which are basically their sterling deposit liabilities with original maturities of two years or less). However, there is some debate as to whether these deposits can be viewed in the context of the banks using the Bank of England as their banker, as the banks have no alternative but to make these deposits if they wish to maintain their authorisation to operate in the UK. These deposits cannot be withdrawn at will, and they can only be reduced if the Bank of England decides to lower the prescribed ratio for all banks, or if a bank should find that its eligible liabilities fall, or if the bank is wound up.

Similarly, whilst the Bank is willing to *offer advice* to individual banks on financial and operational matters, there is some uncertainty as to whether this can be separated from the Bank's formal duties in respect of banking regulation and supervision. In this context, some of the 'advice' given to banks is far from optional, and banks are expected to act in a manner compatible with the advice, or be willing to explain to the Bank why they have not complied. Nevertheless, certain aspects of the Bank's activities, such as the provision of *commentaries* on the domestic and international financial situation and the offering of *broad guidance* on the nature of certain forms of banking and other financial services operations, undoubtedly assist individual banks in the formulation of their commercial strategies, and may be viewed in the same light as any commercial bank providing useful market intelligence and professional guidance to its customers.

Finally, it should be noted that the Bank of England acts as banker to a number of *overseas banking institutions, central banks and monetary authorities*. The Bank provides a range of banking facilities for these organisations, including domestic and foreign currency deposit facilities, international payments services, management of international payments arising from exchange market intervention, advice on investments and borrowing, and general support in respect of financial and monetary matters.

(c)   *The production and distribution of banknotes*

The Bank of England has the exclusive right to print and issue banknotes within England and Wales; and although the Scottish and Northern Ireland clearing banks still issue their own notes, these must be backed by an equal value of Bank of England notes. New notes are drawn into circulation through the accounts held at the Bank by commercial banks, some building societies, and various government departments.

Banknotes are liabilities of the issuing bank, and today the balance sheet counterpart of Bank of England notes is comprised solely of securities. In other words the UK has a *fiduciary note issue*, and this may be raised with the permission of the Treasury. Therefore, in theory at least, government policy sets the limit on the total volume of notes in circulation. However, the actual net issue of new notes (having accounted for the replacement of dirty or damaged notes) is largely determined by the level of demand from the private sector; although the authorities may attempt to influence the overall demand for notes as part of their more general monetary control objectives. The profits generated by the note issuing activity (which are basically the difference between the costs of producing the notes and the interest earned on the securities backing them) are paid to the Exchequer.

4.3.3 The Bank of England's monetary policy role

The Bank's role in relation to the formulation and implementation of government monetary policy is very closely related to its role as the Government's banker. There are several aspects to this activity, which may be directed towards influencing the rate of growth of the money supply and/or the level of interest rates. For example, the Bank may undertake *money market intervention*, and by buying or selling bills from the discount houses may influence the level of liquidity within the banking sector and level of short-term interest rates. (For detailed examination of this topic, see Chapter 5, at 5.3.3.) Alternatively, the Bank may use *non-market (direct) controls*, perhaps involving the setting of minimum liquid reserve ratios or interest rate ceilings on bank deposits, or the issuing of directives on the types of lending which banking institutions should undertake (see Chapter 8, at 8.5.2(b)). The Bank also acts as an *adviser to the Treasury* on monetary policy matters, being able to draw upon the specialist expertise of its staff and long-established comprehensive data bases. Whilst the Treasury has ultimate direction of monetary policy, in practice, the Bank's high reputation in financial circles endows its advice and recommendations with a unique force which it is hard for the Government to ignore. The introduction of an inflation target by the Government in October 1992, and the requirement placed upon the Bank to produce a quarterly Inflation Report (see Chapter 8, at 8.7.3), has strengthened the Bank's position in this respect.

4.3.4 The Bank of England's supervisory role

The Bank of England performs an important supervisory role within the UK financial system, with particular emphasis placed upon the *supervision of banking activities* and certain *wholesale financial market operations*.

The Financial Services Act 1986 and the Banking Act 1987 have led to the Bank's position in respect of financial supervision becoming much more formalised than in earlier years, although since the enactment of the Banking Act 1979, the Bank has had legal duties to supervise the operations of banks and certain other deposit-taking institutions. Currently, the Bank is responsible for ensuring that institutions operating as banks or participating in the UK's wholesale sterling money, foreign exchange and bullion markets meet rigorous authorisation requirements designed to maintain the quality of activities. Of particular importance for banks are its *liquidity and capital adequacy requirements*.

In addition, the Bank has become increasingly involved with issues relating to the supervision of international banking activities, especially via the work of the Basle Committee (representing the world's major central banks). (For detailed discussion of the Bank's supervisory role, see 4.10 below.)

4.3.5 The independence of the Bank of England

Since the signing of the Maastricht Treaty, relating to European Monetary Union (EMU), in December 1991 (see Chapter 10, at 10.4.6), there has been a growing debate on the form that the relationship between the Bank of England and the Government should take. One aspect of the movement towards EMU is the proposal that a *European System of Central Banks* should be established, which would require each EC member's central bank to support the policies of a *European Central Bank*, and to be *independent of its own country's government*. Already, several EC central banks have such independence, but, as stated above, the Bank of England is subordinate to the Treasury. Thus, whilst the Bank is largely free to manage its own day-to-day operations, these must be directed towards achieving the Government's policy goals. This means that the Bank is obliged to bow to the Government's wishes, which may be influenced by *political expediency* rather than by the best interest of the economy. For example, the economic situation may suggest that interest rates should be raised in order to damp down money supply growth and ease inflationary pressures. But an impending by-election or party conference may cause the Government to instruct the Bank of England that interest rates should not be allowed to rise, and, if possible, should be reduced. Thus, short-term political gain may take priority over the long-term needs of the economy. By contrast, if the Bank was independent of governmental pressure, and was given the *duty* and the *necessary powers* to control the *rate of inflation* via monetary means and/or to stabilise the *exchange value of sterling*, operational decisions would be taken solely on the grounds of economic necessity. Political expediency would not be allowed to distort the implementation of monetary policy. It should also be noted that such independence would not interfere with the Bank's ability to undertake its banking and supervisory functions. In fact, if the Bank's roles were clearly defined in this context, political independence might endow it with even greater authority across the whole range of its activities.

The proponents of political independence for the Bank of England often point to the success achieved, in respect of monetary policy goals, by the relatively independent central banks of Germany, the USA and Switzerland. However, the evidence on the relationship between a central bank's independence and its country's inflation rate is rather mixed, and there are several examples of countries achieving a good inflation performance whilst their central banks have been closely tied to their respective governments. Also, it must be remembered that although central bank independence may create monetary conditions which are conducive to the control of inflation, the impact that this regime may have on monetary variables may be detrimental to other aspects of a country's economic performance. For example, there is some evidence to suggest that countries with less independent central banks have tended to generate higher *economic growth* rates than other countries over a significant part of the post-war period. Consequently, the case for giving the Bank of England political independence is not without controversy. Indeed, within a democratic nation there is the important question of *accountability* of the Bank to be resolved, and the appropriate mechanism for the *setting of the Bank's policy objectives* and the *monitoring of its performance* would have to be established. Notwithstanding the pressures which are likely to be generated as a result of the EC's movement towards EMU, there is certain to be much debate on what the term 'political independence' would mean *in practice* for the Bank of England.

4.4 THE COMMERCIAL BANKS

4.4.1 The main banking groups within the UK

At the end of February 1993 there were no fewer than 508 authorised banking institutions operating within the UK, of which 255 were branch operations of overseas banks. Banking institutions within the UK are grouped by the Bank of England as follows:

(a) *Retail banks:* These are banks which have extensive branch networks in the UK and which participate directly in the UK clearing system.

(b) *British Merchant banks:* These are wholesale banks which are members of the British Merchant Banking and Securities Houses Association.

(c) *Other British banks:* Comprise all other UK-registered banking institutions and certain banks in the Channel Islands and Isle of Man which are either independent companies, or are controlled by UK companies or individuals.

(d) *American banks:* Comprise the branches and subsidiaries of US banks, including certain offices in the Channel Islands and Isle of Man. The branches and subsidiaries of US companies which are not banks in the USA are included in the 'other overseas banks' group.

(e) *Japanese banks:* Comprise the branches and subsidiaries of banks based in Japan, including certain offices in the Channel Islands and Isle of Man. The branches and subsidiaries of Japanese companies which are not banks in Japan are included in the 'other overseas banks' group.

(f) *Other overseas banks:* Comprise the branches and subsidiaries, including certain offices in the Channel Islands and Isle of Man, of all foreign companies other than United States and Japanese banks.

(g) *Consortium banks:* These are UK-registered banks which are owned jointly by other financial institutions, one of which must be based overseas, and none of which must own more than 50% of the shares. Since July 1987, separate balance sheet data for this group have not been made available by the Bank of England, and statistics for consortium banks are now included with those for 'other overseas banks'.

Groups (a) to (c) form the *British banks* in the official statistics, whilst groups (d) to (g) form the *overseas banks.* An alternative division is into *retail banks* (group (a)) and the *wholesale banks* (groups (b) to (g)). The distribution of deposit liabilities between these two groupings at March 1993 is shown in Table 4.1. It is interesting to note that whilst the retail banks have a comfortable lead in respect of sterling deposits, the wholesale banks heavily dominate foreign currency activity; and as almost 60% of total bank deposits are foreign-currency-denominated, the wholesale banks also dominate deposit holdings overall. Furthermore, it may be observed that overseas banks accounted for almost 60% of banking sector deposits, with a very heavy emphasis upon foreign currency business. These figures illustrate the international character of the UK banking system. At the end of March 1993, total foreign currency deposits with UK banks amounted to the equivalent of approximately £753b, within a total deposit base of £1,282b.

4.4.2 The retail banks

The institutions comprising the retail banks group are rather mixed in character, ranging from the long-established major clearing banks, such as Barclays and National Westminster, through to Girobank which only became a clearing bank in 1983. Indeed, within the group, the Bank of

Table 4.1 Distribution of deposit liabilities for retail/wholesale and British/overseas banks in the UK: 31 March 1993

	Percentage of all banking sector sterling deposits	Percentage of all banking sector foreign currency deposits	Percentage of all banking sector deposits
Retail banks	61.7	13.9	33.6
Wholesale banks	38.3	86.1	66.4
British banks	72.8	17.7	40.4
Overseas banks	27.2	82.3	59.6

Source: *Bank of England Press Release*, 6 May 1993.

England Banking Department is the odd one out in the sense that the bulk of its activities are quite different to those of the other retail banks. It should also be noted that since July 1989, Abbey National has been included in the group, despite the fact that its operations are still much more closely aligned to those of the building societies than to those of the other retail banks. Nevertheless, its inclusion within the retail banks group is quite reasonable in the light of the substantial volume of retail banking activities which it undertakes. It also emphasises that Abbey National now falls within the regulatory framework applied to banking institutions.

For purposes of analysis, the retail banks may be taken as a group, although the discussion in the remainder of this section is most closely applicable to the main clearing banks, and has only limited relevance for the Bank of England Banking Department.

A key characteristic of the retail banks is their large *branch networks*, which form an important element of their function as providers of *domestic payments services*. Specifically, these banks offer cheque payment services (with cheque guarantee cards to enhance the acceptability of payment by cheque), bank giro credit facilities, standing orders, direct debits, electronic funds transfer (via the Bankers' Automated Clearing Service and the Clearing House Automated Payments System), electronic funds transfer at point of sale (EFTPOS), and credit card facilities. In addition to the payments services, and the necessary holding of customers' current accounts, the retail banks also offer a wide range of *other banking services*, including:

● savings accounts
● personal loans (secured and unsecured)
● overdraft facilities

135

- mortgage loans
- corporate financing (ranging from working capital to long-term secured loans)
- automated teller machines (ATMs) and home-banking via telephone (allowing out-of-hours transactions)
- corporate cash management schemes
- leasing and hire purchase (often via subsidiaries)
- export financing and documentation facilities
- payroll services
- financial management advice for business customers
- travellers cheques and foreign currencies
- international financial transfers
- advice on taxation and financial matters for personal customers
- executor and trustee facilities.

As implied above, the package of financial services offered differs between individual retail banks, although most retail banks do provide the full range of banking services, at least to some degree. It should also be noted that these services tend to evolve according to the pressures of customer demands and the dictates of the wider financial environment. In more recent years retail banks have also entered into 'non-banking' services such as insurance broking, the running of unit trusts, and the provision of personal equity plans.

Table 4.2 shows a summary balance sheet for the retail banks as at 31 March 1993. A brief examination of this balance sheet provides a useful insight into the nature of the financial intermediation activities undertaken by the retail banks.

(a) *Sterling assets*

   (i)   *Cash and balances with the Bank of England.* With the exception of the cash ratio (non-operational) balances which banks are required to hold with the Bank of England, these are the most liquid of all assets, and are vital for the day-to-day transactions of retail banks. The operational balances are used to meet commitments arising from payments-clearing activity.

   (ii)   *Market loans.* These are wholesale loans, usually made at market-related rates, and sometimes through the agency of a broker. A significant proportion of these loans is made to other UK banking institutions, and large amounts of secured funds are placed with the discount houses (see 4.5).

   (iii)   *Bills.* The most important of these instruments are eligible bank bills. These are commercial bills of exchange which have been 'accepted' (i.e. underwritten) by banks having eligibility status

Table 4.2   UK retail banks: Summary balance sheet as at 31 March 1993

Assets	£b	£b
Sterling:		
Cash and balances with the Bank of England		4.1
Market loans		69.2
UK banks	50.6	
Certificates of deposit held	8.5	
UK local authorities	0.3	
Overseas	9.8	
Bills		13.2
Eligible bank bills	11.0	
Others	2.2	
Advances		255.4
UK private sector	252.4	
Others	3.0	
Investments		24.2
Foreign currency:		
Market loans and advances		83.8
UK	31.6	
Overseas	52.2	
Bills		4.1
Investments		22.5
Miscellaneous assets		29.0
Total assets		505.5
Liabilities		
Sterling:		
Notes issued		1.8
Sterling deposits		326.2
UK banks	34.0	
UK private sector	240.3	
UK public sector	4.0	
Overseas residents	23.4	
Certificates of deposit issued	24.5	
Foreign currency deposits		104.6
UK	27.0	
Overseas residents	63.3	
Certificates of deposit issued	14.3	
Miscellaneous liabilities (including capital)		72.9
Total liabilities		505.5

Source: *Bank of England Press Release*, 6 May 1993.

(i.e. banks meeting certain minimum criteria, set by the Bank of England, in respect of the quality of their acceptance business). Where a commercial bill has been accepted by a bank without such status, then a normal (non-eligible) bank bill is created. In addition

137

to both types of bank bills, Treasury bills and local authority bills are also held.

(iv) *Advances.* These assets form by far the largest single element on retail banks' balance sheets. The UK private sector is the dominant recipient of these loans, which are made available for fixed terms or on overdraft facilities. The original maturity of term loans may vary from a few months to upwards of 10 years; and since the early 1980s increasing volumes of mortgage loans have been made, with nominal maturities of up to 25 years. The interest rate arrangements on advances are also extremely variable, with rates being either fixed or floating, and depending upon the maturity of the loan, the amount borrowed, the creditworthiness of the borrower, and so on.

(v) *Investments.* A major element here is the holdings of British government and government-guaranteed securities.

It is clear that sterling assets dominate the retail banks' balance sheets, with sterling advances to the UK private sector accounting for around one-half of all assets held. It should also be noted that the potentially high profit, but illiquid and risky, advances are 'balanced' by substantial holdings of liquid assets, with particular weight being given to market loans to other UK banks. This position reflects the highly liquid nature of the retail banks' sterling liabilities.

(b) *Foreign currency assets*

The types of foreign currency assets held are very similar to the sterling assets, however, market loans dominate foreign currency business, with advances accounting for only about one-quarter of the total. The most important debtor of the retail banks in this respect is the overseas sector, although the UK banking sector accounts for a significant proportion of the total.

(c) *Miscellaneous assets*

This balance sheet item is the residual element on the asset side, and comprises the banks' own premises, plant and equipment through to the value of cheques which have been credited to customers' accounts, but which are held overnight before being presented or paid into the banks' own accounts with other members of the banking sector or banks overseas.

(d) *Sterling liabilities*

(i) *Notes issued.* These are the sterling banknotes issued by the Scottish and Northern Ireland clearing banks. They are backed pound for pound by Bank of England notes.

(ii)   *Sterling deposits.* These form the major liabilities item on the retail banks' balance sheet, with the UK private sector being the major creditor of the banks. In 1993, around 50% of sterling deposits were in the form of *sight deposits*, and a significant proportion (around 80%) of these was interest-bearing. All sight deposits are withdrawable on demand (without interest penalty), and they may be transferred through the chequing system or via electronic means. *Time deposits*, which are of a similar magnitude to sight deposits in balance sheet terms, include both retail and wholesale deposits with nominal terms to maturity ranging from a few days to several years. However, for all practical purposes, a large proportion of retail banks' time deposits are available either on demand (if the depositor is willing to bear an interest penalty) or with only a short period of notice required, thus making their sterling deposit liabilities highly liquid. The retail banks also raise a significant amount of funds through the issue of *sterling certificates of deposit.* These are fixed term (usually 28 days to five years) negotiable bearer securities, issued in denominations of £50,000 and above, and normally carrying fixed rates of interest. The utilisation of these instruments reflects the importance of wholesale money market deposits as a source of funds.

(e)   *Foreign currency liabilities*

These are largely wholesale time deposits, with a high proportion being held by the overseas sector. Foreign-currency denominated certificates of deposit are also issued, although until recently these have been a relatively minor source of funds.

(f)   *Miscellaneous liabilities*

This item includes credit balances received but not yet credited to customers' accounts, and standing orders and credit transfers debited to customers' accounts but not yet transferred to the payee. It also includes the very important element of shareholders' funds. These funds are held to cover the possibility of borrowers' defaults and capital losses on investments, and hence are crucial to the maintenance of depositors' confidence in their banks (as is explained in detail at 4.4.5(b) below).

4.4.3   The changing environment for the retail banks

Since the early 1980s the environment within which the retail banks operate has become increasingly competitive. Their traditional dominance of the provision of certain types of banking services, to both personal and corporate customers, has come under attack largely as a result of deregulation in financial markets, innovation in the provision of financial services, and an increased awareness on the part of customers of alternative suppliers of services. In respect of *personal customers*, a major challenge has been posed by the *building societies*. Indeed, even prior to the enactment of the Building Societies Act 1986, which gave building societies powers to offer a wider range of financial services than had previously been possible, the societies had been moving into banking-type activities, often in collaboration with other institutions (including banks themselves). The banks' response to these developments has taken several forms, and understandably has focused upon the maintenance of the personal customer base. In particular, the banks have broadened the range of savings facilities available, and have improved the flexibility of access to funds, whilst offering more competitive interest rates. Interest-bearing current accounts are becoming increasingly common, and various automatic overdraft facilities and free banking services have been introduced. Banks have also attempted to attack the building societies in their own traditional area of mortgage lending, and have not only allocated large amounts of funds to this purpose, but also have introduced various innovations, including fixed rate mortgage loans for fixed periods. In addition, the banks have become somewhat more aggressive in their marketing and advertising strategies, and have attempted to acquire a more up-to-date and accessible image. There is now much more explicit recognition of customer needs, through longer opening hours (especially Saturday morning opening) and the provision of ATMs. Indeed, the banks have once again begun the take the initiative in respect of the implementation of computer technology.

In relation to *corporate business*, the retail banks have experienced intensified competition resulting largely from the *deregulation of the capital market* and innovations in the provision of facilities for the raising of funds for businesses. The easier access to the capital market for corporate borrowers and larger investors has tended to encourage the raising of funds outside of conventional banking channels by corporate customers. The higher degree of competition within the market has tended to reduce the relative costs of raising funds via securities issues, and the range of sophisticated facilities made available to both borrowers and lenders has stimulated activity still further. The retail banks have, to some extent, responded to this disintermediation trend by improving their existing facilities for corporate customers; but there are limits to the commercial viability of such actions, especially in the light of the high credit ratings of many corporate borrowers (and hence their ability to attain low rates on issues of securities). Therefore, the main response of the banks would appear to have been an increased involvement in securities transactions. Effectively, banks have decided to harness the disintermediation trend to their own advantage. This has come about through acquisitions of capital market firms involved in broking and market-making activities, and through increased involvement in merchant banking, via wholesale subsidiaries. Several banks have also become involved in managing issues of commercial paper, and effectively acting as market-makers in this context. (Recent developments within the capital market are discussed in more detail in Chapter 5 at 5.5.5.)

As a result of the pressures experienced in respect of financial intermediation activities, the retail banks have been paying much closer attention, across both wholesale and retail operations, to the provision of *nonintermediation financial services*. *Fee incomes* have tended to become a relatively more important element of total earnings. This development was largely to be expected given the much reduced '*endowment effect*' (as non-interest-bearing deposits have declined in importance as a source of funds for on-lending) and the *intense competition* for both interest-bearing deposits and high quality borrowers.

The major difficulties which UK retail banks have had to face up to in recent years have largely been caused or precipitated by the *recession* of the early 1990s. This had a serious impact on most banks, across the whole range of their activities. A particular problem was the *record level of provisions* required in respect of the *bad debts* caused by small and medium-sized corporate and other small business insolvencies. Substantial losses also accrued in respect of personal sector lending and a small number of high profile large corporate failures. Taking the period 1990 to 1992, for the largest seven retail banks alone, the total value of domestic commercial provisions was almost £16b. In addition, the weakness of the UK economy, reinforced by a slowdown in economic activity throughout much of the Western world, meant that there were *few opportunities* to expand low risk lending business. In general, many companies drew back from debt financed capital investment projects, instead wishing to strengthen their financial positions; and often those companies approaching banks for increased funding did so because of cash flow problems, thus effectively requiring their banks to engage in *distress lending*. Whilst the pressures faced by the retail banks were never thought to be threatening to their fundamental stability, fears were nevertheless expressed by some commentators that borrowers might face a '*credit crunch*', whereby the banks would only be willing to lend to the most creditworthy of customers, and even then only on increased lending margins. This perception was probably partly responsible for the growing number of *well-publicised complaints* that the banks were treating many of their customers (and particularly their small business customers) harshly. The subsequent media and parliamentary criticism of the banks culminated in a number of *official investigations* into aspects of banks' lending and charging policies, which largely exonerated the banks of allegations of collusion and unfair practice, but did little to improve their tarnished image.

By 1993 the environment within which UK retail banks operated was markedly changed from that which existed during the years of rapid expansion of activities in the second half of the 1980s. Most retail banks were engaged in programmes of *retrenchment*, involving the rationalisation of branch networks and reductions in staff numbers, and many also admitted to harbouring only modest plans for future growth. The banks themselves would argue that they are now leaner and *more efficient* organisations, and it should be recognised that throughout the recession, in aggregate they experienced increasing net interest and non-interest earnings, whilst their total costs as a percentrage of earnings was reduced. The banks would also claim that via their new *Codes of Practice* and *improved communications* with their customers, they have responded positively to criticisms of treating them unfairly and arbitrarily. However, it will only be when a sustained economic recovery occurs in the UK that the banks will be able to prove that they have maintained the capacity to meet the reasonable demands of their customers at the high level of quality now expected of them. In the aftermath of their recent chastening experience, there is little doubt of the retail banks' need to maintain customer loyalty via the provision of *high quality services*, and to engage in the *prudent pricing of loans* (with perhaps more recognition being given to the cash flow of borrowers relative to the security offered).

4.4.4 The wholesale banks

The institutions comprising the wholesale banking sector form a rather mixed group, with individual banks performing somewhat different functions and providing different sets of services to their customers. Nevertheless, a brief examination of the group's summary balance sheet (Table 4.3) still provides a useful insight into the typical forms of intermediation undertaken by these institutions. It also draws attention to the key differences in assets and liabilities structures between the wholesale bank group and the retail bank group.

The aggregate balance sheet of the UK wholesale banks is much larger than that of the UK retail banks. However, it must be recognised that there are currently only 20 retail banks, as opposed to around 490 wholesale banks. Consequently, the average wholesale bank is much smaller, in terms of its asset/liability base, than the average retail bank. A further significant difference is the wholesale banks' emphasis on *foreign currency-de-nominated* activities. At March 1993, about 76% of total deposit liabilities were foreign currency denominated, and of these some 75% were attributable to overseas residents. The *international* dimension of wholesale banking activity is clear. Also, as might be expected, *market loans and advances* dominate the assets side of the banks' portfolios, with holdings of

Table 4.3   UK wholesale banks: Summary balance sheet as at 31 March 1993

Assets	£b	£b
Sterling:		
Cash and balances with the Bank of England		0.6
Market loans		77.7
UK banks	40.6	
Certificates of deposit held	11.8	
UK local authorities	1.1	
Overseas	24.2	
Bills		0.5
Eligible bank bills	0.1	
Others	0.4	
Advances		125.4
UK private sector	113.0	
Others	12.4	
Investments		15.8
Foreign currency:		
Market loans and advances		567.1
UK	132.6	
Overseas	434.5	
Bills		8.3
Investments		77.5
Miscellaneous assets		32.5
Total assets		905.1
Liabilities		
Sterling deposits		202.9
UK banks	54.7	
UK private sector	67.4	
UK public sector	1.7	
Overseas residents	51.5	
Certificates of deposit issued	27.6	
Foreign currency deposits		648.3
UK	109.0	
Overseas residents	486.6	
Certificates of deposit issued	52.7	
Miscellaneous liabilities (including capital)		53.9
Total liabilities		905.1

Source: *Bank of England Press Release*, 6 May 1993.

bills and investments being relatively minor elements. The extremely limited exposure to retail banking activities for the wholesale banks is reflected in the very small holdings of cash and balances with the Bank of England. In addition, only a small proportion of liabilities are in the form of sight deposits (about 3%).

The emphasis of wholesale banks' intermediation activity is based upon the taking of *term deposits* and the making of *term loans*. Consequently, and in the light of the wholesale nature of operations and the varied currency denominations utilised, these banks tend to engage in the *matching of assets with liabilities* according to both *term to maturity* and *currency of denomination*. Matching according to term to maturity is intended to minimise the risk of cash flow (liquidity) problems, although, of course, maturity transformation of funds still takes place. The matching of assets with liabilities according to currency of denomination reduces the exchange rate risk that the bank has to face. The degree of mismatching will depend upon the level of risk that the banker is willing to accept in exchange for potentially higher profits. In general, wholesale banking is more risky than retail banking, primarily because retail banks have a much larger base of customers, meaning less likelihood of excessive fluctuations in net flows of funds.

Taking each of the major categories of wholesale banks separately, it is possible to identify a number of key characteristics in relation to their activities.

(a)   *British Merchant banks*

A traditional element of the business of these banks has been to '*accept*' *bills of exchange*. An acceptance arises when a commercial bill, drawn by a customer of the bank, is signed by a representative of the bank in order to signify that the bank will guarantee payment upon maturity to whomsoever purchases (discounts) the bill. The bank receives a fee for providing this underwriting service, and it bears the risk that the customer may default on discharging the underlying debt when the bill matures. By making bills much more marketable, the acceptance activity encourages the utilisation of bill finance and facilitates the efficient working of the money markets.

The acceptance business, which is also undertaken to some degree by most other groups of banking institutions, has become progressively less important for British Merchant banks, as they have *diversified* into new areas of activity. Today, these banks are much more like their overseas counterparts involved in '*investment banking*'. Thus, many of them now offer a wide range of corporate banking services, including the management and underwriting of new capital issues; they act as management consultants with particular emphasis on financial matters, and including the provision of advice on proposed mergers and acquisitions; they provide portfolio management services for pension funds, insurance companies, unit trusts and investment trust companies; they undertake operations in the gold and silver bullion and foreign exchange markets; and they are important players in the eurocurrency market.

Since the mid-1980s there has been a certain amount of restructuring within the British Merchant banks group, with some institutions becoming part of *larger banking groups* involving both British and overseas parent companies. These changes have been encouraged by the *deregulation* which has taken place within the UK capital market. *Intensified competition* in traditional wholesale banking markets has also influenced the strategy of diversification and the increasing willingness of banks to surrender their independence in the quest for long-term financial stability.

(b) *Other British banks*

The principal area of activity for these banks is overseas. Many were formed in the nineteenth century when London bankers provided the financial expertise of branch banking in British colonies. However, as former colonies have gained independence, the justification for maintaining head offices in London has diminished, although London still has the advantage of being at the heart of one of the world's major financial systems, with good communications and a relatively stable economic and political environment.

(c) *Overseas banks*

At March 1993 there were 255 foreign banks operating branches within the UK, and with an aggregate balance sheet of around £800b their financial power is immense. The number of institutions within this group has grown rapidly since the early 1970s, with the development of the Japanese banks being especially noteworthy.

The banks within this group are very diverse in terms of size and the range of operations undertaken, but a common characteristic is the overwhelming emphasis on foreign currency-denominated activities at a wholesale level. It is not unusual for well in excess of 80% of assets and liabilities of individual banks to be denominated in foreign currencies.

Many of these banks came to the UK initially to service the trading and business requirements of corporate customers based in their own countries. Today, in addition to the provision of normal corporate banking services, they are also important participants in eurocurrency market activities, and some members of the group even have a limited involvement in retail financial services, such as the provision of mortgage loans to personal customers. Deregulation of the UK capital market in the mid-1980s provided further opportunities for these institutions to diversify their operations, and a number have taken over or merged with stockbroking and jobbing firms, as well as more broadly-based financial services companies.

During the early years of the 1990s, UK wholesale banks suffered very similar pressures to those experienced by the retail banks (as described above in 4.4.3.). In particular, the *increasingly competitive nature of corporate financing*, involving both inter-bank rivalry and direct recourse to money and capital markets by corporate borrowers, provided the background for a rising tide of *defaults on loans* and a *stagnant market* for most of the major wholesale banking services and products. The extent of these adverse conditions was highlighted when, in May 1993, the *Bank of England* publicly admitted that during the recent recession it had felt obliged to *provide support* to a number of smaller wholesale banks, which had been viewed as being particularly vulnerable on account of the concentration of their assets portfolios and financing sources. Banks with *high exposure to property lending* or *property-based security for loans* were felt to be especially at risk, due to the unusually depressed state of the residential and commercial property markets. The closure of a number of small banks during late 1990 and early 1991, followed by the closure of BCCI (see 4.10.8 below) in July 1991 tended to *undermine confidence* in wholesale funding markets, creating difficulties for some smaller wholesale banks. The Bank of England kept a total of 40 smaller wholesale banks under review, and provided them with *technical assistance* to adjust the balance of their activities. In a few cases, where there was doubt about the ability of banks to meet capital adequacy requirements (see 4.4.5(b)), assistance was given to wind down their businesses in an orderly manner. The Bank of England also made available *liquidity support* to some institutions facing shorter-term cash flow problems. The outcome of this rather exceptional intervention by the Bank would appear to have been broadly successful, with the stability of the wholesale banking sector being sufficiently robust by early 1993 for the Bank to feel confident enough to publicise an account of the events which had occurred.

The problems which have beset wholesale banking in recent years, not just in the UK but also on a global scale, largely explain the concurrent *steady decline in the total number of wholesale banks* operating in the UK. Some institutions took the strategic business decision to cease taking deposits in the UK, and hence surrendered their authorisations; other banks were taken over or merged. These developments were clearly reflected in the aggregate balance sheets for the sub-groups of wholesale banks, which, over significant periods of time, showed *marked contractions in the scale of intermediation activities*, with certain groups of overseas banks being seriously affected. As with UK retail banks, an important test of the wholesale banks' collective strength is likely to be the extent to which they are able to meet the rising demand for loans and other financial services which might be expected to result from economic recovery. Also, for many wholesale banks, the importance of *international economic and financial conditions* cannot be emphasised too strongly.

4.4.5 Liquidity, capital adequacy and profitability of commercial banks

The concepts of liquidity and capital adequacy are central to the financial intermediation operations of commercial banks, and have important implications for the profitability of activities. Even in the absence of official requirements in respect of liquidity and capital adequacy, commercial factors would require their careful management. Hence it is useful to consider these variables independently of the technicalities of the official requirements which will be dealt with later (at 4.10.4 and 4.10.5).

(a) *Liquidity*

The liquidity of commercial banks relates to their ability to meet their obligations as they fall due. Banks require adequate liquidity, relative to their commitments, in order to maintain the *confidence* of their customers (particularly their depositors) and their shareholders. The specific reasons for banks requiring liquidity include the need to be able to cover withdrawals of funds by customers; to meet inter-bank indebtedness, which may arise on a day-to-day basis following the payments clearing process; to be able to meet any unforeseen borrowing requests from customers; and to be able to cope with interruptions to their normal cash inflows. In addition to these commercial factors, there are also official requirements laid down by the Bank of England in respect of banks' liquidity positions.

A bank may provide for liquidity by holding a *range of assets* embodying varying degrees of liquidity. The most liquid assets are, of course, notes and coin, and these are held in large quantities by retail banks. The liquidity of all other assets is measured in terms of how quickly they may be turned into cash without capital loss and without loss of interest. Thus, other assets held by banks, which are generally regarded as being liquid, include balances at the Bank of England; secured call money with institutions such as discount houses, Gilt-Edged Market Makers and Stock Exchange money brokers; Treasury bills; eligible bank bills; certificates of deposit; government securities nearing maturity; and money market loans (often to other banks or other reputable financial institutions). The broader definition of liquidity recognises the general marketability of assets, as an element influencing their liquidity, although care must be taken in respect of possible capital losses resulting from forced sales. This problem does not arise where the bank holds a range of assets the maturity of which generates a *stream of cash inflows* appropriate for the financing requirements of its maturing liabilities.

On the liabilities side of the balance sheet, the bank may attempt to hold deposits from a *wide range of sources*, and it will also seek to maintain a *good reputation* in the financial markets in general, in order to be able to attract new funds when liquidity needs are pressing, without incurring undue costs. Indeed, the techniques of both liability and asset management, so crucial to the matching operations of the wholesale banks, are increasingly being practiced throughout the whole of the banking sector, leading to something of a reduction in the importance of the traditional liquid asset holdings. Nevertheless, as demonstrated above, retail banks, being closely involved with the operation of the domestic payments system, still hold a relatively high proportion of their assets in liquid form, in order to cover their highly liquid liabilities.

(b) *Capital adequacy*

The capital of a commercial bank may be defined as the value of its net assets (i.e. total assets less total liabilities). The capital base effectively comprises the bank's paid up share capital and its accumulated capital reserves (although subordinated loan stock issued by the bank may also be included within the capital measure under certain circumstances).

The capital base of a bank is vital for the *protection of its creditors* (its depositors), and hence for the maintenance of *general confidence* in its operations, and the underpinning of its *long-term stability and growth*. If the bank suffers from defaults on advances or incurs losses on investments, these will reduce the value of net operating profits. However, large provisions for bad debts (for example, as have arisen for many banks in respect of corporate and small business lending in recent years) may be greater than the concurrent gross operating profits of the bank, and hence these excess losses will have to be absorbed by the bank's capital base. In other words, it is the bank's shareholders who incur the loss (through reduced capital reserves, as well as lower dividends), rather than the bank's depositors.

The adequacy of any given capital base depends not only upon the absolute *volume of assets* to be covered, but also is affected by the *quality of those assets*. Thus, the more risky are the assets, the greater must be the cushion of capital funds, in order to maintain a given level of capital adequacy.

In order to raise its capital base, and hence, other things being equal, its capital adequacy, a bank must raise the value of its assets relative to its liabilities. It may do this by generating *profits* which are retained within the business (rather than being distributed to shareholders), or by raising *new capital funds*, perhaps via a rights issue (or via the issue of subordinated loan stock). Both of these procedures would raise the proportion of shareholders' funds relative to liabilities. Alternatively, the bank may attempt to *improve the quality* of its assets by refining its internal loan assessment and investment evaluation procedures, thus reducing the risk associated with its assets, and hence increasing the adequacy of a given capital base. Indeed, any policy which seeks to reduce the risks faced by the bank, whether on- or off-balance sheet, would have a similar effect. For example, the selection of assets so as to match their interest rate characteristics and their currency of denomination with those of liabilities held, will help to bolster the financial stability of the bank (although it could be at the cost of reduced profitability, at least in the shorter term).

(c) *Profitability*

By definition, commercial banks exist in order to generate profits for their shareholders. Strictly, it is important that sufficient profits are generated so as to allow for *dividends* to be paid to shareholders, and, if it is at all possible, for some funds to be ploughed back into the business in order to finance *future growth* (perhaps via the physical expansion of existing facilities or via the take-over of other businesses). Retained profits also add to the capital reserves of the business (part of shareholders' funds) and hence raise the *capital adequacy* of the bank, thus strengthening the institution against future losses on assets and providing the necessary base for expansion. The accumulation of capital reserves is likely to be reflected in the bank's share price, which not only provides capital gains for the existing shareholders (should they wish to liquidate their holdings), but also should reduce the cost of raising further capital funds in the future via rights issues.

In order to generate profits from their financial intermediation activity, commercial banks must be able to on-lend at a rate of interest which is high enough to leave a surplus after covering their own cost of funds and all other operating costs (including defaults on loans). Thus, banks will seek out *profitable on-lending opportunities*, but in order to reduce the risks which they face, they will also seek to ensure that they hold well-diversified portfolios of advances and other loans. In addition, banks will often hold a range of investments (perhaps forms of government or company securities) which it is hoped will generate income and possibly (in the case of marketable instruments) capital gains on sales before maturity. Once again there are risks involved, and diversification and careful asset selection are of the utmost importance.

A major problem which all banks face is the *inherent trade-off* between liquidity, profitability and risk within assets portfolios. In general, other things being equal, the greater is the liquidity of an asset, the lower will be the return that it generates. Conversely, it is often the case that assets which offer the prospect of high returns are also riskier than low yield liquid assets. Thus, the requirement for adequate liquidity will tend to constrain the extent to which a bank may place its funds into high yield but relatively illiquid assets. Similarly, the need to maintain capital adequacy will constrain the amount of risk which a bank is able to carry within its assets portfolio, although opposing pressures are exerted by the desire to generate profits in order to build up the capital base of the bank.

Finally, it should be remembered that the structure of the bank's liabilities portfolio will be an important determinant of its liquidity requirements, and hence the extent to which it is able to move into more profitable, but relatively illiquid, assets (notwithstanding the limitations set by the riskiness of the assets). Consequently, the bank's structuring of the liabilities side of its balance sheet will play a vital role in achieving an optimal position in respect of generating profits and maintaining both adequate capital and liquidity.

4.4.6 Government economic policy and the commercial banks

Any government policy which affects the operation of the economy may potentially influence the activities of the banking sector. Clearly, the Government's *monetary policy* is likely to have direct and significant effects on the banks, as are certain elements of *fiscal policy*; there are also the indirect effects of these policies to consider. However, it must not be forgotten that policies on the exchange rate, prices and incomes, industrial issues, the distribution of income and wealth, and the degree of public ownership of productive resources may have important implications for banks. It may be the case that banks are affected directly by the policies; for example, strict enforcement of exchange controls would limit banks' freedom in respect of international operations. Banks may also be affected through the influence of the policies on the financial activities of their customers, and hence through the demand for banking services.

(a) *Monetary policy*

As the banking sector plays an important role in the determination of money supply growth, it is to be expected that the implementation of monetary controls will have significant implications for banking activities. The details of monetary control instruments will be examined in Chapter 8; however, for the moment, it should be recognised that these instruments may affect both the size and the structure of banks' assets and liabilities portfolios, and consequently may influence banks' strategic decisions in respect of fee-earning activities. Thus, for example, the authorities may impose reserve asset ratios, specifying minimum required holdings of specific assets relative to a designated sub-group of liabilities. They may then attempt to put downwards pressure on banks' credit creation by undertaking open market operations involving the purchase of reserve assets from the private sector. Alternatively, the authorities may impose ceilings on interest rates in an attempt to limit banks' ability to bid for funds in the markets, and issue lending guidelines in an attempt to direct bank lending towards certain sectors within the economy. The precise controls implemented will depend upon the authorities' policy objectives and their beliefs as to the efficiency of the various alternatives available. However, it is clear that, to the extent that the controls affect the freedom of banks to make commercial decisions, they are likely to distort their competitive position relative to both domestic and overseas financial intermediaries which are not affected by the controls.

Banks, like other financial institutions, are also likely to be affected via the influence of the monetary policy itself on key economic variables. Thus, for example, to the extent that a firm monetarist policy is successful in reducing the rate of inflation, financial stability and confidence in the future strength of the economy may be established. This may ultimately create a lower risk environment for on-lending activities, and hence improve the future prospects for banking operations. However, high interest rates are a familiar by-product of strict monetary control, and banks are obviously affected by this occurrence. To the extent that the demand for loans is reduced, turnover will be adversely affected. A similar effect may occur if the policy pushes the economy into a period of recession as inflation is squeezed from the system. If banks do find that their current domestic activities are put under pressure, the natural response is to seek out new lines of business, or at least to develop services which have hitherto been seen as merely supplementing their core business. This, of course, is likely to bring banks into increased competition with each other as well as with non-bank financial intermediaries. A good example of this type of occurrence was the massive increase in mortgage lending undertaken by UK retail banks during the early 1980s. In addition, banks may seek to develop their overseas business interests, although experience has shown that hasty decisions in this respect may come to be regretted in the longer term.

(b) *Fiscal policy*

Fiscal policy relates to government decisions on public expenditure, taxation and public sector borrowing. Given that all government expenditure must be financed, the decisions in respect of these variables are mutually dependent. Thus, for example, decisions on the level of taxation and government expenditure will automatically imply a value for public sector borrowing.

As *taxation* and *government expenditure* flows normally pass through bank accounts, changes in these variables are likely to affect the utilisation of money transmission services. Moreover, if the net flow of funds is altered, this may have important implications for banks' reserve bases, as funds move between the banks' accounts and the Government's accounts at the Bank of England. In addition, changes to the level or structure of taxation or government expenditure may affect both personal and corporate demands for both borrowed funds and other types of banking services.

Public sector borrowing may also have crucial implications for banking activities, as banks may be involved directly in providing funds to cover government budget deficits (through the purchase of securities). Banks' portfolios may also be affected to the extent that customers withdraw deposits in order to purchase government debt instruments. Indirect effects may be experienced if government borrowing influences the level and/or structure of interest rates. This may affect both the costs and returns associated with financial intermediation activity, as well as the level and nature of that activity. In addition, government debt instruments created by the borrowing process may affect the stock of assets suitable for inclusion in the reserve bases of banks, and hence may have implications for the credit creation potential of the banking system.

It should also be recognised that a government may run budget surpluses, and so have to deal with a *public sector debt repayment*. The effects on the banking sector are basically the opposite of those outlined above, with the critical factors being the sectors of the economy from which debt is repurchased and the consequent impact on the level and structure of interest rates. For example, if the authorities repurchase debt from the personal sector, this will probably (at least in the first instance) result in funds flowing into bank accounts, and hence making good the outflows which are the counterpart to the budget surplus. There may also be downwards pressure exerted on interest rates, which may stimulate the demand for bank loans within the economy as a whole.

Finally, to the extent that the fiscal policy influences the level of *economic activity* and *expectations* of future economic conditions, banking operations may be affected indirectly. Thus, an expansionary policy may lead to an increase in the demand for banking services, and reduced risk in respect of business loans. Profitability may improve to the extent that turnover increases and provisions for bad debts are scaled down. However, if the policy is seen to be excessively expansionary, and merely leads to fears of future inflation problems and international payments difficulties, any initial boost to banking activity may quickly subside, as the implications of the policy are absorbed by the financial community.

4.5 THE DISCOUNT HOUSES

4.5.1 Functions

The discount houses are a very special group of banks, which act as money-market dealing counterparties of the Bank of England. At June

1993 there were seven such institutions. They occupy a unique position within the UK financial system, and their activities are central to the Bank of England's operations in respect of monetary control and the adjustment of liquidity within the banking sector. (These primary money market activities are dealt with in detail in Chapter 5, at 5.3.3.) In addition, by virtue of their ability to take up large volumes of funds and repay them at very short notice, the discount houses are able to smooth flows of funds between the clearing banks, thus helping them to manage fluctuations in their cash positions which may arise when payments clearing operations occur.

The major specific functions of the discount houses are as follows:

(a) *To accept deposits of short-term wholesale funds.* These come mainly from other banking institutions, and a large proportion is taken on a call or overnight basis, thus providing an important source of liquidity for the banks.

(b) *To trade in short-term financial instruments*, such as:

    (i) Treasury bills – these may be purchased directly from the Bank of England (primary market purchases), thus providing short-term finance for the government sector, or from other holders (hence making a secondary market for these bills);

    (ii) short-dated public sector stock, including government gilt-edged securities and local authority bonds;

    (iii) commercial bills – activities involve both discounting (i.e. purchasing from the issuers) and re-discounting (i.e. purchasing from other holders) eligible bank bills, non-eligible bank bills and trade bills of exchange, thus providing both short-term finance for industry and commerce, and a secondary market for these bills;

    (iv) certificates of deposit – the secondary market created provides an important means for banks and building societies to adjust their liquidity positions.

(c) *To place short-term deposits* with other banking institutions and building societies.

(d) *To underwrite the weekly Treasury bill tender*, thus ensuring that the Government is always able to cover its short-term financing needs.

(e) *To act as a buffer between the Bank of England and the banking sector* for monetary control and liquidity adjustment purposes.

The above-listed functions are clearly reflected in the structure of the summary balance sheet for the discount houses (Table 4.4). It may be

Table 4.4   Discount houses: Summary balance sheet as at 31 March 1993

Assets	£m	£m
Sterling:		
Cash ratio deposits with the Bank of England		7
Bills		3,504
Treasury bills	57	
Local authority bills	4	
Other bills	3,443	
Funds lent		5,627
UK banks	198	
UK banks' certificates of deposit	3,700	
Building society certificates of deposit and time		
deposits	701	
Other UK	921	
Overseas	107	
Investments		222
Other assets		93
Foreign currency:		
Certificates of deposit		35
Bills		3
Other		142
Total assets		9,633
Liabilities		
Sterling: Borrowed funds		9,209
(of which call and overnight)	(8,442)	
Bank of England	—	
Other UK banks	7,523	
Other UK	1,677	
Overseas	9	
Foreign currency: Borrowed funds		174
UK banks	41	
Other UK	66	
Overseas	67	
Other liabilities (including capital)		250
Total liabilities		9,633

Source: *Bank of England Press Release*, 6 May 1993.

observed that sterling assets and liabilities dominate the discount houses' balance sheet, and that a very high proportion (normally around 90%) of sterling deposit liabilities are available at call or overnight, giving them the most liquid liabilities portfolio of any banking group. In this respect, a critical factor is the discount houses' immediate access to funds from the Bank of England (effectively in a lender of last resort facility – see Chapter

5 at 5.3.3), which may be utilised when liquidity pressures arise due to the withdrawal of deposits. It should also be noted that holdings of 'other bills' (which are largely commercial bills) together with 'UK banks' certificates of deposit' dominate the assets portfolio. Treasury bills are now of relatively minor significance, although their position may alter periodically, due to changes in government debt financing policy.

4.5.2 The changing environment

The importance of the discount houses within the UK financial system is undisputed; and on many occasions in recent years the authorities have reaffirmed their support for the role of the discount houses. Nevertheless, a number of official actions since the early 1980s have had a significant impact on the operations of the discount houses, and have put them under increasing competitive pressure. Thus, for example, since the October 1986 'Big Bang' deregulation of Stock Exchange activities, the authorities have allowed many more participants to engage in the trading of gilt-edged securities, which has tended to squeeze discount house operations in respect of short-dated gilts. More recently, the 'club money' arrangement was abandoned. This arrangement, which had been in force since August 1981, had required banks seeking eligibility status (for their acceptance business) from the Bank of England, to maintain a certain percentage of their funds in the form of deposits with the discount houses. Its abandonment clearly undermined their bargaining position in relation to the bidding for funds from banking institutions, and forced them to take on a more competitive posture. In addition, since the mid-1980s, the discount houses' role as a channel for official financial support to the banking system has been weakened somewhat by the Bank of England's use of REPO (sale and repurchase) agreements with selected commercial banks. These agreements provide direct help to banks facing short-term liquidity problems, and hence by-pass the intermediation function of the discount houses.

During the 1970s and 1980s (at least, that is, until 1989) the number of discount houses diminished steadily, and an increasing proportion of those remaining in existence lost their independence, being taken over by powerful financial services groups, including commercial banks. For example, in 1984, Alexander Discount and Jessel, Toynbee and Gillet were purchased by Mercantile House. In early 1986, Citicorp (one of the world's largest banks) took over Seccombe, Marshall and Campion, the Bank of England's former 'special buyer' in the discount market. Indeed, it was largely the loss of independence by Seccombe, Marshall and Campion which caused the Bank to introduce direct dealing with the discount market through its own dealing room. However, further official actions, taken in 1988, led to a reversal of the previous trend (albeit only a relatively modest and ultimately short-lived reversal), as two additional institutions were granted dealing relationships with the Bank of England.
continued on next page

In October 1988, the Bank of England published a revised version of a consultative paper (first issued in June 1988) relating to the Bank's operations in the money markets. This paper outlined the Bank's intention to extend its dealing relationships beyond the then existing eight discount houses. It also included an open invitation for institutions to apply to the Bank, at any time, with the view to establishing a money market dealing relationship. In other words, the Bank now allows suitable institutions to apply for discount house or similar status. The paper specifies the criteria which institutions must satisfy if their applications are to be successful, including requirements relating to capital adequacy, the quality of management, internal control systems, and the ownership of the institutions. It also lists the obligations which they must be prepared to meet, including being willing to help maintain the liquidity of the money markets by taking deposits at call from banks and making markets in bills, acting as a counterparty to the Bank in money market transactions, and participating in the underwriting of the weekly Treasury bill tender.

In February 1989, S G Warburg Discount was successful in achieving discount house status. At the same time Greenwell Montague Gilt-Edged established a dealing relationship with the Bank of England, but technically did not become a full discount house. These moves, together with the pressures faced in the traditional areas of activity of the discount houses, merely served to heighten the debate on their future development. In fact, since the mid-1980s there has been an observable trend for individual institutions to diversify, and several have become heavily involved in activities such as futures market and leasing operations, which have met with only variable success. Indeed, it may be noted that the downwards trend in the number of discount houses soon resumed after the Bank of England's change of policy, with the well-established Quin Cope ceasing to operate as a discount house. In 1992, S G Warburg Discount relinquished its discount house status, after just three years.

4.6 THE BUILDING SOCIETIES

4.6.1 Background issues

Irrespective of the measure chosen, building societies form *an extremely important group of financial intermediaries* within the UK financial system. At March 1993, their total assets amounted to approximately £269b, and with around 90 separate societies with just under 6,000 branches spread across the whole of the UK, there is little doubting their significance as competitors to the retail banks. Like many other retail financial institutions, building societies have experienced fast growth since the beginning of the 1970s. In 1970, their total new lending was little over £1.9b; in 1990 the comparable sum amounted to £43.1b, and thus even taking into account the effects of inflation, the real growth in activities has been substantial. It is interesting to note that during the same period of time, the number of societies diminished from 481 to 117, largely through agreed mergers and takeovers within the sector; whilst the branch network expanded three-fold. However, since 1990 the growth of building society lending has *slowed down markedly*, largely due to the depressed state of the UK economy, which caused the housing market to stagnate. In 1992, total new lending by building societies was £32.4b, which was the lowest level since 1985. Also, the recessionary conditions of the early 1990s, marked by rising unemployment and relatively high rates of interest, tended to undermine the generally good record of building societies in respect of *mortgage loan defaults*. By 1992 these had reached record levels, with societies being involved in a rising number of residential property possessions. Fortunately, whilst building societies' *profits* were adversely affected by these developments, their exposure to corporate lending was extremely small, and hence they did not suffer the same pressures as experienced by the retail banks in this respect.

The *rapid growth* of building society activities during the 1970s and 1980s is often attributed to the high demand for mortgage loans, encouraged by the tax relief on mortgage interest payments and the apparent investment value of residential property over that period. For many years the retail banks also alleged that the societies were given an unfair advantage, in respect of attracting retail savings, through the application of the composite rate tax system (which reduced the effective rate of tax paid on interest earnings by tax-paying members and other depositors). However, when the system was extended to the retail banks in 1985, it soon became apparent that this had not been the only factor explaining the buildings societies' competitive position. Indeed, of greater importance has probably been the generally more cost effective branch networks of the societies, and the relative attraction of most of the savings facilities which they offered. In addition, until 1980, the banks were limited in their ability to compete with the societies due to the existence of direct monetary controls, although until the early 1980s, the societies themselves operated a form of interest rate cartel which tended to restrict competitive pressures.

Prior to the early 1980s the activities of the building societies were largely restricted to attracting savings deposits from their members and other depositors and on-lending funds, in the form of mortgage loans for the purchase of residential property. This was despite the fact that the building society sector had come to be dominated by a small number of very large societies, with a large number of very small societies accounting for only a small fraction of the total assets of the sector. A major reason for the very narrow role of the societies within the UK financial system, was the *restrictive legislative framework* within which they were forced to operate. A crucial aspect of this was their *mutual* legal status, and the traditional view that they were to be operated for the benefit of their members on a non-profit-making basis. In other words, the ethos of the building societies was not primarily directed towards commercial objectives, as was the norm for other major financial institutions.

During the early 1980s the financial environment for the building societies began to alter significantly. In particular, the societies began to find that they were being challenged, especially by the retail banks, in areas of activity in which they had been the dominant force for many years. The removal of direct monetary controls in 1980 and 1981 allowed the banks to enter into mortgage lending on a grand scale. Formerly this type of lending had not been attractive for banks within the regulatory framework operating, and in the light of other, more lucrative lending opportunities. However, greater freedom of action in respect of the raising of funds, and the deteriorating state of overseas sovereign lending and domestic corporate lending, created great interest in the mortgage loan market for the banks. The customers of this market were also seen as an important potential outlet for the banks' other services.

A second major development, closely related to the increasing competition being experienced by the building society sector as a whole, was the abandonment of the interest rate fixing cartel, which had operated within the sector for much of the post-war period. Under pressure from some of the larger societies, which believed the interest rate restrictions to be inhibiting their ability to meet their customers' requirements efficiently, the societies began to compete much more explicitly in respect of both deposit and on-lending rates; and in consequence the range of savings products and mortgage facilities available began to expand. Indeed, the success of the societies in this respect is often seen as being a crucial factor in stimulating the clearing banks to improve their own range of savings products and services for personal customers. A further factor drawing the activities of the building societies closer to those of the retail banks was the granting of permission for them to raise funds in the wholesale money markets from 1981 onwards. Initially the amounts of funds involved were relatively modest, but nevertheless this development provided the larger societies with the ability to diversify their sources of funds and hence compete on more equal terms with the retail banks. The extension of the composite rate system to interest payments made on retail deposits by the retail banks, and alterations to the tax rules governing the holding of gilt-edged securities by the building societies, provided further evidence of the authorities' willingness to see freer competition within the retail financial sector, and to treat banks and building societies more equitably.

Thus, by the mid-1980s, important changes had occurred in respect of building societies' activities, relative to only a few years earlier. In particular, their operational environment had become much more competitive, and the nature of their services increasingly sophisticated and varied. It was becoming increasingly common for societies to act as agents for other types of financial institutions (for example, in respect of insurance activities), and several societies were collaborating with banking institutions to provide services which were beyond their own abilities (and powers). However, despite these developments, the restrictions imposed by the Building Societies Act 1962 severely limited the scope of their operations relative to those of the retail banks. A cause of particular concern was the inability of societies to provide unsecured loans to customers, and hence to provide directly key banking services such as overdraft facilities and cheque books with cheque guarantee cards.

4.6.2 The Building Societies Act 1986 and its implications

The major event in respect of the permissible activities of building societies was undoubtedly the enactment of the *Building Societies Act 1986*. This Act, the bulk of which came into force in January 1987, formally recognised the building societies as being major players in the UK financial system, and attempted to provide them with a regulatory framework which would allow them to develop the provision of financial services for their customers, without losing their basic identity as savings and mortgage loan institutions. Indeed, if societies wish to undertake activities falling outside of the provisions of the Act, they now have the option to renounce their mutual status (with the permission of their members), and to become *public limited companies* operating within the same regulations as the retail banks. Those societies which opt to retain their mutual status must now submit to the supervision of the *Building Societies Commission*, which was established in September 1986 to oversee the implementation of, and compliance with, the requirements of the Building Societies Act. In addition to setting guidelines for the liquidity and capital adequacy of societies, the Commission may veto the provision of specific services, and the undertaking of specific operations, by individual societies which are thought to be unsuitable for such roles.

The 1986 Act, together with the subsequent review of Schedule 8 of the Act at the beginning of 1988, has opened up a wide range of new opportunities for building societies to develop their operations:

(a) Of fundamental importance is the ability to make *unsecured loans* to customers, albeit for strictly limited amounts for individual borrowers, and within an overall constraint that this type of loan must not exceed a specified proportion of a society's total commercial assets (see below for details). This provision allows building societies to offer *key banking services* such as personal loans and overdraft facilities, and consequently full current account facilities, including the issue of cheque books with cheque guarantee cards.

(b) Access to *wholesale funding* has been broadened, thus providing additional flexibility to institutions in the raising of funds and in their ability to respond to changes in market pressures. Currently, the ceiling for wholesale funding for any individual society is 40% of its total outstanding liabilities to members and other depositors. By the end of March 1993, societies had wholesale debt outstanding to the tune of £47.7b, and involving wholesale deposits and syndicated borrowing, as well as issues of certificates of deposit, commercial paper and bonds. Indeed, a number of societies have taken advantage of the facility available in respect of foreign currency debt, and in aggregate around £7.7b of total debt outstanding was foreign currency denominated.

(c) Societies may now become involved with the provision of a *range of financial services* which were formerly out of bounds, and some of which have little direct relevance to their mainstream housing finance activities. For example, they may take equity stakes in both life and general insurance companies; undertake fund management; establish and manage Personal Equity Plans and unit trusts through associated bodies; take equity stakes in stockbroking firms; and engage in the provision of various forms of banking services.

It must be emphasised that despite the above-listed powers now available to building societies, they are still *restricted* in the scope of their activities relative to retail banks. As might be expected, the restrictions are most severe in respect of their on-lending activity. For regulatory purposes *commercial assets* (that is, those assets which represent building societies' on-lending to customers) are divided in three categories:

Class 1 – Loans secured by first mortgage of an owner-occupied residential property.

Class 2 – Other loans secured on property.

Class 3 – Unsecured loans and secured loans not coming within Classes 1 and 2, land and property for residential use, and investments in subsidiaries and associates.

Initially, the Building Societies Act 1986 specified that societies must hold no more than 5% of their commercial assets in the form of Class 3 assets, and no more than 10% in the form of Class 2 assets. In addition, Class 1 assets had to account for at least 90% of total commercial assets (meaning that the total of Classes 2 and 3 together could never exceed 10% of commercial assets). Subsequently, these limits were relaxed slightly, and since the beginning of 1993, the limits for Classes 2 and 3 have been set at 25% and 15% respectively, whilst the Class 1 minimum has been set at 75%.

Table 4.5   UK building societies: Summary balance sheet as at 31 March 1993

Assets	£b	£b
Liquid assets:		42.9
Notes and coin	0.3	
Sterling bank deposits and CDs	28.3	
Bank bills	1.5	
Building society CDs	1.9	
British government stock	4.1	
Other public sector debt	6.8	
Commercial assets:		221.7
Class 1	208.8	
Class 2	7.7	
Class 3	5.2	
Other assets		4.4
Total assets		269.0
Liabilities		
Retail shares and deposits		194.6
Wholesale liabilities		47.7
(of which, foreign currency)	(7.7)	
CDs	7.7	
Deposits and commercial paper	21.6	
Syndicated borrowing	2.2	
Bonds	16.2	
Other liabilities and reserves		26.7
Total liabilities		269.0

Source: *Bank of England Press Release*, 6 May, 1993.

A good indication of the broad nature of the building societies' financial intermediation activities is given by the summary balance sheet for the sector, as shown in Table 4.5. It may be observed that some six years after the implementation of the Building Societies Act 1986, the impact on the summary balance sheet had only been modest. Thus, whilst the societies as a whole have clearly taken advantage of their new powers, their operations fell well within the limits specified by the Act. Class 1 assets accounted for about 94% of commercial assets at the end of March 1993, with the much riskier Class 3 assets being only 2.3% of the total. Indeed, mortgage loans accounted for almost 78% of total assets, which is only a slightly smaller proportion than was recorded throughout much of the 1970s and early 1980s. This implies that the Classes 2 and 3 assets have been taken on at the expense of liquid asset holdings (the 'other assets' being largely the business premises and equipment owned by the societies).

On the liabilities side of the balance sheet, the impact of the recent changes has been somewhat more dramatic, with wholesale funding amounting to 19.7% of total deposit liabilities at the end of March 1993. In 1980, all building society funds emanated from retail sources. In addition, prior to 1987 all liabilities were denominated in sterling. This is clearly no longer the case.

Irrespective of the recent changes in their balance sheet structure, the building societies continue to undertake very significant amounts of *maturity transformation of funds* through their financial intermediation activity. Thus, in nominal terms, whilst the original maturity of a mortgage loan is often in the region of 25 to 30 years, a large proportion of deposit and retail share liabilities are effectively available on demand or at very short notice. Consequently, building societies depend heavily upon the stability of their retail deposit bases, as well as being able to draw upon their substantial liquid asset holdings should demands for withdrawals of funds be unexpectedly high. Portfolio management has also been assisted by the increased access to wholesale funds in recent years. In addition, the financial stability of these institutions is underpinned by the generally high quality of the security for their major commercial assets (mortgage loans). Despite the more recent problems in the UK housing market, history has shown that mortgage lending in the UK has been a relatively low risk activity, with the market price of residential property, in the longer term, tending to outpace the general rate of inflation, often by a significant margin.

4.6.3 Conversion to plc status

Despite the increased powers endowed upon building societies by the 1986 Act, there have been strong criticisms of the regulatory framework from several societies, as well as from a number of independent commentators. It has been argued that the constraints placed on societies' activities, especially those in respect of Class 3 assets, make it difficult for them to provide the range of financial services which they claim that their members desire. In consequence, there has been substantial debate on the merits of building societies taking up public limited company (plc) status, and hence escaping from the Building Societies Act regulations.

In order to convert to plc status, a building society must first obtain the *permission of its members*. Specifically, a society requires at least a 75% majority of lending members who vote in the conversion ballot, and voting members must constitute at least 20% of all lending members. The society must also obtain the approval of a majority of those borrowing members who care to vote on the issue. Having obtained the permission of its members, the society must then apply to the *Building Societies Commission* for approval of its conversion plan. The Commission's role in this respect is to ensure that members' interests are protected throughout the conversion process. It must also satisfy itself that the ballot procedures were conducted fairly and without bias. Finally, before conversion can be completed, the society is obliged to seek *authorisation from the Bank of England* in order to be able to continue operating a deposit-taking business once its mutual status has been renounced. If the Bank is satisfied that the building society meets its authorisation requirements, it may then take up plc status, and hence join the ranks of the retail banks.

(a) *The advantages of plc status*

The advantages normally identified as flowing from conversion to plc status include:

- Freedom from the Building Societies Act 1986, and in particular the strict limits on unsecured lending, transactions with the corporate sector, and wholesale funding.
- The ability to engage in a much wider range of on-lending activities, including to corporate and overseas customers.
- The ability to raise equity capital in the open market, and hence accelerate the growth of business.
- The ability to offer a much wider range of financial services.
- The opportunity to engage in takeovers of, and mergers with, other financial institutions, in order to make substantial and rapid additions to the range of facilities offered to customers.
- The enhancement of financial and career incentives for both senior managers and other staff within a commercially-orientated organisation, and hence the achievement of greater operational efficiency.

(b) *The disadvantages of plc status*

However, plc status is not without its problems, and a number of potentially important disadvantages may be identified:

- Supervision by the Bank of England, within the provisions of the Banking Act 1987, is no less rigorous than that under the Building Societies Commission, and, at least in the first instance, compliance with somewhat different technical requirements may prove onerous.
- The plc may find itself under pressure to pay higher dividends to shareholders, and consequently may increasingly seek short-term solutions to business problems.
- As time passes, shareholdings may become concentrated with institutional investors, who may seek to exercise some degree of influence on the activities of the plc.

- All plcs are susceptible to takeover bids, which may not be in the best interests of customers.
- The loss of mutual status may have adverse effects on the institution's image with customers, and may undermine its ability to compete with the building societies which remain as mutuals.
- The commercial ethos of a plc may drive up its operating costs as it bids for appropriately qualified staff against other employers in the banking sector.

(c) *The utilisation of the conversion facility*

In March 1988, Abbey National (at that time the UK's second largest building society, with assets of around £30b) became the first building society to announce its intention to seek the permission of its members to convert to plc status. Despite a strenuous campaign against conversion by a group of Abbey National members, and a significant amount of adverse comment as to the way in which Abbey National directors put the case for conversion to the membership, the subsequent ballot came out heavily in favour of conversion. Thus in July 1989, shares in Abbey National plc were floated on the Stock Exchange, and it became the first mutual building society in the UK to convert to a retail bank.

The Abbey National conversion generated substantial public interest in the process, and it is believed that several other major building societies undertook detailed evaluations of their own positions in this respect. However, by the summer of 1993 no other building society had activated the conversion process, and there was little evidence to suggest that any announcements on this issue were imminent. The major reason for the general loss of interest in the conversion option is undoubtedly related to the markedly *changed circumstances* of the UK financial system in 1993, relative to those which existed in the late 1980s. The recent *recession* affected the UK housing market very badly, and has both undermined the demand for new mortgage loans and caused mortgage lenders to become especially prudent in respect of the conditions of lending. Consequently, the scope for expansion of traditional areas of business, at least in the shorter term, has been significantly reduced, and hence so too has building societies' needs for *additional capital* (easier access to which is seen as a major benefit of plc status). Indeed, technical changes to the regulatory framework for building societies in 1991, now allows them to raise capital via the issue of *permanent interest-bearing shares* (PIBs). These instruments are very similar to bank preference shares, and they may be issued by building societies wishing to strengthen their capital bases using external funds, but without the need for a stock market flotation. PIBs are normally traded through investment banks or similar institutions which are committed to making markets in particular issues, and hence they are likely to be of most interest to sophisticated investors seeking marketable interest-bearing claims on major financial institutions. The issues of PIBs which have been made so far would appear to have been well received by investors.

A further factor limiting the attractions of the freedom that plc status would give to a building society, has been the rather *mixed experiences* of retail financial institutions that pursued strategies of *significant diversification* during the mid- to late 1980s. Many such institutions have subsequently felt obliged to *rationalise* their operations, often at *substantial cost* to their shareholders and capital bases. It is interesting to note that the relative success of Abbey National amongst the retail banks is, at least in part, due to the fact that it has taken a very cautious approach to expansion, and did not rush into new areas of activity which have been proving so damaging to the profitability of other retail banks. Whether or not Abbey National would have been better placed remaining as a mutual institution is a debatable issue, although it cannot be denied that it now has an enviably *strong capital base* and a *flexibility* to respond to changes in retail financial markets which is not open to building societies. Of course, it may also be argued that Abbey National will be an attractive target for takeover bids, from institutions wishing to expand into UK retail financial services, once the interim restrictions on its shareholder base lapse in 1994.

The strategy to be pursued by the building societies into the medium term is likely to be heavily influenced by the nature and extent of the UK economy's recovery from the early 1990s recession. Thus, whilst a number of leading building societies have stated explicitly that, at least for the foreseeable future, they have no intention of seeking plc status, the *competitive pressures* which may be released should a sustained economic recovery materialise, may give rise to second thoughts. For the moment, the *larger societies* would appear to be pursuing strategies involving the *development of a wider range of services*, related primarily to their core mortgage loan business, and the *selective exploitation* of the opportunities for expansion made available within the framework of the 1986 Act. The *smaller societies* are likely to concentrate on *niche markets*, depending for their success on their *specialist knowledge* of local market requirements, and the provision of *high quality low volume financial services*.

4.6.4 The convergence of building society and retail bank activities

As a result of the natural evolution of the UK financial system, and the changed regulatory framework during the past decade, the activities of the retail banks and the building societies (especially the large ones) have converged markedly. Indeed, several large building societies are now members of the clearing house system, and in many ways they are leading the banks in the provision of interest-bearing cheque accounts with associated payments facilities. However, it must be emphasised that with the exception of the raising of wholesale funds, the convergence of activities has been almost wholly in respect of retail personal sector business. There are several quite fundamental differences to be found between the two groups of institutions, especially in relation to their wholesale, corporate and international activities. Thus, whilst the building societies have limits placed on their access to wholesale funding, banks have no specific restrictions applied to such operations; and neither are they limited in respect of their ability to undertake transactions with the corporate sector or with overseas residents. Consequently, a large proportion of retail banks' lending is to the corporate sector, whilst building society lending is almost wholly directed towards the personal sector. Also, the banks offer a much wider range of banking and related financial services to their much more diverse customer base. This is especially so if the retail banks are defined to include their subsidiary and associated companies.

Furthermore, as explained above, the banks and the building societies differ in respect of the regulatory frameworks within which they must operate; although, in relation to certain investment activities, both groups of institutions do fall within the same body of controls, as specified by the Financial Services Act 1986. Also, it may be expected that as the activities of each group converge further, there is likely to be an increased level of co-operation between the official regulatory bodies, and it seems probable that some degree of harmonisation in respect of liquidity and capital adequacy requirements will emerge over time.

4.7 OTHER DEPOSIT-TAKING FINANCIAL INTERMEDIARIES

4.7.1 The National Savings Bank

The National Savings Bank is part of the Department for National Savings, and provides deposit facilities and other simple banking services through the UK's 20,500 post offices. There are two types of account offered:

(a) *ordinary accounts*, which currently guarantee a fixed rate of interest for the calendar year, with exemption from taxation for the first £70 of interest per annum. There is relatively easy access to funds, and account holders are provided with standing order and direct payments facilities.

(b) *investment accounts*, which pay fairly competitive interest rates with funds being subject to one month's notice. Interest is paid gross, but is liable to income tax.

The funds collected by the NSB are invested exclusively in *British government securities*, and their value is effectively underwritten by the Treasury, thus making investments with the NSB virtually risk free. The Government's desire to finance its borrowing requirement in a non-inflationary manner is a very important factor in determining the competitiveness of interest rates on NSB accounts. At the end of March 1993 the total amount of funds held in investment accounts was around £8.9b; ordinary accounts held just £1.4b (an amount which has hardly altered since 1985).

4.7.2 Finance houses

There is some ambiguity as to which institutions should be included within the finance houses category of financial institutions. The major reason for this is that, with the enactment of the Banking Act 1979, some of the larger finance houses took on the status of *banking institutions*, and are today included within the 'other British banks' category of the official statistics. However, a large number of finance houses (many of them quite small individually) are included within the *non-banking sector finance house group*, and their activities have remained largely within their traditional area, which is the provision of *medium-term instalment credit* to individuals and businesses wishing to purchase consumer durables, machinery, and other capital equipment.

Finance house credit is often arranged at the point of sale by the retailer of goods. The retailer may have discretion over the allocation of a block of finance house funds, or individual applications for credit may be passed on to the finance house for processing. Since the beginning of the 1970s, there has been a shift in finance house activities towards the provision of credit to the corporate sector. Initially this was driven by official controls on the extending of consumer credit, and then subsequently by the easier access for personal borrowers to credit card facilities, overdrafts and personal loans from banks and building societies. This change in the balance of their business is reflected in the increased operation of subsidiaries involved in leasing and factoring (i.e. the buying up of debts of another company at a discount).

Finance houses raise a large proportion of their funds on the wholesale money markets, through the issue of commercial bills and other marketable instruments. They also take substantial amounts of wholesale deposits from the banking sector. Consequently, much of their intermediation activity involves the breaking up of blocks of wholesale funds into smaller amounts for on-lending.

At the beginning of 1993 the non-banking sector finance houses had approximately £8b of credit outstanding.

4.8 NON-DEPOSIT-TAKING NON-BANK FINANCIAL INTERMEDIARIES

4.8.1 Insurance companies

The basic operation of insurance companies relates to the evaluation of risk and the spreading of risk between individuals and institutions wishing to protect against it. Activities may be divided into two broad categories:

(a) *General business* involves the provision of insurance against specific risks such as theft, fire, and accident. The insurance policy holder pays a predetermined premium covering a fixed period of time, and in return may make a claim for compensation against the insurance company if a loss is incurred within the terms of the policy.

(b) *Long-term business* relates to the provision of life assurance policies, which pay a capital sum on the death of the person whose life is insured, and to the operation of long-term savings schemes, which may involve an element of life cover should the person named in the policy die before the policy matures.

The insurance companies are extremely important players on the *UK capital market*, being important purchasers of new issues of gilt-edged securities and equity shares, and in respect of their transactions in the secondary market in such instruments (see Chapter 5, at 5.5.1). At the beginning of 1992 their total assets relating to long-term business amounted to £282.6b, whilst other assets were valued at £51.2b. Within these totals, the market value of gilt-edged securities held amounted to £42.9b, whilst UK company securities accounted for £128.8b. In addition, these companies own substantial amounts of real property, make significant volumes of mortgage and other loans, and hold a large amount of funds on deposit with the banking sector. It is interesting to note that many insurance companies regularly make losses on their underwriting business (i.e. the claims made upon them for losses and other payments plus their operating costs exceed their income from premiums), and hence their profitability depends upon the income and capital gains from their investments.

4.8.2 Pension funds

Many individuals are members of *occupational pension schemes*, which operate to collect payments from contributors during their working lives, and to provide some form of regular pension after retirement age. Where members of schemes are employees, it is often the case that payments into the funds are fixed as a percentage of income, with employers making an additional contribution. These schemes are operated on what is known as a *funded* basis, with contributions being used to purchase assets, and with the income and capital gains being used to meet pension payments. The increasingly popular *personal pension* arrangements have very similar characteristics. (The current state pension scheme operates on the 'pay-as-you-go' principle, using current contributions to pay current pensions.) A key aspect of a pension fund's operations is the evaluation and spreading of risk, both in terms of life expectancy of contributors (and hence pension income requirements), and in terms of the selection of the fund's assets portfolio.

Pension funds may be divided into three categories:

(a) *insured schemes*, where an insurance company manages the contributions and guarantees pension benefits;

(b) *managed funds*, where the pension contributions are used to buy a share of an insurance company's managed fund. The return on the contributions, and hence the ultimate pension, depends upon the performance of the fund;

(c) *self-administered schemes*, where the contributions are used to make direct purchases of assets; but even here it is common for outside management (perhaps from merchant banks or insurance companies) to be brought in to oversee the investment portfolio.

In the UK these funds have benefitted greatly from favourable tax treatment. Pension funds which are approved by the Inland Revenue are known as 'gross funds', and they do not have to pay tax either on their investment earnings or on capital gains on assets. Partly due to increased contributions from members experiencing rising incomes, and partly due to the boom in the equity markets between 1980 and 1987, UK pension funds have grown rapidly since the early 1980s. At the beginning of 1992 their total asset holdings amounted to £344.3b, of which approximately £24b was held in the form of gilt-edged securities and £182.4b in the form of UK company securities. Clearly, the activities of the pension funds are very important to the operation of the *UK's capital market*, in respect of both primary and secondary market transactions.

4.8.3 Unit trusts

Unit trusts are funds in which individuals and companies may invest, in order to obtain a share in the income and capital gains generated by the trusts' assets. Unit trusts operate under trust deeds which specify the terms and conditions governing the management of the funds which they hold. Those running unit trusts are required to comply with the provisions of the Financial Services Act 1986 in respect of official authorisation, which

169

means that they must either be members of a Self Regulatory Organisation or be authorised directly by the Securities and Investments Board.

There are always two independent companies involved with the operation of each unit trust:

(a) the *management company* is responsible for the investment decisions of the trust, and for the administration of selling and repurchasing 'units';

(b) the *trustee company*, which is normally a bank or an insurance company, acts as the guardian of the trust's assets and income on behalf of the unit holders, and ensures that the provisions of the trust deeds are met by the management company.

Unit trusts are 'open-ended' in the sense that they may expand or contract according to customer demand for 'units'. There is no secondary market in units; rather the unit trust will create new units according to demand, and will sell them directly to the purchaser (perhaps via the agency of a bank, stockbroker, solicitor or accountant). Furthermore, the unit trust will repurchase units from holders on demand. Thus, unit trusts provide a convenient means for investors to obtain a share in a much larger and diversified portfolio than they are likely to be able to hold directly. The price at which units are sold by the trust (the offer price) and the price at which the units are repurchased (the bid price) will reflect the market value of the trust's holdings. The difference between the buying and selling prices is accounted for by administration and trustee expenses, brokerage charges, contract stamp, and the profit of the management company.

During the middle years of the 1980s investments in unit trusts grew rapidly. As the bulk of unit trust assets are held in the form of equity shares, the worldwide stock market boom during this period both attracted new investors to unit trusts, and raised substantially the capital value of existing asset holdings. However, as might be expected, the stock market collapse of October 1987 led to a sudden change of fortune for the unit trusts, and it was not until 1989, when a sustained stock market recovery occurred, that the unit trust sector regained its earlier attraction for investors. By the end of February 1993, total funds held had reached a value of £69.2b.

4.8.4 Investment trust companies

Investment trusts are limited companies whose business largely relates to investment in financial assets. They are not trusts proper, and they do not operate within the confines of trust deeds. These institutions obtain funds through the issue of equity shares, through borrowing (primarily from the banking sector), and also from retained income and realised capital gains from previous investments. The bulk of their assets are in the form of listed company securities, around a half of which represent claims on overseas companies. The remainder of their portfolios is spread fairly widely over short-term assets, government securities, unit trusts, and property.

Each investment trust company is under the control of its board of directors, but usually the board concentrates on setting out the broad objectives for the company, whilst delegating the actual investment management and administration to specialist individuals and institutions. It is common for investment trusts to retain the services of the investment management department of a merchant bank in this respect. However, it is possible that an investment management firm may be wholly or partly owned by the investment trust company that it manages.

The broad objectives of an investment trust company will determine the general nature of the assets portfolio held. Some funds are general, whilst others specialise in particular geographical areas or industries; some aim for long-term capital growth, whilst others seek to achieve high levels of income. Shares in listed investment trusts may be bought and sold freely on the Stock Exchange. The investor in an investment trust does not buy the underlying assets held by the trust (unlike the investor in a unit trust); rather, shares in the company itself are held. The price of any trust's shares will reflect the supply of and demand for them on the Stock Exchange, which in turn is likely to be strongly influenced by the performance of the company's investment portfolio.

At the beginning of 1993 the total market value of investments held by investment trust companies was £22.5b. The performance of these institutions was badly affected by the stock market collapse of October 1987, and, in common with unit trusts, it was only really after 1989 that this sector began to recover some of the buoyancy experienced during the mid-1980s.

4.9 THE NATURE OF THE REGULATORY AND SUPERVISORY FRAMEWORK

The recognised importance of the financial system to the economic well-being of the nation, and the serious consequences which may arise for both individuals and institutions of entering into commitments which ultimately prove to be more onerous than initially seemed likely, has led to the activities of financial institutions and markets being subject to a substantial amount of regulation and supervision. This has arisen through both *official channels*, involving the direct intervention of governmental or other public sector bodies, and *self-imposed mechanisms*, designed to protect the integrity of specific parts of the financial system. It is important to emphasise that the purpose of financial regulation and supervision goes well beyond the *protection* of the naive from their own ignorance and the inept from their own greed. The complex interrelationships which exist between financial institutions, and between financial markets, create the potential for chain reaction defaults on outstanding debt, widespread losses of confidence in financial institutions and unmanageable crises within financial markets. Thus, an important factor influencing the development of the supervisory framework, has been a desire on the part of the authorities to protect the *stability of the financial system as a whole*.

Despite the unquestioned importance of the regulation and supervision of financial institutions and markets, the issue has tended to be dealt with very *unevenly* in the UK:

(a) Some institutions have been closely supervised by *government departments*. For example, the Department of Trade and Industry has had important responsibilities in respect of the supervision of insurance companies and unit trusts.

(b) Some institutions have been supervised by *non-governmental public sector bodies*, with greater or lesser degrees of rigour. For example, the Bank of England has responsibility for overseeing the activities of authorised banking institutions in the UK, whilst the Building Societies Commission (and formerly the Registry of Friendly Societies) supervises the operations of building societies.

(c) Some institutions and markets have effectively escaped direct official control, and have only been regulated by the *broad professional ethics* of the individuals concerned, or by *rules of membership* stipulated by those bodies controlling entry to various markets, as with the pre-Big Bang London Stock Exchange.

Traditionally, the emphasis of supervision in the UK has been placed upon the *honesty* of the provider of financial services, rather than upon his or her *technical competence* to provide the services. However, since the beginning of the 1980s, important steps have been taken to improve the quality of financial supervision, and, in particular, to *strengthen the protection afforded to the users of financial services*. A major theme of the recent developments in this respect has been to apply the controls to the providers of financial services in a more *equitable* manner than had hitherto been the case. Also there has been a trend towards the *removal of restrictive practices*, in order to facilitate free competitition. Clearly, a delicate balance must be achieved between the need for *adequate safeguards* for the user of financial services, and the need to encourage *innovation and competition* within the financial system. It is often argued that the latter provides a good check against the exploitation of the user of financial services. But without adequate supervision, free competition can easily lead to the compromising of standards as the providers of those services attempt to cut their costs in order to maintain their market positions; and the desire to generate profits may be put before the maintenance of quality.

The natural evolution of the financial system in recent years has tended to make its efficient and effective regulation more difficult for the authorities. The *increased sophistication of financial instruments* and the *greater complexity of many forms of transactions* have been extremely important in this respect. So too has been the trend towards *diversification by individual financial institutions*, which has led to them becoming involved with unfamiliar activities, or with newly established financial markets. In consequence, since the mid-1980s within the UK, the whole framework of financial regulation has been reappraised, and there has been a general movement away from regulation on the basis of historical institutional classification, and towards regulation according to the *nature of activity undertaken*. Thus, for example, whilst the mainstream activities of banks continue to be supervised by the Bank of England, it is necessary for separate authorisation to be obtained from other regulatory bodies for operations involving life assurance and unit trust management, securities dealing, general investment management, and so on. One implication of this development is that an individual bank (or, for that matter, any other form of financial institution) may be subject to controls from a number of different regulatory bodies, with all the attendant *compliance costs* which that involves. This problem is, to some extent, reduced by the use of a '*lead regulator*', whereby the regulator responsible for the dominant business of an institution also takes responsibility for ensuring that information about the institution is passed on to the other relevant regulators. This clearly reduces the costs associated with the provision of data to the regulatory bodies, but it does little to limit the possible operational problems which may be caused for an institution as a result of having to meet simultaneously differing sets of regulatory requirements.

From the point of view of the authorities, perhaps the most serious problem arising from a regulatory regime which concentrates on activities rather than institutions as a whole, is that *no single regulatory body may have a complete picture of the operations of the large, diversified institutions*. Yet the successful regulation of these institutions is likely to be critical to the long-run stability of the financial system. Indeed, this may provide the authorities with a reason for having a regime which takes an inherently cautious approach to regulation, despite the risk of it being criticised by financial institutions as being excessively detailed in its requirements and bureaucratic.

The remainder of this chapter examines in detail the regulation and supervision of banking activities and investment businesses. It is in respect of these areas that some of the most important developments have taken place in recent years. Brief consideration is also given to the regulatory frameworks relevant for building society and insurance activities. Throughout, it is important to keep in mind the *inherent conflicts* which may arise within the regulatory process, as outlined above, and to appreciate that *individual elements of regulation may necessarily have to limit the freedom of businesses in order to protect the integrity of the financial system as a whole.* Figure 4.1 provides a summary of the framework for financial regulation in the UK, the key elements of which will be described in the following sections of this chapter.

4.10 BANKING SUPERVISION AND REGULATION

4.10.1 Background issues

The Bank of England performs the role of supervisor of the UK banking system. For many years, this role was undertaken in a relatively informal manner, but since the enactment of the Banking Act 1979 it has had a formal legal basis. The Bank may be seen as supporting, advising and supervising the individual members of the banking sector, but above all the Bank's efforts are directed towards *maintaining the integrity of the sector*, and hence *the general public's confidence in its stability*.

The Banking Act 1979, which was introduced in the aftermath of a serious crisis involving a number of UK wholesale banks, provided a framework for banking regulation which divided institutions into two groups.

(a) *Recognised banks.* These institutions had to satisfy the Bank of England of their high reputation within the financial community, and of their integrity, financial prudence and managerial competence. They also, in general, had to offer to their customers a wide range of banking services.

(b) *Licensed deposit-takers.* These were institutions which did not meet the full list of criteria laid down for recognised bank status, but which nevertheless were able to satisfy the Bank of their integrity, financial prudence and managerial competence. LDT status was not necessarily a mark of a second class bank, and in all probability it merely reflected the fact that an institution's operations were relatively specialised, and that it did not cover a sufficiently wide spread of activities to warrant recognised status.

However, following the Bank of England's rescue of Johnson Matthey Bankers (JMB) in the Autumn of 1984, it was announced by the Chancellor of the Exchequer that banking supervision within the UK was to be made more rigorous, and in particular that it was the intention of the Government to introduce legislation to abolish the distinction between recognised banks and licensed deposit-takers. The problems of JMB brought to light the fact that recognised banks, of which JMB was one, were less closely supervised than the licensed deposit takers, and that inexpedient bank management practices could continue undetected for significant periods of time. The implications for confidence in the UK banking system as a whole require no elaboration.

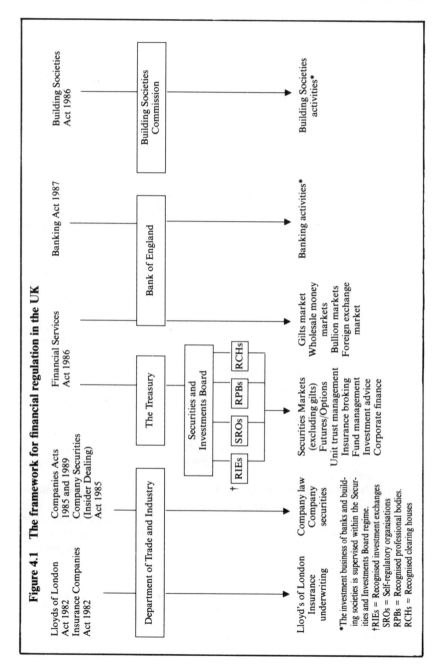

Figure 4.1 The framework for financial regulation in the UK

4.10.2 The Banking Act 1987

The Banking Act 1987 (which repealed the 1979 Act) introduced a unified system of regulation for banking institutions based within the UK. There is now just a *single category of authorised banking institutions*, every member of which must operate within the same statutory supervisory requirements.

Schedule 3 of the 1987 Act specifies the *minimum criteria* which a banking institution must satisfy if it is to gain *authorisation* from the Bank of England. In particular, it is required that:

(a) an institution's directors, controllers and managers are *fit and proper* persons to hold their positions;

(b) the business is *effectively directed* by at least two individuals;

(c) in the case of UK-incorporated institutions, there must be as many *non-executive directors* as are considered to be appropriate by the Bank of England;

(d) the business is *conducted prudently*, in respect of *capital adequacy, liquidity, foreign currency exposure, provisions for bad and doubtful debts, accounting and other records*, and *internal management controls*;

(e) when authorisation is granted, the institution has a minimum value of *net assets* (set at ECU 5m since the beginning of 1993).

In addition, within the provisions of the 1987 Act:

(a) the Bank of England retains the discretion to *set prudential standards on a case-by-case basis;*

(b) the Bank of England has the power to *object to proposed takeovers and mergers* involving UK banking institutions;

(c) it has been made a *criminal offence to provide false or misleading information* to the Bank of England;

(d) *banks' auditors* are expected to pay close attention to the Bank of England's *supervisory information requirements;*

(e) banks are required to give notice to the Bank of England when their *exposure to individual borrowers* is expected to exceed 25% of their capital; and exposures of between 10% and 25% must be reported to the Bank.

Clearly, the Act gives the Bank of England *wide-ranging powers* in respect of the supervision of banking activities within the UK. The Bank also has considerable discretion in relation to the application of prudential controls on liquidity and capital adequacy (which are examined in detail in 4.10.4 and 4.10.5 below), and in determining whether or not an institution is behaving in a manner which justifies its continued authorisation. An important aspect of the supervisory process relates to the *quality of a bank's management* and its *internal management control mechanisms*. This particular emphasis reflects official concern that the management weaknesses apparent in the collapse of JMB should not be repeated. Indeed, a crucial theme of UK banking supervision is that a continual flow of relevant data should be channelled from authorised banks to the Bank of England, and that any factors which may compromise the stability of a specific institution should be brought to the Bank's notice with all possible haste.

The Act also established a *Board of Banking Supervision*. The membership of this Board consists of the Governor and the Deputy Governor of the Bank of England, and the executive director of the Bank responsible for banking supervision (as permanent *ex officio* members), together with six other members selected by the Chancellor of the Exchequer and the Governor of the Bank from outside the Bank on the basis of their relevant skills and experience. These independent members of the Board include senior bankers recently retired or with no current executive responsibilities, and members with legal and accounting qualifications. The function of the Board is to *advise* the Governor on matters relating to the supervision of authorised institutions, the development and evolution of supervisory practice, the administration of banking supervisory legislation, and the structure and staffing of the Banking Supervision Division of the Bank. However, the Governor has the right to ignore the advice of the Board, but must inform the Chancellor of the Exchequer when he does so. Therefore, ultimate responsibility for banking supervision remains within the Bank, and it is this fact which has led to strong criticism from certain quarters. Some commentators argue that the effective regulation of banking activity really requires a completely independent statutory supervisory body, i.e. a body which is free from ties and long-standing relationships with City institutions.

4.10.3 The deposit protection scheme

The Banking Act 1979 provided for the establishment by the Bank of England of a deposit protection scheme, which is aimed at offering a degree of *insurance for ordinary depositors* against the failure of authorised banking institutions. The scheme is financed by a levy on all authorised institutions, set in relation to the size of their deposit balances. The 1987 Act extended this scheme, and currently it covers the first 75% of all sterling deposits up to £20,000 made with an institution's UK offices.

Some commentators, and a number of banks, have criticised the scheme on the grounds that the basis of its financing bears little relationship to the stability of individual banking institutions. That is, it is the larger generally more stable banks which contribute the largest amounts to the deposit protection fund, but it is their depositors who are the least likely to have to call on the insurance facility. Nevertheless, it is broadly agreed that the scheme helps to *maintain confidence* in the banking system as a whole, and that this is of crucial importance to the long-term prosperity of all institutions, irrespective of their individual financial strengths.

4.10.4 Prudential controls on bank liquidity

An important aspect of the Bank of England's supervisory role is to ensure that banks manage prudently their liquidity positions. The current approach to this function was introduced in 1982, and has the broad objective that *institutions should be able to meet their obligations when they fall due.* The major obligations in this context are *sight deposits, time deposits, commitments to lend at a specific date, and unutilised overdraft facilities, where the timing of commitments is uncertain.* Institutions are expected to be able to cover demands for funds made in respect of these obligations via one or more of the following means:

(a) *Cash or other liquid assets may be held,* but it must be recognised that the quality of assets which are liquid by virtue of their marketability may vary due to fluctuations in their market prices.

(b) Asset portfolios may be managed so as to ensure appropriate *cash flows from maturing assets,* with the qualification that a certain amount of default risk may be attached to portfolios.

(c) A diversified deposit base may be maintained, together with an appropriately high standing in the money markets, so that *new deposits may be attracted* as required and without undue cost.

The basic principle of the liquidity controls is one of *self-regulation* by institutions. That is, having established the *broad guidelines* for the evaluation of the quality of assets and for the classification of liabilities, the Bank of England leaves it to the institutions to *select the combination of assets and liabilities which they believe to be optimal,* given their own commercial objectives. In order to ensure adequate liquidity, the management of *an institution may choose any combination of the above-listed approaches.* However, as all banks are required to make regular accounting returns to the Bank of England, and senior managers of all banks are required to meet with Bank supervisors on a regular basis, the Bank is able to *monitor closely* the adequacy of liquidity management. Where an institution is not felt to be pursuing appropriately prudent liquidity management policies, it will undoubtedly be warned by the Bank. Failure to act on such a warning risks the suspension of its authorisation, and hence its ability to continue in business.

It is important to appreciate that the controls are intended to encourage institutions to pursue prudent policies in respect of their liquidity management in the broadest sense. Thus, recognising the increasing internationalisation of financial activities, the controls place emphasis upon the *overall liquidity positions* of institutions, rather than simply concentrating upon the separation of sterling and foreign currency items for liquidity purposes. Also, the Bank must be satisfied that institutions' *internal management systems* are adequate for the roles undertaken, and hence that institutions are suitably equipped for dealing with unforeseen liquidity problems.

Since the introduction of the current prudential framework for bank liquidity, the Bank of England has set no generally applicable liquid asset reserve ratios (i.e. required minimum ratios of liquid assets to some specified category of liabilities for all banks). The emphasis has instead been placed upon flexibility of regulation and minimum standards set for each bank taken on its own merits. This position was reiterated as recently as April 1990, when the Bank rejected proposals for the introduction of a high quality liquidity stock requirement, which would have been embedded within the existing framework. The proposals would have required banks to hold specified liquid assets equal in value to at least a minimum percentage of certain short-term liabilities. However, the fairly rigid nature of the proposals met with fierce resistance from banking institutions, and the ensuing debate demonstrated the controversy which remains in respect of the best approach to prudential controls on bank liquidity.

4.10.5 Prudential controls on capital adequacy

As was explained earlier (at 4.4.5(b)), capital is a *vital requirement for the undertaking of banking activities*. The maintenance of an adequate capital base has been described by the Bank of England as being 'the cornerstone of sound banking'. Since the enactment of the Banking Act 1979, the Bank of England has had a legal duty to regulate the capital adequacy of banking institutions, and this duty was strengthened by the 1987 Act. However, it was only near the end of the 1980s (for reasons to be explained below) that the Bank first stipulated a *common minimum level of capital adequacy* which must be met by *all authorised banking institutions*. Prior to that time, there was no general minimum requirement, and each bank was dealt with separately on its own merits.

Throughout the 1980s, the Bank's approach to measuring capital adequacy was to evaluate the various risks attached to a bank's assets portfolio, and then to *weight the portfolio according to its riskiness*. The

179

more risky the assets held, the greater the weight given to the assets, and hence the larger the amount of capital required in order to maintain a given degree of capital adequacy. In other words, in order to maintain a particular level of protection for depositors against losses on its assets, a bank would have to hold more capital the greater the risk attached to the assets. The Bank also provided a clear definition of the items which could be included within the capital base for regulatory purposes. Consequently, the control regime laid down strict parameters in respect of the treatment of particular assets and capital items, but it left the Bank of England with flexibility to set *specific ratios of capital to risk-weighted assets for individual banks*, reflecting its assessment of each bank's *capacity to manage its risk position, profitability* and *general prospects*. The minimum required capital ratio (referred to as the 'trigger ratio') for any bank was set following discussions with its senior management, but it was expected that in normal circumstances the bank would conduct its operations so as to maintain a margin over this value (thus giving the 'target ratio' for the bank).

To a large extent, the Bank of England has maintained its established approach to the supervision of capital adequacy into the 1990s. However, the UK's acceptance of the proposals on the *harmonisation of capital adequacy standards*, put forward by the Committee on Banking Regulations and Supervisory Practices of the Bank for International Settlements (BIS) in July 1988, has led to the introduction of a more *rigorously defined framework*, and the publication of *minimum required capital ratios* for all banking institutions. Indeed, most of the Western world's major central banks agreed to implement the BIS capital adequacy convergence proposals by the end of 1992. Strictly, these requirements relate only to banks which are internationally active, but the Bank of England has applied them as a *common standard to all authorised banks in the UK*.

The BIS requirements specify *risk weightings* for categories of assets. These include a zero weight for cash; a 10% weight for call money with discount houses; a 20% weight for fixed interest securities issued by OECD central governments; a 50% weight for mortgage loans; and a 100% weight for commercial loans. Account is also taken of off-balance sheet items, such as guarantees, forward currency exchange contracts, and note issuance facilities (which effectively involve underwriting commitments), via the use of 'credit conversion factors' designed to provide a measure *of their value weighted for credit risk*.

For the purposes of the BIS requirements, capital is divided into two types: *Tier 1* (or core) capital comprises shareholders' equity, non-cumulative participating preference shares and disclosed reserves; *Tier 2* (or supplementary) capital comprises revaluation reserves, general provisions, hidden reserves, subordinated term debt, and certain hybrid debt/equity instruments. It is required that banks should have capital equal in value to at least *8% of total risk-weighted assets*. Within this ratio, at least a half of the capital must be of the core variety.

As the Bank of England was fairly confident that the BIS proposals were already being satisfied by the majority of UK banks, it not only accepted the proposals, but also announced that it intended to implement them by the end of 1989, with no transitional arrangements. The Bank also announced that it would make use of the discretion allowed to individual central banks to set capital adequacy requirements *above* the minimum level specified, and that it would continue to set trigger and target ratios for UK banks, in the manner outlined above.

It is hoped that by enforcing minimum capital standards upon all banks involved in international lending, the world's banking system will be *strengthened*, and will be better placed to *weather future adverse conditions* in international financial markets. A further implication of the BIS requirements is that banks based in different countries are now *treated more equitably* in terms of their regulatory controls, and hence competition should take place on a fairer basis. There should also be less incentive for banks to move activities between countries purely on the grounds of the relative ease of regulatory requirements.

4.10.6 The Third World debt crisis and capital adequacy

The BIS proposals on capital adequacy were, to a large extent, motivated by widespread *concern for the stability of banks* heavily involved in *international lending* in general, and in lending to Third World countries in particular. During the 1970s and early 1980s, bank lending to less developed countries (LDCs) grew rapidly, spurred on by increased competitive pressures in the domestic markets of Western nations, and the general belief that lending to sovereign states was not exceptionally risky and could, in fact, prove to be rather profitable. However, at the beginning of the 1980s, when real interest rates began to rise and the United States dollar began to appreciate in value, the ability of many LDCs to service their international debts was called into question. The turning point came in the late summer of 1982, when Mexico announced that it was unable to meet its debt servicing commitments. This precipitated a major crisis of confidence in relation to sovereign debt, with banks drawing back from further lending commitments, at a time when an increasing number of sovereign borrowers were openly expressing fears on their ability to pay interest on outstanding loans let alone make repayments of principal. In fact, the doubts which were raised as to whether some debt would ever be repaid caused the majority of commercial banks involved *to raise substantially their provisions for possible defaults*. It was argued that only by *building up their capital bases* would the banks be able to regain the total confidence of their depositors, and re-establish their credibility with investors. Partly under pressure from central banks, fearing the impact on their countries' financial systems of major sovereign debt defaults, exceptionally large provisions were made, which caused several leading banks (including a number in the UK) to report substantial *accounting losses* on operations over one or more years. Interestingly, the consequent effect on banks' share prices often tended to be positive, as the markets responded favourably to the strengthening of the banks' capital positions. It is now not unusual for provisions to be in the range of 50% to 80% of the value of LDC debt outstanding, and some banks have provided for 100% of their exposure.

In addition to building up capital reserves, some banks have sought ways to *reduce their exposure to LDC debt*. In a number of cases banks have negotiated with borrowers to convert loans into marketable securities, which have then been sold (usually at a large discount on their face value) to other institutions willing to carry the associated risk. Indeed, this process of *securitisation* has sometimes involved the conversion of debt to equity claims on commercial enterprises in the borrowing countries; thus giving the banks a stake in the future industrial prosperity of those countries, as well as the ability to sell off their claims in the capital markets. Also, in line with the Brady Plan for helping debtor countries, there has been a certain amount of writing-off of debt, in recognition of the need to provide substantial relief to certain countries if they are ever to escape from their debt burdens.

Experience has shown that the actions which may be taken by banks to improve their capital adequacy will almost always undermine profitability, at least in the short to medium term. The *writing off of debt* has an immediate impact on profits, and the restructuring of portfolios to increase the proportion of *lower risk assets* is likely to reduce the average return on funds employed. New issues of shares or subordinated loan stock will also tend to reduce the yield per share, at least in the short term. However, if the result of these operations is a better quality assets portfolio, an enhanced capital adequacy, and an improved creditworthiness in international financial markets, the longer-term effects on profitability are likely to be favourable.

For most UK banks, the emphasis placed upon capital adequacy by the authorities, during the second half of the 1980s, proved to be something of a blessing as the UK economy moved into *recession* at the beginning of the 1990s. As stated earlier, *record levels of default* on loans made to a broad range of personal, small business and corporate customers have taken a heavy toll on banks' profits, and *huge losses* have been reported by a number of leading retail banks. However, despite these pressures, the capital strength of UK banks has generally ensured their continued *financial stability*, and, notwithstanding the support provided to a number of wholesale banks by the Bank of England during 1991/92, there have been no major crises of confidence within the banking sector as a whole.

4.10.7 Prudential controls on foreign currency exposures

A further important aspect of the Bank of England's supervisory responsibilities relates to the control of banks' *exposures to foreign currency risks*. As movements in currency exchange rates may have adverse effects on a bank's *net worth*, if its assets and liabilities are not balanced in terms of their currencies of denomination, the Bank seeks to measure, monitor and discuss with banks their foreign currency exposures. It also sets out *guidelines* for the *maximum desirable exposures in individual currencies* and for *total net positions in all currencies*. These controls relating to foreign currency risk are separate from, and additional to, the monitoring of each bank's overall risk position in respect of *large exposures* to individual borrowers or types of assets.

4.10.8 BCCI and banking supervision in the 1990s

In July 1991, the Bank of England moved to close down the UK operations of the *Bank of Credit and Commerce International (BCCI)*, a major international bank incorporated in Luxembourg. At the same time, or shortly afterwards, in a co-ordinated operation, banking supervisors in a number of other countries took similar action in respect of BCCI operations falling within their jurisdiction. The reason for this extraordinary action was the discovery of overwhelming evidence of *gross banking irregularities* and strong suspicion that *massive fraudulent transactions* had been perpetrated by BCCI employees. The complexity of the case is such that the precise losses suffered by BCCI depositors may never be known; but what is certain is that the scale of losses is huge, with conservative estimates being in excess of $5b. When it was closed down, BCCI was one of the largest privately owned financial institutions in the world, holding assets of around $20b and having operations in no fewer than 69 countries.

Whilst the closure of BCCI had extremely serious implications for many of its depositors, the immediate impact on banking markets as a whole was muted. Although, as explained above, the event was probably an important contributory factor in the *erosion of confidence in wholesale banking markets* observed in the UK during the second half of 1991 and early 1992, the major impact of the BCCI affair is likely to be felt in the *longer term* in the way in which international banks are supervised. Following the closure of BCCI, there was *widespread criticism of the failure of banking supervisors to act sooner to protect the interests of deposits*. The Bank of England was a particular target for criticism on account of the importance of UK-based

183

operations for BCCI. Consequently, amid allegations that the Bank had been made aware of improper activities at BCCI several years before its closure, the UK Government appointed Lord Justice Bingham to undertake an *official independent enquiry* into the supervision of BCCI.

The Bingham Report was published in October 1992, and whilst it was not unduly critical of the Bank of England's actions or of the basic system of banking supervision used in the UK, it nevertheless questioned the *emphasis and rigour of the Bank's supervisory activities*, and put forward suggestions and recommendations for improving the supervisory regime. The outcome of the enquiry was a reinforcement of changes which the Bank had already begun to make in respect of its approach to banking supervision. The main issues which were dealt with by the Bingham Report, and the official responses, may be summarised as follows:

(a) The report recommended that the Bank should focus its attention more closely on *banks suspected of improper behaviour*, being particularly alert to evidence of fraud and other malpractice, and should be willing to take *appropriate decisive action without delay*. In response the Bank has established a new *Special Investigations Unit*, which has been given responsibility for following up suspicions of fraud or other criminal activity affecting the financial sector, and for liaising with other relevant authorities. A new *Legal Unit* has also been established to help ensure that the Bank takes full account of its legal powers when dealing with suspect banks. In addition, the Bank is extending the *training* of its supervisors, especially in relation to the handling of malpractice in banks, and is improving its *channels of communication*, both within the Bank and between itself and relevant government departments. Procedures for the involvement of the *Board of Banking Supervision* in operational aspects of supervision have also been strengthened.

(b) The report was critical of the existence of *organisational structures within banks which made it difficult for supervisors to obtain a clear view of their operations*. In response, the Government is to give power to the Bank of England to refuse or to revoke authorisation solely on the grounds that an applicant or authorised bank *cannot be effectively supervised*. This power will be of particular relevance where a bank has or proposes to have *complex internal management structures* or operations in locations which are thought to be *poorly supervised* or allow *excessively secretive* business transactions to occur.

(c) The report argued that *communication and co-operation between banking supervisors in different countries should be improved*. In response, the UK Government is to press for *changes to EC banking legislation* to allow for a *greater exchange of information* to take place between European banking supervisors and other authorities. Also, it has proposed that *reviews of supervision standards* should be undertaken in each country by banking supervisors from other countries.

(d) The report highlighted the need for *closer co-operation* between the various *domestic authorities responsible for banking supervision* and those involved with the *investigation and combating of financial crime*. In response, the authorities have established a *Financial Fraud Information Network*, chaired by the head of the Bank of England's Special Investigations Unit, and supported by the secretariat of the Securities and Investments Board (see 4.11.2), in order to co-ordinate action between UK banking supervisors and investigatory and prosecution authorities.

(e) The report recommended that *banks' auditors* should have a *statutory duty* to provide the Bank of England with *information relevant to the effective supervision of banks*. The Government has responded by putting forward plans to introduce such a duty for auditors and reporting accountants.

Therefore, it may be concluded that the BCCI affair has precipitated a *significant tightening* of the supervisory framework for UK-based banks, with particular emphasis being placed upon the *identification of potentially troublesome* banks *before* their activities are able to put at risk either their depositors' funds or the stability of the banking sector. In addition, the obvious international nature of BCCI's operations has caused the EC Commission to take action to *strengthen relevant aspects of EC banking legislation*; and the Basle (BIS) Committee of Banking Supervisors has put forward *four minimum standards* for banking supervision. These standards relate to the need for all international banks to be supervised by a *suitably competent home country authority*; for *both host country and home country supervisors to give prior approval* for the establishment of overseas branches or subsidiaries; for supervisory authorities to be able to *gather information directly* from banks based in other countries; and for host country authorities to be able to *refuse applications* for authorisation or to *restrict the operations* of an overseas bank where these standards are not met. It is intended that these standards should provide the *internationally-accepted ground rules* for the supervision of international banks, and their application should help to ensure that all such banks have *an identified lead supervisor* able to undertake *consolidated supervision* of their worldwide activities.

4.10.9 Banking regulation within the European Community

The EC's *internal markets initiative*, which was directed towards the completion of the *Single European Market* by the end of 1992, set the goal of completely free movement of goods, services, labour and capital between EC member states. It also gave a major boost to the relevance of EC legislation for banking activities within the UK.

Prior to 1988, the impact of EC legislation was confined to relatively general issues, such as the need for member states to establish systems of authorisation for banking institutions and to set out the minimum criteria to be applied (the *First Banking Co-ordination Directive* 1977); the requirement for the supervision of banking institutions with financial subsidiaries to take place on a consolidated basis (the *Consolidated Supervision Directive* 1983); and the requirement for the structure of banks' accounts to be harmonised (the *Bank Accounts Directive* 1986). Two European Commission Recommendations were also adopted in 1986, relating to large exposures to individual borrowers and deposit protection arrangements, but these were very much in line with the Bank of England's existing position on these matters.

At the beginning of January 1993, the *Second Banking Co-ordination Directive* came into force. This piece of legislation is likely to have *crucial implications* for the future of banking activities within Europe. A major element of this Directive is the introduction of a *single European banking licence*, which allows banking institutions incorporated in any EC member state to obtain automatically *mutual recognition* throughout the EC, by virtue of their home country authorisation (subject to the agreement of their home supervisor). The acceptance of the concept of mutual recognition of authorisation between countries is a fundamental innovation in respect of banking supervision. *Home country supervisors* are now responsible for the *overall supervision of the EC-wide operations of banks* based within their respective countries. However, host country authorities have retained the exclusive responsibility for measures arising from the implementation of monetary policy, and, at least in the short term, primary responsibility for the supervision of liquidity and position risk (i.e. the risk which arises due to unhedged positions on assets and liabilities relating to possible interest rate and exchange rate movements). In consequence, the Bank of England is no longer able, on prudential grounds, to prevent banks authorised in other EC states from establishing branches in the UK, and it only has a very limited role in the day-to-day supervision of such branches.

As might be expected, the introduction of home country regulation and mutual recognition of authorisation is dependent upon the *harmonisation of certain key supervisory standards*. Thus, included within the Second Banking Co-ordination Directive are formal requirements in respect of the minimum level of capital for authorisation and for continuing business (which has been set at ECU 5 million); supervisory control over major shareholders and banks' participations in the non-banking sector; and accounting and internal control mechanisms. These requirements are totally compatible with the provisions of the Banking Act 1987, and hence with existing arrangements within the UK. In addition, since 1988, there has been a wave of EC Directives and Recommendations, which the Bank of England has been required to implement, relating to specific aspects of supervision of financial institutions. For example, the *Own Funds Directive*, adopted in April 1989, sets out the EC's definition of a bank's capital base for supervisory purposes. This Directive was formulated with close reference to the BIS proposals on capital adequacy, and hence serves to reinforce this critical element of regulation. Similarly, the *Solvency Ratio Directive*, the first draft of which was issued in 1988, proposes a uniform risk weighting for banking institutions' assets and a minimum risk asset ratio, which are very much in line with the BIS proposals. The *Bank Branches Directive*, adopted in February 1989, lays down reporting requirements for bank branches whose head offices are outside the member states where the branches are established.

There are also several EC Directives relating to particular types of non-banking financial services and to financial matters in general, which are of relevance to banking institutions. Indeed, without the *Capital Liberalisation Directive*, adopted in June 1988, the practical significance of the removal of many of the other barriers to activities would be very limited, as the free movement of capital funds between EC countries is vital for the provision of many EC-wide financial services. In respect of capital market operations and investment business, the *Investment Services Directive* (issued 1988), the *UCITS* (Undertakings for Collective Investment in Transferable Securities) *Directive* (amended 1988), and the *Admissions Directive* (implemented in 1985, and relating to stock exchange listings for securities) are of great importance.

Without doubt, the recent torrent of EC legislation (which is being implemented in the UK largely via the existing Acts of Parliament relevant to the financial sector), will be of great significance for the future of banking activities in Europe. Already a number of major UK financial institutions have formed alliances with institutions based in other EC countries, with the aim of being well-placed to take advantage of new business opportunities as soon as they arise. Also, the range of regulatory requirements which have been coming into force during the past few years has, for many institutions, necessitated detailed consideration of operating procedures and internal management structures. Even for those banking institutions whose major field of activity is likely to remain the UK domestic market, the impact of freer competition and the harmonisation of the regulatory framework cannot be ignored.

4.11 THE SUPERVISION AND REGULATION OF INVESTMENT BUSINESS

4.11.1 Background to the Financial Services Act 1986

In 1981 the British Government commissioned Professor Jim Gower to undertake an independent investigation of the regulation of investment business and investor protection in the UK. The resulting *Gower Report*, the final version of which was published in January 1984, showed that the regulatory framework left a great deal to be desired. The report highlighted the *variable quality* of supervision relating to different aspects of investment business, and suggested that it was often *excessively complicated, uncertain and inequitable*. The report also concluded that there was an *unnecessary diversity of regulations and regulators*. In short, the regulation of investment business in the UK was shown to be *wholly inadequate and inefficient*, thus threatening both the interests of the investor and the longer-term prospects of the UK as an international financial centre.

The ultimate outcome of the Gower Report was the enactment of the *Financial Services Act 1986*. This Act lays down a comprehensive framework for the *regulation of investment business and investor protection* in the UK. A crucial aspect of this framework is its dependence upon a *formalised system of self-regulation*. In arriving at this position, the authorities accepted the view that the regulation of sophisticated and diverse financial services activities is best undertaken by *practitioners* who understand the detailed operations of the financial markets. However, they also recognised the need for a degree of *overall external supervision*, in order to resist the pressure for self-regulatory bodies to degenerate into trade associations whose primary aim is to protect the interests of their members. Thus, the Financial Services Act established the *Securities and Investments Board* to oversee the regulation of investment businesses via *self-regulatory bodies*. The precise operational structure for supervision is illustrated in Figure 4.2.

4.11.2 The framework for regulation

The Financial Services Act made the *Department of Trade and Industry* (DTI) responsible for the regulation of investment business in the UK. In turn, the Secretary of State for Trade and Industry *delegated operational powers of regulation to the Securities and Investments Board* (SIB). In June

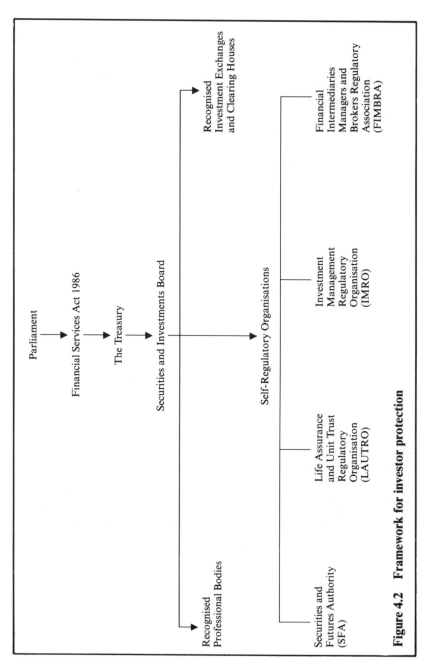

Figure 4.2   Framework for investor protection

1992, the DTI's responsibilities in respect of the Financial Services Act were transferred to the Treasury, in order to consolidate a wide range of financial regulation under one ministry. An initial function of the SIB was to formulate *codes of conduct and regulations* for institutions and individuals involved in the provision of investment services. These codes and regulations form the basis of the SIB's rule book, and they establish the standards expected of the self-regulatory bodies' own rules. The SIB's rule book had to be submitted to the *Director General of Fair Trading*, whose job it was to ensure that the rules embodied therein did not encourage or facilitate *restrictive practices* or *anti-competitive behaviour* within the financial services sector. In fact, the Director General made several important criticisms of the likely effects of SIB's rules on competition between investment businesses. However, he also admitted that it would have been virtually impossible to formulate effective supervisory rules without having some restrictive effect on the free market mechanism. Consequently, and following a few minor amendments by the SIB, the rule book received the approval of the Secretary of State, and in April 1987 the formal powers of regulation and supervision of investment businesses were transferred to the SIB. As will be explained below, these powers are substantial, which makes it all the more surprising that the SIB is formed as a *private company* with no financial support from the public sector. Indeed, the whole regulatory framework beneath the Treasury is financed via a system of levies and fees paid by the institutions and individuals whose activities are being supervised.

Once the SIB had been vested with supervisory authority, it was then able to set about the task of delegating specific responsibilities to a number of *self-regulatory organisations* (SROs), whose areas of competence taken together cover the bulk of investment activities as prescribed by the Financial Services Act. Initially, there were five SROs, but this was subsequently reduced to four by the merger of two of their number. As at summer 1993, the SROs and their areas of responsibility were as follows:

(a) *The Securities and Futures Authority* (SFA). This organisation was formed in 1991 from the merger of *The Securities Association* (TSA) and the *Association of Futures Brokers and Dealers* (AFBD). The overlap in the responsibilities of these two SROs made their amalgamation a logical development. TSA supervised the activities of the members of the London Stock Exchange, whilst the AFBD supervised the trade and broking in financial and commodities futures and options. The SFA has now assumed these responsibilities.

(b) *The Life Assurance and Unit Trust Regulatory Organisation* (LAUTRO) is responsible for supervising the marketing and management of unit trusts and life assurance businesses.

(c) *The Investment Management Regulatory Organisation* (IMRO) is responsible for the activities of independent investment managers and advisers, especially those managing institutional funds, collective investment schemes and in-house pension funds.

(d) *The Financial Intermediaries, Managers and Brokers Regulatory Association* (FIMBRA) is responsible for independent financial advisers who deal with the general public in respect of investments such as unit trusts and life assurance. It also covers the activities of licensed dealers and those providing investment management services for retail clients.

In order to obtain delegated regulatory power, each SRO had to produce its own rule book, which had to be approved by both the SIB and the Director General of Fair Trading. Each rule book must embody the *principles and standards* upon which business is to be conducted by the members of the respective SRO, and these principles and standards are expected to give investors '*equivalent protection*' to the rules developed by the SIB itself. Recognising the weight of detail embodied in the SIB's rules, this authorisation process was not an easy one for several of the SROs. Indeed, the formal basis of the SIB/SRO structure was widely criticised by investment firms as being *excessively legalistic and detailed in its requirements*, and hence as being potentially damaging to investors' interests. Many commentators argued that the regulatory framework would needlessly restrict the freedom of well-managed businesses, leading to *reduced choice* and *increased expense* for the investor. As a result of this criticism, which was largely accepted by the authorities, the SIB subsequently simplified its operating procedures, and reduced the complexity of its regulatory requirements. Thus, since April 1990 investment firms have been expected to operate in line with 10 broad principles laid down by the SIB, and covering their relationships with clients, with the markets in which they operate and with the regulatory bodies. The second phase of this process of rationalisation involved the publication, in January 1991, of a series of 'core rules' by SIB, which are now used as the basis for the production of simplified rule books by the individual SROs. Fewer than half of these core rules apply to dealings between professional investors, thus reducing the level of regulation applied to such transactions and recognising the complaints made in respect of the initially more detailed requirements.

Within the SIB framework there are also *Recognised Professional Bodies* (RPBs), *Recognised Investment Exchanges* (RIEs) and *Recognised Clearing Houses* (RCHs). The RPBs include the Law Societies of England and Wales, Northern Ireland and Scotland, The Institutes of Chartered Accountants in England and Wales, Ireland and Scotland, The Chartered Association of Certified Accountants, The Institute of Actuaries, and the Insurance Brokers Registration Council. Where an individual undertakes investment business as only a *minor element* of his or her total professional activities, then so long as *certification* is obtained from one of the RPBs, there is no need for full authorisation to be obtained from an SRO or from SIB itself. Clearly, this is a valuable concession for accountants, solicitors, and the like, allowing them to offer a range of investment services to their clients without the costs that full authorisation would entail. However, a professional body will only be granted recognised status by the SIB if its own standards and codes of practice are *compatible* with the SIB's own regulatory principles.

RIEs, such as the London Stock Exchange and the London International Financial Futures and Options Exchange, and RCHs, such as TALISMAN (the clearing house for the London Stock Exchange), are responsible for regulating specific financial markets and transactions which take place therein. It is only via recognition by the SIB that these exchanges and clearing houses escape direct supervision of their activities, although the general conduct of business is still supervised by the relevant SRO or RPB, or even by the SIB itself.

Finally, it must be emphasised that whilst the Financial Services Act is directed towards achieving a comprehensive framework for the regulation of investment business, the SIB system does not cover all activities which might be included under this heading. In particular, the Act explicitly makes the *Bank of England* responsible for the regulation of the gilt-edged securities market, the bullion markets, the wholesale money markets and the foreign exchange market. (Any individual or institution wishing to conduct business in any of these markets must first be authorised by the Bank of England to do so, which involves being deemed to be 'fit and proper' to participate in the markets, and being willing to meet capital adequacy criteria and formal codes of operational practice.) Furthermore, the *DTI* still possesses considerable direct regulatory powers over the operations of insurance companies and unit trusts, and has an important regulatory role in respect of insider dealing (which involves the improper use for personal gain of confidential information likely to influence the market price of securities). Indeed, the implementation of the massive body of company law, which is of both direct and indirect relevance for investment and other financial services businesses, is largely the responsibility of the DTI, although specialist matters are often dealt with by the *City Panel on Takeovers and Mergers, the Monopolies and Mergers Commission,* and *The Serious Fraud Office.*

4.11.3 Authorisation of investment businesses

For the purposes of the Financial Services Act, investments are defined to include equity shares in British and overseas companies; debenture stock;

loan stock; bonds; certificates of deposit; gilt-edged securities; local authority bonds; securities issued by foreign governments and international organisations; warrants; depository receipts for shares, bonds, or warrants; units in collective investment schemes; options on currency or on other investments; futures contracts for commodities; and insurance policies which constitute investments (such as endowment and unit-linked policies). A person will be deemed to be carrying on an investment business if he or she buys or sells investments (unless acting in purely a personal capacity), arranges for others to buy or sell investments, manages investments on the behalf of others, advises others on their investments, or operates a collective investment scheme.

Since the major provisions of the Financial Services Act came into force, in 1988, it has been a *criminal offence for any person to operate an investment business within the UK without prior authorisation* as defined by the Act, and unless otherwise exempted by the Act (as are, for example, tied agents working directly for authorised businesses). This offence is punishable by fines and/or imprisonment, and the offending party will be unable to enforce contracts and may be subject to a 'restitution order', requiring the repayment of any profits made by the business and the covering of any losses incurred by other parties as a result of the operation of the business.

Individuals and institutions wishing to undertake investment business may obtain authorisation in one of five ways:

(a)   The *SIB* has the power to authorise investment businesses directly, although its fees structure is set so as to discourage the use of this particular route. Quite simply, the SIB wishes to concentrate its attention on the *policy-making aspects of regulation*, and does not wish to become involved with significant amounts of day-to-day supervision. Although the SIB route may be required for certain cases, perhaps involving institutions undertaking an unusual mix of business.

(b)   Membership of an *SRO* recognised by the SIB is deemed to provide the required authorisation. Each SRO is expected to limit the scope of business which its members are entitled to undertake. Thus, in practice, the provision of an array of investment services by any individual or institution is likely to necessitate membership of more than one SRO, or may involve authorisation via more than one route. The bulk of investment business in the UK is now supervised via the SROs.

(c)   Certification by an *RPB* provides the required authorisation where the investment services offered form only a minor part of the authorised person's business activities.

(d)   Insurance companies and insurance intermediaries involved in the provision of advice on endowment and unit-linked policies may obtain authorisation from the *Secretary of State for Trade and Industry*, within the provisions of the *Insurance Companies Act 1982*. (For further detail on the regulation of insurance business, see 4.13 below.)

(e) An investment business may be operated in the UK if the person or institution undertaking that business is duly *authorised by another EC member state*, and where that state's requirements in respect of investor protection are judged to be *at least as rigorous* as those in force in the UK. Furthermore, this recognition of overseas authorisation is only available to businesses which do not have a permanent place of residence in the UK for purposes of providing their services. The only current exception to this provision relates to the UCITS (Undertakings for Collective Investment in Transferable Securities) Directive of the EC, which was implemented in October 1989. This Directive sets minimum requirements for the authorisation of unit trusts and similar funds and allows such funds authorised in any one EC member state to be marketed throughout the EC without further authorisation, subject only to notification and local marketing rules.

In order to obtain authorisation either directly from the SIB or indirectly via membership of a recognised SRO, it is necessary for a firm to establish that it is *'fit and proper'* to run an investment business. To do this it must satisfy various criteria relating to its *capital adequacy*, its *previous business record*, the arrangements to be put in place to ensure *compliance with supervisory requirements*, and the *good character of its owners, directors and employees*. In addition, the firm must produce a *business plan* which specifies the nature of business and type of customer proposed, the means for dealing with complaints, and the arrangements in respect of compliance officers within the organisation. The content of the business plan is of great importance, as this sets the *approved limits* of investment business which may be undertaken. Once authorisation has been obtained against a particular business plan, any proposed extension of activities must be approved separately, and may even require authorisation from a different SRO. The precise nature of the authorisation criteria vary between the authorising bodies, and depend upon the characteristics of the applicant and the proposed lines of business. Nevertheless, the standards required for authorisation must be *comparable* to those laid down for authorisation by the SIB itself.

In order to maintain authorised status, an investment firm must comply with the *conduct of business rules* laid down by its particular regulator. These rules cover a wide range of operational issues such as advertising, the disclosure of commissions to clients, the segregation of clients' funds from those of the business itself, and the making of unsolicited calls on actual or potential clients. They also seek to ensure that the client is treated fairly at all times and is made absolutely clear of the commitments which will be involved with particular forms of investment. In this respect investment firms are expected to ascertain sufficient details about the clients' financial position and requirements, so as to be able to give the *best advice* or *establish whether or not particular investment products are appropriate.* A *customer agreement* must also be provided which sets out the terms and conditions upon which business is undertaken, and *full records* must be kept of advice given, services provided and products sold, and these must be made available to the relevant authorities in the event of a complaint being made.

Where the activities of an investment firm are suspected of falling below the standards required by the authorities, the relevant SRO may *investigate* the firm, and depending upon its findings may *take action* to protect the firm's clients. This may involve the issue of private or public warnings, the issue of orders to limit the scope of activities which may be undertaken, the suspension of authorisation or the withdrawal of authorisation. The SIB also has the power to investigate the activities of *any* authorised business (as well as those of any business which is suspected of undertaking investment activities without authorisation), and may seize documents and require people connected with the business to give evidence to an enquiry. The SIB's powers, which override those of the SROs and other recognised bodies, include those available to individual SROs, and, in addition, allow it to apply to the court for a winding-up order (where the firm is unable to meet its debts or because 'it is just and equitable to do so') and to undertake *criminal prosecutions* in certain cases where serious violations of regulatory requirements are alleged. The very wide range of weapons available to the SIB and the SROs means that they are able to respond appropriately to breaches of standards of differing magnitudes. This helps to *avoid needless destabilisation* of the investment markets, recognising the complex relationships which may exist between individual investment businesses. It also means that 'first offenders' may be warned to put their houses in order, with the threat of more severe sanctions to follow if this should not occur.

Clearly, the regulatory powers possessed by the SIB are substantial, and given the serious implications which they generate for the livelihoods of individuals and those working in firms accused of breaching the rules of conduct, it is right to expect that there would be some form of *independent appeals procedure* against the stronger of the SIB's remedies for aberrant activities. Thus, other than in cases where court action is taken, which offers the normal appeal procedures of the British legal system, those who believe that they have cause for complaint against the SIB's actions may appeal to the specially constituted *Financial Services Tribunal.* The chairman of the Tribunal will be a lawyer appointed by the Lord Chancellor, and at least one of the other members (both of whom are appointed by the Chancellor of the Exchequer) must have relevant practical experience of the financial services sector. The Tribunal will investigate cases laid before it, and its decisions are binding upon the SIB.

4.11.4 Compensation Fund

An important event in respect of the protection of ordinary investors was the setting up, under the provisions of the Financial Services Act, of a compensation fund. The purpose of this fund is to provide compensation to investors who lose money either as a result of the *insolvency* of an authorised investment firm or because of *fraud* involving such a firm. The fund provides full cover for the first £30,000 of individual investments with authorised firms, and 90% cover for the next £20,000 of investments. The fund is administered by the SIB and is financed by a levy on the SROs, which is fixed according to the gross annual income of their members. The SROs recoup their contribution to the fund via levies on their individual members.

When claims are made against the compensation fund, the initial burden is placed upon the members of the SRO which authorised the firm in respect of which the claims are made. If these claims exceed a specified total within any given calendar year, then the other SROs must also contribute, up to an overall total compensation commitment for all SROs of £100m in any calendar year.

Whilst the introduction of the compensation fund was generally welcomed as providing a much-needed safety net for investors incurring losses due to fraud or insolvency, it has certainly not been free of criticism. A fairly obvious limitation of the scheme is the relatively low upper limit for compensation claims, which is, in fact, lower than on some of the individual compensation schemes which it replaced. One possible outcome of the compensation limit, is that risk averse investors might be encouraged to spread their investments around a number of firms, entrusting no more than £30,000 to any single firm. The arbitrary nature of the £100m per annum ceiling on total payments from the fund is also the subject of criticism, as is the apportionment of the burden of financing the fund, which is quite independent of the risk associated with individual firms' operations. Large, stable businesses involved in fairly low risk activities may justifiably claim that they are being forced to underwrite the riskier (and potentially more profitable) operations of smaller firms; although it is generally accepted that the maintenance of investors' confidence is likely to be beneficial for the long-term prospects of the sector as a whole.

4.11.5 The future development of regulation and supervision

As mentioned in 4.11.2, the SIB has recently taken important steps to *simplify* the basis of its regulatory framework, via the introduction of *core rules* which apply across all areas of investment business for which it has responsibility.

continued on next page

In addition, as at summer 1993, discussions were taking place on the establishment of the *Personal Investment Authority*, which it is proposed will be formed by merging LAUTRO, FIMBRA and the part of IMRO's activities relating to large independent financial adviser members. The intention here is to create a single, self-regulatory body for those individuals and institutions involved directly in the provision of investment services to the *general public*. It is hoped that this initiative will both *strengthen* and *streamline* the regulatory framework, *reducing the overlapping areas of responsibility* between the SROs, and will help to keep the *costs of regulation* within reasonable bounds.

A major criticism of the SIB regime, since its launch, has been the *high level of costs* which it imposes upon investment businesses. In this respect, the fees which have to be paid for authorisation, and the ongoing membership subscriptions to the relevant SROs and RPBs represent only the tip of the iceberg. For many investment firms the ongoing compliance costs are many times greater, especially in terms of the appointment of compliance officers to ensure that the supervisory requirements are met, the preparation of documentation and accounts for the supervisory bodies, and the keeping of detailed records of all transactions with clients. In addition, contributions are likely to be required to the SIB's compensation fund. Clearly, the more detailed are the supervisory requirements, and the more severe are the penalties for violation of these requirements, the greater become the costs of running the investor protection mechanism. Moreover, as most of the costs of protection are likely to be borne ultimately by the investor, by way of higher fees and lower net returns on investments, the question arises as to the overall net benefit to the investor of such elaborate regulation.

A further criticism of the SIB framework is that it may have *reduced the choice* of investment products and services available to the investor. In particular, not only do detailed rules of operation tend to create pressures for the *standardisation* of investment products and services, they may also *restrict innovation*, as investment firms are forced to grapple with the complexities of achieving appropriate authorisation. An especially contentious issue relates to the SIB's role on *polarisation*. This rule states that any person selling financial products such as life assurance and unit trusts must *either* act as an *independent intermediary* (advising clients on the whole range of products available and either charging a fee for this advice or earning a commission when sales result) *or* as a *tied company representative*. The primary objective of this rule is to ensure that investors are absolutely clear as to the status of the person with whom they are dealing. An important implication of this rule is that clearing banks and building societies are no longer able to offer their own insurance and unit trust products via their branches and also act as advisers on investment products in general (and hence as intermediaries for other companies). Thus, where a bank or building society offers its own range of products, the branch manager is unable to recommend products provided by other institutions even if he or she believes

continued on next page

that these are more suitable for the customer's needs. If the manager's own organisation does not offer any suitable product for the customer, the best that the manager can do is to refer the customer to a separate part of the organisation which is officially authorised to operate as an independent intermediary. As might be expected, both banks and building societies argued strongly against the introduction of the polarisation rule, on the grounds that it reflected badly on the professional ethics of their managers, and that it implied that at least some of their customers were not sufficiently intelligent to differentiate between independent advice and sales talk. The rule was also criticised by the Office of Fair Trading as an unnecessary restriction on competition. As events have turned out, all major clearing banks and most major building societies have opted for tied status, and no longer offer independent advice via their branches, which is somewhat unfortunate given the increasing complexity of investment products.

The implications of excessively costly and restrictive regulations go well beyond the immediate impact on ordinary investors. There are strongly held fears within the investment industry that its longer-term prosperity may be seriously harmed. Thus, whilst costs of regulation may be passed on to the investor, the pressure of competition will ensure that some portion of these costs will be reflected in reduced profitability; and as the demand for investment products and services is likely to be undermined, turnover may also be reduced. Moreover, to the extent that comparable activities in other countries are regulated in a more flexible and less costly manner, the international competitiveness of the sector is called into question. So far, this has not proven to be of great significance, given the inherent difficulties faced by ordinary investors in accessing overseas financial markets. However, the continued development of the single EC market is likely to alter markedly the financial environment. For not only is access to EC institutions and markets set to become easier for British investors, perhaps helped by professional agents, but also it is proposed that investment businesses authorised in one EC state will be able to establish branches and sell products and services within all other EC states, without further authorisation. The relevant legislation in this respect is the proposed *Investment Services Directive*, which is still under discussion as at summer 1993. This legislation will introduce a 'single passport' to EC operations for investment firms, on a parallel basis to the single European banking licence. The Directive is also intended to establish minimum operational standards and supervisory requirements for investment firms. But to the extent that the UK authorities impose a stricter regime, the impact on the competitiveness of UK investment firms may be severe (assuming, of course, that other EC states do not impose correspondingly demanding regulatory frameworks).

A number of critics of the SIB regime have suggested that a much less bureaucratic system of regulation for UK investment firms, together with a supporting compulsory indemnity insurance requirement (to provide compensation to clients in the event of losses due to negligence, fraud or insolvency) would be preferable, and may ultimately become vital if the sector is to maintain its prosperity. However, whilst such changes might reduce the overall costs of supervision, as well as force the more risky investment firms to bear a fairer share of compensation payments to investors (via their insurance premiums), they might also increase the chances of firms getting themselves into difficulties. Recognising that an increasingly large proportion of the adult population now makes use of investment products and services, the implications of this occurrence are hardly attractive. Hence, it would seem reasonable to suggest that *fundamental changes in the framework for investor protection in the UK are unlikely, at least in the foreseeable future.*

4.12 THE REGULATION AND SUPERVISION OF BUILDING SOCIETIES

Building societies in the UK operate within the provisions of the *Building Societies Act 1986*, the major elements of which were explained above at 4.6.2. Responsibility for the supervision of building societies rests with the *Building Societies Commission*. Strictly, the Commission is a corporate body and a legal entity in its own right, and is accountable to the Treasury, and hence, ultimately, to Parliament. The work of the Commission is financed entirely by a general charge and a system of fees levied on all building societies.

The broad functions of the Commission may be summarised as being:

- to supervise and regulate building societies within the provisions of the Building Societies Act 1986;
- to advise and make recommendations to appropriate government departments on matters relating to the operations of building societies;
- to promote the financial stability of building societies;
- to promote the protection of shareholders' and depositors' funds by building societies;
- to promote the principal purpose of building societies, which is to raise funds primarily from members with the view to making mortgage loans to members for the purchase of residential property.

A major concern of the Commission is to ensure that building societies *exercise prudently the powers granted to them by the Building Societies Act 1986.* Within this context the Commission possesses considerable powers to *restrict the activities of individual societies* and to *interfere with their operations*:

(a) The Commission is responsible for the *authorisation* of building societies, and for imposing conditions on and revoking authorisation. In respect of the exercise of these powers, the Commission pays close attention to the criteria for prudent management as outlined below in (b).

(b) The Commission has to ensure that societies meet the *criteria for prudent management* as detailed by the Act. These criteria relate to the maintenance of:

- adequate reserves and other designated capital resources;
- the required structure of commercial assets;
- adequate liquid assets;
- suitable arrangements for assessing the adequacy of securities for advances;
- requisite accounting records and internal systems of control.

There are also requirements in respect of the quality of directors and officers; in particular that they are fit and proper persons to hold office, and that they should conduct business with appropriate professional skills, prudence and integrity. If a society fails to meet any of these criteria, it will be in violation of the provisions of the Act, and the Commission will be required to review the society's authorisation.

(c) Where a society violates the prescribed limits for wholesale funding, deposit liabilities, commercial assets or liquid assets, the Commission may *issue a direction* requiring the society to submit an appropriate restructuring plan to bring its portfolios back to within the statutory limits, or requiring the society to seek the approval of its members to convert to public limited company status. If the society fails to comply with an approved restructuring plan or does not initiate the conversion mechanism, the Commission may *apply to the court* for the society to be wound up.

(d) The Commission has the power to determine whether or not an activity or proposed activity of a building society is within its *existing powers*. If a society continues to undertake an activity which has been declared to be beyond its powers by the Commission, a *prohibition order* will be issued which formally orders the society to cease undertaking the activity.

(e) The Commission has a general power over the *nature and context of advertising* by individual societies, and may direct that advertisements be withdrawn or amended as it believes to be appropriate.

Finally, it should be noted that just as the regulatory framework for banking activities is being increasingly influenced by the *EC's single market initiative*, so too is the regulatory framework for building societies. Indeed, strictly, the legislation described in 4.10.9 within the context of banking activities, relates to all 'credit institutions' within the EC, and hence applies equally to building societies. For example, by the end of 1992, the capital adequacy requirements placed on building societies had been brought into line with those applied to banks. So far, the impact on UK building societies has been limited, but following the implementation of the *Second Banking Co-ordination Directive* at the beginning of 1993, the effect on cross-border activities in the future may be more substantial. However, the ultimate impact of this liberalisaton is most uncertain, given, on the one hand, the stringency with which UK building societies are currently regulated, and, on the other hand, the fundamentally different approaches taken to the provision of mortgage finance in different EC states.

4.13   THE REGULATION AND SUPERVISION OF INSURANCE COMPANIES

The bulk of legislation relating to UK insurance companies is embodied in the *Insurance Companies Act 1982*. This Act both consolidated and extended the pre-existing legislation, and took into account EC Directives on insurance business. The major objectives of this legislation are to *protect the insurance policy holder* from the failure of an insurance company, and to *protect individuals from being sold insurance policies unsuited to their needs*. It is the responsibility of the *Department of Trade and Industry* (DTI) to implement the provisions of the Act and to ensure that its objectives are achieved. In this respect the DTI is given powers relating to the *authorisation* of insurance businesses; the stipulation of *solvency margins* (i.e. the effective capital backing for the business); and the *monitoring* of insurance businesses. It may also intervene in the running of insurance businesses.

The 1982 Act makes it a criminal offence for an individual or company to conduct insurance business in the UK without *prior authorisation*, and this will only be granted if the applicant is deemed to be *fit and proper* to undertake such business. The Secretary of State at the DTI is empowered to withdraw authorisation where, for example, the authorised party has failed to comply with any obligation under the Act. Less extreme sanctions include formal directions to insurance businesses to stop the issue or renewal of policies, to modify investment strategies, or to liquidate or repatriate assets. The DTI maintains regular surveillance of insurance businesses through the required annual returns on premiums and claims, the business accounts, and actuarial statements on life assurance activity, and has extensive powers to investigate the activities of insurance businesses. The DTI's responsibility also extends to the supervision of

Lloyd's of London, although this is under the provisions of the *Lloyd's of London Act 1982*. This Act lays down the framework for the regulation of this unique and world famous element of the UK insurance industry.

The *Financial Services Act 1986* required only minor amendments to the Insurance Companies Act 1982, and left the powers of the DTI largely unaffected. Nevertheless, it did seek to strengthen the framework for controlling the *marketing of insurance products* and the activities of those people who provide *advice on insurance products*. Further changes in regulation and supervision are proposed under the *EC's single market initiative*. In this respect, legislation is intended both to harmonise the laws relating to the operation of insurance businesses in different EC states, and to increase the freedom of insurance businesses established in one EC state to offer their services in other EC states. However, recognising the complexity of insurance activities, and the significantly different stages of development of such activities to be found in different EC states, the proposed legislation includes substantial requirements relating to the protection of policy holders where the insurance company is based in another EC state, and the time horizon for the implementation of some parts of the legislation is already set as late as 1999.

4.14 EXAMINATION PRACTICE

4.14.1 Questions

The following questions are taken from past examination papers, and are intended to give students an indication of the type of questions which they are likely to face within the topic area of UK Financial Institutions. Students may care to map out answers to these questions before consulting the guidance notes in 4.14.2. Each question carries 25 marks.

(1) (a) What are the basic benefits arising from financial intermediation? (10)

     (b) What do you understand by the term 'disintermediation'? (5)

     (c) Outline the clearing banks' response to:

        (i) challenges from the building societies in the area of financial intermediation;

      ‡(ii) challenges from developments in the UK capital markets in the area of disintermediation. (10)

(April 1987)

(2) (a) What is meant, in the UK financial system, by the term 'the authorities'? Include in your answer reference to the legal and practical relationships between the parties involved. (9)

     (b) State the functions of a central bank. (7)

     (c) Discuss the case for an independent central bank in the UK. (9)

(October 1990)

(3) Discuss the effects of each of the following on a clearing bank's balance sheet and interest rates:

     (a) regulations concerning capital adequacy; (7)

     (b) the need for liquidity; (11)

  ‡(c) an increased demand for advances. (7)

(May 1990)

(4) (a) What do you understand by the terms 'retail' and 'wholesale' as applied to financial transactions? (7)

     (b) Compare and contrast the activities of the clearing banks and the building societies in:

        (i) the retail market;

        (ii) the wholesale market. (18)

(September 1987)

(5)   (a)   Why does a bank need capital?   (5)
      (b)   Describe in detail the Basle (or Bank for International Settle-
ments) capital ratios.   (10)
      (c)   What action can a bank take to improve its capital ratios? (10)

(May 1993)

(6)   (a)   Outline the areas of responsibility of the main bodies involved
in supervising and regulating investment business in the UK.
(18)
      (b)   What protection do these bodies offer investors against losses
on their investments?   (7)

(May 1992)

4.14.2 Guidance notes

(1) (i) This question covers a wide range of related issues. It is important not to become engrossed with minor details. The major issues should be dealt with concisely.

(ii) In part (a) it is necessary to identify the major characteristics of the *financial intermediation* process, and then to comment upon the *benefits* they generate for ultimate lenders, ultimate borrowers and society as a whole. Excessive detail on the mechanisms of financial intermediation is not required.

(iii) Part (b) requires a clear definition of *disintermediation*. It is also useful to recognise that whilst disintermediation may be encouraged by official restrictions on financial activities, it may also occur as a result of purely commercial factors.

(iv) In part (c)(i) it is necessary to outline briefly the challenges presented by the building societies, in order to appreciate how the banks have *responded*. The emphasis must be placed upon the financial intermediation activity, although it is the whole package of financial services offered which is of relevance to attracting customers in the first place.

(v) Part (c)(ii) requires a brief outline of the trend towards disintermediation for the corporate sector, and recognition that the major *response of banks* has been to harness the trend, rather than compete against it.

Source of relevant material:

Part (a)   4.2.1 (as background) and 4.2.4.
Part (b)   4.2.5.
Part (c)(i)   4.4.3 (paragraph 1) and 4.6.2 (as background).
‡Part (c)(ii)   4.4.3 (paragraph 2) and Chapter 5, 5.5.5 (as background).

(2) (i) In the UK financial system, the authorities are normally taken to comprise the *Bank of England* and the *Treasury*. The answer to part (a) of this question should focus upon these two institutions. However, it is acceptable to mention other legally constituted bodies having regulatory or supervisory responsibilities, such as the Building Societies Commission or the Securities and Investments Board.

(ii) It is not necessary to describe the functions or powers of the authorities in part (a), but the *legal and practical relationship* between the Bank of England and the Treasury must be outlined.

(iii) Part (b) of the question requires a straightforward *listing* of the *functions* of a *typical central bank*. There is no need to discuss these functions or their importance for any particular central bank (for example, the Bank of England) at any given time.

(iv) The answer to part (c) must discuss the *benefits* which are likely to arise from the Bank of England being made *independent of political interference*. It must be emphasised that an independent central bank would still have policy objectives specified by Parliament, but it would be left to pursue these objectives in its own way.

(v) Part (c) does not require a discussion of whether the UK needs a central bank, or whether its functions could be undertaken by a commercial bank. Neither is it necessary to provide an assessment of whether the Bank should be independent.

Source of relevant material:

Part (a) 4.3.1 (paragraph 1) and (as background) 4.9, 4.11.2 and 4.12.
Part (b) 4.3.2, 4.3.3 and 4.3.4.
Part (c) 4.3.5.

(3) (i) The answer to this question must focus upon the effects of the items listed on a clearing bank's balance sheet and interest rates. It is not enough merely to describe the items listed.

(ii) In part (a), it is important to emphasise that a bank's capital is basically the difference between its assets and its liabilities, and that the adequacy of a given amount of capital depends upon the *quality of assets held*. An outline of the *regulations on capital adequacy* is required as the basis for comments on their implications for the balance sheet structure and for the costs incurred by the bank (and hence its interest rates).

(iii) The answer to part (b) requires more than just a listing of *liquid assets* held. It is necessary to mention efficient *asset and liability management*, and the arrangement of *lines of credit*. There is no need for discussion of why liquidity is required.

(iv) Advances are a crucial part of clearing banks' asset portfolios. In part (c) it should be explained that increased advances *must be financed*, either by *running down other asset holdings* or by *raising additional funds* (i.e. by attracting more deposit liabilities or increasing capital funds). The possible effects on both deposit and on-lending interest rates must be noted explicitly.

(v) There is no need to discuss why the demand for advances may have increased, neither is a detailed discussion of the credit creation process required.

Source of relevant material:

Part (a)   4.4.2, 4.4.5(b), 4.4.5(c) and 4.10.5.
Part (b)   4.4.2, 4.4.5(a), 4.4.5(c) and 4.10.4.
‡Part (c)   4.4.2, 4.4.5(c) and Chapter 6, at 6.3.

(4)   (i)   Part (a) of this question requires considerably more than just comments on the size of transactions involved. It is necessary to outline the *general characteristics of both retail operations* (for example, over-the-counter transactions through branch networks, and the provision of money transmission services) *and wholesale operations* (for example, involving the trading of money market instruments).

(ii)   The answer to part (b) should *compare and contrast* the relevant activities; that is, the similarities and differences should be highlighted. The activities undertaken by clearing banks and building societies should not simply be listed separately.

(iii)   It is important to recognise that whilst both the clearing banks and the building societies are classified as retail financial institutions, they are both to some extent involved with wholesale activities.

(iv)   The answer to part (b) should be couched in terms of the typical clearing bank and the typical building society. It is not necessary to give examples of specific institutions.

Source of relevant material:

Part (a)   4.2.6(c).
Part (b)   4.4.2, 4.4.3, 4.6.2, and 4.6.4.

(5)   (i)   Throughout this question, care should be taken not to confuse capital with assets, or with funds available for on-lending or with liquidity.

(ii)   Part (a) of this question requires a *concise* explanation of the *importance of capital* to a bank, emphasising the need to *maintain the confidence of depositors and shareholders.*

(iii)   The answer to part (b) must describe in *detail* the *risk weighting of assets* (including off-balance sheet items), the *definitions of Tier 1 and Tier 2 capital,* and the specification of the required *ratio of capital to risk-weighted assets.*

(iv)   Recognition should be given in part (c) to both the *raising of a bank's capital base* (for a given asset portfolio structure) and the *reduction of risk-weighted assets* (either by switching to lower risk assets or by reducing the asset portfolio size) for a given capital base.

Source of relevant material:

Part (a)   4.4.5(b) (paragraphs 1 to 3).
Part (b)   4.10.5.
Part (c)   4.4.5(b) (paragraph 4) and (as background) 4.4.5(c).

(6)   (i)   Part (a) of this question relates to the *areas of responsibility* of the *main bodies* involved in the supervision and regulation of investment business in the UK. Whilst the Securities and Investments Board and the self-regulatory organisations are at the centre of this activity, it is important not to forget the role of the Bank of England, the Department of Trade and Industry, the Treasury, Recognised Professional Bodies, Recognised Investment Exchanges and Recognised Clearing Houses. Also, the *precise names* of the bodies concerned, together with their *specific duties*, must be listed.

   (ii)   Discussion of the authorisation and regulatory control process is not required, and neither is consideration of the operational performance of investment regulation in the UK.

   (iii)   The answer to part (b) should comment upon the *general protection* offered to investors via the rigorous application of the *authorisation criteria*, and should outline the *compensation arrangements* for investors who have lost money due to *fraud* or *insolvency* of an investment business.

   (iv)   The protection of investors should not be confused with the protection of bank or building society depositors or insurance policy holders.

Source of relevant material:

Part (a)   4.11.2.
Part (b)   4.11.3 and 4.11.4.

4.15   FURTHER STUDY

As should be apparent from the foregoing sections of this chapter, the UK Financial Institutions section of the syllabus requires students to study a substantial amount of material. However, for examination purposes, it is far more important to understand the broad principles and general issues, than it is to be able to recount fine technical details on the operations and activities of specific institutions. Students should not allow their closeness to certain elements of the subject matter to cloud their perception of the importance of the various institutions within the financial system as a whole.

It is especially important that students should understand the nature of operations within the banking sector, and the relevance of the ongoing evolution of the building societies (as the major competitors of the retail banks). They should also attempt to keep up-to-date with the broad developments as reported in publications such as *Banking World, The Banker,* and *Mortgage Finance Gazette.* From time to time, highly relevant articles appear in the *Bank of England Quarterly Bulletin.* This publication is also useful in respect of commentaries on the Bank of England's own activities, although care should be taken to avoid technically detailed items which go well beyond the requirements of the examination. Recent issues of the Bank's *Annual Report and Accounts* and the annual *Banking Act Report* provide an excellent insight into the work of the Bank and its position within the UK financial system.

By its very nature, the material relating to financial supervision and regulation requires an appreciation of the major elements of legislation which impinge upon the activities of individuals and institutions engaged in the provision of financial services. However, this does not mean that a detailed knowledge of specific pieces of legislation is necessary for examination purposes. Rather, it is the *broad principles* embodied within the regulatory framework which are crucial, and students should consider carefully the objectives of regulation, the allocation of responsibilities for the implementation of the major regulatory requirements, and the means by which supervision is enacted. In this context, knowledge of the roles of the Bank of England and the SIB are of great importance, and a general awareness is required of the regulatory and supervisory roles of the DTI and the Building Societies Commission.

As the regulatory framework has a fundamental impact on the nature and scope of the activities undertaken by all UK financial institutions, students should be prepared for examination questions which seek to link the issues of regulation and supervision to the commercial operations of, for example, clearing banks and building societies. In particular, the implications of prudential controls relating to liquidity and capital adequacy for the management of asset and liability portfolios by individual institutions should be considered carefully.

In respect of the Bank of England's regulatory and supervisory role, by far the best source of further information is the Bank's annual *Banking Act Report*, which provides a concise and authoritative survey of recent developments in all aspects of policy and practice. Indeed, most of the regulatory bodies are required to publish annual reports on their fields of activity, although the detail contained therein is normally far in excess of what is required for examination purposes. In relation to the rapidly expanding area of EC legislation, a useful publication is the DTI's *The Single Market: Financial Services*, which is likely to be updated regularly. The booklet contains a brief introduction to the EC's single market initiative, together with summaries of all relevant existing and proposed EC legislation. It also lists points of contact within the DTI and the Treasury from where detailed advice may be obtained.

Substantial changes in the regulatory and supervisory framework tend to be announced well in advance of their implementation. Nevertheless, students should still consult regularly the quality press and professional journals, such as *Banking World* and *Mortgage Finance Gazette*, in order to keep up-to-date with the application of controls in particular cases. It should also be borne in mind that there is still considerable controversy over the appropriate nature of financial regula tion and supervision, and hence articles debating the merits and demerits of different regimes are not uncommon.

Finally, it must not be forgotten that the activities of financial intermediaries are crucial to the determination of the rate of growth of the money supply, and that these institutions are major players in the financial markets. Thus, there are *significant linkages* between the contents of the present chapter and material covered in other parts of this book, especially Chapter 2 (Corporate Sector Finances), Chapter 3 (Personal Sector Finances and the Housing Market), Chapter 5 (UK Financial Markets) and Chapter 6 (The Money Supply). Examination questions may seek to exploit these linkages within the syllabus.

5 UK FINANCIAL MARKETS

5.1 INTRODUCTION

It is difficult to provide a definition of a financial market which is both concise and unambiguous. However, in its broadest interpretation, the term may be used to refer to any organised structure within which individuals and/or institutions may undertake *particular types of financial transactions*. Thus, a financial market may be in the form of a *traditional market place* where parties come together for trading purposes; for example, the London International Financial Futures and Options Exchange. Alternatively, financial markets may have no physical form, but rather may involve the coming together of market participants via *sophisticated communications networks*, using telephone and computer links; for example, the sterling wholesale money markets. In addition, individuals and institutions undertaking particular forms of financial activities, although not directly in contact with each other, may be referred to as being participants in a financial market. The personal savings and loans market and the mortgage market are good examples of this form of market structure.

In respect of the UK financial system, a wide range of financial markets may be identified, all of which contribute to the overall character of the system. However, as the broad nature of the *retail financial markets* is implicit in the foregoing examination of personal sector finances and the UK's major financial institutions in Chapters 3 and 4 respectively, and as the detailed analysis of their operation may become technically complex, discussion of these markets will be taken no further in this book. Rather, the remainder of this chapter is devoted to an examination of the major *wholesale financial markets* concerned with the borrowing and lending of both short-term and long-term funds. The markets to be considered are the *primary sterling money market* (*the discount market*) and the *secondary (parallel) sterling money markets*, whose business involves the borrowing and lending of wholesale short-term sterling funds; the *UK capital market*, with particular reference to the operations of the London Stock Exchange, which is concerned with the raising of long-term funds for both the corporate sector and the public sector, and the trading of existing claims on such borrowers; and the *eurocurrency market*, which involves both short-term and long-term transactions denominated in foreign currencies, and which is extremely important for the banking sector, other corporate institutions and government bodies.

One other financial market which is crucial to international business activities is the *foreign exchange market*. However, as this market is involved with the *buying and selling* of currencies (not to be confused with the borrowing and lending activities of the eurocurrency market), and as its operations determine the structure of foreign currency exchange rates, it will be considered within the more appropriate context of Chapter 10.

5.2 MONEY MARKETS

5.2.1 The nature of activities

Money market activities relate to the *borrowing and lending of short-term wholesale funds*. In the markets for sterling funds the minimum transaction is usually £50,000, and for foreign currency denominated activities the minimum may be as high as the equivalent of US $1 million. In general, the maturity of funds varies from overnight to one year, although occasionally somewhat longer term funds are dealt with by some markets. Transactions may take place either on the basis of straightforward borrowing and lending (secured or unsecured) or through the medium of issues of short-term securities (bought or sold for immediate delivery).

Money markets are intangible in the sense that there is *no physical market place*. Quite simply, the institutions participating in the money markets are brought into contact via sophisticated communications networks, possibly involving telex, telephone and computer links. In addition, whilst individual markets notionally service the requirements of specific groups of users of wholesale funds, it is often the case that individual institutions are active in a number of different markets at the same time, and consequently it is very easy for funds to flow between markets. Indeed, the very nature of money market activities tends to encourage the evolution of an integrated structure of markets, and thus makes the analysis of individual markets in isolation somewhat difficult, and of only limited relevance. Nevertheless, for purposes of exposition it is useful to consider the markets separately, at least initially.

It is possible to identify a number of factors which are likely to facilitate the *growth and development of money markets:*

(a) The larger is the number of potential participants in a market, the greater will be the prospect of the market operating efficiently, and the higher will tend to be the level of liquidity (in the broadest sense)

continued on next page

---

embodied in negotiable money market instruments. Furthermore, competition will tend to be encouraged on both sides of the market, thus reducing the possibility of monopoly positions being established by participants.

(b) The larger is the turnover in a market, the more likely it is that the facilities offered and the instruments traded will become well-known, and hence that further market growth will be stimulated.

(c) The easier it is to move funds around, both within markets and between markets, the more attractive participation in the markets will become. In this context, extensive government regulations for monetary control or prudential purposes, or the existence of complex and expensive tax requirements, may stifle market growth.

(d) The existence of some form of general official supervision over the markets is normally thought to be desirable. For whilst excessive official interference in markets may stifle their growth, it is equally true that unfettered activities may frighten away potential participants. Almost invariably, the central banks of most Western nations have some involvement with the operations of their respective money markets. Indeed, these markets are often regarded as being crucial to the implementation of monetary controls, and they may be used as the channel through which the authorities adjust the liquidity of their country's banking system.

5.2.2 The London money markets

Since the 1950s, London has been a major international centre for money market activities. The particular characteristics of London's financial community, taken against the background of a relatively stable and sophisticated financial system, have tended to encourage the almost continual, and at times rapid, growth of the money markets. London boasts a long-established world-wide reputation as a centre for financial and trading activities, as well as an extremely high concentration of financially powerful institutions, many of which originate from overseas. Also, whilst many of the participants in the markets have been subjected to relatively firm official supervision by the Bank of England, it is generally agreed that this has not been excessive, and has not had detrimental effects on the development of the market.

The recent evolution of the London money markets has been clearly influenced by the steadily growing and increasingly sophisticated demands for financial services, both from within the UK and from overseas. Indeed the very nature of money markets makes them responsive to pressures from the surrounding financial and economic environment. In the 1950s and 1960s the markets were stimulated by official restrictions on the more normal banking and credit facilities within the economy. During the 1980s it was the trend towards securitisation in corporate finance which spawned the most recent addition to the sterling markets (i.e. the sterling commercial paper market).

Notwithstanding the existence of inter-market funds flows, which tend to cloud the boundaries between individual markets, it is possible to separate the London money markets according to the broad nature of their activities. The oldest of the London money markets is the *discount market* (sometimes referred to as the *primary sterling money market*), which has a history dating back to the early nineteenth century. The *parallel* (or *secondary*) *sterling money markets* evolved from the mid-1950s onwards, and today there are six established markets: *local authority, finance house, sterling inter-bank, sterling certificate of deposit, inter-company*, and *sterling commercial paper*. In addition to the sterling money markets, London still hosts the world's largest eurocurrency market, within which a significant proportion of transactions are of a money market nature.

5.3 THE DISCOUNT MARKET

5.3.1 Institutions and instruments

The *discount houses* form the core of the discount market. The other major participants in the market are the *clearing banks*, the *British Merchant banks* and the *Banking Department of the Bank of England*. The clearing banks are the major private sector providers of funds to the market (normally on an overnight or call basis), and along with the merchant banks are important 'acceptors' of commercial bills. It must be understood that only bills of the highest quality are traded in the discount market, and thus the acceptance activity is a crucial aspect of the market processes. Of particular importance are *eligible bank bills* (i.e. commercial bills which have been accepted by eligible banks), as these are rediscountable at the Bank of England. In recent years, these bills have played a major role in discount market trading operations, and the Bank has relied upon them for its market intervention activities (see 5.3.3 below).

The Bank of England's roles in the discount market are to issue *Treasury bills*, by tender on a weekly basis, and to buy and sell short-term instruments in respect of its own portfolios, with due regard to the specific objectives of its market intervention policy. In this respect, the Bank acts as the lender of last resort to the market, standing ready to provide liquidity to the market should conditions dictate. In addition, through the discharge of its broad supervisory responsibilities, in relation to both the market directly and the operations of participating banking institutions, the Bank is able to exercise a considerable influence on the evolution of the market's activities.

In addition to commercial bills and Treasury bills, *short-dated certificates of deposit* issued by UK banks and building societies are of substantial importance to the market's trading activities. Since the late 1980s, other instruments, such as *local authority bills and bonds* and *British government gilt-edged securities*, have been of only minor significance for the market.

5.3.2 Functions

The major functions of the discount market are as described for the discount houses (in Chapter 4, at 4.5.1). To summarise, the market:

(a) provides an important means for the commercial banks to adjust their liquidity positions;

(b) acts as a buffer between the Bank of England and the commercial banks, in respect of the adjustment of liquidity within the banking system and the implementation of monetary policy controls;

(c) makes markets in bills, certificates of deposit, and certain short-term public sector stocks;

(d) provides short-term finance to both the corporate sector and the Government through the discounting of their bills;

(e) underwrites the weekly Treasury bill tender.

Since the early 1970s, almost all of the discount market's functions have come under pressure from *increased competition*. The changes introduced by the Bank of England, in the mid-1980s, in respect of the direct provision of support to institutions other than discount houses, and the opening up of the gilt-edged securities market to a much wider group of participants have already been mentioned (see Chapter 4, at 4.5.2). In addition, the increasing importance of the sterling inter-bank and certificate of deposit markets, as a means for commercial banks to adjust their liquidity positions, has reduced the discount market's significance in this respect. There is also the general deregulation of financial activities, and, in particular, the recent growth of the sterling commercial paper market, which has forced the discount market to compete even harder in relation to its short-term corporate financing role.

The decision of the Bank of England, in 1988, to allow banking institutions to apply for discount house (or similar) status, and the subsequent abandonment of the 'club money' arrangements (whereby the discount houses were assured of substantial deposits from eligible banks), may ultimately prove to be of crucial importance for the development of the discount market. As was mentioned in Chapter 4, the impact of these events has so far been limited, but if significantly more institutions should take on discount market functions, it would in

215

future become increasingly difficult for the specialist discount market institutions (i.e. the discount houses) to survive. Already, most discount houses have, to some extent, diversified their activities away from those traditionally associated with the discount market.

5.3.3 Bank of England money market intervention

Bank of England intervention in the discount market is an extremely important aspect of the market's operations. The Bank intervenes for two main reasons: first, on a day-to-day basis, there may be net flows of funds between the private sector and the government sector, which, without appropriate Bank of England intervention, would cause destabilising fluctuations in short-term interest rates. Thus, for example, on any given day the total payments into the Government's accounts at the Bank, in respect of taxation payments or the purchase of government securities by the private sector, may exceed disbursements from those accounts in respect of public sector expenditures. In this case, there would be a net withdrawal of funds from the commercial banks' accounts with the Bank of England, and hence the effective reserve base of the banking system would be depleted. If the Bank of England did not intervene, the consequent bidding for funds by the commercial banks, in order to replenish their reserve bases, would tend to push up short-term interest rates. Indeed, as net flows between private and government sector bank accounts may, on occasions, be massive, the effects on interest rates could be severe. Therefore, the Bank of England will often intervene in the discount market in order to attempt to smooth out the flows of funds between the government and private sectors and thus attempt to *stabilise interest rates*.

Secondly, the Bank may attempt to implement a specific policy objective by means of *influencing the level and/or structure of short-term interest rates*. In this context the Bank may seek to harness the day-to-day flows of funds between private sector and government sector accounts (as referred to above), or, if need be, it may initiate transactions within the money markets, independently of government financing flows, as a method of carrying out its intervention operations.

Since the early 1980s, the Bank of England has undertaken the bulk of its money market intervention through transactions in *commercial (eligible bank) bills*; although, on occasions, other forms of bills have been utilised, including Treasury and local authority bills. Basically, if the Bank believes that, without intervention, a *shortage of funds* is likely to occur by the end of the day's clearing activities, it will announce the projected shortfall, and effectively *invite the discount houses to offer to it bills* which it will then purchase as the means of supplementing the liquidity available to the discount market, and hence available to the financial system as a whole. However, the Bank does not set a specific price at which it will buy bills, rather the discount houses are expected to make offers to the Bank in respect of the price required for any particular batch of bills. The Bank is then free to *accept or reject* the offers made, depending upon whether or not they are compatible with its *unpublished target band* for short-term interest rates. (The lower the price paid by the Bank for a given batch of bills, the higher is the effective interest rate charged on the underlying funds.) Clearly, the Bank's reaction to offers made sends important signals to the markets as to its intention in respect of short-term interest rates. Acceptance of an offer implies that the Bank is quite content to acquiesce in the rate determined by the market. Rejection of an offer in the face of market shortages of funds is likely to place upwards pressure on interest rates, either because the discount houses are forced to reformulate their offers at lower prices (higher rates of interest), or because institutions experiencing shortages of funds begin to bid up the price of the funds which are available within the market. Therefore, if the Bank merely seeks to smooth flows of funds between the government and private sectors, it will relieve shortages at the going market rate, otherwise, it will take the opportunity to influence rates in the manner desired.

In the event of there being *excessive amounts of liquidity* on the money markets, the Bank will seek to mop up the perceived surplus via the *sale of bills* (normally Treasury bills) to the discount houses. As noted in Chapter 4, the discount houses undertake to purchase the full amount of Treasury bills on offer. Again the discount houses are expected to take the lead in respect of the determination of the implicit interest rate structure, by formulating offers which the Bank is free to accept or reject in the light of its policy objectives.

In recent years, the Bank of England has focused its intervention activity on bills falling within *bands 1 and 2* of the officially-designated maturity classifications for money market instruments (see Table 5.1). That is, trade has taken place largely in respect of bills with maturities of 33 days and less, with particular emphasis placed upon band 1 bills for significant periods of time. The rationale for this approach is that the Bank wishes to leave the determination of the general structure of interest rates to free market forces (insofar as this is feasible in the light of the heavy intervention which is required periodically), whilst having a strong influence on short-term rates. In addition, by purchasing bills which are close to maturity, the Bank is able to maintain a tighter control on money market liquidity, as the scheduled repayments on maturing bills provide a convenient natural out-flow of funds from the private sector, which may or may not be counterbalanced by further official bill puchases, depending upon the Bank's policy position.

Table 5.1   Bank of England money market intervention bands

Band	Days to maturity
1	1 to 14
2	15 to 33
3	34 to 63
4	64 to 91

The above-described mechanism for providing liquidity to the money markets is often referred to as the Bank of England's *lender of last resort* facility. It is important to understand that this function relates to the provision of liquidity to the *banking system* as a whole, and does not involve the bailing out of individual banks which have got into difficulties. In addition to the purchasing of bills, the Bank may also *make loans, at pre-announced rates, directly* to the discount houses against collateral. This form of lender of last resort facility was the most commonly used form of support until the early 1980s, but since that time it has been used only rarely. This form of support may be appropriate when activity in the bill market is only at a low level, or when the Bank wishes to have an immediate impact on the system, perhaps in times of crisis.

Since the mid-1980s the pre-eminence of the discount market's position in respect of Bank of England support to the banking system has been undermined somewhat. In particular the Bank now engages periodically in *REPO agreements* with selected commercial banking organisations. These agreements involve the Bank in purchasing certain relatively illiquid assets from banks on the understanding that the banks will repurchase the assets on a specified future date. Effectively, the Bank is providing a mechanism for selected institutions to raise the liquidity of their assets portfolios, in order to tide them over a period where they might otherwise experience liquidity problems (for example, during the tax gathering season). The nature of these transactions means that, strictly, the Bank is not making loans directly to banking institutions, but rather it is helping them to manage their assets. Nevertheless, this might be thought of as an extension of the traditional lender of last resort activity. In addition, since the Stock Exchange deregulation in 1986, the Bank has provided direct borrowing facilities to institutions such as Gilt-Edged Market Makers and Stock Exchange Money Brokers. This provides yet a further channel for the Bank to influence liquidity conditions in the financial system, independently of the discount market.

5.4 THE PARALLEL STERLING MONEY MARKETS

5.4.1 Background issues

Activities in the parallel (secondary) sterling money markets originated in the mid-1950s; but important developments have taken place as recently as the mid-1980s. An important characteristic of the markets' structure has been the ability to react quickly to the requirements of actual and potential participants, and to provide facilities which have often been denied to them in the more conventional banking channels. In this context, official controls and restrictions placed on normal bank lending have been an important catalyst to the growth of the markets.

Transactions in the parallel markets are *unsecured*, and the lender has to depend upon the 'good name' of the borrower. Also, the Bank of England does not offer a direct lender of last resort facility to these markets. Consequently, there tends to be a somewhat greater degree of risk attached to lending in the parallel markets than in the (secured) discount market. Interest rate structures and differentials between the markets reflect this position. Also, whilst it is usual to talk of a number of separate parallel markets, in practice many institutions are active in several markets simultaneously, and hence funds tend to flow quite freely between market segments. The relevance of identifying the separate markets is in respect of their individual specialist roles.

5.4.2 The local authority market

This market began to evolve in 1955 when the Government restricted local authorities' access to borrowed funds from central government sources. The local authorities quickly became an important force in both bill and bond markets, and also raised substantial amounts of funds via wholesale bank loans. The implicit support of the Treasury for local authority debt instruments has clearly enhanced their attractiveness. However, in more recent years the market has diminished in importance as the Government has attempted to rein in local authority expenditure, and has sought to achieve a greater direct influence over their borrowing activities.

5.4.3 The finance house market

This market is involved with the raising of wholesale funds for UK finance houses. Although this market was important in the early stages of the development of the parallel sterling markets, its significance has diminished somewhat since a number of the larger finance houses gained full bank status in the late-1970s, and began to raise funds on the inter-bank market. Nevertheless, the market is still very active, with regular issues of commercial bills by the finance houses. The non-banking sector houses also raise wholesale funds directly from banking institutions, as well as from insurance companies, pension funds, non-financial companies, and individuals.

5.4.4 The inter-company market

This is the smallest of the parallel sterling markets, and involves lending by companies with surpluses to other companies wishing to borrow, via the agency of a broker. This market originated in 1969 in response to the difficulties faced by fundamentally creditworthy companies in raising finance via normal banking channels. However, as bank lending restrictions have been relaxed, and as facilities for companies to raise funds via issues of securities have become more widely available, the relative attractiveness of this disintermediation activity has diminished, and today this market only operates on a modest scale. It should also be noted that at certain times substantial use has been made of bank guarantees in order to strengthen the financial credibility of borrowers on the market. Indeed, despite the market's title, banks have occasionally participated directly in the market as providers of funds.

5.4.5 The sterling inter-bank market

This market is the *largest*, and perhaps the *most important*, of the sterling parallel markets. Its activities involve the borrowing and lending of short-term wholesale funds between commercial banks, often via the agency of a broker. Also, today, transactions often involve directly large industrial and commercial companies, international institutions, discount houses and building societies. Individual transactions rarely involve amounts of less than £500,000, and many fall in the range of £5m to £20m. Funds may be lent for periods ranging from overnight to around five years, although the typical transaction is for three months or less.

The inter-bank market has become increasingly important as a means through which *commercial banks* may *adjust their liquidity positions* relatively quickly and efficiently. On a day-to-day basis banks are able to place surplus funds on the inter-bank market, and thus earn a reasonably good return whilst maintaining some degree of liquidity for those funds. Conversely, banks experiencing pressure on their liquidity or seeing immediate on-lending opportunities may raise substantial amounts of funds within the market at competitive rates. The use of the market has tended to develop along with the trend towards liability management, whereby banks seek to adjust their liabilities position to reflect their desired assets, rather than adjust their assets to accommodate their liabilities.

The inter-bank rates established by the market determine the *marginal cost of funds* to the commercial banks, and hence movements in inter-bank rates are carefully monitored by the banking community. The key rate in this context is the three-month *London Inter-bank Offered Rate* (LIBOR), which is taken as a crucial indicator of market trends. Today, substantial amounts of commercial bank lending, especially to the corporate sector, are charged at a percentage over LIBOR, and hence changes in this rate have an immediate impact on the financing position of borrowers with such loans outstanding. In addition, changes in inter-bank rates will also have implications for the setting of *base rates*, although the relationship between the two sets of rates is neither direct nor immediate. Rather, base rates tend to follow the longer-term trend in inter-bank rates, but do not react to day-to-day fluctuations. Thus, if inter-bank rates increase, this means that the marginal cost of funds to banks is raised, and, other things being equal, banks' operating margins will be squeezed. But whether or not this occurrence will cause a corresponding increase in base rates, and hence an increase in banks' on-lending rates, will depend upon factors such as the size of the existing operating margin, the proportion of total funds raised by the banks at inter-bank rates, expectations on further movements in inter-bank rates, and the state of competitiveness in on-lending markets. (For further examination of this issue, see Chapter 7 at 7.7.3.)

Due to its nature, the precise size of the sterling inter-bank market is difficult to establish. Nevertheless, using the reported level of sterling deposits held by UK banks emanating from other UK banks as the basis for measurement, the size of the market at the end of February 1993 was £94.2b.

5.4.6 The sterling certificates of deposit (£CDs) market

This market provides an *important alternative source of wholesale funds for the banking sector* and certain large building societies. £CDs are negotiable bearer securities issued by banks and building societies, normally in amounts ranging from £50,000 to £1m. Original maturities are rarely less than 28 days, and may be as long as five years. They provide a useful way for the issuing institution to *raise large sums of money for fixed periods at fixed rates of interest*, thus reducing risk in portfolio management operations. Margins are very competitive, and flows of funds tend to be sensitive to small changes in interest rates paid. Technically, the institutions issuing the £CDs form the primary market in the instruments, whilst institutions which deal in issued £CDs, irrespective of whether or not they are issuers, form the secondary market. The efficient operation of this secondary market is vital to the maintenance of the £CDs' liquidity and hence their attractiveness to lenders.

Banks and building societies often hold large volumes of £CDs in their own assets portfolios in recognition of their *liquidity* and *market related return*, and hence their quality as reserve assets. More generally, there is the possibility that capital gains may be made on premature sale of certificates (especially the longer-term variety), should market rates of interest fall subsequent to the purchase of the certificates. However, of course, there is also the risk of capital losses in the event of an increase in the general level of interest rates. In addition, the purchaser of £CDs also benefits from the fact that tax on interest or capital gains is not withheld on transfer or maturity of the certificates, and there may be benefits arising from the anonymity that transactions in bearer securities allow.

5.4.7 Sterling commercial paper (SCP) market

The SCP market is the most recent addition to the ranks of the parallel sterling money markets, having begun operations in May 1986 following alterations to the provisions of the Banking Act 1979. SCP relates to short-term, marketable, unsecured promissory notes with a fixed maturity, typically between seven days and three months, issued in bearer form at a discount. SCP may be issued by companies (including banks and building societies) in the UK which have a net asset value of £25m or more; these companies or their guarantors (which may be banks) must be listed on the Stock Exchange; and issues of paper must be in minimum denominations of £100,000.

An important advantage of SCP, relative to commercial bills, is that it does not have to be issued as the counterpart to a specific commercial transaction. It may be issued purely as a means of raising *short-term funds for general business purposes*. Also, due to their financial standing, some companies are able to borrow *more cheaply* through issues of SCP than by taking out bank loans, and yet the purchasers of the paper may obtain a higher return than they would through the holding of bank deposits (as the costs associated with financial intermediation are effectively by-passed). Clearly, the development of SCP represents a form of *disintermediation* which is of particular concern for banks in relation to their corporate lending business, although banks may be able to recoup some of their losses through the earning of fees for the management of programmes of SCP issues.

5.4.8 The distinction between the discount market and the parallel sterling money markets

Despite the similarities in the fundamental activities of the discount market and the parallel sterling money markets, it is widely agreed that it is still valid to distinguish between the two types of market. The key differences between the markets, which are implicit in the foregoing sections of the present chapter, may be summarised as follows:

(a) The discount market is the main channel through which the Bank of England influences the liquidity of the banking system, and hence short-term interest rates, for both monetary policy and financial stabilisation purposes.

(b) The Bank of England acts as a lender of last resort, in the traditional context, only to the discount market.

(c) Transactions within the discount market are secured, whereas they are unsecured within the parallel markets.

(d) The high quality of the participants operating in the discount market, together with the high quality of instruments traded therein, normally ensure that interest rates established within that market are somewhat lower than the rates established on parallel market instruments with comparable maturities.

(e) The discount market underwrites the weekly Treasury bill tender.

(f) The parallel markets (specifically the inter-bank and £CD markets) are now the major means through which the commercial banks adjust their liquidity positions.

Whilst recognising the differences between the two types of market, it must never be forgotten that there are *important similarities*. In particular, the banks which have access to the discount market will consider the *competing opportunities* for the adjustment of their liquidity positions. These banks will look for the best deal in respect of depositing surplus funds on either the discount market or the inter-bank market, and the purchase of £CDs provides a further use for such short-term funds. Similarly, in respect of covering short-term deficiencies in liquidity, the discount market, the inter-bank market and the issue of £CDs provide competing sources of funding. In addition, since the mid-1980s, the Bank of England has been willing to inject liquidity into the banking system via means other than discount market intervention. *REPO agreements* provide a good example of the Bank's somewhat more liberal attitude in this respect. Thus institutions active in the parallel markets may, on occasions, have direct access to Bank of England support. Finally, the *regulatory framework* within which both types of market operate has to some extent been *harmonised*. All markets are exempt from the provisions of the Financial Services Act 1986, but are instead supervised by the Bank of England's Wholesale Markets Supervision Division, and are expected to adhere to the London Code of Conduct on money market operations.

5.5 THE CAPITAL MARKET

5.5.1 Capital market activities

The *London Stock Exchange* (LSE) forms the central element of the UK capital market. Activities within the LSE relate to the *issue of long-term securities* by both private sector companies and public sector organisations (this being referred to as primary market activity), and the *trading of existing securities* (referred to as secondary market activity).

The primary market is of great significance for the *raising of funds* to support capital investment in *industry and commerce*. Funds may be raised via the issue of various forms of *equity shares*, which constitute claims upon the profits of the companies issuing them. Dividends will be paid to the shareholders, depending upon the level of profits and the dividend policy of the company involved. The shareholders of the company are its legal owners, and hence they may influence its commercial policies. They also have a claim on the residual value of the company, should it be wound up. Companies may also raise capital funds via the issue of *interest-bearing debt instruments*, such as debentures. Purchasers of these instruments normally have a claim to regular interest payments, and they are creditors of the issuing company. This mechanism for raising funds provides an important alternative to the taking out of bank loans, assuming that banks would be willing to lend funds in the amounts and for the periods of time required by companies. (A more detailed examination of the instruments which may be used by companies for the raising of funds is given in Chapter 2 at 2.6 and 2.7.)

In relation to the *government sector*, the issue of interest-bearing gilt-edged securities has traditionally been an extremely important aspect of budget deficit financing. The ability to issue large quantities of such debt to the non-bank non-building society private sector, as a means of financing a Public Sector Borrowing Requirement, is of great significance for monetary control purposes, as the alternative methods of financing often entail the creation of additional money by the banking sector (as will be explained in Chapter 6, 6.5.1).

The secondary market is also of great importance, as it provides holders of both equities and interest-bearing securities with the opportunity to *liquidate their investments at very short notice*. Indeed, whilst a large proportion of the interest-bearing debt is dated, and hence would mature automatically at some point, some debt instruments, such as government consolidated loan stock (consols), have no fixed maturity date, and the bulk of equities are irredeemable (unless the issuing company deems otherwise). Thus, without the facilities offered by the LSE, it would be considerably more difficult for private companies and the public sector to raise long-term funds, as the borrower would be required to take on a high degree of illiquidity, together with the associated risks.

It should also be recognised that the LSE is not only concerned with the financing of domestic businesses and the UK government sector, it also provides an active market for the trading of securities issued by *foreign companies* and *overseas governments and official institutions*. In addition, the LSE has become increasingly involved with trade in *eurobonds*. Interestingly, it has been developments in respect of international financial activities which have been an important factor in stimulating the deregulation in the capital market which has been experienced since the early 1980s.

Finally, it must be emphasised that whilst the LSE is at the very heart of UK capital market activities, a large volume of trade in securities (especially foreign securities) takes place outside of the LSE, often through *wholesale banks* and *securities houses* (many of which are foreign-owned). Indeed, a substantial proportion of all eurobond activity (see 5.6.1 below) by-passes the LSE entirely. Also, there are *specialist financial institutions* which companies may approach for the provision of capital funds, such as venture capital institutions (for example, Investors in Industry) and government-sponsored regional development bodies. As with normal LSE facilities, such specialist provision may involve the taking of equity stakes in companies, or the making of long-term loans (possibly against the issue of marketable securities).

5.5.2 The raising of capital funds on the LSE

If a company wishes to raise funds on the main LSE market, it must first apply for a *'quotation'*. However, the achievement of quoted status does not mean that the company has been given an official seal of approval; rather it means that relevant information about the financial position and operations of the company has been made public. When a company is going to the market for the first time for funds, this is referred to as a *public flotation* of the company, and would normally be managed by a merchant bank working in co-operation with a broker (although for relatively small companies, a broker may handle the operation alone).

There are two broad approaches which may be taken to a flotation:

(a) *Offer for sale.* Advertisements are published inviting the general public to purchase shares, and the issue will be underwritten by financial institutions (i.e. for a fee, certain institutions are willing to stand ready to purchase, for a fixed price, any shares which are not taken up by the general public).
    The offer may be made –
(i) *at a fixed price*, although if the price is made sufficiently attractive
continued on next page

it may result in 'stagging', whereby individuals and institutions apply for more shares than they desire to hold, in the hope of being able to sell them immediately upon allotment at a profit. There is also the problem of allocating shares when an issue is over-subscribed;

(ii) *for tender*, whereby bidders are allotted shares in descending order of bid price until the issue of shares is exhausted. It is normal to charge all those allotted shares a price which is equal to the price offered by the final bid accepted (this is known as the 'striking price'). Prospective purchasers bidding less than the striking price receive no shares. This approach effectively stops stagging, but it may lead to a concentrated ownership for the shares.

(b) *Placing*. The shares are taken up, usually in large blocks at agreed prices, by a limited number of individuals and institutions. This form of issue incurs less cost than an offer for sale, but the distribution of shares is rarely wide, and hence the company may be dominated by a small number of large shareholders.

Once a company has been successfully floated, it may subsequently raise additional finance through *rights issues* (i.e. by offering additional shares directly to existing shareholders, normally at a discount to the current market value), or through the issue of *debentures*. Unfortunately, where a company does not have a sufficiently long or creditable track record, it may not even be eligible for a quotation on the main market of the LSE. In this case it may still be able to raise funds, either via offers for sale or placings, through the LSE's *Unlisted Securities Market* (USM). The requirements laid down by this market for companies wishing to raise funds are less demanding than those on the main market; for example, only a two-year track record is required, as opposed to three years for the main market. Also, the flotation costs are lower. However, as companies raising funds through the USM are generally less well established than those operating through the main market, there is clearly greater risk for the investor, and hence the prospective yield required on the securities issued is likely to be above that expected from companies on the main market. Nevertheless, during the 1980s, the USM proved to be very successful, with a significant number of companies which had been floated on the market graduating to a full listing on the main market. But since 1990, the relative attraction of the USM for companies seeking flotation has diminished somewhat, due to the reduced entry requirements for the main market. Indeed, the LSE has published plans for the abolition of the USM by the end of 1995, although this proposal was still the subject of intense debate as at August 1993.

Table 5.2 provides a summary of the numbers of securities traded on the LSE at December 1992, together with their market valuation. It may be observed that whilst UK company securities are the most numerous, it is overseas company securities which account for the largest market

continued on next page

capitalisation value, thus reinforcing the LSE's claim to be a truly international stock exchange.

Table 5.2   LSE : Securities traded and market valuations as at 31 December 1992

Security type		Number of securities	Market valuation £b.
Public sector	: UK	198	168.2
	Overseas	212	18.3
Eurobonds		2,403	185.1
Company sector	: Listed UK	3,621	646.4
	Overseas	933	1,561.4
	: USM	331	4.8
Total		7,698	2,584.2

Source: *Quality of Markets Review*, LSE, Winter 1992.

5.5.3   LSE participants

Until 27 October 1986, members of the LSE were divided into two distinct groups:

(a) *Brokers* took orders from clients to buy or sell securities, but they were not allowed to deal with each other, except under special circumstances. Brokers earned their living from the commission paid by clients on each transaction undertaken, and often they supplemented their income by selling related financial services such as portfolio management, research and investment advice.

(b) *Jobbers* dealt in and held stocks and shares as principals (on their own account), and they traded with brokers (executing clients' orders). Jobbers were not allowed to deal directly with the general public. They earned their living by selling securities at prices greater than those at which they purchased the securities.

This *single capacity system* was buttressed by strict rules to keep the activities of the two groups quite separate. In theory, this system should have provided investors with an efficient trading mechanism, as it was in the interest of the broker to seek the best deal for his client, given that commissions had to be charged on a fixed scale, and the competing jobbers should have ensured an active free market, irrespective of whether the investor wished to buy or sell securities. Also, by keeping the broking and jobbing functions apart, it was argued that the investor would be protected from the conflicts of interest which might have arisen had a single firm been holding shares and acting as adviser to and agent of the investor.

In world terms, both broking and jobbing firms were relatively small scale operations. Stock Exchange rules had made it difficult for members to bring in additional capital, with which to support expansion. Indeed, it was not until 1970 that Stock Exchange firms could become limited companies, but even after that time many brokers remained as partnerships; and in any event, despite company status, individual members remained personally liable for losses incurred by their firms, and directors still had to be members of the Stock Exchange themselves. Initially, a maximum of only 10% of the share capital of any firm could be held by any single outsider; this was raised to 29.9% in 1982.

5.5.4 The changing environment

By the early 1980s, the traditional broker/jobber system was becoming outdated. In practice, a broker might have difficulty finding even two or three jobbers willing to quote prices on particular shares, and it was not uncommon for deals to be set up through the broker's own office, with only a token use of a jobber's services in order to comply with Stock Exchange regulations. Thus, an increasing volume of share dealing was by-passing the floor of the Stock Exchange, and some by-passed jobbers entirely. This was particularly noticeable in respect of trading in international securities, the bulk of which took place outside of the Stock Exchange.

An important factor in the changing market conditions was a continuing increase in the importance of *institutional investors* relative to the direct holding of securities by individuals. By 1981, only 28% of UK company equity shares were held by individuals. Insurance companies and pension funds accounted for around a half of all shareholdings, with unit trusts and investment trust companies also being major holders of shares. It should be noted that this trend continued throughout the 1980s. By 1992, individuals accounted for only 20% of UK company equity shareholdings. The major effect of the Government's policies on privatisation and direct investment by individuals has merely been to increase the number of people holding shares, as opposed to increasing the power of individuals in aggregate as shareholders.

As the dominance of institutional fund managers grew, brokers found that they were dealing with increasingly sophisticated investors wishing to transact *increasingly large deals*. Moreover, the structure of minimum fixed commissions which brokers had to charge meant that large institutional clients were heavily overcharged relative to small investors, as rates were set as a percentage of the value of the deal rather than in relation to the work involved for the broker. In addition, as brokers could not compete for custom by altering their charges, many attempted to attract clients by offering research and other related services, either free of charge or at very low prices. Small private clients gained from these services, whilst large institutional clients often did not require the services, having their own in-house research teams. Clearly, the inherent *inefficiency* and *cross-subsidisation* of clients led to a poor deal for institutional investors.

The changing market structure also created problems for the jobbers. As the size of desired transactions grew, the books (i.e. the holdings of securities) maintained by jobbers should really have grown in proportion if the market's requirements were to be satisfied effectively. Unfortunately, many jobbing firms were too small to benefit from the new trend in activities, and the pressures felt on their capital bases made them less willing to meet the market's requirements. This was despite the fact that over the years many jobbing firms had merged and specialisms had been narrowed. Thus, the position of specialist jobbers was increasingly questioned, given that the securities markets can continue to operate so long as some institutions are willing to carry shares until ultimate buyers can be found. Similarly, the need for specialist brokers was also questioned, particularly as in some overseas financial centres the commercial banks dominate the buying and selling of securities. Clearly, once there is doubt in respect of the precise roles of Stock Exchange participants, the rationale for the Stock Exchange itself becomes questionable. This is especially so once it is recognised that London's huge eurobond market operates effectively without any physical market place.

5.5.5 Deregulation in the capital market

The pressures facing the Stock Exchange in the early 1980s did not only emanate from the external sources outlined in the previous section, they were also being generated within member firms themselves, which began to see the restrictive Stock Exchange rules as being a threat to their future prosperity. In particular, the rules had kept member firms much smaller than many of their overseas counterparts, by denying them access to substantial external capital, and by restraining their ability to compete freely. Thus, when the Stock Exchange agreed to modify its rules in 1983, it was not merely to avoid the imminent litigation which had been initiated against it by the Office of Fair Trading (under the Restrictive Trade Practices Act 1976). Possibly more important was the recognition that without the removal of restrictive rules the future prosperity, and even the survival, of some member firms was questionable.

The fundamental nature of the proposed deregulation of the Stock Exchange meant that it was not until 1986 that the new structure of operations was finally in place. However, in the meantime, there was a flurry of activity as non-member institutions began to position themselves in readiness for the opening up of the UK securities market. A particularly noteworthy feature was the interest shown in both broking and jobbing firms by *British and overseas commercial banks*, and other major international financial services organisations. Many such institutions purchased stakes in Stock Exchange firms, within the limitations still in force until the end of February 1986. After that date it became possible for outside institutions to take a *100% stake in Stock Exchange firms*. As a result of this development, many such firms soon lost their independence, and a significant number of major new securities businesses came into being. For example, Barclays Merchant Bank joined with de Zoete and Bevan (stockbroker) and Wedd Durlacher Mordaunt (jobber) to form a new company, Barclays de Zoete Wedd (BZW), in an ambitious move by Barclays Bank to become a major player in global securities trading. A similar move was undertaken by National Westminster Bank, which combined its subsidiary County Bank with Fielding Newson-Smith (stockbroker) and Bisgood Bishop (jobber) to form County NatWest. Many of the banking institutions involved in the formation of new securities businesses believed that the trends towards disintermediation in respect of corporate borrowing, and the increasing securitisation of debt, represented a major threat to their future profitability, which could only be effectively countered by their direct involvement in securities market activities. Furthermore, many argued that the ability to offer their corporate customers a complete range of banking and securities facilities, would be vital if they were to become leading players in what many now regard as global financial markets. Thus, it would appear that many larger banks saw their purchases of Stock Exchange firms as a critical element of their longer-term *strategic response* to the changing financial environment. Consequently, at least at the time, they regarded as a good investment the huge sums which they had to pay in order to acquire such firms; and the inflated salaries offered to key staff as a means of retaining their services for the newly-created businesses, were regarded as inevitable.

The significant amount of takeover and merger activity which took place during the mid-1980s led to a substantial injection of *new capital* into the UK securities market. This was seen by many observers as a crucial aspect of the deregulation process, thus allowing UK securities firms to compete more effectively on world markets. However, of even greater significance for the competitive position of the UK market, were the major operational changes for Stock Exchange activities which came into force on 27 October 1986. These changes, which became known collectively as *'Big Bang'* (due to their implications for the long-established practices of Stock Exchange member firms), included the *abolition of fixed minimum commissions*, thus introducing a competitive pricing basis for trading. The *distinction between brokers and jobbers was also abolished*. There is now a single category of member, namely the *broker/dealer*, who may act as both a broker and a market-maker. In other words, if LSE members so wish, they may take on dual capacity dealing. In practice, many firms retained their specialist broking role, and it has tended to be only the larger institutions, formed through mergers and takeovers, which have offered a full range of securities market facilities.

A further key aspect of Big Bang was the opening up of the *gilt-edged securities market* by the Bank of England. Initially, 27 institutions were granted licences to act as official primary dealers in gilts. (Formerly just two jobbers had accounted for 75% of market-making activity in this sector of the capital market.) These *gilt-edged market-makers* (GEMMs) deal directly with clients, and hence operate on a dual capacity basis. Unfortunately, the subsequent pressure of competition forced several of the GEMMs to withdraw from the market, although a number of new institutions have joined the market since Big Bang. Thus, at the beginning of 1993 there were 19 GEMMs active in the market. At the time of Big Bang, six *inter-dealer brokers* (IDBs) also began operations, in order to provide an anonymous dealing service between the GEMMs; and three new *Stock Exchange money brokers* (SEMBs) joined the existing six SEMBs in providing a stock-lending and financing service for the GEMMs. However, by January 1993 the number of SEMBs had fallen back to eight, and only three IDBs remained active. It should also be noted that the new market structure involved the introduction of telephone trading, with direct lines to major clients, and the closing down of operations on the floor of the Stock Exchange. The Bank of England also established the *Central Gilts Office* in order to provide computerised book-entry transfer facilities and assured payments arrangements for market participants.

Over all, the deregulation of the capital market was intended to lead to a much *freer competitive environment*, offering an improved service to both investors and those wishing to raise finance. As things have turned out there has been a great deal of restructuring within the capital market, and commissions paid by the larger institutional investors would appear to have been reduced significantly. The same cannot be said for small investors, the services for whom were formerly subsidised within the fixed commissions framework. However, there is now a *greater choice of instruments* available through a wider variety of institutions for those organisations wishing to raise funds, and hence also a greater choice for those investors seeking longer-term investment opportunities.

In relation to the LSE members themselves, fortunes have been somewhat mixed since the deregulatory changes occurred. A number of major international banks subsequently withdrew from certain sectors of the market, and many institutions incurred *significant losses* in the aftermath of the stock market collapse of October 1987, which led to a significant slow down in trading activites, as well as falling security prices in the short term. Indeed, the effects of the crash have made it difficult to determine the success of the market deregulation and its true implications for the operation of the UK financial system. However, it is likely that the LSE will maintain its *vitally important position within the UK financial system*, at least for the foreseeable future.

5.5.6 Investor protection

A potential problem which may arise within a deregulated securities trading system is that of *conflict of interest*. For example, when a single institution acts as both a market-maker in shares and a purveyor of advice to investors on possible share transactions, there is always the danger that the advice offered may not be totally impartial and in the best interests of the investor. Consequently, as soon as it became apparent that deregulation of the market was going to occur, a new impetus was given to the ongoing efforts to restructure the legislative framework relating to investor protection. In the event, the resulting *Financial Services Act 1986* goes well beyond the problems caused by potential conflicts of interest, and in fact covers the whole field of authorisation and operation of investment businesses in the UK, as well as giving broad protection to investors' rights.

Today, market participants must convince the authorities of their *honesty, competence* and, where appropriate, *capital backing* before being authorised to operate an investment business; they must adhere to strict *codes of practice* in relation to their dealings with the general public; and they must maintain *detailed records* of transactions and advice given, so that dealings are seen to be executed fairly. In this respect, the development of *sophisticated electronic dealing systems* for securities, with automatic logging of transactions, has become of great importance. This aspect of investor protection has been helped by the rapid transition to electronic dealing systems following Big Bang. Indeed, by the beginning of 1988 the bulk of securities trading had left the Stock Exchange floor, and was being undertaken via telephone and computer links.

5.6 THE EUROCURRENCY MARKETS

5.6.1 The nature of eurocurrency activity

Eurocurrency activity relates to *foreign currency denominated borrowing and lending at a wholesale level*. Thus, for example, a wholesale deposit in a foreign currency with a bank is referred to as a eurocurrency bank deposit; wholesale bank loans denominated in foreign currencies are eurocurrency bank loans, and so on. As such, eurocurrency activity may take place in *any country* in the world, and is not exclusive to Europe (although around a half of all transactions do take place within Europe). Also, *any convertible currency* may be used as the basis for eurocurrency transactions, although the euro-dollar dominates, accounting for around 45% of the total. Other important eurocurrencies include the euro-deutschmark, euro-yen and euro-sterling.

In general, transactions in the eurocurrency markets are for a minimum of US$1 million equivalent, funds are *unsecured* (with the lender depending upon the good name of the borrower), and often the assets created have a maturity of one year or less. An important element of short-term activity relates to *inter-bank deposits*, but tradeable instruments such as *certificates of deposit* are also issued. In respect of longer-term transactions, perhaps the most widely used instrument is the *eurobond* (some $347b worth of these were issued during 1992), although syndicated euro-loans were popular during the 1970s as means of providing sovereign borrowers with large amounts of foreign currency funds (more recently, the Third World debt problem has seriously undermined the attraction of this particular market for lenders).

5.6.2 The growth of the eurocurrency markets

Since the early 1960s there has been substantial growth in eurocurrency activities, with particularly fast expansion taking place between the mid-1970s and the early 1980s. Due to the nature of the markets, and in particular to the high volume of inter-bank lending involved, it is difficult to obtain precise figures for the size of the markets, although the Bank for International Settlements estimates that at the beginning of 1993 total oustanding eurocurrency bank debt amounted to approximately $7,350b, of which around 70% related to inter-bank claims.

Some of the factors which may be cited to explain the undoubted success of the eurocurrency markets are now of only historic interest. These include the removal of currency *exchange controls* in major Western nations during the 1950s and 1960s; the application of *direct monetary controls* in the USA, undermining the international competitiveness of US domestic banking markets; *political tension* between the USA and East European countries, encouraging the latter to hold their dollar balances with European banks; and the major *oil price rises* of 1973/74 and 1978/79, which resulted in a massive recycling of funds, through the eurocurrency markets, between the oil exporting nations and those countries facing massive international payments problems. However, other factors have maintained their importance through the years, and continue to encourage the massive volumes of transactions which still take place within the markets; although some of these factors have begun to lose some of their force in the face of a changing financial environment:

(a) It is generally agreed that the single most important factor explaining the growth of the markets has been their ability to operate on *very fine interest rate margins*. (A detailed examination of the determination of eurocurrency interest rates and their relevance for the foreign exchange market, is given in Chapter 7, at 7.9.) In relation to comparable domestic markets, the eurocurrency markets have often been able to offer *higher rates on deposits* and yet to charge *lower rates to borrowers*. One reason for this has been the very *large scale of operations* which has kept down unit administration costs; a further reason, at least until recently, has been the *absence of specific reserve requirements*, in respect of both liquidity and capital. Thus, banks were able to operate in the eurocurrency markets without the need to hold large volumes of relatively low yield liquid assets, and without the capital backing which would be required for similar domestic operations. Consequently, intermediation costs were kept low, and competitive pressures ensured that a significant part of the benefit was passed on to the customer, thus stimulating activity within the market. (Although it should be recognised that from the ultimate lenders' viewpoint, a greater return on funds will be demanded to compensate for the greater risk involved in eurocurrency market activities relative to normal domestic business.)

However, during the second half of the 1980s important steps were taken to *tighten regulatory controls* on international banking activities, including those falling within the eurocurrency markets. In particular, agreement between the Western world's major central banks to introduce common capital adequacy requirements by 1992 was bound to have a major impact on the markets. Indeed, the general progress towards the harmonisation of controls is believed to have been an important cause of the slow-down in eurocurrency market growth since the late 1980s. (For further details of the regulatory framework for banking activities, see Chapter 4, at 4.10.)

Nevertheless, even with identical supervisory requirements applied to eurocurrency markets and to domestic markets, economies of scale and other attractive operational factors would still persist, and hence the eurocurrency markets may still have a competitive edge in certain circumstances.

(b) The US dollar is still the most widely used international trading currency, particularly in relation to trade in basic commodities. Thus, the international business community has become increasingly accustomed to holding dollar balances (outside of the USA), rather than engaging in the switching of dollar earnings into other currencies, only to have to switch back at a later date in order to meet dollar-denominated commitments. The gains to be achieved are not only in terms of *reduced transactions costs* and possibly *higher interest earnings* on surplus funds, but also there is the *avoidance of exchange rate risks* (as there is always the chance that exchange rates may move adversely between the time that the dollar earnings accrue and the time that the dollar commitments fall due). This financial management factor undoubtedly continues to be of relevance for the provision of funds to the euro-dollar market; and the raising of dollar loans against expected future dollar earnings is likely to explain at least some of the borrowing activity within the euro-dollar market. In addition, it is possible to extend these ideas to other major currencies, such as the deutschmark and the yen, as they become increasingly used for international payments purposes. The continuing trend towards the *internationalisation of business and trading activities* can only contribute further to the support of the eurocurrency markets.

(c) The *inherent flexibility* of the eurocurrency markets has allowed *innovative forms of on-lending* to evolve, and many variants on conventional marketable instruments have been created, without the market participants having to worry about infringements of official guidelines. Bankers have been left relatively free to exercise their own judgment over the prudence of engaging in specific forms of transactions. Indeed, some types of transactions are *only accessible via the eurocurrency markets* for institutions based in some countries, and there are still some *tax advantages* in dealing off-shore. However, as the controls on domestic markets in most major Western nations have been *liberalised*, the advantages claimed by the eurocurrency markets have tended to diminish. In particular, the markets have suffered as a result of the wider array of business financing opportunities now available within domestic markets for both banks and their corporate customers. Since the early 1980s, significant developments have included the easing of banking regulations in respect of the allowable scope of domestic activities (for example, the removal of certain inter-State banking restrictions in the USA); the removal of restrictions on the issue of certain forms of securities by domestic companies (for example, in respect of the issue of sterling commercial paper by UK companies); and the general deregulation of domestic capital markets, allowing many banks to become much more directly involved with activities in areas of the financial system which were formerly largely out of bounds.

5.6.3 The recent development of the eurocurrency markets

Whilst the growth of eurocurrency market activity has continued unabated, there is little doubt that since 1982 this growth has been rather more modest than in earlier years. Furthermore, there have been significant shifts in the distribution of activities, both between geographical centres and between particular types of eurocurrency business. The causes of these changes within the markets are many and varied, and some proved to be only transitory phenomena which have long since ceased to have a direct impact on the markets.

In addition to the issues raised in the previous section, relating to the *regulation* of the eurocurrency markets and the *liberalisation* of financial markets in general, a crucial factor influencing eurocurrency activities has been the *Third World debt problem*. This has its roots in the 1970s and early 1980s when many less developed countries (LDCs) borrowed vast sums of money in the form of eurocurrency bank loans. Quite simply, in the early 1980s, when real interest rates rose as the exchange value of the United States dollar increased, the debt servicing burden for these countries became onerous (much of the debt being denominated in United States dollars and attracting market-related rates of interest). The world recession at that time, and the consequent collapse of primary commodity prices, forced many developing countries to suspend the servicing of their debt, and several threatened outright defaults. The effect of these developments was to *undermine the growth* of the eurocurrency bank lending market. Many banks are now most reluctant to provide new loans to heavily indebted LDCs, and it is often the case that additional funds will only be made available as part of IMF-backed rescheduling exercises. Indeed, many banks have already made huge provisions for the writing-off of LDC debt, and wherever possible such banks have attempted to reduce their exposure to the worst offenders amongst the LDCs. In this context, there have been various attempts to 'securitise' LDC debt held by specific banks, so that they might recoup at least some of the funds lent by selling the debt on international markets, often at a very heavy discount.

The LDC debt problem was also instrumental in pushing the balance of eurocurrency market activities towards transactions involving *developed countries* and *corporate borrowers*. In addition, the advantages for banks of being able to dispose of marketable instruments quickly in the event of liquidity difficulties weighed against the participation of banks in the syndicated eurocurrency loans market, particularly during the middle years of the 1980s. Indeed, the more general trend towards *securitisation of debt* has offered attractive opportunities for eurocurrency market participants to be involved with the management and trading of issues of securities, without necessarily having to accept the on-lending risks of taking debt onto their own balance sheets. Thus, for example, banks now act as agents for euro-commercial paper issues. Nevertheless, since 1987 there has been a major resurgence in the syndicated loans market, and whilst the bulk of this activity has involved the lending of funds to companies in OECD countries, 1989 saw a recovery in such lending to LDCs.

There is little doubt that the *inherent flexibility* and *convenience* of the eurocurrency markets, together with their *low cost bases*, have been critical in driving the *continued growth* of the markets. A further important factor was probably the maintenance of reasonably good rates of *economic growth* in many industrialised nations during the 1980s. More recently, the economies of the major Far Eastern countries have shown a notable immunity to the adverse economic and financial conditions which have affected other parts of the world, and it is likely that this has been instrumental in causing a shift in the distribution of eurocurrency activities in favour of the *Far East*. The importance of the eurocurrency markets in *Japan* and in some *Far Eastern off-shore centres* has increased markedly during the past decade. At the same time, other off-shore centres have lost their former attraction, and so there has been a reduction in the share of activities undertaken in these markets. *Western Europe* has also tended to lose out, with the UK's share of activities falling from around one-third of the world total to about a half of that value since the beginning of the 1980s. Nevertheless, Western Europe still accounts for around one-half of all eurocurrency market activities.

5.6.4 Participants in the eurocurrency markets

The *suppliers of funds* to the eurocurrency markets may be divided into three categories:

(a) *Official institutions*. This group includes central banks, public sector bodies, and international monetary institutions. These organisations were important providers of funds during the early 1960s and again during the mid-1970s (in respect of the recycling of the surplus funds generated by the major oil-exporting nations).

(b) *Commercial banks*. These have become increasingly important as channels for new funds entering the markets, with the banks effectively on-lending on behalf of non-bank customers. It is important to differentiate between this activity, which adds to the total volume of funds available within the markets, and the purely inter-bank transactions, which merely shift funds around within the markets.

(c) *Non-bank private sector institutions and private investors*. These include mainly multinational commercial and industrial companies, and wealthy individual investors.

Many of the advantages in placing funds on the eurocurrency markets have already been mentioned in the foregoing sections of this chapter, including, in particular, the availability of a wide range of flexible investment facilities paying returns which are generally above those to be earned on comparable domestic financial instruments. In addition, for central banks and official monetary institutions, the convenience of being able to hold reserves in the form of interest-bearing liquid assets, denominated in internationally-traded currencies, is obvious. For commercial banks, the eurocurrency markets provide an extremely useful mechanism for the adjustment of liquidity, and are a crucial aspect of asset and liability management operations for some institutions. In the light of the increased volatility of exchange rates during the past decade, the ability to manage the associated risks through the holding of eurocurrency deposits and marketable instruments has been of great significance for both financial and non-financial institutions. Indeed, as implied above, the ability of the eurocurrency markets to assist with the financial management of institutions involved in international business activities is likely to become an increasingly important justification for eurocurrency operations, as the traditional interest rate advantage is eroded by the tightening of the regulatory framework.

Turning to the *users of funds* from the eurocurrency markets, there are again three groups which may be identified:

(a) *Official institutions.* During the 1970s and early 1980s, central governments of less developed countries and certain East European countries borrowed massive sums of money from the eurocurrency markets. However, due to the subsequent debt servicing problems of many of these countries, the flow of funds to these particular users fell markedly. Consequently, until the beginning of the 1990s, when large loans were made to official institutions (independently of officially-sponsored support packages for developing countries), they were almost invariably the central governments of developed countries carrying high credit-ratings in international financial markets. More recently, confidence has begun to build in some developing country borrowers, especially in Latin America, and hence they have once again been granted access to new funds on a relatively large scale.

(b) *Commercial banks.* These institutions are very active in raising funds on behalf of their customers, although large volumes of inter-bank borrowing take place, which, of course, does not remove funds from the markets in aggregate.

(c) *Non-bank private sector institutions.* This group is now the main ultimate user of eurocurrency funds. In this respect large multi-national corporations are particularly important, raising funds via a range of eurobonds and short-term paper, as well as through the more traditional syndicated bank loans.

The general advantages accruing to users of eurocurrency funds have already been explained above, and include, in particular, attractive interest rates, the availability of flexible terms, and the possibility for issuing innovative debt instruments. In addition, central banks and official monetary institutions find it especially useful to be able to raise funds independently of political overtones or explicit policy commitments (which might be sought by official lenders). In the past, this has been especially relevant to many developing and newly-developed countries, where the need for borrowed funds is often high, but the willingness to accept political ties or strict conditions from international monetary organisations is low.

For corporate borrowers, direct access to large amounts of funds denominated in foreign currencies is often very useful when international trading or investment activities are planned. Also, it may be the case that there are official controls in force on borrowing or on capital investments in a company's parent country, which limit the availability of funds for international financial operations. Thus, the eurocurrency markets may assist with the by-passing of official constraints on international business activity (although, such restrictions are becoming increasingly rare, at least within the developed Western world). Commercial banking institutions may also take advantage of the eurocurrency markets in a similar manner; with their usage for liquidity adjustments and asset and liability management being especially important.

Therefore, despite the difficulties which the eurocurrency markets have had to face in recent years, it is clear that they continue to play a vital role within the international financial system. Whilst it is unlikely that they will return to the rapid rates of growth experienced during the 1970s, at least in the foreseeable future, it would seem reasonable to suggest that their inherent characteristics and advantages for specific groups of users will ensure their continued existence. Of course, the precise nature of their future development will depend critically upon the evolution of the individual domestic financial systems, and the extent to which there is further international co-operation in respect of the supervision of financial activities.

5.7 BROAD TRENDS WITHIN THE UK FINANCIAL SYSTEM

When examining the nature and operations of UK financial institutions and markets (as in Chapter 4 and in the foregoing sections of the present chapter), it is very easy to be overwhelmed by the variety of activities undertaken and the complexity of the details of operations. However, careful consideration of these activities and operations leads to the conclusion that, in recent years, there have been a number of broad trends identifiable within the UK financial system. Most of these trends are to be found within most of the sectors of the financial system, although in respect of individual institutions and markets, it is possible to find cases which contradict some of them. Nevertheless, recognition of these trends facilitates the appreciation of the recent evolution of the UK financial system, and hence the present chapter concludes with a brief summary of those trends.

5.7.1 Growth

Since the beginning of the 1980s there has been a tremendous growth in the size of the UK financial system. The portfolios of both bank and non-bank financial intermediaries have grown substantially in real terms, and there has been a large increase in the provision of non-intermediation services (such as financial consultancy, portfolio management, the provision of advice on investments, and so on). Within this growth, there has been an increase in the size of individual institutions, as well as many new entrants into particular areas of activity. There has also been a corresponding increase in the number of financial markets, and their real turnover has increased markedly.

5.7.2 Innovation

In addition to the increase in the volume of funds passing through financial institutions and markets, there has been a very high incidence of financial innovation. Many new forms of financial instruments have been devised, and new operational techniques have been introduced. These changes have arisen in response to customer demands and as a result of institutions' attempts to deal with a more volatile environment.

5.7.3 Diversification

There has been a high level of diversification of activities by financial institutions. Increasingly, many have been offering a wider range of services to their customers, which transcend the traditional bounds of activities for particular types of institutions. For reasons of profitability and longer-term stability, institutions have developed new products, and mergers and takeovers have occurred. Some institutions now offer complementary services within an integrated organisational framework, although for others the structure chosen is one of a loose grouping of related companies.

5.7.4 Internationalisation

Increasingly, activities within the financial system have become more international. This goes well beyond the provision of normal banking facilities in relation to the financing of international trade and payments. There has been a general internationalisation of outlook in the management strategy of financial institutions. Branches and subsidiaries have been established overseas, and foreign companies have set up operations in the UK. Also, trade in overseas securities has increased markedly, and the operations of financial markets have become more susceptible to developments within the financial systems of major overseas countries.

5.7.5 Intermediation, disintermediation and securitisation

In relation to personal sector activity, there has been a shift towards the use of financial intermediation. In particular, direct holdings of equities have diminished markedly in importance for individuals, whilst holdings of claims on financial intermediaries which invest in equities have risen substantially. However, more recently, for the corporate sector, there has been a trend towards the issuing of marketable securities rather than borrowing through bank loans; whilst other institutions have been willing to purchase such securities rather than place funds on deposit with banks. (This process of disintermediation is discussed in detail in Chapter 6, at 6.9.1.) Consequently, the markets through which securities are issued, and within which they are traded, have become increasingly important to both the short-term and the long-term financing of industry and commerce, and to the investment decisions of both the personal and the corporate sectors of the economy.

5.8 EXAMINATION PRACTICE

5.8.1 Questions

The following questions are taken from past examination papers, and are intended to give students an indication of the type of questions which they are likely to face within the topic area of UK Financial Markets. Students may care to map out answers to these questions before consulting the guidance notes in 5.8.2. Each question carries 25 marks.

(1) †(a) How does a commercial bank provide for liquidity? (13)
    (b) Explain in detail how the Bank of England ensures that there is always adequate liquidity in the banking system. (12)

(April 1987)

(2) (a) Discuss the role of the parallel sterling money markets in London. (15)
    (b) Is it still valid to distinguish the parallel markets from the discount market? (10)

(May 1988)

(3) Why and how does a bank raise funds in the following markets?
†(a) the retail market; (5)
†(b) the wholesale market; (10)
†(c) the capital market. (10)

(May 1991)

(4) Discuss the role of the following in the UK financial system:
†(a) Treasury bills; (8)
†‡(b) gilt-edged securities (gilts); (8)
†(c) eligible commercial bills. (9)

(October 1990)

(5) (a) During the 1970s, some of the most active borrowers in the eurocurrency markets were the developing nations. How have conditions in the eurocurrency markets changed since then for this group of countries? (8)
    (b) Identify the main borrowers and lenders (other than developing countries) in the eurocurrency markets, and discuss the characteristics that attract them to these markets. (17)

(October 1989)

5.8.2   Guidance notes

(1) (i)   The answer to part (a) of the question must focus upon the various actions taken by commercial banks to provide for liquidity. This involves more than just the *holding of liquid assets*. Do not forget *prudent portfolio management* (including the matching of assets with liabilities), and the maintenance of a *range of sources of funds* (including inter-bank and sterling certificates of deposit). It is also useful to mention the difference in requirements between retail and wholesale banks.

(ii)   Discussion of why banks need liquidity or official requirements in respect of liquidity is not required.

(iii)   Part (b) relates primarily to the Bank of England's discount market intervention. A *detailed* explanation should be given of how the Bank undertakes its bill purchases, and hence provides support for the *banking system*. Direct assistance to the discount houses and REPO agreements should also be mentioned.

(iv)   Whilst reference may be made to the Bank's liquidity guidelines for *individual banks*, it is important to explain their relevance within the context of ensuring adequate liquidity for the *banking system*.

Source of relevant material:

†Part (a)   Chapter 4, at 4.4.5(a) and (as background) 5.4.5 and 5.4.6.
Part (b)   5.3.3 and (as background) Chapter 4, at 4.10.4.

(2) (i)   The question relates to the sterling money markets, and therefore it is not necessary to discuss the eurocurrency markets or the foreign exchange markets.

(ii)   Part (a) requires a clear outline of the *nature* of parallel sterling money market activities, as well as a brief discussion of the operations of each of the major parallel markets.

(iii)   The answer to part (b) should explain the ways in which the activities of the discount market *differ* from those of the parallel markets, and hence should evaluate the extent to which it is valid to distinguish between the two types of market. The major *similarities* of the markets should also be noted explicitly.

(iv)   Detailed discussion of the operations of the discount market is not required, although clearly it is necessary to provide a broad outline of its functions in order to be able to compare and contrast the market with the parallel markets.

THE MONETARY AND FINANCIAL SYSTEM

Source of relevant material:

Part (a)   5.4.1 to 5.4.7.
Part (b)   5.4.8 and (as background) 5.3.1 and 5.3.2.

(3)   (i)   This question requires an answer which focuses clearly upon *how* and *why* a bank may raise funds in three different financial markets. It is not an invitation to ramble about banking activities or financial markets in general.

(ii)   Throughout, care should be taken not to confuse the *raising of funds in financial markets* with the *generation of profits* from the efficient utilisation of those funds.

(iii)   The answer to part (a) of the question should emphasise the raising of retail funds for *lending purposes*, and the establishment of *business relationships* with retail customers. The *main means* by which a bank may *attract retail funds* must be discussed.

(iv)   The answer to part (b) must differentiate between *retail banks*, which supplement their retail funds from wholesale sources, and *wholesale banks* which rely exclusively on the latter. The needs for funds for *lending activities, liquidity management* and *foreign currency matching* (via the eurocurrency markets) should be considered, and the *main wholesale sources of funds* listed.

(v)   The answer to part (c) must emphasise the importance for a bank of having *adequate capital*, and brief mention may be made of the *official capital adequacy requirements*. It is also necessary to consider the raising of capital by banks via the *issue of new equities* and *loan stock*.

Source of relevant material:

†Part (a)   4.2.6(c) (as background) and 4.4.2.
†Part (b)   4.2.6(c) (as background), 4.4.2, 4.4.4, 5.4.5, 5.4.6 and 5.6.4.
†Part (c)   4.4.5(b) and 5.5.1.

(4)   (i)   It is important to deal with each part of this question separately, and to *discuss the roles* of the instruments listed. It is not enough merely to describe the characteristics of the instruments.

(ii)   The answer to part (a) should draw attention to the role of Treasury bills in *financing short-term government budget deficits* and to their importance in *official money market intervention*.

(iii)   The issuing of gilt-edged securities to cover *long-term government budget deficit financing requirements* should be emphasised in the answer to part (b). Also, the importance for *monetary control purposes* of gilts sales to the non-bank non-building society private sector should be noted, as should official repurchases of gilts when *budget surpluses* occur.

(iv) In part (c) it is necessary to define the term *'eligible'* and to explain the role of eligible commercial (bank) bills in respect of *official liquidity and monetary policy operations*. The role of commercial bills in *company financing* should also be mentioned.

(v) Care must be taken not to confuse Treasury bills with commercial bills, and both of these instruments with sterling commercial paper or sterling certificates of deposit.

Source of relevant material:

†Part (a) 5.3, Chapter 1 at 1.6(c) and Chapter 4 at 4.3.2(a) and 4.5.1.
††Part (b) 5.5.1, Chapter 1 at 1.6(d), Chapter 4 at 4.3.2(a), and Chapter 6 at 6.5.
†Part (c) 5.3, Chapter 2 at 2.5.3 (as background), and Chapter 4 at 4.4.2(a)(iii) and 4.5.1.

(5) (i) The focus of the answer to part (a) must be upon how *conditions in the eurocurrency markets have changed*, since the early 1980s, for *less developed countries* (LDCs). The problems faced by the LDCs in *raising new money* must be emphasised.

(ii) Whilst the broad nature of the LDC debt problem must be mentioned, it is not necessary to discuss its causes or possible solutions to that problem.

(iii) The answer to part (b) must list the *broad groups of borrowers and lenders* (other than the LDCs) in the eurocurrency markets. Examples of specific institutions or countries are not required.

(iv) The *broad advantages* of operating in the eurocurrency markets should be discussed in part (b). It is not necessary to describe individual instruments or types of transactions.

Source of relevant material:

Part (a) 5.6.3 and 5.6.4 (paragraphs 3(a) and 4).
Part (b) 5.6.4.

5.9 FURTHER STUDY

For the past decade the subject matter of the UK Financial Markets section of the syllabus has been extremely topical. The free market stance of government policies, significant moves towards the removal of restrictions on competition in financial markets, Big Bang and the stock market collapse, have all served to keep alive academic, professional and media interest in the activities and operations of the markets. Consequently, a great deal has been written (and continues to be written) on all aspects of the UK Financial Markets topic, and a wide array of material, of varying depth and complexity, is available for those students wishing to develop their knowledge of the subject area. However, students should take care not to become enmeshed in the minor details of market operations, but rather should use the framework established within the foregoing sections of the present chapter as a guide to the issues which are of relevance for examination purposes, and as an indicator of the depth of study required.

An excellent source of information on developments in the discount market and the gilt-edged securities market is the *Bank of England Quarterly Bulletin*. Each issue contains a commentary on official operations in these markets, and changes in the markets' activities are quickly and accurately reported. Also, periodically, there are detailed feature articles on specific issues and developments within the whole field of UK financial markets. On a daily basis, the money and capital markets pages of the *Financial Times* provide a first rate insight into the ongoing operations of the markets. Relevant articles in *The Banker* and *Banking World* should also be consulted, particularly in respect of the broader evolution of the financial system.

The best single source of information on capital markets developments is, perhaps, *The Quality of Markets Review* (published by the LSE). *Euromoney*, together with its regular supplements, provides an excellent insight into the operations of the fast moving eurocurrency markets and international banking in general.

Finally, students are advised to remain alert to the overlaps which exist between the material embodied in the present chapter and other key areas of the syllabus; and hence should be prepared for examination questions which may straddle several topic areas. In particular, the operations of financial institutions (Chapter 4) have a fundamental influence upon developments within financial markets, and vice versa. Also, the direct relevance of the discount market and the gilt-edged securities market for the implementation of monetary controls and for interest rate determination (Chapters 6, 7, and 8) must be recognised.

6 THE MONEY SUPPLY

6.1 INTRODUCTION

This chapter examines the factors which influence the supply of money in a modern economy. From the outset it is important to appreciate that the nature of any discussion of the determinants of the money supply will depend crucially upon the definition of money employed. The narrower the definition, the smaller will be the range of assets which are included, and hence the fewer will be the determinant factors requiring consideration. In addition, it must be remembered that, as time passes, the groups of assets which are recognised by the conventional money supply measures tend to alter, in response to developments within the financial system. This evolution of the money substance merely serves to make the problem of explaining money supply growth increasingly complex.

A major problem relating to any discussion of money supply growth is in separating what might be referred to as the *'natural'* influences on the money supply, from the effects of *official monetary controls* which are explicitly directed towards achieving a particular monetary policy objective. Quite simply, the monetary authorities might not wish to see the rates of money supply growth which would be generated if the monetary system were left to its own devices, and hence they may seek to influence the creation of money within the private sector. However, the importance of official monetary policy and control in contemporary Britain is so great that it is dealt with in detail separately in Chapter 8. In the present chapter there is merely a brief introduction to the topic, which flows naturally from the discussion of the other determinants of the money supply. Nevertheless, the effects on the money supply of government budget financing and of the Government's exchange rate policy will be considered in the present chapter. The reason for this approach is that these monetary effects may be both significant and unintended. That is, whilst the authorities may utilise fiscal (budgetary) policy and exchange rate policy as means of influencing monetary conditions, there is no reason why this should be the case. These policies may be implemented quite independently of monetary considerations, and hence it is important to recognise their potential implications for money supply growth.

6.2 THE CASH BASE

In most Western nations banknotes and coin in circulation form a *relatively small proportion of the total money supply*, according to all except the narrowest of measures. Cash is literally the small change of the financial system, where the payments mechanism in value terms is dominated by the transfer of bank and building society deposits, through the cheque clearing system and via electronic funds transfer.

In the UK, coin is produced under royal prerogative at the Royal Mint. It is sold for its face value to the Bank of England, which is responsible for its distribution through the banking system. Any surplus over costs earned by the Royal Mint is paid to the Treasury. It is generally agreed that the issue of coin is a public service, and the amount in circulation has little economic significance. Thus, the overall supply of coin is largely dictated by public demand, although the authorities may occasionally attempt to influence the mix of denominations for production economy reasons.

As was explained in Chapter 4, the UK has a fiduciary note issue (which is managed by the Bank of England) and hence, in theory at least, it is *government policy* that determines the volume of notes in circulation. At the extreme the Bank could simply deny notes to the banking system, or it could seek to reduce the volumes already in circulation, either by selling securities to the private sector or by using its monetary control powers to force banks to place funds into frozen accounts at the Bank. However, for all practical purposes, the Bank has never denied notes to the banking system when they have been required, and it *accommodates* all seasonal fluctuations in the demand for notes. The only qualification to this position is that the Bank may attempt to influence the mix of denominations of notes in circulation, and the proportion of new notes to old notes, in order to keep the costs of note issue within reasonable bounds.

As cash pays no interest, an increase in the market rate of interest will raise the opportunity cost of holding cash, and, consequently, is likely to depress demand for this most liquid of assets. Thus, whilst it is quite correct to think of the supply of cash as being largely *demand-determined*, this does not mean that the supply is not affected by Bank of England monetary policy actions. In addition, as was explained in Chapter 5, the Bank is able to harness the flows of funds between the private and public sectors as a means of influencing interest rates, and hence monetary conditions in the economy as a whole. An important aspect of this mechanism is the banking sector's desire to hold minimum amounts of *high-powered (base) money*, which is effectively cash and balances at the Bank of England. Therefore, the importance of cash in respect of money supply growth goes well beyond its own direct contribution to the volume of money available.

6.3   CREDIT CREATION

In the modern economy, bank deposits and building society deposits (and shares) are money by virtue of the fact that people have confidence in the financial system, and, in general, are willing to accept the transfer of bank and building society deposits, via cheque clearing and electronic payment systems, in discharge of debt. With the sole exception of M0, all money supply measures are dominated by such deposits, and hence the factors determining their creation are *crucial* to an understanding of money supply growth.

Bank and building society deposits may be created by way of a *customer paying cash into his or her account*. However, this *does not add to the total money supply*, as the cash is taken out of circulation as the deposit is created. Thus, in effect, one type of money asset (cash) is swapped for another type (deposits).

The deposit creation which does add to the money supply is the sort which occurs when *a bank or building society makes a loan to a member of the private sector*. Thus, for example, if an individual is successful in obtaining a bank loan, it is most unlikely that he or she will be given cash, at least directly. The normal occurrence is that the borrower's current account is credited with the amount of the loan, or an overdraft facility is made available. The borrower is then able to draw upon this bank-created money, which is virtually as good as cash in the modern financial system. When the borrowing and lending transaction takes place, there is the creation of a financial liability against the bank (the deposit), which is held by the borrower in the first instance, and a financial asset, held by the bank in the form of an interest-bearing claim (the loan) against the borrower. Thus, the act of credit creation leads to an equal increase on both sides of the bank's balance sheet. The same effect is experienced when loans are made by building societies operating in the same mode (i.e. offering full current account services). This privately created money is sometimes referred to as *low-powered money*.

6.3.1 Limitations on the credit creation process

The credit creation process *cannot continue without limit*. Experience shows that a proportion of a credit-creating institution's deposits (whether the original cash deposits made by customers or the deposits created by the institution as the counterpart to loans) is likely to be *withdrawn* in cash at some stage. It is most unlikely that an institution's customers will wish to undertake all of their transactions via the chequing system or via electronic funds transfer. Therefore, it is necessary for all credit-creating institutions to hold *reserves of cash and other liquid assets* ready to meet withdrawals by customers. In addition, individual institutions may negotiate *lines of credit with other financial institutions*, which may be called upon should their own reserves prove to be inadequate.

The desired ratio of liquid reserve assets to total deposits for any given credit-creating institution will be influenced by its *past experience* of patterns of withdrawals of deposits by customers. It will also be influenced by the *risk aversity* of the institution's management. In selecting the desired reserve ratio, the *liquidity* of the asset portfolio has to be balanced against the commercial need to generate satisfactory *returns* from the business activity. Thus, whilst the holding of zero interest cash and low yield liquid assets is vital to the maintenance of customers' confidence in the institution, it is also necessary that sufficient funds are channelled into higher yield, but normally less liquid assets, in order to maintain the profitability of the institution. Cutting back the reserve ratio, in order to extend the level of credit creation, may raise the net return on the institution's portfolio, but it will also raise the *risk* that liquid reserve holdings will prove to be inadequate to meet customers' demands for withdrawals of funds. Whilst this occurrence need not be fatal, it might entail expensive emergency support in the short term, and may damage the business credibility of the institution in the long term. Thus, even in the absence of official controls, which may enforce minimum reserve requirements, prudent financial management will ensure that sufficient reserves are always held in order to *maintain confidence* in the institution.

Given the need for sufficient reserves, the next issue to be resolved relates to how much credit will actually be created. There are several dimensions to this problem. An important aspect is the *availability of reserve assets* (and especially high-powered money) for the credit-creating institutions to hold. This will depend upon how much of the total supply of such assets in the economy is pre-empted by non-credit-creating institutions and individuals within the private sector. Normal portfolio selection behaviour will probably lead to the holding of interest-bearing liquid assets as well as cash by these elements of the private sector. The implication here is that if credit-creating institutions are able to raise the rate of interest that they pay on deposits, they may be able to attract more of the total available pool of reserve assets. Ultimately, of course, the size of the pool is limited; and much depends upon the supply of cash and other potential reserve assets controlled by the monetary authorities. In this respect, as will be explained in 6.5 below, the Government's fiscal policy position, and in particular the size of the public sector borrowing requirement or debt repayment and the methods of financing chosen, may be extremely significant for the level of credit creation.

A further factor which affects the credit-creating potential within the economy as a whole is the existence of *leakages* of funds from the financial system. For example, the personal sector may wish to hold additional cash balances, which effectively denies reserve assets to the credit-creating institutions. Alternatively, funds may flow overseas for the purchase of imports or for investment purposes, and hence may be held by foreigners. Funds may also be used to purchase government debt instruments, thus leading to a transfer of deposits out of the private sector, which will again reduce the reserve base of the credit-creating institutions. These leakages are in addition to the normal day-to-day fluctuations in payments flows within the financial system, which require individual institutions to maintain liquid reserves for the purpose of meeting inter-institution indebtedness.

A credit-creating institution may also be limited in the expansion of its deposit base by an *insufficiency of capital*. As was explained in Chapter 4, at 4.4.5(b)), minimum holdings of capital relative to risk-weighted assets are vital for the maintenance of depositors' confidence in an institution, and, in addition, minimum capital adequacy requirements are enforced by the authorities. Thus, where an institution's capital adequacy is at the desired minimum, it will either have to raise additional equity or sub-ordinated loan capital, or be willing to retain profits within the organisation, if the level of credit creation is to grow further.

Assuming that credit-creating institutions are not constrained by an insufficiency of capital, it will be the interaction of past experience of deposit withdrawal patterns, the trade-off between liquidity and return on assets, risk aversity, the availability of reserve assets, leakages of funds from the financial system, and the possibility of inter-institution indebtedness, which determines the *minimum reserve ratio* desired by those institutions, and hence the *maximum credit multiplier* for the financial system. This multiplier indicates the maximum amount of credit which might be created on the basis of an injection of liquid reserve assets into the financial system. Thus, for example, if a credit-creating institution received a cash deposit of £1,000, and its desired reserve ratio was 20%, then the following balance sheet adjustments would occur if the full credit multiplier was utilised:

Period 1: £1,000 cash deposit

Liabilities		Assets	
Deposit (in cash)	+ £1,000	Cash	+ £1,000

Period 2: £1,000 cash holding used as reserve base for the making of loans to customers

Liabilities		Assets	
Deposit (in cash)	+ £1,000	Cash	+ £1,000
Deposit (created to cover loans)	+ £4,000	Loans	+ £4,000
	+ £5,000		+ £5,000

£1,000 of cash backs £5,000 of deposits, and hence the reserve ratio is the desired 20%. The credit multiplier is said to have a value of 5 (although credit worth only four times the original cash deposit is actually created).

It should be recognised that the modern credit-creation process outlined above does not require a sequence of funds being deposited with financial institutions, followed by a large proportion of these being lent out to customers, followed by these funds being redeposited, and so on. Rather, the sophistication of the financial system means that credit-creating institutions may utilise the whole of a new cash deposit as reserve base, and hence immediately create credit up to the maximum multiplier value.

In reality, the actual reserve ratio held by any given credit-creating institution at any given time may be above the desired minimum ratio. The reason for this is that in order for credit to be created, there must be a *demand for loans* from the credit-creating institutions. However, as lending institutions always seek to earn at least a minimum interest rate on their on-lending, in order to meet their profit requirements, a point will be reached where *the market for credit becomes satiated*. In addition, lending institutions are only willing to lend to *creditworthy borrowers*, and will prefer to hold excess reserves assets rather than take on undue risk of default.

Finally, it must be emphasised that the credit creation process described above is on the basis of the *free operation of commercial forces*. In practice, the monetary authorities may seek to interfere with the process by enforcing minimum reserve requirements above those thought necessary for commercial purposes, by dictating the nature of appropriate reserves, by setting lending and interest rate ceilings, and so on. Thus, credit creation may be limited by *official monetary policy actions*. Currently, in the UK, there are no such direct controls operating, although banks must maintain (cash) deposits with the Bank of England in non-operational balances, as a condition of authorisation by the Bank. Similarly, liquidity guidelines are laid down by the Bank of England and the Building Societies Commission as a means of encouraging prudent financial management. Adherence to these guidelines may constrain credit-creation relative to what would occur in their absence.

6.4 THE EFFECTS OF BANK AND BUILDING SOCIETY LENDING ON THE MONEY SUPPLY

As implied above, bank and building society lending in sterling to the non-bank non-building society domestic private sector will add to all measures of the money supply (other than M0), as new bank and building society deposits are automatically created as the counterpart to loans made.

The effect of the building societies making loans in their more traditional (pure financial intermediation) context is less clear, but nevertheless they still add to the money supply as defined by M2, M4 and M3H. This is because in order to make additional loans to the non-bank non-building society private sector (outside of the credit creation process) the building societies must either run down their cash holdings or (more likely) their bank balances, and hence add to the money stock held by the non-bank non-building society private sector, or they must attract new deposits of funds. These new funds may come either from the banking sector, in which case the money supply is raised as soon as the funds are on-lent, or from the non-bank non-building society private sector, which, in the first instance, alters the composition of the asset holdings of that sector, but then adds to the money supply when the funds are on-lent and ultimately redeposited with the banks or building societies. Sales of government debt holdings to finance new loans by the building societies to the remainder of the private sector would have the same effect on the money supply.

6.5 PUBLIC SECTOR FINANCING AND THE MONEY SUPPLY

6.5.1 Public Sector Borrowing Requirement (PSBR)

The PSBR relates to the difference between the total expenditure and the total receipts of the public sector. In this context, the public sector includes the central government, local authorities and public corporations. Public sector expenditure includes spending on defence, health services, social security payments, education, and so on. Public sector revenue is derived mainly from taxation on income and expenditure, local council tax and business rates, and the operating surpluses generated by public sector enterprises. Sales of public sector assets make one-off contributions to official revenue. To the extent that revenue does not cover expenditure, it is necessary for the public sector to *borrow funds*, either from the *domestic private sector*, or from the *Bank of England*, or from *overseas*. The amount of this borrowing, the sources of finance employed and the debt instruments issued by the authorities may each have a fundamental influence on the growth of the money supply. (Given its recognised importance, the M4 measure of the money supply will be used as the basis for the following analysis.)

(a) *Borrowing from the domestic non-bank, non-building society private sector*

This form of budget deficit financing has *no direct effect on the money supply*. This is because the excess of government expenditure over receipts is covered by *borrowing money which is already in existence* within the private sector. *No new money is created* by this borrowing, which normally takes place through the issue of gilt-edged securities and National Savings instruments, and the taking of deposits through the National Savings Bank. In effect, the borrowed funds are *recycled* to the private sector through government expenditure.

However, it may be noted that this form of deficit financing may have a minor effect on the holding of bank and building society deposits, insofar as the government borrowing/expenditure process redistributes funds between different groups within society which have differing propensities to use the services of financial institutions. For example, relatively better off members of society may lend funds to the Government, whilst poorer groups are the main recipients of government transfer payments. The latter groups are less likely to hold bank or building society accounts, and more likely to undertake the bulk of their expenditures using cash. In the short term, at least, this will tend to deny cash to the credit-creating institutions, although ultimately much of it will probably be recycled to them.

(b) Borrowing from the Bank of England

Normally, when the Government borrows from the Bank of England the Bank creates deposits which are credited to the Government's accounts in exchange for either Treasury bills or gilt-edged securities. The Government may then spend the deposits at its disposal, either by drawing newly created cash from its accounts and distributing this through various official agencies which deal directly with the private sector, or, more usually, by transferring funds by cheque or giro to members of the private sector. This latter occurrence will lead directly to a transfer of deposits from the Government's accounts to commercial bank or building society accounts at the Bank of England, as a result of the payment clearing process. In either event, *not only does the money supply rise by the amount of the government borrowing, but also the increase is entirely in the form of high-powered money*; that is, the total of cash held by the private sector plus banks' and building societies' balances at the Bank of England rises pound for pound with the Government's budget deficit financing. It should also be noted that the Bank makes available to the Government 'ways and means' advances in order to cover very short-term financing requirements. These advances effectively operate as overdraft facilities for the Government, which are paid off as soon as somewhat more permanent funding is available. Their effect on the money supply is exactly the same as that which occurs when the Bank purchases securities from the Government.

In addition to the immediate effect on the money supply, it is quite possible that government borrowing from the Bank of England could lead to *secondary increases in the money supply* as time passes. The reason is, of course, that the high-powered money created by the borrowing forms the ultimate reserve base for further credit creation.

(c) *Borrowing from the commercial banks and building societies*

The purchase of government debt by banks or building societies will *always add to the money supply*, as measured by M4, by an amount equal to the government borrowing. The mechanism is exactly the same as that explained in 6.4 above, which occurs when banks and building societies make sterling loans to the domestic private sector. However, whilst the money created by the lending process is *low-powered money*, which cannot itself be used as the basis for further credit creation, the securities purchased by the credit-creating institutions, as the counterparts to the loans to the Government, may be suitable as reserve base. Indeed, as the securities purchased by banks and building societies have often been Treasury bills and shorter-dated gilts, there is a reasonable probability that, if not immediately, then at some future date, the government borrowing may lead to secondary effects on the money supply as the credit-creating capacity of the financial system is enhanced.

(d) *Borrowing from overseas residents and in foreign currencies*

When the Government borrows *sterling* from overseas residents, normally via the sale of gilt-edged securities, there is a reduction in the value of funds that has to be borrowed domestically. The effects on the domestic money supply will depend upon where the sterling was originally held. Thus, if the sterling was held by overseas residents in *UK bank deposits*, then upon being transferred to the domestic private sector through government expenditure, there will be an *increase in the money supply* equal to the value of the funds borrowed. There is no reason why this transfer of funds should affect the credit-creating capacity of the financial system. However, if the sterling balances were initially held *overseas*, then not only would the domestic money supply increase by the amount of the borrowed funds, but also the *high-powered money base* of the financial system would rise, with clear implications for future credit creation. Of course, if overseas residents bought gilts using *sterling purchased from UK residents*, there would be *no net effect* on the money supply, as the Government would ultimately recycle the borrowed funds to the UK private sector via its expenditure.

The Government may also borrow funds via the issue of *foreign currency instruments* (including ECU-denominated Treasury bills and bonds), and may do so from private sector institutions and individuals, both domestically and overseas, and from official bodies, such as the International Monetary Fund and overseas central banks. The impact on the domestic money supply of government borrowing in foreign currencies depends upon how the Government uses the funds. Thus, if the Government's aim is to bolster the *UK's official foreign currency reserves*, the borrowed funds will be paid into the Exchange Equalisation Account (EEA), held at the Bank of England, in exchange for sterling. However, this does not mean that the Government's demand for sterling borrowed funds is reduced, as the Treasury still has to find the sterling used to purchase the foreign currencies by the EEA. In the presence of a PSBR, this sterling would have to be borrowed by the Government in one or more of the ways outlined above, with the associated effects on the money supply as indicated. Alternatively, the Government may borrow foreign currencies for the purpose of *supporting the value of sterling* by intervention on the foreign exchange market. The sterling purchased by the authorities through this mechanism may then be used to displace sterling borrowing, with the impact on the money supply depending upon the counterparties to the intervention transactions. For example, if the foreign currency is purchased by UK residents using sterling balances held with UK banks, there will be no overall effect on the money supply. In this case, the sterling proceeds are used to cover the Government's deficit spending, and hence are recycled to the UK private sector. Where the foreign currency is purchased by overseas residents, the effect on the money supply is basically the same as that explained above in respect of purchases of sterling debt by overseas residents, and depends upon the initial location of the sterling funds used in the transactions. It may also be noted that the selling of official foreign currency reserves for sterling would have the same impact on domestic borrowing needs and on the money supply.

(e) *Interest rate effects of the PSBR*

In addition to its direct effects on the money supply and the reserve base of the financial system, government borrowing may also affect money supply growth via its influence upon the level and/or structure of interest rates, and hence upon the *willingness of members of the non-bank non-building society private sector to borrow*. Thus, for example, government borrowing may add to the demand for borrowed funds within the economy across the whole spectrum of maturities, and so lead to a *general increase in interest rates*, other things being equal. This will tend to *depress the private sector's demand for loans*, and hence credit creation. However, in the short term, there could be perverse effects as corporate borrowers find themselves having to raise additional loans, in order to deal with cash flow problems deriving from high debt interest payments. Alternatively, if government borrowing is concentrated on longer-term debt maturities, this might tend to *raise long-term rates of interest* relative to short-term rates, and might lead to a crowding-out of business borrowing through longer-term debt issues. Thus, companies may *raise their demand for short-term finance*, which is primarily in the form of bank loans, in the hope of being able to re-finance their debt for a longer period at a future date, and thus avoid being locked into high interest rate long-term commitments. Clearly, this is likely to raise the level of bank credit creation, and hence the growth of the money supply.

(f) *The absolute size of the PSBR*

The size of the Government's borrowing requirement is also of relevance in determining the type of impact which it is likely to have on money supply growth. At a very basic level, the larger the PSBR, the more difficult it becomes to finance it exclusively through debt sales to the non-bank non-building society private sector, and hence the more likely it becomes that the money supply will be affected. However, as should be clear from the foregoing discussion, an isolated observation of the absolute size of the PSBR, even when considered relative to the level of the national income, is not enough to lead to firm conclusions on its monetary effects. For example, a given PSBR financed by one particular combination of sources of funds, may have less impact on the money supply than a markedly smaller PSBR financed in some other way. In addition the announcement of a projected PSBR may affect expectations of future economic conditions, and hence business confidence. This, in turn, is likely to influence the demand for bank loans and hence money supply growth.

6.5.2 Overfunding of the PSBR

To the extent that a PSBR is financed by the sale of public sector debt to the non-bank non-building society private sector there is no direct impact on the money supply. However, if sales of public sector debt to the non-bank non-building society private sector *exceed* the value of the PSBR during any given time period, there is said to be *overfunding of the PSBR*, and an overall *negative public sector contribution to the growth of the money supply*. Effectively, the authorities draw more bank and building society deposits from the private sector, as a result of debt sales, than they feed back into the private sector via deficit spending. The overall result is to reduce the amount of money available within the private sector.

During the first half of the 1980s overfunding was pursued quite extensively in the UK. At the time it was seen as a useful means of counteracting the effect on the money supply of excessive growth in bank lending to the domestic private sector. Unfortunately, this policy was not without *difficulties*, for in order to restore the high-powered money base of the financial system, and hence avoid undesired fluctuations in short-term interest rates, a large proportion of the funds withdrawn from the private sector had to be recycled by means of open market purchases of short maturity instruments, through the money markets. This operation not only created technical problems for the Bank of England, as it accumulated a very large volume of commercial and other bills, but also, and more disturbingly, it distorted the relationship between bill rates and other money-market rates, in a manner which tended to boost money supply growth. (This arbitrage problem is dealt with in 6.9.2 below.) In any event, the practice of deliberate overfunding of the PSBR was officially abandoned in late 1985. An example of the effect of over-funding on the growth of the money supply is shown in Table 6.1 (at 6.8), within the context of M4 for the year to 30 June 1985.

It is interesting to note that the policy of overfunding the PSBR is virtually indistinguishable from open market operations which seek to sell long-term government debt to the non-bank non-building society private sector, and simultaneously purchase short-term debt from the financial sector. The implications for the money supply of the closely-related national debt management activity are examined in 6.5.5 below.

6.5.3 Reducing the PSBR

As the size of the PSBR is likely to have important implications for the growth rate of the money supply, it would appear reasonable that the Government should wish to manipulate the size of the PSBR if it is attempting to bring the money supply under control. As it is unlikely that the PSBR would be used as an instrument for raising the rate of money supply growth, it is the ways in which the PSBR may be reduced which are of relevance for policy purposes. The main approaches which may be taken may be summarised as follows:

(a) *Tax revenue* may be raised by increasing, for example, the rates of income tax, VAT or duties. Clearly, for total revenue to be raised, it is necessary that the higher rates of taxation do not have proportionately greater adverse effects on the tax bases, i.e. on the level of earnings (for income tax) or total expenditures (for VAT or duties). Additional revenues may also be generated by the levying of higher National Insurance charges or higher council tax and business rates.

(b) Public sector revenues may also be increased through the *public corporations* in aggregate *operating more profitably*. Individual organisations may seek to raise their profitability or reduce their losses, through greater productive efficiency and the reduction of unit costs and/or the raising of sales volume and/or prices.

(c) *Public expenditure* may be reduced. For example, spending on major programmes such as health, education and defence may be curtailed. Alternatively, the rates of state benefits paid to the unemployed or to pensioners may be reduced; although the overall effect on expenditure will depend upon the number of claimants for such benefits. It should also be noted that reductions in public expenditure may depress economic activity and may raise the number of claims for state benefits.

(d) *Public sector assets* may be sold in order to increase the Government's revenue and so reduce the PSBR. The privatisation of British Gas and British Telecom, and the sale of shares in BP are examples of such asset sales in the UK in recent years. However, it should be recognised that in some countries privatisation receipts are regarded as a means of financing a PSBR, rather than reducing it, due to their one-off nature and the implications for future public sector earnings.

6.5.4 Public Sector Debt Repayment (PSDR)

During the 1987/88 to 1990/91 tax years, *UK public sector receipts exceeded expenditures* by a total of £26.4b, and hence the authorities had to cater for the effects of substantial PSDRs. The effects on the money supply of a PSDR are largely the *reverse* of those considered above in respect of a PSBR. Thus, for example, if the authorities utilise their surplus funds to repurchase public sector debt from the *Bank of England*, this will reduce the high-powered money base of the financial system (as the funds which are transferred from bank and building society accounts, in order to make payments to the public sector, are not recycled to the private sector), and hence the potential for future credit creation is also reduced. Where debt is repurchased from the *non-bank non-building society private sector*, there is no effect on the money supply, as the surplus funds are merely recycled to the private sector. The effect of debt repurchases from *banks or building societies*, in the first instance, is to reduce the money supply by the amount of the debt repurchased; that is, deposits with these financial institutions are run down by customers as the counterpart to the Government's budget surplus. The official repurchase of debt from the institutions merely alters their asset structures (with securities being exchanged for balances at the Bank of England, which makes good the initial reduction in such balances resulting from the net payments flows to the Government). However, there may be longer-term implications for the institutions' credit-creating potential, depending upon whether or not the debt repurchased is in the form of assets which may be used for reserve purposes. Debt repurchases from *overseas residents* will have a similar impact to repurchases from banks and building societies, if the funds are deposited with those institutions. If overseas residents deposit their sterling proceeds with overseas institutions, the effect is to reduce the UK's high-powered money base, with possible second round effects via the reduced potential for future credit creation.

A PSDR may also affect the level and structure of interest rates and hence may influence the demand for loans and credit creation. Clearly the *pattern of debt repurchases* will be critical to the interest rate effects, which may either stimulate credit creation (if rates in general are reduced) or depress it (if longer-term rates are reduced relative to short-term rates, thus encouraging long-term bond issues by corporate borrowers). Thus, whilst the existence of a PSDR may be of direct assistance to the authorities in their task of holding down money supply growth, it is possible that the indirect effects arising from the financing of the PSDR will not be quite so favourable. Table 6.1, at 6.8, shows the PSDR for the year to 30 June 1989, and illustrates clearly how its negative impact on money supply growth was largely offset by the repurchase of public sector debt from the non-bank non-building society private sector.

6.5.5 National debt management

In the UK, as in many other Western nations, there is a large outstanding national (public sector) debt. This debt generates an almost continual stream of maturing instruments which require funding; that is, replacing with newly-issued debt. The existence of a PSBR adds to the national debt, and to the amount of debt instruments which must be issued. A PSDR means, in effect, that an amount of maturing debt need not be replaced, and hence the total national debt is reduced. The flows of funds associated with this debt management activity, and the effects which they have on the structure of the outstanding national debt, may have important implications for money supply growth. For example, by replacing maturing debt by long-dated gilts, and by using similar instruments to finance an ongoing PSBR, the authorities may be able to reduce the volume of liquid assets within the financial system, thus limiting the potential reserve base for credit creation. They may also be able to affect the structure of interest rates, by appropriate sales and repurchases of debt, and hence affect the borrowing plans of the private sector.

However, the rate of turnover of outstanding public sector debt, and the ongoing levels of budget financing, may generate only slow changes in the overall structure of outstanding debt. Therefore, to speed up the process of debt management, the authorities may engage in open market operations, whereby the Bank of England enters the market and attempts to buy certain types of debt, and perhaps to sell other instruments drawn from official holdings. Thus, for example, the Bank may sell gilt-edged securities to the non-bank non-building society private sector. The effect of this action is to

continued on next page

reduce the money supply by the amount of the debt sale, as bank and building society deposits are drawn upon to pay the Bank of England for the securities. This also reduces the high-powered money base, as bank and building society balances at the Bank of England are reduced when the cheques drawn by the purchasers of the gilts are cleared. This form of operation should not be confused with the sale of gilts to the non-bank non-building society private sector as a means of financing a PSBR. In this case the borrowed funds are recycled to the private sector, via government expenditure, and, as explained above, there is little marked effect on the money supply.

It is important to recognise that the precise nature of open market operations, in terms of the forms of instruments traded and the elements of the private sector participating in the activity, is critical to the ultimate impact on money supply growth. Thus, whilst sales of gilt-edged securities to the non-bank non-building society private sector have an immediate negative effect on the money supply, the same debt sales to the banks or building societies would have no immediate impact. In effect these institutions would merely create new deposits with which to puchase the debt. However, whilst this would not affect non-bank non-building society money holdings, it must not be forgotten that such purchases of debt by banks or building societies will entail a transfer from their own accounts with the Bank of England, and hence the available reserve base would be reduced with clear implications for the future credit-creating potential of the financial system. A similar result may occur if gilt-edged securities are sold by the Bank of England to overseas residents. In the first instance there is no effect on the money supply, as foreigners' holdings of sterling are not part of any measure of the domestic money supply. In the longer term, if the sterling was initially held in the form of deposits with UK banks or building societies, the purchase of gilts by foreigners would result in a reduction in banks' and building societies' balances at the Bank of England, and hence the reserve base of the financial system would once again be reduced.

Finally, it should be noted that debt management policy need not be directed exclusively towards supporting official monetary control objectives. The operations may be used for stabilising financial markets, by accommo-dating changes in demand for various forms of official debt instruments, and there is also the underlying desire of the authorities to minimise the costs of servicing the national debt, in so far as this is compatible with other policy objectives. In addition, it is possible that debt management operations aimed at objectives other than the control of the money supply may have undesired implications for the growth of the money supply.

6.6   BALANCE OF PAYMENTS FLOWS AND THE MONEY SUPPLY

6.6.1   Balance of payments deficits and surpluses

In simple terms, a *balance of payments deficit* occurs when, over an accounting period, the total value of a country's current account imports and capital outflows exceeds the total value of its current account exports and capital inflows. Taking the UK as an example, a balance of payments deficit means that the *supply of sterling* on the foreign currency exchange market (from domestic residents wishing to obtain foreign currency in order to pay for imports or to make capital payments overseas) *is greater than the demand for sterling* (from overseas residents wishing to purchase UK exports or make capital payments in the UK, and willing to supply foreign currency in exchange). However, as the balance of payments must always balance in accounting terms (as will be explained in Chapter 9), *official financing* must cover this deficit. Basically, this means that *the authorities buy up the excess sterling* on the foreign currency market in exchange for foreign currency drawn from the official reserves (technically, from the Treasury's Exchange Equalisation Account held at the Bank of England). This operation clearly reduces the level of official gold and convertible currency reserves (unless, of course, the authorities simultaneously engage in official overseas foreign currency borrowing in order to replenish the reserves), and it also *reduces the amount of sterling held by the domestic private sector*. In addition, not only do bank and building society deposits decline, but also, as the sterling funds representing the deficit are transferred to the public sector, there is a reduction in the high-powered money base of the financial system. In short, a balance of payments deficit causes an immediate pound for pound *reduction in the domestic money supply*, and it also has longer-term implications for the credit creation capacity of the financial system.

When a *balance of payments surplus* occurs (i.e. when the total value of UK current account exports and capital inflows is greater than the total value of UK current account imports and capital outflows), the effects on the domestic money supply are the opposite of those outlined above. Thus, there is an *excess demand for sterling* on the foreign currency market, which is met by *the authorities selling sterling* in exchange for foreign currencies. The result of this operation is an increase in the UK's official reserves, and an immediate *increase in the domestic money supply* (as the sterling is effectively required for the purchase of goods and services from the UK or for capital payments within the UK). The high-powered money base of the domestic financial system is also raised.

6.6.2 The exchange rate regime

It is important to recognise that the above discussion implicitly assumes that the authorities are operating either a *fixed exchange rate regime* or a *managed floating exchange rate regime*, and hence that they stand ready to buy and sell currencies in the foreign currency market, whenever a balance of payments deficit or surplus begins to emerge. If this was not so, and the authorities instead operated a *clean floating exchange rate regime*, then there would be no official financing, and balance of payments flows would have no direct impact on the domestic money supply. Market forces would be given complete freedom to determine exchange rates via the interaction of the supplies of and the demands for currencies as deriving from international trade and capital transactions. In theory, there should be neither balance of payments deficits nor surpluses (in the conventional sense), for as the authorities are neither adding to nor drawing from the available pool of foreign currencies on the exchange markets, payments for imports (both current and capital) must be covered by earnings from exports (both current and capital). Thus, for example, if a deficit occurs on the current account, it must be financed by a net inflow of foreign currency through the capital account. (The mechanics of exchange rate determination are explained in detail in Chapter 10.)

Whilst a clean floating exchange rate regime precludes any direct effect on the domestic money supply of balance of payments flows, there may still be indirect effects, which might also occur within a fixed exchange rate regime or a managed floating regime. These effects may arise due to the impact on the demand for bank and building society loans of *interest rate movements* stimulated by the need for the private sector to finance its international payments. Indeed, the authorities may deliberately attempt to influence interest rates as a means of attracting foreign financial investment and hence foreign currency inflows. This form of policy may be pursued where the authorities are attempting to hold the currency exchange rate within a particular target band.

6.6.3 Sterilisation of the effects of balance of payments flows

The existence of a balance of payments deficit or surplus may have serious implications for the rate of growth of the domestic money supply. However, the above discussion of such implications implied that the authorities would behave mechanistically in respect of foreign currency flows, and within a fixed or managed exchange rate regime would allow them to influence the domestic money supply unimpeded. In practice this may not be the case, and the authorities may take deliberate actions to sterilise the balance of payments effects. Thus, for example, in the face of a *balance of payments surplus*, the UK authorities might undertake open market operations, and *sell gilt-edged securities to the domestic private sector*. This would lead to funds being transferred from private sector bank and building society accounts to the Government's accounts at the Bank of England, and hence would lead to a reduction in the high-powered money base of the financial system. In effect, the authorities would mop up the additional base money injected into the system as a result of the net inflow of currency through the Exchange Equalisation Account. In the face of a *balance of payments deficit*, the policy would simply be reversed, and

263

the authorities would seek to *purchase* an appropriate amount of *debt instruments from the domestic private sector.*

6.7 NET NON-DEPOSIT STERLING LIABILITIES OF BANKS AND BUILDING SOCIETIES

Bank and building society capital reserves (i.e. the issued share capital for corporate organisations or the initial owners' capital for mutual institutions, plus retained profits) are not included in any measure of the money supply. Therefore, when the volume of these non-deposit sterling liabilities alters, there are implications for the money supply. For example, if banks and building societies *reduce* their *non-deposit sterling liabilities, M4 will be raised.* Quite simply, if the institutions should distribute to their shareholders amounts greater than their current net profits, then in net terms funds are transferred from their capital reserves (which are not part of M4) to bank or building society deposits (which are part of M4). Conversely, an *increase in non-deposit sterling liabilities*, as would occur following a rights issue of shares or the retention of profits, implies that funds have been transferred from the non-bank non-building society private sector, and hence means that the *money supply is reduced.*

When banks and building societies make *sterling purchases of investments in other institutions and of other non-financial assets* (such as premises and equipment) from domestic residents, this transfers funds to the non-bank non-building society private sector, and hence causes the *money supply to grow.* Sales of such assets by banks and building societies to the non-bank non-building society private sector have the opposite effect. These sterling asset sales and purchases are taken together with changes in bank and building society non-deposit sterling liabilities to give a single value, referred to as the *change in net non-deposit sterling liabilities.*

6.8 COUNTERPARTS TO CHANGES IN M4

A commonly quoted identity which summarises the factors explaining changes in M4 is shown in Table 6.1. In the light of the discussion in the preceding sections of this chapter, the rationale for the counterparts identity should be fairly clear. However, the main points may be summarised as follows:

- If a *PSBR* is covered entirely by *sales of public sector debt to the non-bank non-building society private sector*, there is no direct effect on the money supply. Borrowing from the Bank of England, the commercial banks or the building societies will lead to an increase in M4 as new bank and/or building society deposits are created. A *PSDR* financed by the repurchase of debt from the non-bank

non-building society private sector will have no direct effect on M4.
- *Sterling lending by banks and building societies* to the non-bank non-building society private sector will always lead to the creation of new bank and building society deposits.
- *Sterling lending to the overseas sector* will only add to the domestic money supply if the deposits created are used to finance payments to domestic residents.
- If there is an increase in *sterling deposits held by the overseas sector*, then, in the absence of new bank or building society lending or official sterling transfers to the overseas sector, M4 will be reduced.
- *Net flows of currency* through the Exchange Equalisation Account will raise or lower the value of M4 depending upon whether the Bank of England purchases/sells foreign currency from/to the private sector.
- If banks or building societies raise their holdings of *net non-deposit sterling liabilities* this means that money is effectively taken out of circulation and the value of M4 is reduced.

Table 6.1   Counterparts to changes in M4 (£m)

		Year to 30 June 1985	Year to 30 June 1989	Year to 30 June 1992
	PSBR(+)/PSDR(−)	8,174	−12,612	17,453
−	Net purchases of public sector debt by UK non-bank non-building society private sector	−11,644	12,195	−15,824
+	Bank sterling lending to UK non-bank non-building society private sector	19,071	57,214	12,548
+	Building society sterling lending to UK non-bank non-building society private sector	14,430	26,702	19,662
+/−	External and foreign currency transactions of banks and building societies	1,603	−8,898	6,731
+/−	External and foreign currency finance of public sector	−2,448	1,073	−4,289
−	Increase in net non-deposit sterling liabilities of banks and building societies	−5,072	−14,715	−10,237
=	Increase in M4	24,114	60,959	26,044

Source: *Bank of England Quarterly Bulletin*, August 1989 and February 1993.

Table 6.1 shows the values for each of the counterpart items for the year to 30 June 1985, the year to 30 June 1989 and the year to 30 June 1992. A number of interesting points are clearly apparent:

(a) During the 1984/85 year the positive impact of the PSBR on M4 growth was more than counterbalanced by the higher level of public sector debt sales to the non-bank non-building society private sector. This provides a good example of the *over-funding* policy pursued by the authorities during the first half of the 1980s. The 1991/92 year produced a much larger PSBR which was *under-funded*, meaning that domestic public sector financing had a positive impact on M4 growth during that year. By contrast, had it not been for substantial *repurchases* of public sector debt from the non-bank non-building society private sector during the 1988/89 year, the large PSDR would have caused public sector finances to generate a significant reduction in M4 growth.

(b) During the three years shown, *bank and building society lending* was by far the most important factor causing M4 to grow. It may be observed that there was a substantial absolute increase in lending between 1984/85 and 1988/89, reflecting the relatively high rate of economic growth experienced by the UK over this period. However, the impact of the subsequent recession, especially on the demand for bank loans, is apparent in the equally large reduction in lending between 1988/89 and 1991/92.

(c) In aggregate, *external and foreign currency flows* had a negative impact on M4 growth during both the 1984/85 year and the 1988/89 year. By contrast, during the 1991/92 year, these flows contributed towards the growth of M4.

(d) The effect of banks and building societies increasing their *capital bases* was quite substantial during all three years shown. Had this accumulation of net non-deposit sterling liabilities not occurred, M4 growth would have been significantly greater than was actually recorded.

6.9 DISTORTION OF MONEY SUPPLY MEASURES

It is important to recognise that there are a number of factors which may tend not only to influence the growth of the money supply, but also to distort the interpretation of changes in specific aggregates. The operation of these factors is especially relevant when considering the implementation of monetary controls, as they may interfere with the relationship between monetary aggregates and private sector spending decisions. The most important distorting factors are disintermediation/re-intermediation, arbitrage and high interest rates.

6.9.1 Disintermediation and re-intermediation

Disintermediation refers to the situation where lenders and borrowers come together directly, and thus bypass the established financial intermediation channels. The disintermediation process may occur when there are *official restrictions* placed upon the free market mechanism (such as the application of direct monetary controls to bank and building society lending), which results in creditworthy borrowers being unable to raise the funds that they require through normal bank or building society channels. It is also necessary that there are individuals or institutions willing to lend funds directly to borrowers, albeit for higher rates of interest than they could earn on deposits with banks or building societies. The activity may be facilitated by the existence of agents whose role is to seek out parties who are willing to be involved with direct borrowing and lending. The sterling inter-company money market was formed on this basis in 1969. An alternative cause of disintermediation may be that the borrower possesses a *very high credit-rating*, and hence is able to raise funds more cheaply by going direct to lenders than by operating via a financial intermediary. The evolution of the sterling commercial paper market provides a good example of this form of disintermediation.

Irrespective of its cause, an important effect of disintermediation is that the borrower obtains the spending power desired, but as no funds pass through either banks or building societies, there is no change in the measured value of the money supply on this account. Thus, whilst the money supply as measured by the conventional aggregates may be under tight control, this may not have the restraining effect on the level of private sector expenditure that might be expected. In other words, the existence of disintermediation raises serious doubts as to the viability of money supply measures, which focus upon the liabilities of financial institutions, as indicators of economic activity.

Somewhat ironically, if the underlying cause of the disintermediation is removed, the ensuing *re-intermediation* may cause further distortion to monetary aggregates. Quite simply, as it once again becomes possible or commercially attractive for the parties involved in disintermediation to undertake borrowing and lending via normal bank and building society channels, these activities will be brought back within the bounds of the conventional money supply measures. In consequence, the values of these measures will be inflated, but there will be little impact upon the real expenditure decisions within the economy.

6.9.2 Arbitrage

Arbitrage (which is sometimes referred to as '*round-tripping*' in respect of money market operations) describes the process whereby individuals or

continued on next page

institutions seek to take advantage of price differentials between two closely related markets. Basically, an arbitrageur buys in the market with the lower price, and sells in the market with the higher price. Whilst this activity may be part of the normal market adjustment mechanism, its occurrence within financial markets may lead to distortions in monetary aggregates. A simple example of arbitrage is where a large company borrows from a clearing bank on overdraft at, say, base rate plus 1%, and then immediately on-lends the funds in the inter-bank market at a higher rate of interest. This opportunity for the company to make a profit on a pure financial transaction arises because base rates do not adjust immediately in response to changes in money market rates. Clearly, the possibility that arbitrage may occur provides an incentive for clearing banks to close the gap between their own on-lending rates and money market rates. But in the meantime the arbitrage leads to an increase in bank lending (and hence money supply growth), without having any corresponding impact on private sector expenditures. The company has borrowed purely for the financial gain which may accrue.

During the mid-1980s there was a certain amount of concern expressed that *bill arbitrage* might be having a significant adverse impact on the operation of monetary controls in the UK. This form of arbitrage involves a company drawing a bill of exchange and having it discounted by a bank. The funds raised are then re-deposited with the banking sector. If relatively low yields are available in the bill market, perhaps due to high levels of official bill purchases, then this activity is likely to be stimulated, and the values of the conventional money aggregates raised. If the deposit made with the banking sector is of the same maturity as the bill, then the company avoids the risk of adverse movements in interest rates during the period of the bill, as it knows precisely the cost of funds borrowed against the bill and the interest rate to be paid on the term deposit. Clearly, for the activity to be profitable it is necessary for the interest rate differential to be more than sufficient to cover the acceptance fee paid by the company and any associated transactions costs. This form of arbitrage, which once again inflates the money supply without having any direct impact on domestic expenditure is referred to as '*hard*' arbitrage. '*Soft*' arbitrage occurs where bill transactions are undertaken in order to allow the company to pay off existing bank loans. Effectively the company swaps one form of debt for a cheaper form, and as the initial bank loans are extinguished in the process, there is no effect on the money supply. Hence soft arbitrage is not a problem in respect of the interpretation of monetary aggregates.

6.9.3 High interest rates

Significant upwards movements in interest rates, particularly when they are largely unexpected, may cause serious cash flow problems for borrowers with outstanding loans charged at market-related rates. Consequently, it may be

continued on next page

necessary, at least in the short term, for such borrowers to raise additional loans to tide them over their period of financial difficulties. If new loans are taken out from banks or building societies the money supply will be raised, but as the funds are effectively required to cover the higher interest payments on outstanding debt, there is no implication for the level of demand within the economy. Clearly, this form of response to higher interest rates is likely to be of more relevance for corporate borrowers than personal borrowers. If it occurred on a large enough scale it could make the interpretation of monetary conditions difficult as the authorities seek to tighten monetary policy.

6.9.4 The practical relevance of distortions to the money supply

The extent to which the factors outlined above have led to significant distortions of money supply aggregates is difficult to determine. In particular, there is no easy way to separate out what might be referred to as the purely financial distorting transactions from the massive amount of normal business and personal transactions which do affect private sector expenditure decisions. Nevertheless, it would appear reasonable to suggest that the *high interest rate factor* is likely to be only relatively short-lived. The possible boost given to money supply growth in the short term will almost certainly unwind as time passes and borrowers adjust their financial positions to the higher cost of borrowed funds. Indeed, as higher interest rates are likely to depress the demand for loans in general, the apparently perverse effect on some borrowers with floating rate debt may merely reduce the short-term depressing impact on money supply growth.

On a number of occasions during the 1980s, the Bank of England examined the possibilities for *arbitrage* to occur, and came to the conclusion that, in general, it had not been a major problem in respect of monetary control objectives. The Bank found that when bill arbitrage did occur, it was often of the 'soft' variety, and also that most cases of 'hard' arbitrage tended to involve only relatively small amounts. The Bank's major concern would appear to have been that the markets might misinterpret money supply statistics if they believed that arbitrage was taking place, even if in practice any amounts involved were relatively insignificant.

The major distorting effect on money supply growth may have come via *disintermediation*. The rapid growth in new financial instruments and related money market activities, bears witness to the huge amounts of borrowing and lending which no longer appear on the balance sheets of financial institutions. The recent evolution of the sterling commercial paper market illustrates how *securitisation of debt* may prove to be attractive for borrowers, relative to normal bank loans.

6.10   INTRODUCTION TO MONETARY CONTROL

The identity showing the counterparts to changes in M4, as specified in Table 6.1 above, is extremely useful for drawing attention to the possible lines of attack which may be taken by the monetary authorities when one of their policy targets is to reduce the rate of growth of M4. Thus:

(a)   *A PSBR may be reduced*, or *a PSDR may be raised*, for any given level of net sales of public sector debt to the non-bank non-building society private sector. This policy may, of course, involve an increase in taxation or a reduction in the level of government expenditure.

(b)   The level of *net sales of public sector debt to the non-bank non-building society private sector may be raised* for a given value of PSBR. Alternatively, where a PSDR exists, *net debt repurchases* from the non-bank non-building society private sector may be *reduced.*

(c)   The level of *bank and building society sterling lending may be controlled* through the standard monetary control instruments (to be discussed in Chapter 8).

(d)   *Foreigners could be encouraged to hold sterling balances* (perhaps via interest rate incentives), thus avoiding their seepage into the domestic private sector.

(e)   A policy of *reducing a balance of payments surplus* or even *encouraging a balance of payments deficit* might be attractive as a means of holding down money supply growth, however it would hardly be a preferred option for most governments. Therefore, *sterilisation* of balance of payments effects on the money supply might have to be undertaken, which throws the issue back to point (b) above.

(f)   The authorities might try to *encourage banks and building societies to raise their holdings of capital reserves*, perhaps via the use of fiscal incentives.

It should also be recognised that occasionally, for policy reasons, the authorities may seek to stimulate money supply growth. In order to do this, the above-listed policies may simply be put into reverse, and hence the monetary control position relaxed.

Finally, it must be emphasised that as time passes, it is quite probable that the nature of the money substance in a sophisticated financial system will tend to evolve. So long as it is profitable to do so, institutions will continue to develop financial instruments to meet the needs of customers. If these instruments are thought to embody sufficient liquidity, they may become widely accepted into the category of near-money assets. Consequently, the forms of control used by the authorities, together with their range of application, will also have to evolve if the efficiency of the monetary control mechanism is to be maintained.

6.11   EXAMINATION PRACTICE
6.11.1   Questions

The following questions are taken from past examination papers, and are intended to give students an indication of the type of questions which they are likely to face within the topic area of The Money Supply. Students may care to map out answers to these questions before consulting the guidance notes in 6.11.2. Each question carries 25 marks.

(1)   (a)   What is meant by the term 'Public Sector Borrowing Requirement' (PSBR)?   (5)
      (b)   Assuming that the PSBR is zero, discuss the factors which could generate an increase in a country's money supply.   (11)
      (c)   Can the credit creation process be carried on indefinitely?   (9)

(May 1988)

(2)   (a)   Explain how a government's public sector borrowing requirement (PSBR) might be:
            (i)   reduced;
            (ii)   financed.   (16)
      †(b)   Why are the size and method of financing the PSBR of importance for commercial banks?   (9)

(October 1988)

(3)   †(a)   Define the measure of money supply known in the UK as M4.
                                                                                (6)
      (b)   Explain how M4 would be affected by each of the following:
            (i)   sales of gilt-edged securities to finance a budget deficit;
                                                                                (10)
            (ii)   the payment by companies of tax liabilities;   (5)
            (iii) an increase in sterling bank lending to the overseas sector.
                                                                                (4)

(October 1991)

(4)   (a)   Discuss the factors which cause the M4 money supply aggregate to grow.   (17)
      (b)   To what extent have each of the factors you have identified in (a) been responsible in recent years for causing M4 growth? (8)

(May 1991)

(5)   (a)   What are the main instruments of finance available to:
            †(i)   UK companies;   (6)

(ii)   the UK Government?   (4)

(b)   How does the use of each of these instruments affect the level of money supply (M4)?   (15)

(October 1992)

6.11.2 Guidance notes

(1) (i)   This question relates to *general concepts* and *theoretical issues*, and hence details on the current position in the UK or any other country in respect of the PSBR and the level of credit creation are not required.

    (ii)   Part (a) requires a *full definition of the PSBR*, and not simply general comments on central government borrowing.

    (iii)   Part (b) should be interpreted in terms of the PSBR being held at zero throughout, and hence the factors which may cause the money supply to increase in the *absence of any net change in outstanding public sector debt* should be identified.

    (iv)   Attention must be focused upon the fundamental factors affecting money supply growth, such as *bank and building society sterling lending* and *foreign currency flows*. It is also acceptable to mention *national debt funding policy* in this context. Detailed discussion of the credit-creation process is not required.

    (v)   In respect of part (c), it must be remembered that there are factors other than *official constraints* limiting credit creation. In particular a *liquid reserve assets base* is vital to the process, *leakages* from the financial system may occur, and there must be the requisite *demand for credit*.

Source of relevant material:

Part (a) 6.5.1 (paragraph 1).

Part (b) 6.8 (the counterparts identity provides a useful starting point), 6.3 (for background information), 6.4, 6.5.5, 6.6, 6.7 and 6.10.

Part (c) 6.3.1.

(2) (i)   Reducing the PSBR involves *raising government revenues* and/or *reducing government expenditures*. In part (a)(i), it is necessary to outline the ways in which this may be done, giving specific examples of revenues and expenditures.

    (ii)   Do not confuse the ways in which a PSBR may be *reduced* (part (a)(i)) with the ways in which a *given* PSBR may be *financed* (part (a)(ii)). The latter requires a discussion of the sources of borrowed funds and the instruments which may be utilised by the Government.

    (iii)   There is no need to discuss government policy on the PSBR or the progress of the PSBR in recent years; neither is anything required on the monetary control issue.

(iv) The emphasis in part (b) should be placed upon the *direct effects on commercial banks' balance sheets* of the PSBR, with particular attention paid to the implications of a large PSBR and to the sources of funds and instruments issued. However, it is quite acceptable to mention briefly the more *general effects* on the economy of the PSBR, so long as the implications of these effects for the commercial banks are made clear.

Source of relevant material:

Part (a)(i)   6.5.3.
Part (a)(ii)   6.5.1.
†Part (b)   6.5.1 and Chapter 4 at 4.4.6(b) (paragraphs 3 and 5).

(3) (i)   Part (a) requires a *precise definition of M4*. There is no need to discuss the definition or to comment upon the factors affecting the growth of M4.
     (ii) In the answer to part (b) it is necessary to explain how each of the three events listed affects the value of M4. It is not necessary to discuss the background to the events listed.
     (iii) The answer to part (b)(i) must recognise the different implications for M4 depending upon *who purchases the securities* (within the domestic private sector and the overseas sector). Consideration must be given to the impact of the sale of securities together with the associated government *budget deficit expenditure.*
     (iv) In part (b)(ii) the payment of tax liabilities must be taken in isolation. This involves the transfer of funds from the private sector to the government sector, and hence the effect on M4 depends upon whether payment is made from *existing bank accounts* (M4 being reduced) or from *newly-created bank loans* (M4 is unaffected).
     (v)   All sterling bank lending adds to total sterling bank deposits. However, sterling lending to the *overseas sector*, as specified in part (b)(iii), has no effect on M4 unless the funds flow back to the *domestic non-bank non-building society private sector.*

Source of relevant material:

†Part (a)   Chapter 1, at 1.8.
Part (b)(i)   6.5.1 (a) to (d).
Part (b)(ii)   6.4 and (as background) 6.5.1 (paragraph 1), 6.5.3 and 6.8.
Part (b)(iii) 6.4, 6.6.1 and 6.8.

(4) (i)   It is important to note that part (a) of this question relates to the factors which *in theory may cause M4 to grow*, whereas part (b) requires comments on the factors that have *caused M4 to grow in practice* in recent years.

(ii) A good starting point for part (a) of this question is the *M4 counterparts identity*. This effectively provides a checklist of the factors which should be *discussed* in respect of the growth of M4.

(iii) In part (b) it is necessary only to identify the factors that have *caused M4 to grow in recent years*, and to comment briefly on their *relative importance*. There is no need to examine the reasons for the factors themselves occurring.

(iv) Discussion of official monetary policy and controls is not required.

Source of relevant material:

Part (a) 6.8 (counterparts identity as a useful starting point), 6.4, 6.5.1, 6.5.5, 6.6.1 and 6.7.

Part (b) 6.8.

(5) (i)   Part (a) of this question merely requires a *listing of the main instruments* of finance *available* to UK companies and to the UK Government. For full marks, mention must be made of money market instruments, capital market instruments and bank finance in respect of companies, and both short-term and long-term debt issues, including National Savings instruments, in respect of the Government. It is acceptable to include taxation as a means of government financing in this context, along with the standard deficit financing instruments.

(ii) In part (a) it is not necessary to discuss the sources of finance (that is, the purchasers of the instruments).

(iii) The extent to which the various instruments are used in practice is not relevant to this question.

(iv) The answer to part (b) requires *explanation* of the impact on M4 of using each of the instruments identified in (a). In respect of company financing, the key factor is whether or not *new bank or building society deposits are created* as part of the financing process, recognising that sterling funds held by *overseas residents* may be used for the purchase of instruments. For government financing, the *type of purchaser* of the instruments is of crucial significance, and especial care must be taken in respect of *overseas purchasers* and *foreign currency borrowing*.

(v)   In relation to the impact on M4 of government financing, the answer must make clear whether or not the effects of the *associated deficit spending* are included.

Source of relevant material:

Part (a)   †(i)   Chapter 2, at 2.5, 2.6 and 2.7.1.
Part (a)   (ii)   6.5.1.
Part (b)   6.3 (for background information), 6.4, 6.5.1 (a) to (d), 6.5.5 and 6.8.

6.12 FURTHER STUDY

As the contribution to UK money supply growth from each of the determinant factors may alter over time, it is useful to keep up-to-date with broad trends in the government sector financing position, bank and building society lending, and the overall balance of payments position. The Economic Commentary in the *Bank of England Quarterly Bulletin* and the financial pages of the quality press are useful in this respect, as are relevant articles in *Banking World, The Banker*, and *The Economist*.

For examination purposes, the most important requirement is a broad understanding of the major factors which influence money supply growth, and hence an appreciation of the nature of the problem faced by the authorities in attempting to control the money supply. Monetary control issues are examined in detail in Chapter 8. Students should also recognise the links between changes in the money supply and changes in other major economic variables such as inflation, interest rates, national output and the balance of payments, as discussed in Chapters 1, 7, 8, and 9 respectively.

7 INTEREST RATES

7.1 THE NATURE OF INTEREST RATES

7.1.1 The central role of interest rates within the financial system

Interest rates have a critical role in the financial intermediation process within the modern financial system. Indeed, almost every *borrowing and lending transaction* involves an interest payment being made in some way or other. Consequently, an understanding of interest rate determination is extremely important for the study of monetary and financial activities. Unfortunately, there is a tendency for commentaries on economic developments, especially those given in the popular media, to refer to 'the rate of interest', or, at best, 'the level of interest rates'. The use of these phrases can only serve to mislead those who are making serious efforts to study the operation of the monetary and financial system. Even a cursory glance at the Money Markets page of the *Financial Times* illustrates graphically the vast array of interest rates to be found in the modern economy, and the rates reported in this publication represent only a small fraction of the total number which actually exist within the UK financial system.

The present chapter examines in detail the factors which influence the *general level of interest rates*, the determination of the *pattern of rates* and the *relationship between the different rates* within the economy. From the outset it is important to appreciate that the interest rate topic is relatively complex, and has significant linkages with other key areas of study such as the operations of financial intermediaries, monetary policy and control and exchange rate determination. Also, it should be recognised that whilst a clear understanding of the theory of interest rate determination is most desirable, a full appreciation of interest rates can only be achieved by relating the theoretical concepts to the *operation of the modern financial system*. Therefore, this chapter also attempts to explain how real world monetary and financial events have influenced (and are continuing to influence) interest rate levels and structures, and how changes in interest rates may themselves have fundamental implications for other major economic variables, and for the operations of banks.

7.1.2 Definition of an interest rate

An interest rate is a price established by the interaction of the supply of and the demand for future claims on resources. Prospective borrowers wish to

279

obtain resources today, and are willing to offer in exchange claims against themselves at a future date (i.e. they are willing to provide a supply of future claims). Prospective lenders have resources available today which they are willing to give up in exchange for claims on resources at a future date (i.e. they provide a demand for future claims). The interest rate is effectively the price at which these claims change hands. It is only if the lender is to be repaid, at a future date, a claim to resources of an exactly equal value to the claim originally given up, that the rate of interest is zero. In general, interest rates are positive, and hence the lender receives, at a future date, claims to resources in excess of the amount initially lent out to the borrower.

There are three related reasons why interest rates are normally positive:

(a) *The lender requires compensation for giving up current consumption possibilities.* Human nature tends to favour consumption in the current period, rather than at some time in the future, although individuals will tend to vary in respect of their time preference. However, it should also be recognised that people may wish to abstain from current consumption in order to build up sufficient financial claims to be able to make a relatively expensive purchase at a future date.

(b) *The lender requires compensation for giving up liquidity.* Although the prospective lender has more funds available than are required for current consumption purposes, the fact that these funds are held in money form means that immediate purchasing power is retained. However, as soon as the funds are lent, the lender's financial wealth becomes less liquid. Indeed, if a fixed term loan is made, the funds may be quite illiquid until the time that the loan matures. Consequently, the interest payment offers some recompense for the loss of convenience experienced by the lender.

(c) *The lender requires compensation for the risk attached to lending.* When funds are lent, there is always some risk that the borrower may default on interest payments and/or repayment of principal. When a number of loans are made, either simultaneously or over a period of time, the losses arising from occasional defaults may be covered by charging appropriate rates of interest on all loans made. Indeed, even where the possibility of default is negligible, for example when government debt instruments are purchased, the lender may still incur losses if the debt has to be liquidated at a time when market prices are relatively low. Thus, interest payments help to cover the possible capital losses which may be experienced if the lender wishes to retrieve his or her funds prior to the maturity of the debt instruments purchased.

7.2 REAL AND NOMINAL RATES OF INTEREST

7.2.1 Definitions

A *nominal* rate of interest is the actual money rate paid (or received) on a financial liability (or asset). A *real* rate of interest is a nominal rate adjusted to take account of the effects of *inflation*. Thus, for example, a building society share account may pay a nominal interest rate of 8% per annum. However, the real return on an investment in this account will only be 8% if the purchasing power of money remains constant over the period of the investment, i.e. the real return will only be equal to the nominal return if there is a zero rate of inflation. As soon as inflation occurs, the purchasing power of money falls, and hence the real return falls below the nominal return. For example, if the rate of inflation over the period of the investment quoted above averages 6% per annum, the real rate of interest received will be only 2% per annum. In other words, three-quarters of the nominal return on the investment is required simply to make good the lost purchasing power on the principal sum invested. If the rate of inflation should have an average level above 8% per annum, then the real return on the investment would be negative, as the nominal interest payment would be insufficient to maintain its real capital value.

7.2.2 Measuring the real rate of interest

As implied above, measuring the real rate of interest for a past period presents no major problem. It is merely necessary to choose an appropriate *price index*, and then 'deflate' the actual nominal rate of interest paid. As explained in Chapter 1, however, price indices are formulated on the basis of samples of prices of particular goods and services in predetermined quantities, and there can be different price indices depending upon the base of sample components chosen. Therefore, it is important to appreciate that there are no definitive measures of real rates of interest, only *reasonably adequate approximations*.

A major problem in dealing with real rates of interest is that for investment purposes it is the real rate of interest that an asset *will* pay in the future which is of relevance. However, for a given fixed nominal rate of interest, future real rates can only be *expected* rates, as the ultimate outcome will, of course, depend upon future rates of inflation, which are extremely difficult to predict accurately, especially into the longer term. Thus, if expectations turn out to be over-optimistic in respect of the rate of inflation, funds may be lent out at a fixed nominal rate of interest which proves to be too low to protect the real value of the principal lent.

One way for the lender to gain some protection for the real return on his investment may be to lend the funds at a *market-related rate of interest*. Experience has shown that market rates of interest tend to reflect movements in the rate of inflation, and hence a higher than expected rate of inflation may be compensated for by a higher than expected rate of interest. Unfortunately, as illustrated by the inter-bank rates shown in Table 7.1 at 7.4, the evidence would suggest that floating rates do not guarantee a positive real return in all time periods. The reason for this is quite simply that factors other than the rate of inflation also influence the level of nominal interest rates, and these factors may alter as the rate of inflation changes.

The only way for the uncertainty over the real rate of return on funds lent out to be removed is by the use of *indexation*. This concept was discussed in Chapter 1, and as will be recalled the principal sum is linked to an appropriate price index, so that the amount eventually repaid has the same purchasing power as the amount initially borrowed. An interest payment is then made on the indexed principal sum, thus guaranteeing a real return (notwithstanding, of course, the possibility of outright default on the loan). This guaranteed real return, which is offered by the British Government on certain issues of gilt-edged securities and National Savings Certificates, transforms the risk associated with the return into one related to the nominal amount to be paid and received.

7.3 THE GENERAL LEVEL OF INTEREST RATES

7.3.1 Theories on the general level of interest rates

There are two major theories which seek to explain the general level of interest rates: the *classical (loanable funds) theory* and the *Keynesian (liquidity preference) theory*. It must be emphasised that whilst these two theories appear to take markedly different approaches to the problem of interest rate determination, in fact they may be reconciled fairly easily in terms of the time horizon to which they apply. In addition, it should be recognised that the theories are concerned solely with the overall level of rates and changes in the level over time; they do not deal with the patterns of rates which may be found at any given point in time.

7.3.2 The classical (loanable funds) theory

The classical theory focuses upon the *real* rate of interest, and argues that its level is determined by the interaction of the supply of and the demand for

continued on next page

loanable funds. *The supply of loanable funds* is determined by the level of saving in the economy. It is argued that, other things being equal, the higher the rate of interest the greater is the opportunity cost of consuming goods and services today (i.e. the greater is the amount of future interest earnings which have to be given up), and hence the higher the level of saving is likely to be. *The demand for loanable funds* depends upon the level of desired capital investment within the economy. If people wish to invest more than the amount of their own surplus income (after consumption) they must borrow, and it is argued that the higher the rate of interest the greater is the cost of borrowed funds, and hence the lower the level of investment is likely to be. These relationships are illustrated in Figure 7.1.

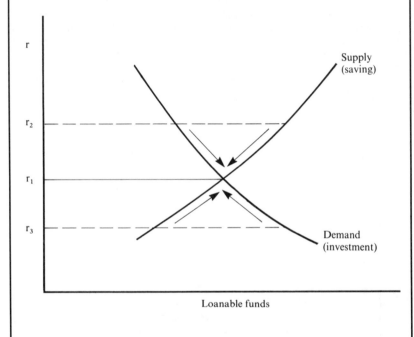

Figure 7.1   Supply of and demand for loanable funds

In relation to Figure 7.1, it is only at a rate of interest of r_1 that the demand for and the supply of loanable funds are in equilibrium. If the rate of interest was at, say, r_2, there would be an excess supply of loanable funds, and it is argued that market forces would push down the 'price' of these funds until the market was cleared. As the rate of interest falls towards r_1, the amount that people wish to save decreases, whilst there is an increase in the demand

continued on next page

for funds as marginal investment projects became increasingly attractive. Conversely, if the rate of interest was at, say, r_3, there would be an excess demand for loanable funds, and as prospective borrowers vied with each other for the available supply, the rate of interest would be pushed upwards, towards r_1. As this happened, the supply of funds on the market would increase.

According to the classical theory, it is only if there are changes in the real economic factors, which determine the underlying relationships between interest rates and saving, and interest rates and investment, that the equilibrium real rate of interest will alter. Thus, for example, if attitudes towards thrift within society alter, and people wish to save a larger amount of their income at every rate of interest, the supply curve for loanable funds will shift to the right, and the equilibrium real rate of interest will fall. This is illustrated in Figure 7.2. Alternatively, technological advances may raise the productivity of capital investment, thus making potential investment projects more profitable, and hence raising the demand for loanable funds at every rate of interest. As Figure 7.3 shows, the consequent rightwards movement of the demand for loanable funds curve has the effect of raising the equilibrium real rate of interest.

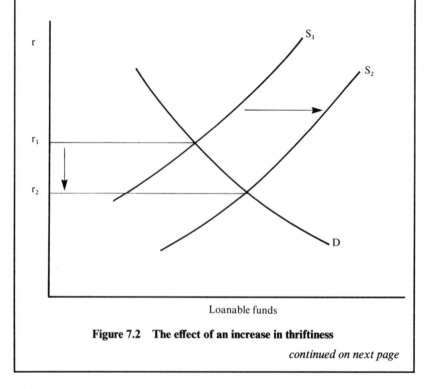

Loanable funds

Figure 7.2   The effect of an increase in thriftiness

continued on next page

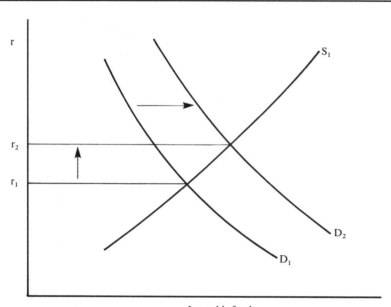

Loanable funds

Figure 7.3   The effect of an increase in capital productivity

It should be noted that the classical theory has no explicit role for the money supply. The theory argues that changes in the money supply affect only the absolute level of prices, and have no effect on real variables such as consumption and investment. Thus, if the money supply is increased, it is assumed that the additional liquidity created will be absorbed quickly and completely into the day-to-day transactions which take place at a higher price level (as was explained in Chapter 1). Therefore, changes in the money supply have no effect on the real rate of interest, unless, of course, the smooth adjustment mechanisms of the classical system fail.

7.3.3   The Keynesian (liquidity preference) theory

The Keynesian theory argues that it is the supply of and the demand for liquidity (or money, in the simplest version of the theory) which determines the level of interest rates. The rate of interest is seen as being the price which someone must pay if they wish to obtain liquidity (money) via borrowing; it is also the opportunity cost faced by someone who wishes to hold liquidity (money). Thus, the higher the general level of interest rates, the greater is the

continued on next page

return which will be forgone by holding zero-interest money (which is perfectly liquid), and hence the more willing wealth holders will be to lend the funds (converting their assets into a less liquid form). In effect, the cost of convenience related to the holding of immediate purchasing power is weighed against the return to be obtained from holding interest-bearing illiquid assets.

Starting from equilibrium, if the stock of money was to rise, in the first instance this would mean that individuals would find themselves holding a greater volume of money balances than they desire for their existing day-to-day transactions requirements and their financial asset portfolio requirements. In other words, there would be excess holdings of liquidity, which would generate pressure for a desired change in financial portfolio structures. Specifically, the Keynesian theory assumes that money and other financial assets are close substitutes, and hence the demand for these other assets would rise as individuals attempted to unload their excess money holdings. This action would effectively result in an increase in the amount of funds available for lending (including via the purchase of marketable securities), and hence the rate of interest would be depressed.

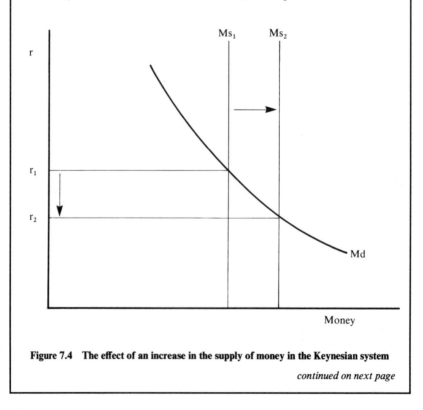

Figure 7.4 The effect of an increase in the supply of money in the Keynesian system

continued on next page

In the event of a reduction in the money supply, the above described adjustment would occur in reverse. Thus, interest rates would be pushed upwards as individuals sold interest-bearing financial assets and refused to renew maturing loans, in an effort to restore the liquidity within their financial portfolios to the desired level. The higher rate of interest would then tend to reduce the desire to hold money. The upwards pressure on interest rates would continue until the financial portfolios which existed were all held willingly, and there was no further desire to make adjustments.

The effect of a change in the money supply in the Keynesian system is illustrated in Figure 7.4. An increase in the money supply from Ms_1 to Ms_2 results in a reduction in the rate of interest from r_1 to r_2. It should also be noted that for simplicity it is assumed that the money supply is fixed by the monetary authorities independently of the rate of interest. In reality, the higher the rate of interest the more willing banks and building societies are likely to be to create credit, and hence the greater the supply of money will be. Thus the money supply curve may be shown as sloping upwards from left to right.

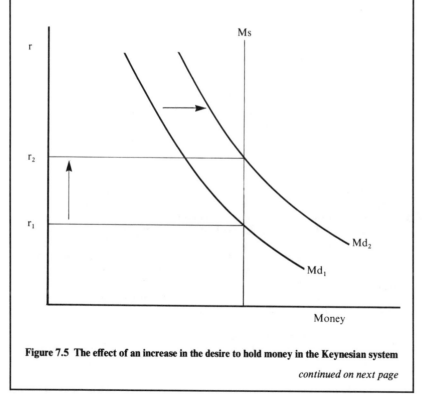

Figure 7.5 The effect of an increase in the desire to hold money in the Keynesian system

continued on next page

A shift in the money supply curve may be brought about by government policy, perhaps resulting in the relaxation of monetary controls. Alternatively, banks and building societies may decide to alter their reserve ratios and hence create additional credit on the existing reserve base. In either case, the additional liquidity made available within the financial system will tend to depress its price, i.e. the rate of interest.

Changes in the demand for money for any given supply position are also likely to affect interest rates. Thus, for example, if there is a boom in the economy, people may wish to hold additional amounts of money in order to finance their higher level of day-to-day expenditures, and hence the demand for money curve will shift to the right. As illustrated in Figure 7.5, the rate of interest is raised as pressure is placed on the available supply of money.

Finally it should be recognised that the Keynesian theory is a monetary theory, and it relates to nominal rates of interest. However, as the basic Keynesian analysis plays down the effects of changes in the supply of and the demand for money on the general price level, the theory implies that any change brought about in nominal interest rates will be reflected in a corresponding change in real rates of interest.

7.3.4 Reconciliation of the classical and Keynesian theories

At first sight, the classical and Keynesian theories would appear to be seriously in conflict. The classical theory argues that money is irrelevant for the determination of interest rates, whilst the Keynesian theory makes money central to the analysis. In fact, the theories may be easily reconciled by the introduction of time into the analysis, and the acceptance of a more realistic approach to the operation of the economy by both sides.

Thus, in general, the classical school accepts that in reality the economy does not adjust immediately and smoothly to changes in the money supply. Hence, they also accept that an increase in the money supply will, in the short term at least, raise the real supply of loanable funds, causing a reduction in the real rate of interest (and perhaps stimulating an increase in real investment expenditure, as suggested by the Keynesians). Conversely, most Keynesians accept that, in the long run, changes in the money supply are likely to be reflected in the price level. Thus, whilst an increase in the money supply might tend to reduce the rate of interest in the short term, as prices rise the increased demand for money to cover day-to-day transactions will tend to push interest back up in the longer term. Clearly, perfect price adjustment, as proposed by the classical school, would soak up all of the additional liquidity put into the economy, thus removing any possible permanent effect on the real rate of interest (unless, of course, the real determinant factors within the economy are affected by the adjustment process).

7.3.5 Changes in the level of interest rates

It is possible to identify a number of factors which are likely to cause the general level of interest rates to alter. The following factors are of especial importance in placing upwards pressure on the general level of *nominal interest rates*:

(a) Higher actual and/or expected rates of *inflation* will tend to push nominal interest rates upwards, as lenders seek to protect the real purchasing power of their nominally-denominated financial assets.

(b) A tightening of *official monetary controls* may result in higher nominal rates of interest. The authorities might, for example, reduce the supply of liquid assets via open market operations; and a higher rate of interest might be seen as a deliberate policy target in order to depress the demand for borrowed funds.

(c) Higher interest rates in *overseas financial markets* may place upwards pressure on domestic interest rates. This may occur naturally as domestic financial intermediaries seek to protect their deposit base in the face of more attractive overseas rates, or it may result from official policy actions designed to avoid excessive outflows of capital funds and hence downwards pressure on the domestic currency's exchange rate.

(d) An increase in the level of *economic activity* will tend to raise the overall demand for money, to cover the higher level of day-to-day transactions, and hence a shortage of liquidity may emerge at the initial level of interest rates. Unless the supply of money is allowed to accommodate, interest rates will tend to move upwards.

(e) An increase in the underlying *real rate of interest*, for any of the reasons discussed below, will put upward pressure on nominal rates for any given state of actual and expected inflation rates.

Clearly, when the above-listed factors operate in *reverse*, there will tend to be *downwards pressure* exerted on nominal interest rates. For example, if the rate of inflation is expected to fall, the nominal compensation required by lenders will tend to diminish correspondingly, for any given underlying desired real rate of interest.

It is also possible to identify a number of factors which may cause the *real rate of interest* to rise:

(a) Any factor which causes *nominal rates of interest* to increase without leading to an increase in the rate of *inflation* will cause the real rate of interest to rise. For example, if the authorities intervene in the money markets to produce an increase in short-term rates, this will have the effect of raising the real rate of interest. By the same token, any factor which is able to reduce the rate of inflation whilst leaving nominal rates of interest unaltered (or at least whilst reducing them by a smaller percentage amount) will also raise real rates of interest. The strict application of a prices and incomes policy by the Government may have this type of effect.

(b) In the longer term, the *real economic factors*, such as the productivity of new capital equipment and the desire of individuals to save, will be crucial to the level of real interest rates established. Thus, for example, technological innovation, which offers the prospect for improved profitability for capital investments, is likely to lead to an increased demand for loanable funds, which, without any corresponding increase in the desire to save within the economy, will tend to push up real rates of interest.

(c) The Government's *fiscal policy* position determines the public sector's borrowing requirement, and this may have important implications for the total demand for borrowed funds within the economy as a whole. Thus, if the Government's policy entails a large budget deficit, this may contribute to the maintenance of high real interest rates. A widening deficit could well result in higher long-term real rates as the public sector's increased requirements add to pressure on available funds.

(d) For *monetary policy* to constrain the growth of the money supply, it may be necessary not only to raise nominal rates of interest, but also to raise real rates. Thus, the authorities may have to hoist nominal interest rates well above the ruling, and (probably) the generally expected, rates of inflation in order to make the policy effective.

(e) An increase in the level of *uncertainty* within the financial environment, perhaps arising from political or social upheaval either domestically or in important overseas countries, may cause a higher premium to be placed on borrowed funds. Quite simply, the higher risk attached to lending will warrant a higher real return.

In order to explain a *reduction* in real rates of interest, the operation of the above-mentioned factors needs only to be *reversed*. For example, if the Government moves from a position of large budget deficit to one of large budget surplus, this will reduce the overall demand for borrowed funds within the economy, and other things being equal, real interest rates are likely to be lower than they otherwise would have been.

7.4 UK INTEREST RATES SINCE 1980

Throughout much of the 1970s in the UK, *real rates of interest* on most retail, and on many wholesale, financial assets were *negative*. Since the

Table 7.1 Selected UK interest rates: Nominal and real, 1980 to 1992, annual average percentages

Year	Retail price inflation	Retail banks' base rate		Inter-bank 3 months		20-year gilt-edged securities	
		Nominal	Real	Nominal	Real	Nominal	Real
1980	18.0	16.3	−1.7	16.6	−1.4	13.8	−4.2
1981	11.9	13.3	1.4	13.9	2.0	14.7	2.8
1982	8.6	11.9	3.3	12.3	3.7	12.9	4.3
1983	4.6	9.8	5.2	10.1	5.5	10.8	6.2
1984	5.0	9.9	4.9	10.0	5.0	10.7	5.7
1985	6.1	12.3	6.2	12.2	6.1	10.6	4.5
1986	3.4	10.9	7.5	11.0	7.6	9.9	6.5
1987	4.2	9.7	5.5	9.7	5.5	9.5	5.3
1988	4.9	10.1	5.2	10.9	6.0	9.4	4.5
1989	7.8	13.9	6.1	14.3	6.5	9.6	1.8
1990	9.5	14.8	5.3	14.8	5.3	11.1	1.6
1991	5.9	11.7	5.8	11.2	5.3	9.9	4.0
1992	3.7	9.6	5.9	9.4	5.7	9.1	5.4

Source: *Financial Statistics*, Central Statistical Office, various issues.

beginning of the 1980s the position has altered markedly, as inflation rates have fallen to relatively low levels, whilst nominal rates of interest have fallen less significantly. This return of *positive real interest rates* is reflected in the figures shown in Table 7.1. These statistics are typical of those generated for a wide range of comparable financial assets to be found within the UK financial system. Indeed the broad trend which they demonstrate in respect of real interest rates was fairly common throughout much of the Western World during the period covered.

Whilst it is difficult to provide a definitive explanation for the precise levels of UK interest rates and movements therein over time, it is possible to identify a number of major events which have probably had a fundamental influence on these rates:

(a) *Inflation.* During the inflationary period of the early 1980s, it appeared that nominal rates of interest adjusted more quickly and more strongly than they had done during the inflationary periods of the 1970s. Thus, real interest rates held up much more noticeably than they had done during the 1970s, although significant negative real rates were still to be found during this period. It may be that lenders had learned the lesson of the 1970s, and had become better informed about developments in the financial environment. However, irrespective of the initial cause, it is clear that as the rate of inflation fell during the early 1980s, nominal rates of interest fell more slowly. This may have been partly due to lags in the adjustment of expectations of inflation, or it may perhaps have reflected a belief in the markets that the lower rates of inflation were unlikely to be permanent. Subsequent experience would suggest that any such belief was not wholly misplaced. More recently, the rate of inflation has fallen again substantially, but concurrent reductions in nominal interest rates, encouraged by a change of emphasis in government economic policy, have tended largely to offset the impact on real rates of interest.

(b) *Government monetary policy.* During the second half of 1979 and the early years of the 1980s, the central theme of the Government's economic policy was the defeat of inflation via the use of strict monetary controls. One of the outcomes of this policy was an upwards pressure on real interest rates. Indeed, to the extent that a policy of restricting money supply growth is successful in reducing the rate of inflation, the natural by-product of associated higher nominal interest rates will always be higher real rates of interest. This trend was supported by the authorities' desire to finance as much of the Public Sector Borrowing Requirement as possible through the sale of gilt-edged securities and National Savings instruments to the non-bank non-building society private sector. Such sales help to limit the monetary effect of budget deficit financing, but they also necessitate attractive interest rates, especially on longer-term instruments. Since the mid-1980s the Government has taken a somewhat more pragmatic approach to economic policy, initially elevating the sterling exchange rate as a target for monetary controls, and then subsequently emphasising the need to stimulate economic growth in the face of a deepening recession. The turning point in this respect was the withdrawal of sterling from the Exchange Rate Mechanism (ERM) of the European Monetary System in September 1992. (This important development will be discussed in detail in Chapter 10.) Within a few months of this major change of government policy, a significant reduction had occurred in the level of nominal interest rates in the UK. However, the impact on real rates of interest was relatively small, as lower mortgage lending rates helped to reduce an already depressed headline rate of inflation.

(c) *United States economic policy.* During the first half of the 1980s, fiscal expansion in the USA, involving large government budget deficits, coupled with relatively strict monetary policy, tended to maintain high nominal rates of interest in the USA. In addition, as inflation rates were quite modest, the USA also experienced fairly high real rates of interest. As funds may be moved relatively freely both into and out of the USA and the UK, and as London is one of the world's major financial centres, the economic conditions prevailing within the USA exerted considerable pressure on UK financial markets. In particular, given the inherent strength and stability of the US economy, UK financial institutions felt obliged to offer rates of interest at least comparable to those available in the USA in order to protect their deposit bases. This force persisted throughout much of the 1980s. However, since 1991 there has been a significant relaxation in the US monetary policy position, largely in response to deteriorating economic conditions in the USA. By early 1993, this trend had led US short-term nominal interest rates to fall to levels not seen since the early 1970s, generating negative real rates of interest on some financial instruments. This development can only have contributed to the creation of a financial climate within which the UK authorities felt able to relax their monetary policy.

(d) *Sterling exchange rate.* For the first half of the 1980s, the UK monetary authorities appeared content to see the foreign currency exchange value of sterling steadily diminish. The continuation of UK inflation rates in excess of those experienced by most of its major trading partners made this occurrence almost inevitable, if the UK was to maintain its relative competitive position in international markets. However, by late 1984 the steady fall in the value of sterling had turned into a major slide, and there were fears that a collapse in the exchange rate would have serious consequences for the UK financial system, as well as providing an unwelcome stimulus to domestic inflationary pressures (by pushing up the sterling price of imports). Consequently, since that time the authorities have paid much more explicit attention to the sterling exchange rate in the setting of monetary policy controls, and interest rates have often tended to respond more directly to signals from the foreign exchange market. As might be expected, the massive deterioration in the UK's current account on the balance of payments during the late 1980s (to be discussed in detail in Chapter 9), provided a severe test of the Government's resolve to protect the exchange rate. However, it was probably the Government's decision to place sterling in the ERM, in October 1990, which led to the maintenance of relatively high rates of interest in the UK during 1991 and 1992, despite a falling rate of inflation and a slight improvement in the UK's current account position. In particular, high interest rates in Germany, maintained to combat growing inflationary pressures resulting from German reunification, meant that the UK authorities had little choice but to pursue a high interest rate policy. This was thought to be necessary in order to prevent outflows of capital funds from the UK, and hence to hold the value of sterling within its deutschemark parity band. The UK's position was not helped by a growing body of opinion that the exchange value set for sterling within the ERM was unsustainably high, in the light of the UK's weak international trading position and rapidly rising level of unemployment. In the event, a collapse of confidence led to massive sales of sterling by international investors, and, as mentioned above, sterling had to be withdrawn from the ERM in September 1992. This event precipitated a substantial depreciation in the exchange value of sterling, and allowed other economic policy objectives, requiring lower rates of interest, to take priority.

(e) *International economic and financial problems.* At the beginning of the 1980s, the world financial environment became somewhat more unstable than it had been for most of the post-war years. In particular, fears of massive defaults on the international debts of many less developed countries undoubtedly raised the risk premiums sought by many financial institutions on international lending. The large volumes of provisions made by UK banks in order to protect their capital bases against possible defaults are also likely to have been reflected in the interest rates set by these organisations. In addition, the worldwide recessions of the early 1980s and the early 1990s were probably responsible for further upwards pressure on interest rates. During both of these periods of economic downturn, the effects on the UK economy, particularly in terms of the level of unemployment, were perhaps more severe than in most other Western countries, with the result that business confidence was undermined, whilst the risk attached to business transactions was raised. Indeed, the record losses sustained by UK banks on corporate and small business lending since 1991, have made banks more wary of increasing their exposure to all but the most creditworthy of customers. Fears have been voiced that, in consequence, downwards movements in market rates of interest may not be fully translated into lower bank lending rates for certain categories of business customers.

(f) *The behaviour of financial intermediaries.* Since the early 1980s, the degree of competition between UK financial intermediaries, especially at the retail level, has increased markedly. Despite the many economic and financial problems experienced, the number of relatively attractive outlets for private sector savings has grown significantly. At least until the recent period of recession, beginning in 1990, it seems likely that this competition was partly responsible for holding up the level of interest rates paid on retail deposits. What appeared to be an almost insatiable demand for mortgage loans and consumer credit, during the latter half of the 1980s, allowed these higher finance costs to be reflected in the rates charged to borrowers from financial intermediaries. By contrast, the markedly reduced demand for borrowed funds from the UK private sector, during the early 1990s, severely limited the freedom of intermediaries in this respect, and probably goes some way towards explaining their acquiescence in the lower rates of interest observed since the Autumn of 1992.

(g) *Private sector financial sophistication.* An after-effect of the inflationary periods of the 1970s and early 1980s would appear to be an increased sensitivity of private sector lenders to the real rate of interest received on financial assets. Today, there is a reduced willingness to lend funds at low nominal rates of interest, against the background of uncertain expectations of future inflation rates. This increased financial sophistication within the private sector has probably been important in encouraging the growth in competition between financial intermediaries.

(h) *The long-term trend in interest rates.* Citing statistical evidence, some economists have argued that the low (often negative) real rates of interest experienced during the 1970s and early 1980s in the UK were really an aberration from the more normal situation. Fast monetary growth, together with only a slow adjustment of inflationary expectations, simply allowed real rates of interest to slip downwards. Thus, a return to relative monetary stability, and the evolution of a better educated population and a more responsive financial sector, have allowed the longer-term trend to reassert itself.

7.5 THE TERM STRUCTURE OF INTEREST RATES

7.5.1 Definition

The term structure of interest rates refers to the spread of interest rates paid on the *same type of assets with different terms to maturity*. The concept is relevant only to fixed-interest, fixed-term financial assets, such as government gilt-edged securities or sterling certificates of deposit.

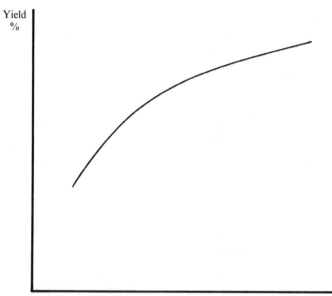

Figure 7.6 The 'normal' yield curve

The diagrammatic representation of the term structure of interest rates is known as the *yield curve*, and a typical example is illustrated in Figure 7.6. It is conventional to work in terms of the yield on an asset, which depends upon the interest income plus or minus any capital appreciation or depreciation (arising from changes in the market value of the asset, when it constitutes a marketable instrument). However, in the present context it is acceptable to use the terms 'yield' and 'interest rate' interchangeably. It should also be noted that the yield curve analysis is related to nominal rates of interest rather than real.

The yield curve shown in Figure 7.6 is referred to as a 'normal' yield curve, and is constructed on the basis that there is no specific expectation of interest rate movements, but that there exists an uncertain financial environment. The upwards slope of the normal yield curve is explained in terms of the risk attached to lending and the liquidity preference of the lender.

7.5.2 Risk and liquidity preference

In general, the longer is the term to maturity of a loan, the greater is the associated risk for the lender, and hence the higher is the interest premium required by the lender. There are various types of risk to consider:

(a) *Default:* where the borrower cannot or will not repay the debt.
(b) *Capital loss:* which arises where marketable securities have to be liquidated prior to their maturity at unfavourable prices.
(c) *Erosion of purchasing power of funds lent:* arising due to inflation rates proving to be higher than expected at the time when the rate of interest on the asset was agreed.
(d) *Change of circumstances:* which might require the lender to make unplanned alterations to his or her financial portfolio.

Lenders also normally require compensation for the loss of access to immediate purchasing power, which is entailed when funds are used to make fixed-term loans. The longer the term to maturity of the loans, the greater the amount of compensation which is required by the lender. This point is still valid even when marketable securities are purchased, as the risk of capital loss from premature sale means that liquidity is lost in the strict sense.

The intensity of lenders' preferences for liquidity, together with the nature of the perceived risk attached to lending, will determine the slope of the yield curve. The tendency for the normal yield curve to flatten out at longer maturities merely reflects the fact that it becomes virtually impossible to differentiate between intensities of risk and degrees of liquidity preference beyond a certain number of years into the future.

7.5.3 Expectations of interest rate movements

The existence of risk and liquidity preference explains why longer-term rates of interest are higher than shorter-term rates when there are no specific expectations of interest rate movements. However, when expectations of interest rate movements do exist, additional forces are exerted on the shape of the yield curve.

(a) *Expectations of an increase in interest rates*

If there are general expectations of an increase in interest rates, this will tend to *push up long-term rates of interest relative to short-term rates*. This occurs because lenders, wishing to avoid being locked into relatively low yield assets, will increasingly prefer to lend short term in the hope that when the loans mature they will be able to re-invest the funds at the expected higher rate of interest. Thus, there is an increase in the supply of short-term funds, and a corresponding reduction in the supply of long-term funds. Conversely, borrowers will wish to borrow long term today at the currently relatively low rates of interest. They would be foolish to borrow short term only to have to re-borrow the funds at higher rates of interest at some time in the future. Thus, there will tend to be an increase in the demand for

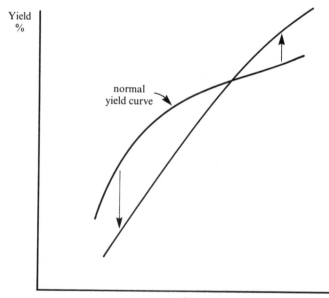

Years to maturity

Figure 7.7 Expectation of higher rates of interest

long-term funds, and a reduction in the demand for short-term funds. Therefore, considering the behaviour of both lenders and borrowers, the effect of an expected increase in interest rates is to create an excess demand for long-term funds and an excess supply of short-term funds, at the initial term structure of interest rates. This will tend to result in *market forces pushing down short-term rates and pushing up long-term rates, thus making the yield curve steeper*, as illustrated in Figure 7.7.

(b)   *Expectations of a reduction in interest rates*

If there are general expectations of a reduction in interest rates, this will tend to *push down long-term rates of interest relative to short-term rates*. This occurs because lenders will wish to avoid lending short term, as this would imply having to re-lend funds at the expected future lower rates of interest. It would be far better to lend long term today, and hence lock the funds into a relatively high yield asset. Thus, there will tend to be an increase in the supply of long-term funds, and a corresponding reduction in the supply of short-term funds. Conversely, borrowers will wish to borrow short term, in the hope of being able to roll-over their debt at expected future lower rates of interest. This will tend to cause an increase in the demand for short-term funds, and a reduction in the demand for long-term funds. Taking the demand and supply considerations together, at the initial interest rate structure, there will be an excess demand for short-term funds and an excess supply of long-term funds. The net result is to *push up short-term rates and push down long-term rates, thus causing the yield curve to become flatter*, as illustrated in Figure 7.8.

Where there are particularly *strong expectations* of interest rate reductions, it is possible that the 'expectations effect' may swamp the underlying risk and liquidity preference effects, thus producing a yield curve which *slopes downwards from left to right*. That is, it is possible for a term structure of interest rates to show *lower rates of interest for longer maturities than for shorter maturities*. This form of relationship is illustrated in Figure 7.9, in respect of recent UK experience. The precise shape of any particular yield curve is influenced by the detailed nature of expectations of future interest rate movements.

7.5.4   Yield curves for UK financial instruments

Throughout most of the period between late-1979 and September 1992, the yield curves generated by longer-term UK financial instruments such as gilt-edged securities, sloped downwards from left to right, at least over the higher maturities. Typical yield curves for gilts are shown in Figure 7.9. Their general shape indicates that expectations can only have been for future reductions in interest rates of a magnitude sufficient to overcome

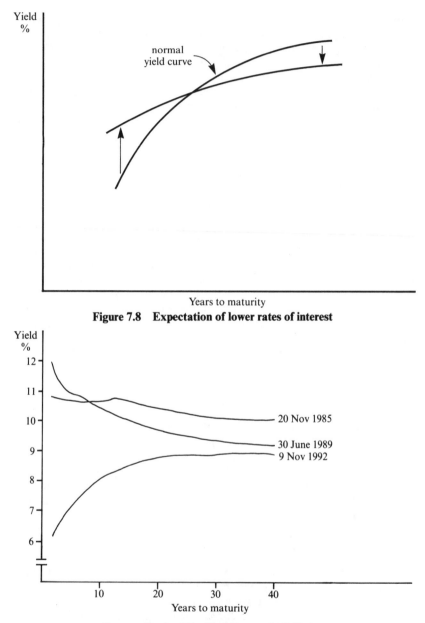

Figure 7.8   Expectation of lower rates of interest

Source: *Bank of England Quarterly Bulletin*
Figure 7.9   Yield curves for UK government gilt-edged securities

the risk and liquidity preference factors. This clearly reflects the unusually high nominal rates of interest which were ruling in the UK for significant periods of time during these years, together with the general belief that the Government was intent upon reducing the rate of inflation. The emphasis upon the use of monetary controls by the authorities, as the major means of controlling inflation, was probably responsible for there being only limited expectation of lower rates of interest in the short term. However, during 1989 the yield curves for gilts were, on occasions, downwards sloping along the whole of their length, implying that the then current high rates of interest were seen largely as a short-term expedient for monetary policy purposes. The sudden change in the Government's monetary policy position following the withdrawal of sterling from the ERM in September 1992, had a dramatic impact upon market expectations of future interest rate movements, and consequently upon the shape of yield curves for UK financial instruments. The return of relatively steep upwards sloping (from left to right) yield curves, of the type illustrated in Figure 7.9 reflected the widely-held view that not only were short-term rates of interest in the UK likely to remain low and perhaps fall even further in the shorter term, but also that the relaxed monetary regime would lead to inflationary pressures in the longer term. Fears of future inflation lead to expectations of higher nominal rates of interest (for both monetary control and commercial reasons) in the longer term, which support the underlying risk and liquidity preference factors pushing for upwards sloping yield curves.

7.6 INTEREST RATE DIFFERENTIALS BETWEEN DIFFERENT TYPES OF ASSETS

The structure of interest rates in a modern financial system depends upon *a wide range of factors influencing borrowing and lending transactions* (and hence *the supply of and the demand for financial assets*). Many of these factors have already been discussed in the foregoing sections of this chapter. Nevertheless, it is useful to draw together those factors, and to introduce additional ones, as a means of emphasising the broad array of issues which must be taken into account when considering the determination of specific interest rates. Also, it is important to recognise that not all of the factors to be listed below are relevant for each type of borrowing and lending transaction undertaken. Indeed, it is the operation of various combinations of the factors, in varying intensities, which explains why there are *so many different rates of interest ruling at any given time within a modern financial system.*

The major factors affecting the nature of borrowing and lending transactions may be summarised as follows:

(a) *Risk.* In respect of most types of loan, there is always some risk that the borrower will default on the payment of interest or the

301

repayment of principal. In general, the lower is the creditworthiness of the borrower, the greater will be the risk premium sought by the lender. Banks normally charge a percentage margin over base rate or LIBOR, to reflect the perceived creditworthiness of the customer.

(b) *Time to maturity.* For fixed-maturity fixed-interest loans, in the absence of strong expectations of future reductions in interest rates, the longer the term to maturity the higher will be the rate of interest required by the lender. Also, as explained at 7.5.3 above, expectations of interest rate movements over the period of a loan will influence the interest rate which it actually commands.

(c) *Absolute size of transaction.* A large (wholesale) deposit with a financial intermediary may attract a higher rate of interest than a smaller (retail) deposit. This reflects the lower unit administration costs associated with wholesale activities, and the ability of intermediaries to negotiate the rate on each wholesale deposit separately. Conversely, large scale loans may justify higher rates of interest than small loans, as the lender must forgo the opportunity to spread portfolio risk more widely.

(d) *Business strategy.* The interest rate structure established by a financial intermediary will be affected by its strategy for developing its business. Thus, the intermediary may set rates so as to maintain a stable depositor base, rather than simply to maximise short-run profits.

(e) *Eurocurrency and international interest rates.* Domestic money market rates of interest, and ultimately most domestic interest rates, are likely to be influenced by changes in the ruling rates of interest in competing international financial markets. (This point is taken up in 7.8 below.)

(f) *Marketability of an asset.* Where a debt is in the form of a marketable security, the easier it is to buy and sell the lower is likely to be the rate of interest, other things being equal.

(g) *Level of guarantee of interest rate.* The extent to which an interest rate is fixed, and the mechanisms which exist for renegotiating 'fixed' rates, will have an important influence upon the rate which the lender is willing to accept. Facilities may also be offered for fixing rates in real terms via the use of indexation.

(h) *Type of loan.* Banks and building societies may offer funds as term loans (on which interest must be paid irrespective of whether or not the funds are used by the borrower) or as overdraft facilities (where only the portion of the funds used attracts interest). There may also be some form of agreement on the rolling-over of fixed maturity debt.

(i) *Tax treatment.* The tax positions of the borrower and the lender, and tax concessions available in respect of specific forms of debt instruments, may affect the interest rate structure established.

(j)   *Expectations of inflation and interest rate movements.* Expectations are likely to differ between individuals at a point in time, and within society over time. Thus, the nominal rates of interest acceptable to lenders, for any given underlying desired real rate of interest, will tend to variety between individual transactions and over time.

(k)   *Market imperfections.* Unusually powerful participants may dominate sectors of particular financial markets, or legal constraints on the holding of particular forms of financial instruments or on participation in specific markets, may cause patterns of interest rates to occur which may appear inconsistent when considered on the basis of normal market criteria.

(l)   *Official intervention.* All financial institutions are subject to some form of official regulation, and this may affect cost structures, and hence influence both absolute and relative interest rates within the financial system. In addition, the monetary authorities, in seeking to control money supply growth, may implement policies which directly or indirectly affect the structure of interest rates. Mechanisms such as interest rate ceilings and officially-administered rates have an obvious direct impact, but it must not be forgotten that open market operations and various forms of reserve requirements are also likely to influence the pattern of interest rates. Indeed, the financing of government budget deficits and surpluses may have differential effects on interest rate structures, depending upon the types of instruments traded and the individuals and institutions involved with the transactions.

7.7   KEY UK INTEREST RATES

7.7.1   London sterling money market rates

As was explained in Chapter 5, the London sterling money markets form an extremely important part of the UK financial system. The interest rates generated within these markets are of direct relevance to the activities of a wide range of financial institutions and other commercial organisations; and, eventually, changes in money market rates are likely to influence indirectly all commercial borrowing and lending transactions.

Table 7.2 shows a selection of London sterling money market interest rates. Whilst the pattern of rates illustrated is typical of those generated by the market during the early months of 1993, it should be recognised that rates may alter continually, and an explanation of interest rate differentials must look to the factors influencing the supply of and the demand for each of the separate instruments involved. In terms of the analysis in the

Table 7.2   London money market interest rates: percentage per annum; 6 April 1993

	Overnight	7 days' notice	One month	Three months	Six months	One Year
Inter-bank offer	6¾	5⅞	5¹⁵⁄₁₆	5¹⁵⁄₁₆	5¹⁵⁄₁₆	5¹⁵⁄₁₆
Inter-bank bid	5	5½	5¹³⁄₁₆	5¹³⁄₁₆	5¹³⁄₁₆	5¹³⁄₁₆
Sterling CDs	—	—	5¹³⁄₁₆	5¹³⁄₁₆	5¹³⁄₁₆	5²⁷⁄₃₂
Local Authority Deposits	6	5⅞	5¹³⁄₁₆	5¹³⁄₁₆	5¹³⁄₁₆	5¹³⁄₁₆
Discount Market Deposits	8	6	—	—	—	—
Company Deposits	—	—	—	—	—	—
Finance House Deposits	—	—	5¹³⁄₁₆	5⅞	5⅞	5⅞
Treasury Bills (Buy)	—	—	5¹¹⁄₁₆	5⁹⁄₁₆	5½	—
Bank Bills (Buy)	—	—	5¾	5⅝	5⁹⁄₁₆	—
Fine Trade Bills (Buy)	—	—	—	—	—	—

Source: *Financial Times*, 7 April 1993

Note: No transactions were reported on the date specified for either company deposits or fine trade bills.

preceding sections of this chapter, the short-term nature of money market operations implies that the Keynesian liquidity preference theory (see 7.3.3) is appropriate in providing an explanation of the general level of rates. However, a particularly important factor relates to the position of the *Bank of England*, in respect of its *liquidity and monetary control operations* through the primary (discount) money market. Furthermore, as all of the London money markets (including those dealing in eurocurrencies, i.e. foreign currency denominated transactions) are, to some extent, interconnected, the Bank's influence may percolate quickly through the whole market system.

Since the introduction of the present monetary control regime, the Bank of England has tended to concentrate its attention on very short-term rates, especially within its designated bands 1 and 2 (instruments with up to 33 days to maturity). Hence, the official monetary policy position is of critical direct relevance to corresponding very short-term money market rates. It is then via portfolio adjustment that private sector financial institutions and other financial wealth holders transmit the effects of official policy changes through the market. Thus, for example, a tightening of monetary controls, limiting the supply of the most liquid assets in the market, is likely to raise the rate of interest on very short-term funds, making slightly longer-term funds appear more attractive to prospective borrowers, but relatively less attractive to lenders. The effect is likely to be an upwards pressure on slightly longer-term interest rates, and so on.

The precise relationships between the interest rates generated on any given instrument with different terms to maturity may be explained within the *term structure* analysis, involving the characteristics of risk, liquidity preference and expectations of interest rate movements. Clearly, general expectations on matters such as changes in government monetary policy, exchange rate movements, short-term economic prospects and trends in inflation are likely to be of greatest relevance in this context. It is interesting to note that the data for most instruments reported in Table 7.2 suggest yield curves which are either horizontal or have slightly negative slopes at the longer maturities, hence implying expectations within the market for future reductions in interest rates at the time when the data were collected.

Interest rate *differentials* between different money market instruments are influenced by the *set of characteristics* which each instrument embodies. Thus, even where instruments have the same term to maturity, the interest rates which they generate may differ due to their inherent risks, ease of marketability, role in respect of official market intervention operations, and so on. Also, especially in the short term, there may be apparent the results of market imperfections and unusually large transactions within specific areas of the market. In respect of the data contained in Table 7.2, it may be observed that for given maturities, Treasury bills have *marginally lower* rates than the secondary market instruments; and within the latter group, rates for finance house deposits tend to be slightly higher than rates for inter-bank (bid) and sterling CDs. Against the background of normal market conditions, this pattern is largely to be expected.

7.7.2 Bank base rates

Bank base rates are one of the most important sets of interest rates to be found within the UK financial system. Their level is often regarded as being a crucial indicator of the state of health of the economy, and movements in base rates have tended to acquire an almost political status as far as governments are concerned. Yet it must be remembered that base rates are only the *starting point* for the calculation of actual lending rates by banks. A percentage margin is always added to base rate according to the bank's assessment of the *creditworthiness* of the customer. For example, a high quality (blue-chip) corporate customer may be offered funds at 1% over base rate. In addition, a significant proportion of bank term loans are now *linked directly to money market rates* (usually the London Inter-bank Offered Rate, LIBOR), thus by-passing base rates entirely. Nevertheless, an understanding of the determination of base rates is crucial to an appreciation of banking operations, and changes in base rates have important implications for the financial position of borrowers, both directly and indirectly, via their impact on other lending rates within the economy.

The setting of bank base rates depends heavily upon the *cost of funds* to the bank. Thus, the rate of interest which the bank has to pay in order to raise deposits, whether they be from retail or wholesale sources, provides the starting point for the base rate calculation. On top of the cost of funds, the bank adds an *operating margin* which reflects its overhead costs, such as the running of a branch network and contributions to the running of the cheque clearing system, provisions for bad debts, and taxation levied on activities. In addition, the bank's *commercial (profit) objectives* must be taken into account, as it is necessary for the bank to generate sufficient income from its on-lending to cover all costs associated with the intermediation process and provide a profit for its shareholders. The position is made more complex by the degree of competition which now exists within the financial system, and the tendency for the majority of banks to fix their base rates at the same level over most periods of time. Consequently, the control of costs is critical to a bank's profitability, as is the ability to generate profits from non-intermediation activities. However, general conditions within the financial system are likely to influence base rate decisions in aggregate. For example, when economic activity is buoyant and the demands for borrowed funds are high, base rates may be pushed upwards, as a result of the cost of funds to banks being raised (through competition for available deposits) and a general desire of bank managers to maintain their institutions' profitability.

7.7.3 Relationship between commercial bank lending rates and sterling money market rates

Commercial banks are extremely important participants in the London money markets. These markets not only provide profitable short-term outlets for surplus funds, but also they are used extensively by banks as a source of short-term finance. In particular, the *inter-bank market* is thought to be critical to the *adjustment of banks' liquidity positions.* Therefore, it is to be expected that movements in money market interest rates, and especially inter-bank rates, will have potentially significant effects on banks' decisions in relation to the interest rates on their on-lending.

Short-term inter-bank interest rates provide a good measure of the *marginal cost of funds* to individual banks attempting to adjust their liquidity positions. (The three-month London Inter-bank Offered Rate (LIBOR) and the three-month London Inter-bank Bid Rate (LIBID) are often taken as benchmark rates in this respect, due to their relative stability and the importance of the three-month maturity in money market operations.) The importance of the inter-bank market cannot be over-emphasised, for it must be remembered that it is virtually impossible for a bank to adjust its short-term liquidity position through retail funds flows (i.e. through deposits made by ordinary personal customers and small business customers). Indeed, not only does it often take a significant period of time for retail deposits to react to changes in interest rates, but also changes in rates must apply to all deposits within the categories affected, and hence the cost of raising marginal funds via retail channels may be excessive. By contrast, the inter-bank market is sensitive to relatively small changes in rates, terms for individual transactions are negotiated separately, and the sophisticated communications networks ensure that financing needs can be met quickly and efficiently.

The effect of changes in short-term inter-bank interest rates on commercial bank lending rates depends very much upon the *types of lending activity* involved and upon the *nature of the changes* in inter-bank rates. Thus, in relation to on-lending at a *fixed margin above inter-bank rate*, the relationship is direct. For example, a wholesale loan may be made to a corporate customer at a fixed percentage over the three-month LIBOR, and consequently an increase in inter-bank rates will cause an immediate increase in the rate charged to the corporate customer.

Where lending rates are *linked to base rates* the relationship is somewhat more complex. Base rates tend to follow *the general trend* in short-term inter-bank rates, but are not adjusted to reflect every short-term fluctuation in such rates. The reason for this is that the cost of inter-bank funds is *only one factor* in the determination of base rates. The direct effect on a bank's profit margin of having to pay a higher rate for inter-bank funds would have to be weighed against the cost of adjusting base rate, both in terms of the *administration expenses* and the effect on *customer loyalty*. Banks are more willing to raise base rates, and hence on-lending rates, the greater is the increase in inter-bank rates; the more permanent is the increase in inter-bank rates expected to be; the larger is the proportion of total funds that the bank raises at inter-bank rates; the finer is the bank's pre-existing profit margin; and the greater is the response of competing financial intermediaries. Banks will also be alert to the possibilities for corporate customers to undertake *roundtripping* at their expense (i.e. borrowing funds that have been made available on overdraft facilities at a small margin over base rate, and then redepositing the funds on the money market at a higher rate). In order to restrict the chances of this happening, banks will seek to limit the differential between base rates and money market rates. In this respect the short rates (overnight to seven days) are particularly important, as it is more likely that customers will attempt this arbitrage activity if they are able to limit the risk of being caught out by a sudden upwards movement in base rates. The shorter the period of time required for them to retrieve the on-lent funds, the smaller is that risk.

Finally, it should be recognised that some on-lending by commercial banks takes place at *fixed rates*. However, changes in inter-bank rates are still likely to influence the average of such rates, as term loans mature and are re-negotiated and as new loans are made at rates reflecting the new (and future expected) cost of funds to the bank.

7.7.4 Relationship between short-term interest rates and mortgage loan rates

In recent years, experience has shown that mortgage lending rates may respond significantly, and relatively quickly, to movements in short-term money market interest rates. An important factor here is that *most mortgage lending rates are variable* upon a reasonable period of notice being given by the lender, and hence the fact that the original period of maturity for mortgage loans is often around 25 years, is of only limited relevance to the determination of the interest rate charged. The *lender has to raise funds on a much shorter-term basis* in order to finance the mortgage loans; and hence in order to maintain profitability, increases in the cost of funds to the mortgage lender will often be passed on to the mortgage borrower. For example, if the Bank of England seeks to raise short-term rates of interest (via its intervention in the bill market), it may easily cause an increase in mortgage rates in the relatively near future, to the extent that changes in money market rates are perceived to be more than transitory and are significant in their magnitude. Clearly, the greater the proportion of its funds which the mortgage lender raises in the money markets, and the greater is the actual change in money market rates, the more likely it becomes that mortgage rates will be altered in step with market rates, and with only a limited lapse of time. However, even where the mortgage lender raises most of its funds via retail markets, it is probable that the cost of funds will be affected, as the changes in money market rates percolate through the financial system. Quite simply borrowers and lenders will adjust their positions in respect of amounts and maturities of funds, and changes in the shortest money market rates will tend to initiate a *ripple effect* along the whole term structure of rates in the financial system, although expectations of future money market changes will be critical in determining reactions within the remainder of the system.

Having suggested that Bank of England money market intervention has an important influence upon mortgage rates, it must not be forgotten that there are other factors relevant to the determination of both mortgage rates and, indeed, money market rates themselves. Some commentators would, in fact, suggest that relative to the *broader market forces*, the Bank of England's influence is quite limited, especially in the *longer term*. Thus, the general nature of the supply of and demand for long-term mortgage funds is crucial in establishing the level of rates charged for such funds. Related to this issue are the factors affecting the level of interest rates in general, such as expectations of future *inflation rates*, the *competitive pressures* within the markets for borrowed funds, the general state of health of the economy as a whole, and broad trends in saving and investment within the private sector. Finally, it should be recognised that there does tend to be some stickiness in the responsiveness of mortgage rates to changes in short-term money market rates. It may simply be that it takes time for the effects of changes in the market to percolate through, although a significant proportion of mortgage loans now involve annual reviews of rates, whereby the actual charges to borrowers are altered at most once per year; of course, new borrowers may be affected much sooner. There are also some mortgage loans which involve guaranteed fixed rates for a fixed number of years, thus altering the more conventional balance of interest rate risk between borrower and lender.

7.8   DOMESTIC AND INTERNATIONAL INTEREST RATES

In 7.3.5 it was noted that changes in the level of interest rates ruling in *overseas financial markets* may have significant implications for the level of *domestic interest rates*. As the UK has one of the most open financial systems in the world, the factors which link domestic and overseas rates of interest are of particular importance. In this respect, whilst the precise relationship between any two countries' interest rates is likely to be extremely complex, it is possible to identify three broad factors which are thought to be of fundamental importance to international interest rate differentials:

(a)   *Relative actual and expected inflation rates.* A country with a relatively high current rate of inflation is likely to experience nominal rates of interest which are higher than those payable on comparable assets to be found in a low inflation country, assuming that the underlying real rates of interest are basically the same in both countries. Similarly, relative interest rate term structures are likely to reflect the patterns of expected future inflation rates.

(b)   *Expectations of currency exchange rate movements.* If there are general expectations that the exchange value of the domestic currency is about to depreciate relative to major foreign currencies, then, other things being equal, domestic interest rates are likely to carry a premium, in order to compensate for the expected loss of international purchasing power embodied in assets denominated in the domestic currency. The absence of the interest rate differential might lead to sales of such assets, and the switching of the proceeds into other currencies, thus tending to make expectations of domestic currency depreciation self-fulfilling. Clearly, when there are general expectations of domestic currency appreciation, assets denominated in that currency are likely to carry a discount on their interest rate, relative to comparable overseas rates, due to the anticipated international purchasing power gain to be made.

(c)   *General economic environment.* A strong high growth economy will usually bolster business confidence, and may reduce fears of defaults on loans, thus pushing for lower real rates of interest on funds lent. Conversely, lending in economies which are politically or socially unstable may attract a sizeable risk premium. Indeed, international interest rate differentials may also reflect the more subtle differences between countries' economic policy positions. Thus, for example, the fear of excessive government intervention in private investment activities, may place a premium on the rates of return required by investors in the country concerned.

Changes in any of the above-listed factors in any one country are likely to alter the relative attractiveness of that country's pre-existing interest rates, and this in turn is likely to generate pressures for interest rate movements. For example, if a change in government policy leads to fears of higher domestic rates of inflation, then domestic nominal rates of interest will appear less attractive relative to overseas rates. Consequently, domestic financial institutions are likely to raise their deposit rates in order to protect their deposit base; the Government may also push for higher rates of interest as a means of protecting the domestic currency's exchange rate.

7.9 EUROCURRENCY INTEREST RATES

7.9.1 The determination of eurocurrency interest rates

The term 'eurocurrency' refers to *foreign currency denominated wholesale borrowing and lending activities*. (These activities are discussed in detail in Chapter 5.) The level of interest rates paid on eurocurrency deposits and charged on eurocurrency loans is broadly determined by the forces of *supply and demand* for eurocurrency funds, taking into account the operating costs of the banking intermediaries involved with the transactions. However, given the special nature of the eurocurrency markets, it is possible to identify a number of specific key factors which affect the level of interest rates in these markets:

(a) The rate of interest paid on a eurocurrency deposit or charged on a eurocurrency loan reflects the level of *interest rates ruling in the country from which the relevant currency originates* (rather than the rates ruling in the country where the eurocurrency market is based). The reason for this is that for activities to take place, banking institutions must obtain foreign currency funds, and these will only be forthcoming if the rates of interest offered on deposits are at least as good as those available in the country from where the currency originates. In addition, market forces ensure that the rates charged on eurocurrency loans will not drift too far away from the rates charged on comparable domestic funds. (Indeed, as will be explained below, the euromarkets have the ability to undercut many domestic markets as a means of attracting borrowers.) Therefore, the factors which affect the level of interest rates within any particular domestic market also influence the level of rates to be found for the same currency in the eurocurrency market. Thus, important factors include the current and expected rates of domestic inflation; the official monetary policy position of the domestic authorities; the general economic environment, including the international payments position and prospects for future economic growth; the confidence of investors in future economic and financial prospects; and the risk premium required by investors in the light of the inherent political and economic stability of the country.

(b)   Until the mid-1980s, eurocurrency market activity was largely *unregulated*. Intermediaries were not required to hold low yield liquid assets or to maintain specific capital backing for their liabilities, and hence they were able to operate on very fine margins. The large scale of transactions has also tended to hold down unit administration costs. Thus, for any given maturity of funds, the rates paid on eurocurrency deposits have tended to be somewhat higher than those rates paid on comparable domestic deposits; whilst the rates charged to borrowers have often been lower than rates charged for comparable domestic loans. However, in recent years the *comparative advantage of the eurocurrency markets has been eroded* by the movement towards the *harmonisation of regulation within international banking markets*. This has come about through both the strengthening of domestic supervisory requirements and the pressures exerted by the Basle Committee agreement (requiring all banks to achieve minimum capital adequacy standards in respect of all forms of intermediation activities). In consequence, the differentials between eurocurrency and comparable domestic interest rates have tended to narrow somewhat in recent years.

(c)   In the past, a number of countries have operated *exchange controls* on movements of capital funds. Where this has occurred, the differential between interest rates in eurocurrency markets and the rates in the comparable domestic markets has sometimes been greater than might be explained purely on the basis of economic factors. In such cases the normal market forces are distorted as funds are stopped from flowing freely to where returns are the most attractive. However, today, there are very few Western countries operating exchange controls, and their number is set to decline further in the near future.

Table 7.3 Selected eurocurrency interest rates: percentage per annum; 6 April 1993

	Short term	7 days' notice	One month	Three months	Six months	One year
Sterling	$5\frac{3}{4}$–$5\frac{1}{2}$	$5\frac{5}{8}$–$5\frac{1}{2}$	6–$5\frac{7}{8}$	6–$5\frac{7}{8}$	$5\frac{15}{16}$–$5\frac{13}{16}$	$5\frac{15}{16}$–$5\frac{13}{16}$
US Dollar	$3\frac{3}{16}$–$3\frac{1}{16}$	$3\frac{1}{8}$–3	$3\frac{3}{16}$–$3\frac{1}{16}$	$3\frac{1}{4}$–$3\frac{1}{8}$	$3\frac{3}{8}$–$3\frac{1}{4}$	$3\frac{5}{8}$–$3\frac{1}{2}$
Dutch Guilder	$8\frac{1}{8}$–8	8–$7\frac{7}{8}$	$7\frac{15}{16}$–$7\frac{13}{16}$	$7\frac{11}{16}$–$7\frac{9}{16}$	$7\frac{5}{16}$–$7\frac{3}{16}$	$6\frac{13}{16}$–$6\frac{11}{16}$
Swiss Franc	$5\frac{1}{2}$–$5\frac{1}{4}$	$5\frac{1}{2}$–$5\frac{1}{4}$	$5\frac{3}{8}$–$5\frac{1}{4}$	$5\frac{3}{16}$–$5\frac{1}{16}$	$4\frac{15}{16}$–$4\frac{13}{16}$	$4\frac{3}{4}$–$4\frac{1}{2}$
Deutschmark	$8\frac{1}{4}$–$8\frac{1}{8}$	$8\frac{1}{4}$–$8\frac{1}{8}$	$8\frac{3}{16}$–$8\frac{1}{16}$	$7\frac{15}{16}$–$7\frac{13}{16}$	$7\frac{1}{2}$–$7\frac{3}{8}$	$6\frac{15}{16}$–$6\frac{13}{16}$
French Franc	$10\frac{5}{8}$–$10\frac{3}{8}$	$10\frac{1}{2}$–$10\frac{1}{4}$	$10\frac{1}{2}$–$9\frac{7}{8}$	$9\frac{3}{4}$–$9\frac{1}{2}$	$9\frac{1}{8}$–$8\frac{7}{8}$	$8\frac{3}{8}$–$8\frac{1}{8}$
Italian Lira	$12\frac{1}{2}$–$10\frac{1}{2}$	$11\frac{7}{8}$–$11\frac{3}{8}$	$12\frac{1}{8}$–$11\frac{5}{8}$	$12\frac{1}{8}$–$11\frac{5}{8}$	12–$11\frac{5}{8}$	$12\frac{1}{8}$–$11\frac{5}{8}$
Japanese Yen	$3\frac{1}{8}$–$3\frac{1}{16}$	$3\frac{3}{16}$–$3\frac{1}{8}$	$3\frac{1}{4}$–$3\frac{3}{16}$	$3\frac{9}{32}$–$3\frac{7}{32}$	$3\frac{5}{16}$–$3\frac{1}{4}$	$3\frac{3}{8}$–$3\frac{5}{16}$

Source: *Financial Times*, 7 April 1993.
Note: Short-term rates are 'call' for US Dollars and Japanese Yen; others, two days' notice.

Table 7.3 shows a selection of interest rates for major eurocurrencies on 6 April 1993. Taking any particular time to maturity and looking down the column, the differentials between rates are quite clear. The relatively high rates on euro-deutschmark, euro-guilder and euro-French franc reflect the tight monetary policy being pursued at that time by the German authorities, in an attempt to subdue inflationary pressures, and the linkage between the three currencies through the EC's Exchange Rate Mechanism. Underlying the low rates on euro-yen was the low inflation and strong exchange rate position of Japan; whereas the much higher rates for the euro-lira may be explained by the much weaker position of Italy in respect of these variables. The low rates for euro-dollars were caused primarily by the policy of the US authorities to keep US interest rates low in an effort to stimulate economic expansion.

7.9.2   Eurocurrency interest rates and foreign exchange rates

The level of interest rates ruling for any given eurocurrency may have important implications for the exchange rate of the currency involved. Taking as an example the most important eurocurrency, the euro-dollar, the effects of changes in eurocurrency interest rates may be illustrated. Thus, an increase in the level of euro-dollar rates, other things being equal, is likely to lead to an increase in the volume of euro-dollar deposits. However, in order to make euro-dollar deposits, investors must obtain the necessary dollars. Some investors may initially be holding bank balances denominated in other currencies, and these may be used directly to purchase dollars on the foreign exchanges. Alternatively, investors might have to sell assets denominated in other currencies, and then switch the funds generated into dollars for depositing with banks outside of the USA.

Consequently, and irrespective of the precise portfolio adjustments undertaken, a *higher level of euro-dollar interest rates is likely to lead to an increase in the US dollar spot exchange rate*, as investors raise their demand for dollars for the purpose of making euro-dollar deposits. A reduction in euro-dollar rates is likely to have the opposite effect, as investors liquidate their euro-dollar deposits and switch to investments denominated in currencies which now offer relatively more attractive returns.

Changes in euro-dollar rates, other things being equal, will also have implications for forward transactions on the foreign currency exchange markets. This is because the *premiums and discounts on forward exchange rates* reflect the *differences between interest rates* on assets denominated in the currencies involved. The relationship can best be explained via a simple example. Thus, a UK-based bank may agree to sell dollars to a customer in three months' time. The bank will immediately purchase an appropriate amount of dollars on the spot market, and will then use these dollars to make a euro-dollar deposit with a three months maturity. Thus, the bank effectively converts an amount of funds which would otherwise have been held as interest-bearing sterling assets into an equal value of interest-bearing dollar assets. If the rate of interest which can be earned on the euro-dollars is less than that which can be earned on comparable sterling assets on the domestic market, the bank will charge a premium on the forward transaction in order to cover the interest rate differential, which amounts to a cost imposed on the bank. (This premium is in addition to charges which the bank will make for the various administrative expenses incurred.) Consequently, the *higher is the rate of interest* which the bank is able to earn on the *euro-dollar deposit*, the *smaller is the premium* which it will charge the customer. The existence of competitive financial markets will ensure that the premium is reduced, and that benefits from the higher euro-dollar rate are passed on to the customer. Alternatively, if the rate of interest paid on the euro-dollar deposit is initially higher than that which could be earned on domestic sterling deposits, the bank will offer a discount on the forward sale of dollars for sterling relative to the ruling spot rate. In this case, an increase in the euro-dollar rate will cause the *discount* to be *raised*, as the bank benefits from the increased interest rate differential in favour of euro-dollars. *A fall in the euro-dollar rate* would lead to a *reduction in the discount or an increase in the premium* on forward dollar sales to the bank's customer, depending upon the magnitude of the reduction in the euro-dollar rate and the value of the initial interest rate differential.

7.10   THE ECONOMIC EFFECTS OF CHANGES IN INTEREST RATES

The importance of interest rates for the operation of the modern economy cannot be overemphasised. Movements in interest rates are potentially of relevance to the *economic well-being of every individual and business organisation* in the country, and the *credibility of government economic policy* is often measured in terms of the level of key interest rates.

Therefore, to conclude this chapter on interest rates, it is appropriate to consider briefly the effects of changes in interest rates on major elements of the domestic economy. For clarity of exposition, the following discussion examines the main implications of an *increase* in interest rates; however, of course, the effects of a reduction in interest rates are largely the reverse of the effects to be analysed below. It should also be noted that the increase in interest rates is assumed to be an increase in real rates, unless otherwise stated.

7.10.1 Balance of payments

An increase in domestic interest rates, other things being equal, is likely to attract an *inflow of foreign short-term investment funds*, and may encourage the *repatriation of domestic funds held overseas*. In addition, domestic investors contemplating investing short-term funds overseas are more likely to keep their funds within the domestic economy. These effects, relevant for the portfolio investment elements of the capital account of the balance of payments, are likely to generate *upward pressures on the domestic currency's exchange rates*. If exchange rates are allowed to float freely, then the rates for the domestic currency may be pushed upwards. On the other hand, if the authorities seek to limit the movement of exchange rates, through the official purchase of foreign currency on the exchange market, then there is likely to be an increase in the country's foreign currency reserves or perhaps a reduction in outstanding official overseas debt, which will be reflected in the values of the relevant official elements of the capital account (see Chapter 9).

The effects on other elements of the capital account are *uncertain*, and much will depend upon both domestic and foreign investors' expectations of the likely influence of the higher level of interest rates on the growth and prosperity of the domestic economy. Thus, if it is believed that domestic economic activity is to be depressed for the foreseeable future, then there may be reduced inwards flows of direct capital investment, and perhaps increased outwards flows (as domestic investors seek better opportunities overseas). However, such investments are usually made on the basis of assessments of long-term prospects, which are *unlikely to be markedly affected* by an increase in interest rates. Indeed, as the portfolio flows would tend to constitute largely *short-term 'hot money'* responding to changes in interest rate differentials, it might only require some further relatively minor change in the financial environment to reverse the flows, and hence change the direction of the pressure placed on the domestic exchange rates.

The effect on the *current account* of the balance of payments will depend upon the extent to which *exchange rates* alter. If exchange rates for the domestic currency do rise, then exports will become less competitive overseas, and imports will become cheaper in domestic currency terms. This is likely to lead to an adverse movement in the volumes of trade, with more goods and services being imported and less exported; but the ultimate effect on the current account will depend upon the *elasticities of demand for traded goods and services.* As will be explained in Chapter 9, if elasticities are sufficiently high, the current account position will deteriorate, and ultimately the ability of the nation to pay its way internationally is likely to be called into question. The position is made slightly more complex by the possible depressing influence of higher interest rates on the level of domestic demand. Clearly, to the extent that this occurs, the growth of imports might not be as great as it otherwise would be.

In respect of both current and capital account adjustments, it must be acknowledged that *expectations* of future changes in interest rates, inflation rates and exchange rates may affect the response of traders and investors to current changes in interest rates. Thus, the higher level of domestic rates may simply be a response of the markets to expected inflation or perhaps a depreciating currency implied by a weak balance of payments position overall. Also, it is quite possible that other factors, such as comparable interest rate movements in major overseas countries, may cancel out any incentive created by changes in domestic interest rates to move funds between countries.

7.10.2 The personal sector

A major direct effect of higher rates of interest for the personal sector is likely to arise via the increase in *mortgage loan interest payments.* For those with outstanding mortgage loans, the amount of disposable income available for other expenditure purposes will be reduced, and hence their living standards are likely to be eroded. However, it should be recognised that the effects may only occur with a time lag, as some mortgage lenders alter rates on an annual basis, and others have arrangements for easing the effects of higher rates, perhaps via the addition of the extra interest charges to the outstanding capital sum.

Consumers' expenditure may also be discouraged by *higher rates on credit facilities* (overdrafts, personal loans, credit card balances, and so on). However, this effect will depend upon the *sensitivity* of borrowers to the interest element in the total debt repayment costs. Also, where rates of interest on consumer borrowing are in some way related to market rates of interest, the expectation of future reductions in rates may soften the effect of higher current costs of funds, as may expected higher rates of inflation.

The spending behaviour of those members of the personal sector who are running financial surpluses may also be affected, as higher rates of interest may encourage *higher levels of saving* (especially if higher fixed rates are on offer, and there is the expectation that rates are unlikely to rise any further in the foreseeable future). However, many economists believe that saving is relatively insensitive to interest rates, and that the level of total income is a far more important determinant. Indeed, for those individuals already holding funds in building society or bank accounts, there is likely to be an increase in their interest earnings, and this might even encourage them to raise their levels of expenditure.

Taking a somewhat broader perspective, to the extent that higher interest rates have a detrimental effect on the *business sector*, perhaps by *undermining capital investment and economic growth*, members of the personal sector may suffer via reduced *job prospects* and a slower improvement in *living standards*. However, if the increase in interest rates represents a real increase relative to rates ruling in major overseas economies, then it is probable that the domestic currency's *exchange rates* will be pushed upwards, and, at least in the shorter term, domestic consumers will find that the prices of imported goods and services will become relatively cheaper. In the longer term, the possible detrimental effects to the current account of the balance of payments are likely to reverse the initial movement in exchange rates, and whilst this will reduce the international purchasing power of the domestic currency, it will probably also improve the prospects for domestic employment, by providing a stimulus to the export industries.

7.10.3 The corporate sector

Higher rates of interest are likely to undermine the level of *capital investment* undertaken by companies. Where funds are already held (perhaps as a result of retaining profits), the opportunities offered for higher returns on safe financial investments (for example, in bank accounts or in government stocks) may make any previously marginal capital project proposals look unattractive. Similarly, where funds have to be borrowed, their now *higher cost* may reduce the expected profitability of projects to such a level that they no longer appear viable. In addition, if the business community believes that the higher rates of interest will lead to a general reduction in the level of domestic economic activity, as well as higher domestic currency exchange rates (at least in the shorter term), there is likely to be a downwards adjustment in *expectations of future business prospects*, which will further reduce the viability of capital investment projects. The *longer-term profitability and growth* of companies is, therefore, likely to be impaired. However, the strength of these effects depends very much upon the extent to which the higher rates represent higher real rates (which, in turn, depends upon expectations of future levels of inflation) and the period of time for which the rates are expected to remain high. Thus, for example, where an increase in rates is expected to be only a temporary phenomenon, capital investments may merely be delayed, and, indeed, where funds are to be raised at floating rates of interest, the increase in rates may have little significant effect.

To the extent that companies have large amounts of outstanding debt at floating rates, or find it necessary to borrow funds at the higher rates of interest, their total operating costs will be raised. Unless the additional cost can be passed on to the customer (and much will depend upon the state of competition in the markets for the companies' outputs), the level of profitability will be adversely affected. Conversely, where a company holds substantial amounts of surplus funds, in the form of deposits or marketable instruments which pay market-related rates of interest, its returns from these assets will be raised, and so too will be the contribution to the profitability of the company from this source. However, the evidence would suggest that this type of effect is unlikely to be of great significance for most companies.

7.10.4 The commercial banks

For wholesale banking activity, a rise in the general level of interest rates is likely to have its major effect in terms of depressing the *demand for loans*, whilst perhaps stimulating the *supply of funds* on to the markets. A great deal will depend upon what happens to the *profit margin*. If the margin remains unaltered, then a lower level of *turnover* will lead to a reduction in profitability; if the margin can be widened (which should be possible given the reduced demands for funds from borrowers, and hence the reduced need for banks to raise funds), then profitability may be maintained.

For retail banking, the situation is somewhat more complex. To the extent that banks have the use of funds deposited in non-interest-bearing sight accounts, a higher level of interest rates on loans enhances the '*endowment*' *effect*, although the higher rates may also depress the demand for loans, thus pulling in the opposite direction in relation to profitability levels. Further, there is the problem that *base rates* are administered by banks, and they tend to be moved only periodically, whilst in recent years an increasing proportion of funds has been raised at market-related rates; and therefore *margins may be squeezed* as market rates of interest rise. This effect may be particularly pronounced if banks have doubts as to the durability of the interest rate rise; expectations of future rate movements are crucial. However, banks may attempt to widen the margin between deposit rates and lending rates if the *demand for loans* is reduced by the higher rates of interest, thus reducing the amount of funds that banks have to raise.

For all banking institutions, higher rates of interest are likely to spell *capital losses* on holdings of *fixed interest securities*. There is also the problem that the value of some assets charged as security for bank loans may be eroded. The possible effects on banks' profits are clear. In addition, there is the possibility that higher interest rates may put more debts at risk. Inability to service loans may force business customers into liquidation and could lead to the bankruptcy of personal customers. If banks fear that this may occur, they may raise their level of *provisions*. Profits may also be hit to the extent that *economic activity* in general is depressed, thus reducing the demand for banking services, or if the domestic currency value of *overseas earnings* is reduced by any appreciation in the domestic currency which may be caused by the higher interest rates.

Finally, once again, it should be recognised that *expectations* of future inflation rates may be crucial in determining the actual outcome of an increase in nominal interest rates. Banks and their customers may not be unduly concerned if nominal interest changes are seen merely to compensate for expected price level changes.

7.11 EXAMINATION PRACTICE

7.11.1 Questions

The following questions are taken from past examination papers, and are intended to give students an indication of the type of questions which they are likely to face within the topic area of Interest Rates. Students may care to map out answers to these questions before consulting the guidance notes in 7.11.2. Each question carries 25 marks.

(1) (a) What factors determine the general level of interest rates in a country? (12)

(b) State the factors which are of specific relevance in determining:
(i) short-term interest rates;
(ii) long-term interest rates. (8)

(c) Are short-term interest rates always lower than long-term rates? Give reasons for your answer. (5)

(October 1991)

(2) (a) What is a yield curve? (5)

(b) Why is an upward sloping yield curve considered normal? (10)

(c) To what extent does the shape of the yield curve depend on expectations about the future? (10)

(May 1992)

(3) †(a) Explain in detail how the Bank of England influences money market interest rates. (10)

(b) To what extent do changes in money market rates lead to changes in:
(i) bank base rates; (5)
(ii) bank mortgage rates; (5)
(iii) gilt yields? (5)

(May 1992)

(4) (a) What is meant by the 'real' rate of interest and how is it calculated? (6)

‡(b) For what reasons might the UK Government reduce interest rates? (6)

†(c) What effect might a reduction in UK interest rates have on the banks? (13)

(October 1992)

319

(5) (a) Discuss the factors which determine the level of eurocurrency interest rates. (13)

   (b) Why are changes in eurodollar rates of importance to the foreign exchange markets? (12)

(May 1989)

(6) Analyse the effects of a rise in a country's interest rates on:

   (i) the personal sector;
   (ii) the corporate sector;
   †(iii) the commercial banks;
   ‡(iv) the capital account of the balance of payments.

(October 1988)

7.11.2 Guidance notes

(1) (i) This question relates to *what might happen in theory*. There is no need to discuss actual experience in respect of interest rates in the UK or in any other country.

(ii) The answer to part (a) requires an outline, *in general terms*, of the factors that influence the *general level of interest rates*. Key factors to mention include the rate of inflation, government economic policy, market expectations of future interest and inflation rates, interest rates in major overseas economies, and the supply of and demand for borrowed funds in general.

(iii) In part (b) it is necessary to *identify separately* the factors which specifically affect *short-term* interest rates and those which affect *long-term* rates. For part (b)(i), official money market intervention and market expectations in respect of such intervention must be emphasised. For part (b)(ii), the broad market forces dominate, including trends in the demand for longer-term investment funds and the size of the PSBR.

(iv) Part (c) requires a *brief explanation* of the factors affecting the *term structure of interest rates*, with particular reference to *expectations of lower rates of interest*, which may cause long-term rates to fall below short-term rates.

Source of relevant material:

Part (a)   7.3.5 and (as background) 7.3.1, 7.3.2, and 7.3.3.
Part (b)   (i)   7.3.5 (especially paragraph 1) and (as background) 7.3.3.
Part (b)   (ii)   7.3.5 (especially paragraph 2(b), (c) and (e)) and (as background) 7.3.2.
Part (c)   7.5.1, 7.5.2 and 7.5.3.

(2) (i) Part (a) of this question requires a *concise and precise definition of a yield curve*.

(ii) The answer to part (b) must *explain in detail* why a yield curve slopes upwards (from left to right) when there are *no general expectations of interest rate movements*. For full marks, the *various types of risk* associated with lending must be identified, and the relevance of *liquidity preference* must be explained.

(iii) In part (c), an explanation is required of how *expected higher rates of interest* will cause a yield curve to become steeper than it otherwise would be, and of how *expected lower rates of interest* will cause a yield curve to become flatter or even to slope downwards.

(iv) Simple diagrams in support of the answer to part (c) are helpful.

(v)   Discussion of actual experience of yield curves in the UK or in any other country is not required.

Source of relevant material:

Part (a)   7.5.1 and (as background) 7.5.2 and 7.5.3.
Part (b)   7.5.2.
Part (c)   7.5.3.

(3)   (i)   The answer to part (a) must focus upon Bank of England intervention in the money markets, and should include a clear description of how the Bank currently engages in *transactions in bills* as a means of influencing short-term interest rates. *Direct lending* by the Bank to the markets and *REPO agreements* should also be noted.

   (ii)   Discussion of why the Bank of England intervenes in the money markets or the nature of UK monetary policy and control is not required.

   (iii)   Throughout part (b) recognition must be made of *the extent to which* the items listed are influenced by changes in money market interest rates.

   (iv)   In part (b)(i) emphasis should be placed upon the *marginal cost of funds* to banks effectively being measured by the inter-bank lending rate. It must be explained that bank base rates tend to follow the *general trend* in money market interest rates, and do not reflect every minor fluctuation in the latter.

   (v)   The answer to (b)(ii) is very similar to that required for (b)(i), except that bank mortgage rates are more prone to the influence of factors such as *building society mortgage rates* and *expectations* of future interest rate movements.

   (vi)   In part (b)(iii) it should be recognised that gilt yields are determined by *the supply of and the demand for gilts.* Hence, whilst money market interest rates will be taken into account by gilts market participants, *other factors* such as expectations of inflation or government financing policy may be more important.

Source of relevant material:

†Part (a)   Chapter 5, at 5.3.3.
Part (b)   (i)   7.7.3.
Part (b)   (ii)   7.7.4.
Part (b)   (iii)   7.7.1.

(4) (i) The answer to part (a) requires a *clear definition* of a real rate of interest. The difference between a *known past real rate* and an *expected future real rate* should be noted. Also, as the calculation of a real rate of interest involves the use of a *price index*, the associated problem of *accuracy* should be recognised.

(ii) The answer to part (b) should outline the main reasons why the Government *might* wish to *reduce* interest rates. Discussion should not be restricted to the specific policies on interest rates which are currently being pursued, or have been pursued at some time in the past, in the UK.

(iii) Part (c) requires an examination of both the *direct and indirect effects* on banks which might be caused by a reduction in UK interest rates. The indirect effects should include those arising via the possible impact of a reduction in interest rates on *general economic prospects* and on the *exchange value of sterling*.

Source of relevant material:

Part (a) 7.2.1 and 7.2.2.
‡Part (b) 7.3.5 (paragraph 1(b) and paragraph 3(a)), 7.10 (as background), and Chapter 8, at 8.4.2.
†Part (c) 7.10.4 and (as background) Chapter 4, at 4.4.2 and 4.4.4.

(5) (i) Eurocurrency markets relate to *foreign currency denominated borrowing and lending*. Do not confuse these markets with the foreign exchange markets which relate to the buying and selling of currencies.

(ii) Part (a) of the question requires a discussion of both the factors determining the *absolute level* of eurocurrency interest rates, and the *general relationship* between the level of eurocurrency rates and the rates to be found in comparable domestic markets.

(iii) Discussion of the growth of the eurocurrency markets or the problems which they face is not required.

(iv) Part (b) of the question relates to the *euro-dollar*, rather than eurocurrencies in general. Also, it asks about the effects of changes in euro-dollar rates on foreign exchange markets, and not vice versa.

(v) In part (b) it is necessary to discuss the effects of changes in euro-dollar interest rates on both *spot and forward exchange markets*. Do not confuse euro-dollar interest rates with dollar exchange rates.

THE MONETARY AND FINANCIAL SYSTEM

Source of relevant material:

Part (a)   7.9.1.
Part (b)   7.9.2.

(6) (i)   The emphasis of the answer to this question must be placed
            upon *the effects of a rise in interest rates*. There is no need to
            discuss issues relating to the determination of interest rates or
            to recent UK experience in respect of interest rates.

     (ii)   Take care not to drift into a broad discussion of the role of
            interest rates in the economy as a whole. Maintain the focus of
            the answer on the specific aspects listed in the question.

     (iii) Note that a rise in *nominal* interest rates need not constitute a
            rise in *real* interest rates. In other words, it is necessary to take
            into account concurrent changes in the domestic rate of
            inflation. Changes in overseas interest rates are also relevant
            when considering the relative level of domestic interest rates.

     (iv)   Remember that changes in interest rates may have both direct
            and indirect effects on the various sectors of the economy, and
            that some of these effects may occur with a time lag.

     (v)   Do not confuse the personal sector with the private sector.

     (vi)   Do not confuse investment in real capital equipment with
            investment in interest-bearing financial assets.

Source of relevant material:

Part (i)   7.10.2.
Part (ii)   7.10.3.
†Part (iii) 7.10.4 and (as background) Chapter 4, at 4.4.2 and 4.4.4.
‡Part (iv) 7.10.1 (paragraphs 1, 2 and 4) and (as background) Chapter 9,
            at 9.2.2(b) and 9.5.3(a) and (b).

7.12 FURTHER STUDY

The interest rate topic is one of the most important within the syllabus for The Monetary and Financial System. Students should not only attempt to master the basic principles relating to the determination of the level and structure of interest rates, but also they should recognise the practical significance of interest rates for issues such as the growth of the money supply, the operations of financial institutions and markets, the implementation of official monetary policy and controls, exchange rate determination and the balance of payments. It is important that theoretical concepts should be related to the operation of the modern financial system, and care should be taken not to confuse possible theoretical alternatives with what has actually happened in the UK or in any other major economy.

Therefore, having studied the contents of the present chapter, students would be well-advised to consult regularly the financial pages of the quality press, remaining alert for commentaries on developments relating to interest rates and their effects on business and the personal sector. Analyses of the Government's monetary policy position are also of great relevance, and once again the *Bank of England Quarterly Bulletin* provides an excellent source of up-to-date material.

The Money Markets page of the *Financial Times* and *The Economist's* Economic and Financial Indicators pages (to be found at the end of each issue) together with supporting analyses, provide a wealth of useful factual material. The Economics page of *Banking World* is relevant for broader background issues.

8 ECONOMIC POLICY

8.1 INTRODUCTION

8.1.1 Background issues

During the 1980s, in most Western nations, monetary policy, directed towards the control of the money supply, tended to take an extremely important position in respect of government economic policy. As far as the UK was concerned, it is probably correct to suggest that monetary policy came to dominate the Government's approach to its management of the economy, with other policies being relegated to merely a supportive role. However, the 1980s may be thought of as being somewhat special in the post-war history of economic policy. The more usual approach, which began to re-emerge during the later years of the 1980s, has tended to involve a balanced application of a *range of policies* designed to achieve a *set of economic policy objectives*. In this context, government decisions have focused upon the selection of the 'correct' mix of policies, with the view to achieving an optimal outcome in respect of the running of the economy.

Strictly, the term 'economic policy' may relate to the Government's position on any aspect of economic activity, from help which may be provided for the establishment of small businesses, through to the application of economy-wide counter-inflation initiatives. However, the discussion in the following sections of this chapter will focus primarily upon policies which relate to the operation of the economy as a whole. Such policies are often referred to as *macroeconomic policies*, and they are the ones which most people tend to think of within the context of the economic policy debate. The policies which relate to the operation of individual firms or industrial activities in particular regions (i.e. the microeconomic policies) are beyond the scope of this book.

8.1.2 The nature of economic policy

Economic policy may be defined as the position taken by the Government in respect of its *discretionary interference* with the operation of the economy. At one extreme the Government may engage in substantial deliberate manipulation of major economic variables. At the other extreme the official policy may be one of minimal intervention, with an implied dependence on the natural forces of the free market system to take the economy towards a desired optimal position. Irrespective of the

Government's political views or its beliefs about how the economy operates, it will always take some position on all major aspects of economic policy. This is because all governments are aware of the policy options, and hence merely to do nothing in relation to some aspect of policy is clearly a consciously taken decision, which, it may be presumed, is aimed at helping to secure some desired policy objective.

The major forms of economic policy may be summarised as follows:

(a) *Monetary policy* involves the control of some measure(s) of the money supply and/or the level and structure of interest rates. This policy is examined in detail at 8.4 below, but for the moment it should be recognised that it forms just one, albeit important, part of the Government's policy package. This fact helps to explain some of the difficulties which are faced in respect of the implementation and operation of monetary policy. Furthermore, the importance attached to monetary policy by the Government will depend not only upon its perception of the effects on the economy of changes in the money supply or interest rates, but also upon its ordering of policy objectives. Thus, where strict control of the money supply is seen as being paramount, perhaps with the view to controlling the rate of inflation, the monetary policy will be the major element of the economic policy package. The other components of the package may then be structured so as to support the monetary policy. Alternatively, the monetary policy itself may be used to support other policies, which may take a dominant role.

(b) *Fiscal policy* involves decisions on the level and structure of taxation and government expenditure, and hence, by implication, the public sector borrowing requirement or debt repayment. (As explained in Chapter 6, the PSBR or PSDR forms an important link with the operation of monetary policy.) Traditionally, fiscal policy has been regarded as a major means of managing aggregate (total) demand within the economy, and hence of influencing, for example, the level of output and employment. It is common for fiscal policy to be used in concert with other policies. Thus, for example, an expansionary fiscal policy, designed to raise the level of demand within the economy and hence raise total output, may be accompanied by a monetary policy designed to accommodate any ensuing changes in the demand for money, and hence to stabilise interest rates. However, it may be the case that the authorities take a pragmatic view of policy, and whilst not wishing to see excessive monetary expansion in the longer term, may be willing to countenance some accommodation to changes in the demand for money, in order to avoid excessive fluctuations in interest rates. (The nature of fiscal policy and demand management are dealt with in more detail at 8.3 below.)

(c) *National debt management policy* is closely related to monetary and fiscal policies, and involves the manipulation of the outstanding stock of government debt instruments held by the domestic private sector. This policy may be aimed at influencing the level and structure of interest rates or the availability of liquid reserve assets to the banking sector. (For further discussion of national debt management policy, see Chapter 6, at 6.5.5.)

(d) *Exchange rate policy* may be directed towards achieving some target for the exchange value of the domestic currency in terms of foreign currencies, perhaps with the objective of influencing the country's international trading and investment patterns. This particular policy may be regarded as being a member of a broader group of policies designed to affect current account flows on the balance of payments, and including the use of instruments such as tariffs on imports, import quotas and exchange controls. (General issues relating to exchange rate policy are examined in Chapter 10, at 10.6.)

(e) *Prices and incomes policy* involves the implementation of either statutory or voluntary restrictions on the setting of prices and/or wages, with the obvious aim of influencing the rates of price and wage inflation. The levels of dividend payments by companies and interest charges on borrowed funds may also be restricted. These policies may form part of a broader demand management policy as will be explained below at 8.3.1.

It is important to appreciate that whilst the various forms of economic policy may be listed separately, in reality there is *considerable overlap* between policies in relation to both their implementation and their operation. Indeed, it is quite possible that the successful outcome of one policy may be frustrated by the side-effects flowing from the operation of another policy. For example, the Government may introduce a monetary policy directed towards holding down the rate of growth of the money supply, but if, at the same time, it is running a fiscal policy which necessitates large amounts of public sector borrowing from the banking sector, the desired effect of the monetary policy may be frustrated. Similarly, a policy of keeping the domestic currency's exchange rate below a particular value in terms of other major currencies, may be undermined by the operation of strict monetary controls, which push up domestic interest rates and hence cause foreign currency capital inflows, which, of course, will put upwards pressure on the exchange rate (see Chapter 10, at 10.3.1(b)).

8.2 THE OPERATION OF ECONOMIC POLICY

8.2.1 The objectives of economic policy

It is generally agreed that all governments, irrespective of their political beliefs, would like to achieve the following major economic policy objectives:

(a) *Full employment of the labour force*, or, perhaps more precisely, the provision of suitable employment for all those willing and able to work.

(b) *A stable price level*, or, at least, only a low rate of inflation, in order to avoid the damage which may be caused to the economy by a falling purchasing power of the domestic currency (as was explained in Chapter 1, at 1.10.4).

(c) *A balance of payments equilibrium* in the longer term, or, perhaps, a small surplus, ideally on the current account, as a means of ensuring the country's ability to pay its way internationally, and especially its ability to purchase necessary imports when required.

(d) *A satisfactory rate of economic growth*, in order to ensure that living standards may be raised over time.

In addition, individual governments may attempt to pursue other, more specialised, economic objectives, such as the redistribution of income and/or wealth within society, in order to achieve a desired distribution of benefits from the nation's available resources. There may also be general policies directed towards the ownership of major parts of the nation's industrial or commercial sectors, and it is often thought to be desirable for a developed country to have a sufficiently strong economy in order to allow it to be able to provide foreign aid to less fortunate developing nations.

8.2.2 The implementation of economic policy

All economic policies may be examined within a framework based upon the concepts of instruments, targets and objectives.

- *Objectives* are the ultimate goals of policy, as described at 8.2.1 above.
- *Intermediate targets* are variables through which the authorities attempt to achieve their objectives.
- *Instruments* are variables over which the authorities have some control, and through which they hope to influence target variables.

Table 8.1 Examples of instruments, intermediate targets and objectives

Policy	Instruments	Intermediate targets			Objectives
Monetary	Open market operations (official purchases/sales of debt instruments)	Short-term interest rates	Rate of growth of monetary aggregates		Rate of inflation
Monetary	Ceilings on bank lending	Banks' credit creation	Aggregate demand		Rate of Inflation
Monetary	Special deposits	Banks' holdings of liquid reserve assets	Level of interest rates	International capital flows	Balance of payments
Fiscal	Government expenditure plans	Actual government expenditure on goods	Aggregate demand	Domestic output	Employment
Fiscal	Income tax rates	Disposable income	Aggregate demand	Level of imports	Balance of payments
Fiscal	Tax allowances for capital investment	Level of real capital investment			Long-term economic growth
Prices and incomes	Legislation	Wage demands	Wage settlements	Domestic production costs	Rate of inflation
Exchange rate	Devaluation (within a fixed exchange rate regime)	Relative prices of internationally-traded goods	Levels of exports and imports		Balance of payments
National debt management	Open market operations	Level of long-term interest rates	Level of real capital investment	Domestic output	Employment

Table 8.1 shows a number of examples of economic policies with their associated chains of instruments, targets and objectives. It may be observed that in respect of some policies, there may be a sequence of intermediate targets; whilst other policies have a more direct route to the final objective. Also, it must be emphasised that the examples shown are not exhaustive, and that each row in the table implies a specific view as to how a policy works in practice. Thus, it would be equally acceptable to show a monetary policy using open market operations as the instrument, but aimed at the level of interest rates and aggregate demand, as the intermediate targets, with the level of employment being the final objective.

For economic policies to be able to achieve their objectives, it is necessary that the authorities are able to *control their intermediate target variables via their policy instruments*, and that the *final objectives are sensitive to changes in target variables*. In respect of the former requirement, there are three problems to consider:

(a) *Instruments may not be controllable independently*. For example, when the Government sets the rates of taxation and its expenditure plans, this will imply a particular value for the PSBR or PSDR during the planning period. This clearly limits the freedom of the authorities in respect of the implementation of monetary controls, given the potential importance of the PSBR/PSDR for money supply growth.

(b) *Intermediate target variables may be difficult to define*. For example, there is much uncertainty over the appropriate measure(s) of the money supply for control purposes.

(c) The achievement of a desired change in an intermediate target variable may depend critically upon *how the private sector reacts* to the implementation of a change in the chosen policy instrument. For example, if an increase in the rate of income tax has no effect on work effort or desired hours of work, the level of private sector disposable income will fall, and so total spending within the economy may be reduced. However, the increased income tax rate may cause people to work harder and for longer hours, in order to maintain their net of tax income, and this may frustrate the objectives of the policy by allowing the private sector to maintain its initial level of expenditure.

In respect of the requirement that policy objectives should be sensitive to changes in intermediate target variables, the major problem is quite simply that *inappropriate target variables* may be chosen. Thus, for example, whilst the authorities might be successful in reducing the rate of growth of the money supply, according to a particular measure of money, this may not lead to the control of the rate of inflation (in the manner predicted by the monetarists), if the measure chosen happens to be the wrong one for policy purposes. As a further example, whilst capital investment may be sensitive to changes in interest rates in most instances, a policy of reducing interest rates may fail to stimulate capital investment if there happens to be a massive amount of excess productive capacity, and little prospect of any increase in the demand for its output. In this instance, the level of interest rates is an inappropriate target variable if it is hoped to raise the level of investment.

It cannot be emphasised too strongly that for a policy to be effective, both of the broad requirements specified above must be satisfied. One weak link in the policy's operational chain will be sufficient to undermine its effectiveness. It is also important that policies are implemented at the *correct time*, given the unavoidable lags in their operation. A policy which is implemented at the wrong time may only begin to affect its objective at a time when it is not required, and may end up doing more harm than good to the economy. For example, an expansionary fiscal policy may be introduced in the face of rising unemployment, but may fail to affect total demand in the economy until a time when output is increasing rapidly due to free market forces. Thus, the fiscal policy may only serve to generate unwanted inflationary pressures, rather than helping to stimulate real output and employment. Clearly, successful policies require careful planning on the basis of accurate predictions of future economic prospects. Indeed, it is doubt over the authorities' ability to implement policy changes at the right time which motivates some economists to argue against the use of policy for 'fine tuning' the economy. They would argue that, on balance, discretionary tinkering with policy instruments is likely to damage the economy, and that hence the best approach to policy is for the authorities to create a stable monetary and financial environment within which private sector enterprise may flourish.

8.2.3 The conflict between policy objectives

Experience has shown that, other than for relatively short periods of time, governments have rarely achieved more than two of their major policy objectives (as listed at 8.2.1) simultaneously. In the light of the difficulties surrounding the implementation of policies, as outlined above, this is hardly surprising. However, the government's position is made even more difficult by the existence of *natural inherent conflicts between the achievement of individual objectives when specific policy instruments are applied*.

There are many ways in which policies may conflict. Taking the application of a fiscal policy, for example, the authorities may reduce income taxes with the view to stimulating aggregate demand within the economy, reducing unemployment and perhaps encouraging future economic growth. However, to the extent that the domestic economy is unable to meet the additional demands placed upon it, there are likely to be inflationary pressures generated, and the current account of the balance of payments may deteriorate as imports are sucked into the country whilst potential export goods are diverted to the domestic market.

A further example is the application of a strict monetary policy intended to hold down money supply growth, with the ultimate objective being the defeat of inflation. Unfortunately, in the short term at least, this policy is likely to depress demand for domestic output (as credit is constrained), and the possibly higher rates of interest caused will tend to force up the domestic currency's exchange rates, thus making exports more expensive overseas, and imports cheaper domestically (perhaps undermining the balance of payments position). High rates of interest are also likely to prove detrimental to the achievement of the economic growth objective, as capital investment is depressed, and unemployment may rise.

In the face of these inherent conflicts, the Government is likely to be forced to identify the *trade-offs between policy objectives*, and hence devise a package of measures which aims to achieve an optimal balance in respect of these objectives. For example, a tight monetary policy may be combined with an expansionary fiscal policy, in the hope of holding down inflationary pressures whilst at the same time stimulating demand for domestic output. Of course, the monetarist school of thought would suggest that the defeat of inflation must take priority above all other policy objectives, and all policy instruments must be directed towards this goal. It is argued that the other major objectives of policy will be achieved naturally (indeed can only be achieved in a sustained manner) once inflation has been defeated. Thus, monetarists take a somewhat extreme view of the policy conflicts and select just one policy objective for 'intensive treatment', leaving the remaining objectives to natural economic forces. However, given the inherent policy conflicts which are widely recognised, it is probably correct to suggest that most governments, irrespective of their economic ideology, set priorities for policy objectives, which are likely to vary over time depending upon the political mood and social pressures. The state of knowledge on the economic relationships between inflation and unemployment, between economic growth and the balance of payments, and so on, is also a vital determinant of the ultimate policy framework established.

8.3 DEMAND MANAGEMENT AND FISCAL POLICY

8.3.1 Principles of demand management

Whilst the dominant theme of economic policy during the 1980s was monetary control within the broad monetarist framework (as was outlined in Chapter 1, at 1.10.2), during the 1960s and 1970s policy was of a form which might loosely be described as *demand management*. This approach to policy, which has been slowly re-emerging since the beginning of the 1990s within the economic policy formulations of some Western nations, is based on the theory propounded by J. M. Keynes. This theory is driven by the belief that it is the level of *aggregate (total) demand* within an economy which determines the amount of output produced by that economy, and hence the level of employment. Thus, it is argued that if the authorities are able to influence the components of aggregate demand, they will be able to manage the real economic variables which actually matter to the well-being of the economy.

The components of aggregate demand may be classified as follows:

- Private sector expenditure on consumer goods and services (consumption).
- Private sector investment expenditure, including the purchase of both new capital equipment by firms and newly constructed dwellings by the personal sector (investment).
- Government expenditure on goods and services.

The sum of consumption, investment and government expenditure on goods and services gives a measure of *total domestic expenditure*, which would be equal to aggregate demand if there were no international transactions. However, for an *open economy* it is necessary to take into account internationally traded goods and services:

- Expenditure by foreigners on domestically-produced goods and services (exports) must be added to the value for total domestic expenditure.
- Expenditure by domestic residents on foreign-produced goods and services (imports) must be subtracted from the value for total domestic expenditure, as this represents the portion of the latter that is not matched by domestic output.

Therefore, if the authorities are able to raise any element of consumption, investment, government expenditure (on goods and services) or exports, or reduce imports, they will be able to raise aggregate demand for domestic output, and hence raise the levels of national product and employment, assuming that sufficient productive capacity is available within the economy. This latter assumption is extremely important, for without an appropriate adjustment of *aggregate supply*, any increase in aggregate demand is likely to place upwards pressure on *domestic inflation rates*.

As already mentioned, an important means of managing aggregate demand is via the use of *fiscal policy*, and this will be examined in detail below. However, it should be recognised that the instruments associated with other forms of economic policy may also have a significant impact upon the level of demand within the economy. Thus, for example, whilst strict control of the money supply tends to be associated with monetarist policies directed towards the control of inflation, it must not be forgotten that the level of interest rates and the availability of credit are important factors in respect of private sector investment decisions, and may also influence the level of domestic consumption. Consequently, *monetary policy* may be explicitly directed towards aggregate demand management. Indeed, some economists would argue that it is via the suppression of aggregate demand that the monetarist anti-inflation policy has its major impact upon the operation of the economy.

The manipulation of the *domestic currency's exchange rate* (which is examined in Chapter 10, at 10.6) is of particular relevance to the management of the international elements of aggregate demand. For example, by reducing the exchange value of sterling, other things being equal, UK-produced goods and services are made cheaper in foreign currency terms, with the probable outcome that the demand for UK exports will be raised; conversely, foreign-produced goods and services will become more expensive in sterling terms, thus tending to reduce the demand for imports within the UK. The net effect on real aggregate demand, and hence domestic output and employment in the UK, is likely to be positive. (The precise impact on the current account of the balance of payments will depend upon the elasticities of demand for traded goods and services, as will be explained in Chapter 9, at 9.5.2(a)(i).) Clearly, the exchange rate policy pursued by the authorities may have important implications for overall levels of demand within the economy, irrespective of whether or not this is a chosen target of the policy.

Prices and incomes policy may also contribute to the control of aggregate demand, by way of its impact upon the growth of private sector disposable income, and hence the ability of individuals and firms to purchase goods and services at any given price level. However, such policy is normally seen as being a direct means of holding down the rate of inflation, and its use for explicit demand management objectives would be rather unconventional, and possibly somewhat unpredictable in its outcome.

8.3.2 The nature of fiscal policy

Within democratic nations, governments may not simply seize the resources that they require to carry out their perceived functions, unless, of course, they are facing a dire national emergency. Rather, governments must normally raise funds with which to purchase from the private sector the goods and services required. In other words, governments are bound by a *budget constraint*, which may be specified as follows:

| Government expenditure | − | Tax revenue and income from other sources (including public sector asset sales) | = | Government borrowing requirement |

Fiscal policy relates to the setting of the variables included within the budget constraint, and may have both direct and indirect impacts upon aggregate demand within the economy. *Government expenditure*, to the extent that it involves the purchase of goods and services from the private sector, has a direct effect on the level of aggregate demand. *Transfer payments*, which include state pensions, unemployment pay and grants to students, are also included in the overall figure for government expenditure, but they will only affect aggregate demand indirectly via the spending behaviour of the recipients. Furthermore, some transfer payments may be used for the purchase of imported goods and services, and hence may have no impact on domestic aggregate demand. Changes in *taxation* will also operate indirectly, and may affect aggregate demand to the extent that changes in private sector disposable income influence expenditure decisions.

It is important to appreciate that fiscal policy need not have explicit demand management objectives. For so long as the Government spends, it will require some form of fiscal policy as a means of establishing the required financing. However, irrespective of the policy's precise objectives, in all probability it will have *monetary implications* operating both directly and indirectly. The relevance of the *Public Sector Borrowing Requirement* (or *Public Sector Debt Repayment*), and the precise ways in which fiscal policy may be used to alter its value, have already been examined (in Chapter 6, at 6.5). It should now be recognised that the amount and requisite financing of public sector borrowing (or debt repayment) is likely to be influenced significantly by the effects of the fiscal policy as a whole on the *operation of the economy*. For example, the degree of success of an expansionary fiscal policy, involving a higher level of government expenditure, will determine the amount of additional tax revenues consequently generated, and hence the amount of additional government borrowing which will be required. Furthermore, the effects of a fiscal policy on the level and nature of economic activity may also tend to have monetary implications, arising particularly from any consequent changes in the demand for money balances, and hence interest rates and credit creation by banks and building societies. (Relevant issues in this respect have already been examined in Chapter 4, at 4.4.6(b).)

8.4 MONETARY POLICY

8.4.1 The nature of monetary policy

In Chapter 6, the 'natural' forces influencing the rate of growth of the money supply were examined, on the basis of the assumption that the authorities were not acting deliberately to interfere with the money creation process. However, of course, in reality this assumption may not be valid, as it is possible that the rate of money supply growth, or the level and structure of interest rates, implied by the operation of free market forces, may be incompatible with the authorities' desired economic policy objectives. Thus, the authorities may attempt to pursue an active monetary policy, involving the official manipulation of monetary target variables.

The authorities may attempt to influence either some measure(s) of the money supply or the level and/or structure of interest rates. It is important to understand that in a modern financial system, where a very large proportion of the money supply is created by private sector financial institutions, it is not possible for the authorities to control *both* the money supply *and* interest rates *independently*, at least, that is, other than in the short run, using extremely restrictive monetary controls. Thus, at one extreme, the authorities may attempt to *set the quantity of money* available in the economy, but in this case it will be the nature of the private sector's demand for money which will determine the level and structure of interest rates. At the other extreme, there may be an attempt to *peg the level or structure of interest rates*, in which case the authorities must be willing to allow the supply of money to adjust accordingly in order to meet demand. Alternatively, the authorities may be willing to see some accommodation of changes in the demand for money, in order to avoid excessive movements in interest rates, without following a strict policy of pegging interest rates. But nevertheless, the fact still remains that the authorities cannot choose both money supply growth rates and interest rates independently.

It must be emphasised that the above comments relate to the operation of *free market adjustments* within the financial system. It is, of course, possible that the authorities may impose wide-ranging portfolio constraints (to be examined at 8.5.2(b) below) on deposit-taking and on-lending activities of financial institutions, in an effort to influence both the rate of growth of the money supply, and the level and structure of interest rates. For example, reserve requirements may be stipulated, in an attempt to control the creation of bank and building society deposits, and at the same time directives might be issued to limit the interest rates which may be charged on loans made by banks and building societies. Therefore, these institutions would not be able to utilise the market mechanism to allocate their available funds, and hence would be forced to use some other form of rationing device (perhaps lending funds according to the category of customer, or perhaps simply on a first-come-first-served basis) if demand for loans outstripped their ability to lend at the fixed maximum rate of interest. However, the important issue here is that whilst direct intervention by the authorities may lead to the control of both the money supply and interest rates in the short term, in all probability it will also distort the financial system and generate pressures for *disintermediation* to take place. Basically, this means that borrowing and lending transactions are pushed outside the controlled areas of the financial system as prospective borrowers, frustrated by the monetary controls, seek out potential providers of funds and perhaps offer better returns than are available from the controlled institutions. As mentioned in Chapter 6, at 6.9.1), this disintermediaton activity distorts the interpretation of monetary aggregates which embody primarily the liabilities of the institutions which are being controlled directly, and consequently uncertainty arises as to whether the monetary aggregate being controlled is the right one for policy purposes. Quite simply, the disintermediation activity may cause the measure of the money supply deemed to be relevant to the determination of private sector expenditure decisions to evolve beyond that measure of the money supply which is the target of the authorities' controls. Therefore, the authorities are likely to find that they are no longer controlling a measure of the money supply which is meaningful for policy purposes; and, in any event, the disintermediation process is likely to take place at rates of interest which are different to those ruling within the controlled sector, if the latter are held artificially low.

8.4.2 Intermediate target variables of monetary policy

The possible intermediate targets of monetary policy include the following:

(a) *The rate of growth of the money supply.* This is the well-known target variable of the monetarist policy for dealing with *inflation*, especially in the longer term. Monetarists would argue that the rate of growth of the money supply must be controlled if the price level is to be stabilised. Unfortunately, a major problem in utilising this target variable is in determining which measure of the money supply to use.

(b) *The level and/or structure of interest rates.* This is also a widely-recognised target of monetary policy. The basic notion here may be that by altering interest rates the authorities may be able to influence *interest-sensitive expenditure* relating to both business investment and consumer spending. Changes in interest rates may also have implications for international currency flows, and hence for the balance of payments. In addition, it is important to recognise that changes in interest rates may be used as a means of influencing *other intermediate target variables*, and hence may be part of a chain of intermediate targets. For example, an increase in the level of interest rates may be affected by the authorities in the hope of damping down the demand for bank and building society credit, and hence reducing the rate of growth of the money supply.

(c) *Bank and building society credit creation.* As members of the non-bank non-building society private sector obtain credit primarily to finance expenditure on goods, services and real assets, there is likely to be a predictable relationship between the extension of bank and building society credit and the total level of *private sector expenditures*. It should also be remembered that bank and building society credit creation is an important element in explaining changes in the money supply.

(d) *Currency exchange rates.* These may be a target variable, with the view to affecting the relative prices of exports and imports, and hence influencing the *current account of the balance of payments*, *domestic output* and *employment*, and the *rate of inflation*. There are also implications for business confidence, and hence longer-term international capital movements.

(e) *Nominal domestic expenditure (or national income).* It is quite acceptable to consider the level of domestic expenditure as a target for policy, as ultimately the manipulation of this variable may be expected to have an influence upon the *rate of inflation* and/or the levels of *output* and *employment*. In this case, the monetary policy instruments would be set in the light of the growth of domestic expenditure, and thus the authorities would be able to work via a target variable which is closely related to their policy objective.

Ultimately, the choice of target variable(s) by the authorities will depend upon their views on *how the economy operates* and their beliefs about the *strength and stability of the relationships* between the target variable(s) and the desired policy objective(s). Furthermore, there has been considerable debate about whether or not chosen targets should be *publicised in advance* of their application. Most countries which do adhere to monetary targets do tend to make these widely known in advance, but it would be quite acceptable for targets to be set for internal control purposes by the authorities, without making them known to the general public. The main argument in favour of advance publication of targets is that private sector *expectations* may be influenced, and hence behaviour affected favourably. For example, if tight monetary controls are implied by the target, wage demands and price setting behaviour might be moderated, and the inflation objective facilitated. In addition, it is argued that the actions of the authorities are put in the spot-light, and thus they are less likely to allow *political expediency* to compromise the required monetary policy actions.

However, the advance publication of targets is not without its *disadvantages*, and a particular danger is that rigidity may be built into the economic policy framework, thus making it harder for the authorities to change the course of policy should the economic environment alter. In other words, the authorities will feel obliged to justify explicitly any policy changes which appear to conflict with their published targets. Indeed, the prospect of political embarrassment for the Government when targets are not met, may cause it to continue with policies even when it has become clear that those policies have been overtaken by events. This position is obviously unfavourable for the long-term health of the economy.

8.5 METHODS OF MONETARY CONTROL

8.5.1 Basic principles

In order to formulate methods for the effective control of the money supply and/or interest rates, *it is necessary to identify the potential components of the money supply*. As was explained in Chapter 1, the most widely accepted measures of the money supply embody cash (notes and coin), bank deposits and building society deposits (and shares) held by the non-bank non-building society private sector. Thus, specific controls may be directed towards some or all of these components, depending upon the broadness of the money measure which the authorities seek to control.

In the UK financial system, *cash* is a relatively small element of the money supply, but it must never be forgotten that it forms a crucial element in the *reserve base* required for the creation of credit (deposits) by banks and building societies. Therefore, to some extent, control of the cash base of the economy may be desired by the authorities as a means of influencing the broader money measures. The supply of new cash to the private sector is under the *direct control* of the monetary authorities, and hence there is, in theory at least, no difficulty in controlling the rate of growth of the cash base. Moreover, it is relatively easy for the authorities to manipulate the amount of cash in circulation, using, for example, official open market purchases or sales of government securities from or to the private sector. As a longer-term measure, the Government may regulate the volume of borrowing that it undertakes from the central bank, thus affecting the flow of new cash into the economy via this channel.

The main focus of monetary controls is the *creation of credit* by banks and building societies, which is of overriding importance to the conventional measures of the money supply. At a very basic level such controls may be directed towards attacking the willingness of members of the non-bank non-building society private sector to borrow (that is, the controls may attempt to undermine the *demand for credit*), or the ability and/or willingness of banks and building societies to lend (that is, the controls may attack the *supply of credit*). It should also be recognised that the instruments which may be used in this context, which are outlined in 8.5.2 below, may also have implications for the growth rate of holdings of *other liquid assets* which fall outside of the official measures of the money supply.

8.5.2 The instruments of monetary control

The instruments of monetary control may be divided into three broad groups:

- instruments of market intervention
- instruments of portfolio constraint
- longer-term control mechanisms.

(a) *Instruments of market intervention*

Within the context of the UK institutional framework, instruments of market intervention comprise the Bank of England's *open market operations* and the setting of its *discount rate* (currently referred to as intervention rate). This latter rate is effectively the price charged by the Bank for funds supplied to the discount market in the event of a general shortage of liquidity. In recent years (as was explained in detail in Chapter 5, at 5.3.3) intervention rate has normally represented the rate of discount which the discount houses have been 'forced' to accept from the Bank in respect of their bill sales to the Bank. In addition, in certain circumstances the Bank may be willing to make secured loans to the discount houses, again charged at the discount rate. The influence of this rate on the financial system is pervasive, as it measures the *marginal cost of funds* to the banking system as a whole. Changes in the discount rate give important signals in respect of the likely future trend of interest rates in general, but especially the trend in short-term rates.

Open market operations occur when the Bank intervenes in the markets for securities, either buying or selling depending upon its objectives in relation to the level and structure of interest rates and/or the volume of liquidity in the financial system. The Bank trades extensively in the discount market, and hence its greatest influence is exerted upon short-term interest rates, but it may also buy or sell long-term gilt-edged securities, thus having a somewhat more direct effect on long-term rates. Indeed, open market operations may be used to engineer a shortage of liquidity on the money markets, thus causing the discount houses to sell bills to, or take loans from, the Bank at intervention rate.

The instruments of market intervention are likely to have a fairly *generalised* effect on financial conditions. Thus, if interest rates are pushed upwards, this may dampen the demand for mortgage loans from building societies and hire purchase credit from finance houses, as well as the demand for bank loans. There are clear political and social implications here, and, in addition, there may be perverse effects in the short-term, as corporate borrowers engage in additional borrowing in order to meet their now higher debt servicing commitments (assuming that funds have been borrowed at market-related rates).

(b) *Instruments of portfolio constraint*

Although these instruments could be applied broadly, in practice they are normally applied to specific groups of financial institutions, and hence they tend to operate in a *discriminatory* manner. This is clearly inequitable, and the controls may generate conditions which undermine their own effectiveness in the longer term. In other words, *disintermediation* may occur, as non-controlled institutions attempt to take up any business driven away from the controlled parts of the financial system.

In the UK, portfolio constraints have only ever been applied to banking institutions, but in theory they could be applied to any form of lending institution as relevant for monetary control. The major portfolio constraints are *reserve requirements, special deposits, supplementary special deposits, moral suasion,* and *direct controls on lending and interest rates*:

(i)　In order to create deposits, banks and building societies must hold a *reserve asset base*, usually in the form of cash or other liquid assets. When an institution reaches its minimum desired reserve ratio, assuming that there are unsatisfied demands for loans, it either has to turn away potential borrowers or it has to attract more deposits and/or purchase reserve assets. In either event, it is likely that interest rates will be pushed upwards, which will restrain the demand for loans. Thus, if the authorities are able to influence the total *supply of reserve assets*, perhaps via the use of open market operations or a call for special deposits (see below), or are able to dictate a change in the *required reserve ratio*, they should be able to exert pressure on the level of deposit creation and hence the rate of growth of the money supply.

(ii) The Bank of England may require that certain banking institutions place funds with it, equal to a certain percentage of a selected group of their deposit liabilities. These *special deposits* are then effectively frozen at the Bank, and whilst they appear on the assets side of the banking institutions' balance sheets, they *cannot be used as part of any reserve base*. Thus, a call for special deposits has an immediate impact on the credit creating power within the financial system, other things being equal. Special deposits have a similar ultimate effect to official open market sales of longer-term securities to the private sector, although they tend to act quicker and are useful for mopping up excess reserves held within the banking system. Also, as banks are able to adjust their reserve positions steadily following a call for special deposits, there is unlikely to be undue destabilisation within the financial markets.

(iii) The authorities may fix an *upper target limit* for some category of *deposit liabilities* of banking institutions. In the UK, between 1973 and 1980, the so-called 'corset' mechanism operated periodically. Within this regime, controlled institutions were expected not to exceed a maximum target growth rate for their interest-bearing eligible liabilities (i.e. sterling deposits with less than two years to maturity). If institutions did overshoot the target rate, they would be required to pay *supplementary special deposits* to the Bank of England. These supplementary special deposits were paid on a scale related to the degree of target overshoot; they could not be used as part of the reserve base by banks; and they attracted no interest payment from the Bank of England (unlike ordinary special deposits). The major advantages of this type of control are that it focuses attention squarely upon an important element of the money supply, it makes institutions immediately aware of the costs to themselves of allowing their deposit bases to grow at an excessive rate, and it may be adjusted quickly according to ongoing policy requirements. However, by its very nature, it distorts free market banking activities, and hence the possible associated disintermediation problems may be serious.

(iv) *Moral suasion* occurs where the Bank of England applies *informal pressure* on financial institutions to act in a manner which is conducive 'to the national interest', although this might not be in the best commercial interest of the institutions. The extent to which the Bank is able to exert such influence is questionable in the increasingly competitive financial environment, but its position and powers within the financial system undoubtedly give it some leverage in this respect. For example, the Bank may make suggestions in respect of lending priorities, and may ask institutions to limit the amount of credit granted to certain categories of customers.

(v) *Direct controls* may be introduced in respect of bank lending or interest rates payable on deposits. The Bank of England might, for example, *issue directives limiting the volume of credit creation* in respect of some or all borrowers; it may *specify qualitative lending guidelines*, designed to direct lending towards specific categories of borrowers; or it may *set ceilings on interest rates payable on deposits* (thus limiting the ability of institutions to bid for additional deposits). These forms of controls may be implemented quickly and targetted precisely, and they may be used where the authorities seek to protect particular financial activities or groups within society from the pressures which might otherwise be felt in a regime of tight monetary controls. For example, efforts may be made to direct bank lending towards manufacturers and exporters. However, once again the threat of disintermediation is always present, and many economists would argue that direct controls are only really suitable for short run control requirements, as their effectiveness decreases with the length of time over which they are applied.

(c) *Longer-term control mechanisms*

There are a number of approaches which the authorities may utilise in an attempt to influence the *longer-term trend in money supply growth or the level of interest rates*. These approaches are largely related to the authorities' position in respect of *public sector financing*, and the major issues have already been examined in detail (in Chapter 6, at 6.5). Nevertheless, it is useful to summarise the key issues at this stage, in order to present a complete picture of the ways in which a monetary policy may be implemented.

Of particular importance is the manipulation of the levels of *taxation* and *public expenditure* in a manner designed to reduce the level of public sector borrowing (the PSBR) or to increase the size of public sector debt repayments (the PSDR). If the authorities are able to reduce the PSBR, this not only has a direct effect on demand for borrowed funds within the economy, but also, and particularly to the extent that the PSBR would have been covered by sales of short-term government debt instruments, the supply of potential bank reserve assets is limited. In addition, for any given size of PSBR, the greater is the proportion which is covered by the issue of gilt-edged securities and National Savings instruments to the non-bank non-building society private sector, the smaller are the monetary implications of the deficit financing. Indeed, as existing debt matures, the authorities may pursue a *funding policy* which is aimed at reducing the stock of liquid assets in the economy suitable for reserve asset purposes.

In the case of a PSDR, funds are withdrawn from the private sector, and the money supply will be reduced, unless the authorities use these funds to retire debt held by the non-bank non-building society private sector. Clearly, the greater is the PSDR the greater is the opportunity for reducing money supply growth. On a somewhat broader level, the authorities might attempt to undermine the *willingness* of the non-bank non-building society private sector *to borrow*, perhaps via the use of fiscal disincentives or education programmes.

8.5.3 The effectiveness of monetary controls

The previous section has illustrated the very wide variety of instruments which the authorities may use in order to influence the growth of the money supply and the level and structure of interest rates. However, experience has shown that the authorities in many countries have often had only *limited success* in achieving even apparently modest money supply growth targets, let alone the ultimate objectives of monetary policy. The reasons for the rather mixed performance relate partly to the *inherent weaknesses* of the control instruments, as mentioned above, and partly to the *limited knowledge* which economists possess of how individuals and organisations are likely to react to changes in monetary policy variables within a modern financial system.

To summarise, the extent to which the authorities are able to control their monetary target variables will depend crucially upon:

(a) the central bank having a monopoly in the issuing of cash;

(b) the central bank acting as the lender of last resort to the banking system, and hence to the domestic financial system as a whole;

(c) the authorities being able to influence the overall supply of liquid assets suitable for use as the reserve base for private sector credit creation;

(d) the central bank being able to cause credit-creating institutions to alter their reserve assets ratios;

(e) credit-creating institutions responding positively to the issue of directives by the central bank;

(f) disintermediation activities being insufficient to nullify the impact of official portfolio constraints;

(g) the ability of the Government to finance its PSBR/PSDR in a manner which does not stimulate the creation of additional credit within the private sector.

In addition, even when money supply and interest rate variables can be controlled, this will only have the desired effects on economic policy objectives where the *economic behaviour of individuals and organisations within the private sector is influenced in a consistent manner by the relevant target variables.* The desired results may not come about if:

(a) private sector expenditure decisions are not sensitive to changes in interest rates; for example, people may not be excessively concerned about the interest element in debt repayments, especially where the borrowed funds have been used to purchase assets (such as residential property) which are expected to appreciate in value substantially;

(b) firms react to tighter credit conditions by raising their borrowing, perhaps because of fears that funds may become even more scarce in future, or simply because of cash flow problems created by higher debt servicing commitments;

(c) there are general expectations that changes in monetary target variables are only likely to be temporary;

(d) concurrent changes in other economic variables (for example, the actual or expected rate of inflation) counteract the impact of changes in monetary target variables;

(e) monetary controls are relaxed in an economic environment within which there is excess productive capacity available (thus removing the need for additional capital investment) and where future economic prospects are uncertain (thus undermining the willingness of individuals to borrow for the purpose of funding the purchase of dwellings or consumer durables).

8.6 MONETARY CONTROLS IN THE UK

During the 1970s, the UK monetary authorities placed a very heavy emphasis upon the use of portfolio constraints for monetary control purposes. Special deposits, supplementary special deposits and a variety of direct controls on bank lending and interest rates were used extensively, and it is also believed that moral suasion was applied periodically. These constraints, used in addition to extensive open market operations and manipulation of the Bank of England's discount rate, appear to have been only partly effective. The major problem related to the distortion which they caused to the development of the financial system, and disintermediation is believed to have been widespread.

Since the new monetary control provisions were introduced by the authorities in August 1981, the emphasis has been placed upon the use of *market intervention* and the implementation of policies directed towards the *longer-term control* of the money supply. Portfolio constraints have been largely abandoned. The key aspect of monetary control in the UK has been the manipulation of short-term interest rates. This has been achieved through the use of Bank of England operations in the discount market, involving *transactions in bills* (with purchases of bank bills by the Bank dominating), *purchase and resale agreements* (normally involving bank, Treasury and local authority bills), and, on occasions, *direct lending by the Bank to the discount market* at pre-announced rates. One side effect of this approach to monetary control has been a tendency towards *relatively high real rates of interest* in the UK. This was caused initially by a combination of generally lower rates of inflation and high short-term interest rates (used to restrain the growth of credit creation, and then subsequently to support the exchange value of sterling). Since the withdrawal of sterling from the EC's Exchange Rate Mechanism (ERM) in September 1992 (see Chapter 10, at 10.4, for details), the authorities have felt able to reduce short-term interest rates, in an attempt to stimulate economic recovery. However, concurrent reductions in the rate of inflation, at least through to the summer of 1993, meant that real rates of interest fell only modestly.

A further element of the Government's monetary control strategy has centred upon *public sector borrowing*. At the beginning of the 1980s, the Government announced that it intended to *reduce the PSBR* as a proportion of national income. A rationale for this policy is that the smaller is the PSBR the easier it is to finance in a manner which has little or no implication for money supply growth. It is also argued that longer-term interest rates are likely to be lower than they otherwise would be, which should not only stimulate capital investment, but also encourage corporate borrowers to utilise the capital market rather than raise funds via bank loans (with the associated implication for money supply growth). In fact, due to rapid economic growth during the mid- to late 1980s, the Government managed to generate substantial *budget surpluses* between 1987 and 1991. In themselves, budget surpluses have a contractionary effect on the money supply, which, on this occasion, the authorities chose to neutralise by pursuing a *full-funding policy*; that is, by using the surplus funds to repurchase public sector debt from the non-bank non-building society private sector.

The problem faced by the authorities since 1991 has been the dramatic resurgence of *budget deficits*; with a record PSBR being forecast for the 1993/94 tax year. The rising demands for state support from the unemployed, coupled with depressed taxation revenues, both resulting from the recessionary conditions within the UK economy during the early 1990s, are to blame for a significant part of these budget deficits. Although it is argued by some economists that even without the recession government sector finances would still be weak, with a structural imbalance being the natural outcome of the Government's failure to contain public expenditure as was initially planned, against a background of substantial tax reductions during the late 1980s. In any event, irrespective of their precise cause, the large PSBRs have potentially *serious monetary implications*, although the slow underlying growth of the money supply, at least during the first half of 1993, has meant that the authorities have not shown undue concern about the situation. Indeed, in his March 1993 Budget Speech, the Chancellor of the Exchequer announced that in future *purchases of gilt-edged securities by banks and building societies* would be counted towards the financing of the PSBR; meaning, in effect, that in future the authorities would not automatically attempt to counter the impact on the money supply of such purchases. This development provides an interesting contrast to the *over-funding policy* which was pursued during part of the 1980s, whereby sales of gilt-edged securities and National Savings instruments to the

Table 8.2 UK Monetary Targets, 1980–1993

Target set	Target period	Monetary target	Target growth range (%p.a.)	Actual outcome (%p.a.)
Mar. 1980	Feb. 1980/Apr. 1981	£M3	7–11	18.5
Mar. 1981	Feb. 1981/Apr. 1982	£M3	6–10	14.5
Mar. 1982	Feb. 1982/Apr. 1983	M1	8–12	14.3
		£M3	8–12	11.1
		PSL2	8–12	11.3
Mar. 1982	Feb. 1983/Apr. 1984	M1	7–11	14.0
		£M3	7–11	9.4
		PSL2	7–11	13.1
Mar. 1984	Feb. 1984/Apr. 1985	M0	4–8	5.5
		£M3	6–10	11.6
Mar. 1985	Apr. 1985/Apr. 1986	M0	3–7	3.3
		£M3	5–9	16.5
Mar. 1986	Apr. 1986/Apr. 1987	M0	2–6	5.2
		£M3	11–15	20.5
Mar. 1987	Apr. 1987/Apr. 1988	M0	2–6	6.4
Mar. 1988	Apr. 1988/Apr. 1989	M0	1–5	6.2
Mar. 1989	Apr. 1989/Apr. 1990	M0	1–5	7.3
Mar. 1990	Apr. 1990/Apr. 1991	M0	1–5	1.6
Mar. 1991	Apr. 1991/Apr. 1992	M0	0–4	1.2
Mar. 1992	Apr. 1992/Apr. 1993	M0	0–4	4.8

Source: *Bank of England Quarterly Bulletin*, various issues.

Note: £M3 and PSL2 were renamed in May 1987 as M3 and M5 respectively.

non-bank, non-building society private sector often exceeded the concurrent PSBR, thus having a *negative impact* on the growth of the money supply.

An important aspect of UK monetary policy between 1976 and 1993 was the use of *formal targets* for the growth rates of various monetary aggregates. As Table 8.2 clearly shows, since the beginning of the 1980s the authorities have had only *limited success* in achieving their targets. Even maintaining the narrow measure M0 within its target band has proved to be difficult, and when the rapid growth in bank and building society lending during the late 1980s is acknowledged, serious doubts are raised as to the *effectiveness* of the approach chosen for monetary control in the UK. However, it may be argued that the success of any monetary control regime should be measured in terms of whether or not the ultimate policy objectives are achieved. Unfortunately, as will be demonstrated in the following section, the UK's success in achieving the major policy objectives has itself been rather mixed in recent years.

8.7   UK ECONOMIC POLICY

8.7.1   UK economic policy prior to 1980

Throughout the post-war period until the mid-1970s in the UK, monetary policy played a subsidiary supportive role to fiscal policy. Governments of all political persuasions tended to emphasise the use of demand management techniques in an attempt to 'fine tune' the economy. The recurrent preoccupation with the stabilisation of interest rates, as a means of strengthening business confidence, meant that the money supply was often allowed to accommodate money demand, with little attention being paid (at least publicly) to the possible inflationary implications of this policy. However, in 1976, international payments problems and pressure from the International Monetary Fund (from which the UK found itself having to borrow substantial amounts of foreign currency), caused the Government to make a fundamental reappraisal of the nature of its economic policy. The outcome was that a much more positive role was adopted for monetary policy in the UK, with explicit recognition being given to the control of the money supply as an important element in the fight against inflation.

In the Spring of 1979 a Conservative government was returned to power, and this proved to be a turning point for UK economic policy. The new Government was elected on a platform of freeing the market forces of the economy, in the belief that this would revive the UK's flagging economic performance. Moreover, it was firmly committed to the doctrine of *monetarism*, and hence its primary economic policy objective was to be the *defeat of inflation* through a *strict control of money supply growth*. Thus, monetary policy was brought to the forefront of the economic policy package, and the other policies were seen as being merely supportive to this. For the first time since the 1930s, a British government quite openly placed the control of inflation and the establishment of financial and monetary stability above the objective of full employment. Indeed, it went further and argued that governments could do very little about the level of unemployment and economic growth in the long run. The only thing that governments could do, so it was claimed, was to provide a stable economic and regulatory framework within which the private market economy could operate efficiently. It must be stressed that the Conservative government was not arguing that unemployment did not matter; on the contrary, it was suggested that the only way in which full employment could be assured was for inflation to be squeezed from the economy, and for restrictions on market forces to be removed.

8.7.2 The Medium-Term Financial Strategy

The title 'Medium-Term Financial Strategy' (MTFS) was given by the Conservative government, in 1980, to its broad approach to the implementation of its economic policy. Initially, the overall aims of the MTFS were stated as being to *reduce inflation*, via a regime of strict monetary control; to *reduce the proportion of national resources taken for public sector use*; and to *reduce the burden of taxation on income*, in order to boost incentives for enterprise and hopefully encourage long-term economic growth. During the early years, an important aspect of the MTFS was the setting of *targets and projections* for money supply growth, public spending, taxation and the PSBR for four years ahead, with the strategy updated annually. However, as early as 1982 the Government was becoming more flexible in its use of money supply growth targets, and, as may be observed in Table 8.2, did not follow its original intention of reducing steadily the target bands for money supply growth. By March 1987 only the single target for M0 remained. (The monetary targets which were pursued within the framework of the MTFS have already been discussed in detail in Chapter 1 at 1.8.3.) Moreover, even before this time, the authorities had been placing increased stress upon the need for policy instruments to be set in the light of *a range of indicators of monetary conditions*, and not simply on the basis of the growth rates of precisely defined monetary aggregates. In this context, the authorities looked increasingly towards movements in *sterling exchange rates* during the second half of the 1980s, with the ultimate step in this regard being the placing of sterling into the *ERM* in October 1990. This action undoubtedly constrained the extent to which monetary policy instruments could be directed towards controlling the growth of the domestic money supply, and hence modified further the practical operation of the MTFS.

8.7.3 Economic policy since September 1992

The most fundamental turning point for government economic policy in the UK in recent years came with the *withdrawal of sterling from the ERM in September 1992.* This event followed an apparent widespread loss of confidence in the authorities' ability to maintain the exchange value of sterling within its parity bands relative to other ERM currencies. Massive sales of sterling on the foreign exchange markets by international holders of the currency, created intense pressure on sterling's exchange value. In response, the authorities undertook high levels of *foreign-exchange market intervention,* in order to prop up the value of sterling, using substantial amounts of foreign currency borrowed from overseas monetary institutions and financial markets, and drawn from official reserves. On the day of withdrawal itself (which subsequently became known as 'Black Wednesday', on account of the damage done to the credibility of the Government's economic policy and the costs to the Treasury of the foreign exchange market intervention), the authorities also attempted to support the value of sterling by pushing up *money market rates of interest.* Initially, it was announced that rates would be raised by 2%, in order to take base rates to 12%; then later it was indicated that a further 3% rise in base rates would be required the following day. In the event, following the withdrawal of sterling from the ERM, the latter rise was cancelled, and the next day base rates were allowed to fall back to 10%. As might be expected, the result of withdrawal was a *substantial depreciation in the exchange value of sterling* against most other major currencies. By the end of 1992, sterling had depreciated by 13% against a trade-weighted basket of other major currencies.

Being released from the constraints of the ERM, the Government also felt able to sanction *further reductions in interest rates,* expressing the view that the recessionary forces prevalent in the UK economy were sufficient to counteract any ensuing inflationary pressures. In January 1993 base rates were reduced to 6% (their lowest level since 1977), and when taken with the substantially reduced exchange value for sterling and subdued inflationary forces, it could be argued that in 1993 the UK economy was *well placed for sustained recovery to occur.* Certainly the major boost given to the *UK's international trading competitiveness* by the depreciation of sterling is an important element of recent developments, recognising the underlying weakness of the current account of the balance of payments. Of course, any subsequent resurgence of inflation could easily erode this newly-found competitive advantage, and, in any event, the depressed economic conditions in many of the UK's overseas markets are likely to limit the benefits to be gained by the UK in terms of increased exports.

Notwithstanding the extreme contrast from the strong (stable) exchange rate and high interest rate stance of the economic policy pursued until the final moments before sterling was withdrawn from the ERM, the Government's policy in 1993 continued to be couched in terms of the MTFS (although it is now regarded more simply as providing a framework for achieving sustainable economic growth based on permanently low inflation). However, the events of September 1992 precipitated important changes to the components of the MTFS. Of particular significance is the *inflation target* announced by the Chancellor in October 1992. This target effectively commits the Government to directing its economic policy instruments to the maintenance of the *underlying rate of inflation within the range 1% to 4% per annum* (underlying inflation being measured by the 12-month change in the retail price index excluding mortgage interest payments).

In order to support the implementation of its policy, the Government invited the *Bank of England* to provide a *regular (quarterly) report* on the progress being made towards the achievement of its inflation target. The first such report was published in February 1993, and provided a comprehensive assessment of inflationary trends and prospects for the UK economy. In addition, it is claimed that the *Treasury* is showing more openness in respect of monetary policy matters through the production of its own *Monthly Monetary Report* (first published in December 1992). These developments should lead to a more informed debate on the Government's economic policy, and may make it more difficult for the authorities to take actions which are not wholly consistent with their stated policy objectives. Of course, the fundamental uncertainties surrounding the determination of inflation and the interpretation of economic analysis and predictions are not altered by the new policy. Therefore, there is still scope for the Government to adjust its policy instruments in response to shorter-term political expedients, although perhaps less so than there would otherwise have been.

In the absence of a formal target for the growth rate of a broad measure of the money supply, the abandonment of the ERM commitment in respect of sterling meant that the Government effectively had no credible basis for the direction of its monetary policy. However, by choosing to target the rate of inflation directly, the Government has *by-passed all the conventional formal targets of monetary policy*. Consequently, the relevance of the *monitoring range* announced for *M4* in the Chancellor's 1992 Autumn Statement and the *monitoring range* for *M0* (replacing its former target band) announced in the March 1993 Budget Speech, is in terms of their value as *early warning devices*, indicating when policy may be running off course, and especially signalling any likely build-up in inflationary pressures. The monitoring ranges set for the whole of the period covered by the MTFS (as updated at March 1993) were 0%–4% per annum growth for M0 and 3%–9% per annum growth for M4. If the actual growth of either of these variables deviates from its monitoring range, then this will be *taken into account by the authorities in the setting of monetary controls* (and hence in the fixing of short-term interest rates). In addition, movements in *sterling exchange rates* and *asset* (and especially *house*) *prices* will also be considered, as these have proved to be useful leading indicators for inflation in the past. The setting of formal targets for monetary aggregates would not have been logical in the light of a target being specified for inflation itself.

Finally, it must be noted that the new policy framework continues to recognise the importance of *fiscal policy*, both for the achievement of a sustainable economic recovery, and as a supporting element of the counter-inflation strategy. As was explained in 8.6 above, the recessionary conditions of the early 1990s in the UK have led to *record PSBRs* (of approximately £36.5b in 1992/93, and expected to reach around £50b in 1993/94), and it is anticipated that large PSBRs will remain a feature of economic policy for many years to come. This is despite the Government's stated aim that public sector spending should take a declining share of national income over time, and even taking into account the substantial increases in taxation and National Insurance contributions which were announced in the March 1993 Budget Speech. It is argued by the Government that the high PSBRs are, to a large extent, a *counter-cyclical phenomenon*, and reflect public sector finances responding naturally to a period of *recession*. Economic recovery is expected to reduce significantly the level of PSBRs. Nevertheless, the Government has stated that it will raise taxes further and cut back public expenditure plans if the desired reduction in the PSBR fails to occur. In the meantime, in order to minimise the monetary impact (and hence inflationary implications) of the huge borrowing programme envisaged by the authorities, *full-funding* of the PSBR is to be maintained, although, as already mentioned, the Government now counts *gilt-edged securities purchased by banks and building societies* as falling within this funding total. This means that if banks and building societies should purchase large volumes of gilts there could be a substantial boost to money supply growth, although this would probably only occur if gilts issues were relatively short maturity and their yields were sufficiently attractive. In this context, the Government has made clear that it has no intention to move to a policy of *under-funding*, involving issues of *short-term instruments*, such as Treasury bills, in order to finance the PSBR.

8.7.4 The success of economic policy

The success of the Government's economic policy can best be assessed in terms of the UK's performance in respect of the major economic policy objectives.

(a) *Unemployment*

Table 8.3 shows clearly that the level of unemployment rose rapidly during the early 1980s, to reach about 3.1m adults unemployed by 1986; and it should be recognised that this figure was achieved despite a significant number of changes which were made to the basis for collecting unemployment statistics, most of which tended to reduce recorded levels. However, during the later years of the 1980s, there was a substantial reduction in the level of unemployment, as the UK experienced a period of sustained economic growth. By the beginning of 1990, the total number was down to approximately 1.6m, although it should not be forgotten that this level was still significantly higher than that experienced in 1979, when the present Government came to power. Since 1990, the level of unemployment has risen once again, reflecting the longest period of recession in the UK since the 1940s. By the beginning of 1993 the unemployment rate had risen to 10.5%, representing just under 3m unemployed. There is little doubt that the level of unemployment has remained a major source of disappointment for the Government, although it has tended to be seen as something of a longer-term objective of policy. Also, to be fair to the Government, the trends seen in unemployment in the UK in recent years have been broadly similar to those experienced in most major Western countries.

Table 8.3   Unemployment in the UK, 1980–1992

Year	Unemployed (thousands)	Unemployment rate %
1980	1,561	5.8
1981	2,270	8.5
1982	2,547	9.6
1983	2,791	10.4
1984	2,921	10.7
1985	3,028	10.9
1986	3,098	11.1
1987	2,807	10.0
1988	2,275	8.1
1989	1,784	6.3
1990	1,623	5.8
1991	2,287	8.1
1992	2,767	9.8

Source: *Economic Trends*, Central Statistical Office, various issues.

Note: The unemployment rate percentage is obtained by dividing the total unemployed (excluding school leavers) by the total working population, i.e. those employed, including employees, self-employed and HM forces, plus those registered as unemployed. The figures are annual averages.

(b) *Inflation*

Relative to the first three years of the 1980s, the period 1983 to 1988 saw a marked improvement in the inflation position for the UK, as is shown by Table 8.4. Between 1989 and 1991 there was a resurgence of inflation, which was explained in part by buoyant demand for both consumer goods and certain categories of labour at least until 1990, and a doubling of base rates between mid-1988 and the end of 1989 with a comparable rise in mortgage interest rates. Ironically, the latter trend was created by the actions of the authorities in attempting to depress inflationary forces via a tightening of monetary policy. However, since 1991 the rate of inflation has fallen substantially, reaching a low point of 1.2% in June 1993 (an annual rate not seen in the UK since 1964). The impact of the recession on consumer demand and wage bargaining, and the reductions in mortgage lending rates

Table 8.4   Annual percentage change in UK Retail Price Index, 1980–1992

Year	Percentage change
1980	18.0
1981	11.9
1982	8.6
1983	4.6
1984	5.0
1985	6.1
1986	3.4
1987	4.2
1988	4.9
1989	7.8
1990	9.5
1991	5.9
1992	3.7

Source: *Economic Trends*, Central Statistical Office, various issues.

Table 8.5   Annual percentage change in retail prices for selected OECD countries: 1980, 1985, 1990 and 1992

	1980	1985	1990	1992
France	13.6	5.8	3.4	2.8
Italy	21.0	8.6	6.0	5.4
Japan	8.0	2.0	3.1	1.7
UK	18.0	6.1	9.5	3.7
USA	13.5	3.5	5.5	3.0
Germany	5.5	2.2	2.7	4.0

Source: *Economic Trends*, Central Statistical Office, February 1993.

following the withdrawal of sterling from the ERM were important factors in achieving this position. Consequently, it may be concluded that the Government has had some success in achieving its major objective of economic policy since it came to power; but the success has been somewhat patchy, and, as is illustrated by Table 8.5, the UK's rate of inflation has persistently been above the rates experienced by most of its major trading partners.

(c)   *Balance of payments*

A detailed examination of the performance of the UK's balance of payments since 1980 is to be found in Chapter 9 (at 9.6). At the present stage it is merely necessary to consider the broad trends within the accounts, and in particular the progress of the current account, which reflects the extent to which the country is able to cover its current overseas expenditures on goods and services with its current earnings from the sale of exports. In this respect, following an unusually favourable period during the first half of the 1980s, the position of the current account deteriorated markedly after 1985. During the early 1980s large surpluses on trade in oil were able to hide a gradually worsening non-oil trade position, and between 1980 and 1982, the visible trade account was in very healthy surplus. Between 1982 and 1989 the visible trade position became progressively worse, and in 1989 there was a record deficit of £24.7b. Since that time there has been some improvement in the visible trade balance, reflecting a steady growth in the value of exports and a depressed demand for imports in the UK (especially during 1991). In 1992 the visible trade deficit stood at £13.8b.

Throughout the 1980s invisibles remained in surplus, and until 1987 they were sufficient to hold the overall current account in surplus. The substantial reduction in the invisibles net balance in 1989, coupled with the above-mentioned huge visible trade deficit, left the current account with an overall record deficit of almost £22b in 1989. During the early years of the 1990s, the current account balance improved somewhat, with a deficit of around £12b reported for 1992. This trend was largely due to the above-mentioned recovery in the visible trade balance, with the invisibles balance being rather weak by historical standards, although remaining in surplus. Clearly, the economic policy objective of an equilibrium on the current account of the balance of payments has not been achieved in recent years. Furthermore, the UK has also experienced rather volatile capital account flows, which, at least until recently, involved disturbingly large net inflows of short-term ('hot') investment funds, attracted by the UK's relatively high real rates of interest.

(d)   *Economic growth*

Between 1983 and 1988 the UK's economic growth, as measured by the annual percentage change in gross domestic product (GDP), was significantly above the level experienced during the 1960s and 1970s. Moreover, the growth rate, which averaged 3.8% per annum over this period, was on a par with the rates occurring in many comparable Western nations, and exceeded the rates of others. Overall, and especially by European standards, the UK's economic growth rate was most satisfactory during the second half of the 1980s. Unfortunately, this period of relatively high growth rates was both preceded and followed by serious rounds of recession. The more recent downturn in economic activity had a major negative impact on growth during 1990, and both 1991 and 1992 saw absolute reductions in GDP (which were reflected in the UK's unemployment figures). It was only during the early months of 1993 that output in key sectors of the economy began to show meaningful signs of recovery.

Taking the 1980s as a whole, the UK's average growth rate was little different from that experienced during previous post-war decades, as is illustrated by Table 8.7. More recent events have ensured that economic performance during the early 1990s was well below its long-term trend. Whilst this period of recession was common to most Western nations, and was caused by a complex combination of cyclical business trends and official policy actions, it is generally agreed that the UK's position was exacerbated by the UK authorities' attempts to dampen down the rapid expansion of bank and building society lending during the late 1980s and 1990, against the background of a serious current account deficit on the balance of payments and domestic inflationary pressures. The placing of sterling in the ERM is likely to have contributed to the deflationary trend by requiring a regime of high interest rates to be maintained in the UK, despite an obvious slowing down of economic activity and a falling inflation rate during 1991 and 1992.

As at summer 1993, the UK once again faces the classic economic policy conflict between, on the one hand, achieving a satisfactory growth rate and falling unemployment, and, on the other hand, the need to keep inflation and the current account of the balance of payments within reasonable bounds. Recognising the subdued inflationary pressures within the UK economy, the most helpful development in respect of the major objectives of economic policy would probably be for a sustained recovery to occur in the economies of the UK's major trading partners.

Table 8.6   UK Gross Domestic Product (GDP) at 1985 prices, 1980–1992

Year	GDP index	GDP percentage change per annum
1980	90.7	−2.3
1981	89.6	−1.2
1982	91.2	1.8
1983	94.2	3.7
1984	96.1	2.0
1985	100.0	4.1
1986	103.8	3.8
1987	108.6	4.6
1988	113.5	4.5
1989	115.8	2.0
1990	116.6	0.7
1991	113.7	−2.5
1992	113.2	−0.4

Source: *Monthly Digest of Statistics*, Central Statistical Office, various issues.

Note: The figures relate to annual averages.

Table 8.7   UK Gross Domestic Product (GDP) average annual growth rates 1950–1992

Decade	Average annual percentage growth in GDP
1950–1959	2.6
1960–1969	2.9
1970–1979	2.1
1980–1989	2.3
1990–1992	−0.7

Source: *Economic Trends*, Central Statistical Office, October 1983.
Monthly Digest of Statistics, Central Statistical Office, various issues.

8.8   EXAMINATION PRACTICE

8.8.1   Questions

The following questions are taken from past examination papers, and are intended to give students an indication of the type of questions which they are likely to face within the topic area of Economic Policy. Students may care to map out answers to these questions before consulting the guidance notes at 8.8.2. Each question carries 25 marks.

(1)   (a)   State the main objectives of economic policy.   (4)
     (b)   Why in practice is it difficult to achieve these objectives simultaneously?   (9)
     (c)   To what extent have each of the main economic objectives been achieved in the UK in the past decade?   (12)

(October 1989)

(2)   In seeking to achieve the ultimate objectives of monetary policy the authorities can set intermediate targets.

     (a)   Discuss the intermediate targets that might be selected.   (17)
     (b)   List the techniques that could be used to achieve these targets.   (8)

(October 1988)

(3)   †(a)   Why might a government seek to control the growth of bank lending?   (10)
     (b)   Indicate the policy instruments available to the authorities to achieve control over credit.   (9)
     (c)   Discuss the problems which can arise as a result of implementing controls on bank lending.   (6)

(October 1990)

(4)   (a)   Why and how do governments seek to control the level of demand?   (16)
     (b)   Which methods of control has the UK Government relied on since October 1990?   (9)

(May 1992)

(5)   Describe the following and discuss their role in the operation of monetary policy:

†(a)   gilt-edged securities   (9)
†(b)   commercial (eligible bank) bills   (9)
†(c)   the sale of public sector assets.   (7)

(April 1986)

8.8.2 Guidance notes

(1) (i) Part (a) requires a brief summary of the major *objectives* of economic policy pursued by most governments. Do not confuse objectives with *targets* and *instruments* of policy. Discussion of actual experience of achieving objectives is not required in this part of the question.

(ii) Part (b) requires a discussion of the *natural conflicts* which arise in respect of policy objectives, with comments upon the *trade-offs between objectives* which must be recognised by governments in respect of the formulation of economic policy. *Specific examples* of the conflicts between objectives should be given.

(iii) A relatively detailed knowledge of the trends in the *major economic variables* in the UK during the past decade is required by part (c). It is important to work through the objectives listed in (a) in sequence, rather than simply provide a commentary on the UK economy in recent years.

(iv) Part (c) does not require a description of how the authorities went about introducing policies or the instruments used. The focus must be maintained on the extent to which the main objectives have been achieved.

Source of relevant material:

Part (a) 8.2.1.
Part (b) 8.2.3.
Part (c) 8.7.4.

(2) (i) This question relates to theoretical alternatives – the *intermediate targets* which *might* be selected, and the *techniques* that *could* be used. Consequently it is not sufficient merely to discuss the targets and techniques which are currently being used (or have been used at any particular time in the past) in the UK.

(ii) Do not confuse *intermediate targets* (part (a)) with either the *ultimate objectives* of monetary policy or the *instruments* which may be used to influence the targets (part (b)).

(iii) Whilst the *money supply and interest rate targets* are vital elements of the answer to part (a), the *other possible targets* must not be forgotten. Detailed definitions of possible money supply targets are not required.

(iv) It is not necessary to discuss the general nature or operation of monetary policy and control, either in theory or in practice.

(v)   Part (b) of the question merely requires a straightforward *listing of the techniques of monetary control.* Detailed explanation of their operation is not required, and neither is discussion of any other form of economic control techniques. The emphasis throughout should be placed upon monetary issues.

Source of relevant material:

Part (a)   8.2.2 (as background) and 8.4.2.
Part (b)   8.5.2.

(3) (i)   This question relates to *theoretical possibilities* in respect of the control of bank credit creation. The answer should not concentrate merely upon particular experience in the UK or any other country.

    (ii)   Part (a) of this question relates to the reasons why a government *might* wish to control the growth of bank lending (credit creation). The answer should comment upon the relationship of bank lending to *money supply growth, aggregate demand, inflation,* and *the current account of the balance of payments.* The authorities may also wish to offset the monetary impact of *large PSBRs* by restraining bank lending.

    (iii) The answer to part (b) merely requires a *listing of the monetary policy instruments* which the authorities *might* use in order to control credit creation.

    (iv) Discussion of how the Bank of England influences interest rates is not required.

    (v)   Part (c) requires a brief discussion of the problems which *may arise* for both the authorities and the banks if controls on bank lending were to be implemented. In particular, possible adverse side effects of high interest rates on *exchange rates* and the *balance of payments, economic growth* and *unemployment* should be noted. Direct controls bring the problems of *disintermediation* and *unfairness* to banks (if other lending institutions are not controlled).

Source of relevant material:

†Part (a)   8.2.1, Table 8.1, 8.3.1, 8.4.2(c) and (as background) Chapter 1, at 1.7.4.
Part (b)   8.5.2.
Part (c)   8.4.1, 8.4.2(c) and 8.5.2.

(4) (i) This question relates to *general policy issues*. The answer should not be restricted to specific policies in force at any given time, either in the UK or in any other country.

(ii) The answer to part (a) must outline the *main objectives of economic policy*, emphasising how control of the level of demand may help to achieve these objectives. It must also indicate *how* a government may *use the full range of policies* in order to influence demand.

(iii) Part (b) concerns the policy position of the UK Government since October 1990. It is necessary to outline the use of *monetary policy* (short-term interest rates), initially within the ERM framework, and more recently as a means of stimulating demand. Mention must also be made of *fiscal policy*, which has tended to adjust naturally in response to the recession, although the recognition of the need to deal with the huge PSBR should be noted.

(iv) Discussion of the implementation, operation or success of economic policies is not required.

Source of relevant material:

Part (a) 8.1.2 (as background), 8.2.1 and 8.3.1.
Part (b) 8.6, 8.7.2 and 8.7.3.

(5) (i) This question relates to *clearly defined assets* and their *relevance for the operation of monetary policy*. The answer must be correspondingly *clearly focused*. Wide-ranging waffle on monetary policy is not required.

(ii) The answer to each part of the question should begin with a *concise description* of the items listed. It is then necessary to explain the ways in which these items are *relevant for monetary control purposes*.

(iii) In part (a) it is necessary to explain how the *financing of a PSBR* via the *sale of gilts to different sectors of the economy* will have differential implications for monetary control. The position of gilts in respect of the financing of a *PSDR* should also be mentioned.

(iv) The crucial role of eligible bank bills in the *Bank of England's day-to-day discount market intervention* must be explained in part (b). Care should be taken not to confuse eligible bank bills with Treasury bills.

(v) In part (c) it is important to explain the role of public sector asset sales in *financing government expenditure*, and hence in *reducing the amount of public sector borrowing* that has to be undertaken. It should be noted that the monetary impact of such sales is largely the same as that which arises when the PSBR is financed by the issue of gilts. This helps to explain why the governments of some countries (unlike that of the UK) regard public sector asset sales as a means of financing a PSBR rather than reducing it.

Source of relevant material:

†Part (a) 8.5.2(c), Chapter 1, at 1.6, and Chapter 6, at 6.5.1, 6.5.2, and 6.5.4.

†Part (b) 8.5.2(a), Chapter 4, at 4.4.2(a)(iii), and Chapter 5, at 5.3.3.

†Part (c) 8.5.2(c), and Chapter 6, at 6.5.1 (paragraph 1) and 6.5.3(d).

8.9 FURTHER STUDY

Whilst the basic concepts and principles of economic policy are well established, the actual application of policy in any particular country may alter relatively quickly. This is true both of the ordering of policy objectives and the set of policy instruments and targets utilised by the authorities. Consequently, it is important that students remain alert to changes in the broad policy position of the Government, and the declared means via which the policy is to be implemented. In this respect the Chancellor of the Exchequer's annual Budget speech, now delivered in November of each year (and normally reported verbatim, with accompanying commentaries, in *The Times* and *Financial Times*, as well as in other quality newspapers), provides a mine of useful information. However, given the speed with which events may alter, it is necessary to keep up with interim developments by consulting the economics and finance pages of quality newspapers on a frequent basis.

Publications such as *The Economist, Bank of England Quarterly Bulletin* and *Banking World* provide excellent sources of analysis and discussion of the progress of the UK and other major economies, and of the operational effectiveness of government economic policy. In relation to the nature and operation of monetary policy and controls, the *Bank of England Quarterly Bulletin* is undoubtedly the definitive work. A further useful source of material is the technical economic and business surveys produced by most of the major UK clearing banks. For detailed statistical information *Monthly Digest of Statistics* and *Economic Trends* (both published by the Central Statistical Office) should be consulted; although students should take care not to become enmeshed in the mass of detail to be found in these publications. For examination purposes, it is the broad concepts and principles which matter, supported by a working knowledge of recent economic trends and the actual operation of policy within the UK economy.

Finally, students are reminded of the important overlaps which exist between the material covered within the present chapter and topics appearing within other parts of this book. In particular, the general linkage between Chapter 1 (Money and Inflation) and Chapter 6 (Money Supply) with the sections of the present chapter on monetary policy and control should be noted. Also, there are important linkages with the policy issues raised in Chapter 7 (Interest Rates), Chapter 9 (The Balance of Payments) and Chapter 10 (Exchange Rates). Where specific cross-references are given in the text, students would be well advised to consult the topics stipulated, especially when revising for the examination.

9 THE BALANCE OF PAYMENTS

9.1 INTRODUCTION

The progressive removal of barriers to international trade and capital movements has meant that domestic monetary and financial systems have become increasingly influenced by overseas economic events. Today, the vast majority of financial institutions undertake activities which are, at least to some extent, international in their character. Such activities may range from the provision of international payments services and the trading of securities originating overseas, through to the operation of branches and subsidiaries on a global scale. Consequently, an understanding of the nature of international trade and payments mechanisms is becoming increasingly important to an appreciation of the evolving environment within which domestic financial institutions and markets must operate.

A useful starting-point for the discussion of international monetary and financial relations is an examination of the balance of payments accounts, as these essentially provide a record of the financial aspects of a nation's international economic transactions. Thus, the first part of the present chapter examines the general concept and structure of the balance of payments, and considers the economic and financial significance of the underlying international currency flows. In addition, as a country's balance of payments position may have important implications for domestic output, employment and inflation, it is also appropriate to consider the policy actions which might be taken by the authorities when adverse trends appear in balance of payments flows. The implementation of such policies may in itself have significant effects on the activities of financial institutions and markets.

For the UK the importance of overseas economic relations cannot be over-emphasised. By most measures, the UK has a highly open economy, with both exports and imports of goods and services amounting to around 35% of gross domestic product in recent years. On top of this, there are usually large international capital flows to take into account. This high degree of openness has great significance for the structure of industry and employment within the UK, and the Government has often faced serious policy conflicts in respect of achieving a satisfactory position on the UK's balance of payments, without generating adverse effects on other economic policy objectives. The final part of this chapter examines recent experience in respect of the UK's balance of payments, and considers its relevance for government policy objectives in general.

9.2 BALANCE OF PAYMENTS ACCOUNTS

9.2.1 Basic concepts

The balance of payments accounts may be defined as a systematic record, taken over a given period of time, of *all transactions between domestic residents* (including government agencies and military forces located abroad) *and residents of foreign nations.* In the case of the UK, all transactions are recorded in sterling; and when items are valued in foreign currencies, the conversion takes place at the exchange rate ruling at the time of the transaction.

By convention, all *credit items* (that is, those which increase net money claims on foreigners) enter the accounts with a *positive sign.* Credit items include exports of goods and services; inflows of transfer payments; earnings of interest, profits and dividends from overseas; overseas investment in the domestic economy; and domestic borrowing from overseas. *Debit items* (that is, those which reduce net money claims on foreigners) enter the accounts with a *negative sign.* Debit items include imports of goods and services; outflows of transfer payments; interest, profits and dividend payments made to overseas residents; domestic investment in overseas economies; and domestic lending to overseas residents.

9.2.2 The structure of the balance of payments accounts

The balance of payments accounts may be divided into three parts:

- the current account
- the capital account (referred to in the UK as 'transactions in UK external assets and liabilities')
- the balancing item.

(a) *The current account*

This may be sub-divided into visible trade and invisibles. *Visible trade* relates to the export and import of tangible items such as *basic raw materials, fuels, food, beverages, tobacco,* and *manufactured goods.* The overall position in respect of visible trade is known as the *balance of trade.* *Invisibles* relate to credits and debits for the following items:

(i) *Private sector services*, including sea transport, civil aviation, travel, financial services (such as insurance and banking) and consultancy services.

(ii)   *Government sector services*, including payments for the maintenance of armed forces and embassies overseas.

(iii)   *Interest, profits and dividends*, deriving from international
investments and borrowing/lending activites. These may be
divided into flows attributable to the private sector and to the
government sector.

(iv)   *Private sector current transfer payments*, including remittances
of gifts of money and goods to overseas residents, and emi-
grants' and immigrants' transfers of assets.

(v)   *Government sector current transfer payments*, including subscriptions and remittances to international bodies, such as the UK's
EC budget payments and receipts, and overseas official aid
projects.

The aggregate figure for total debits and credits on visible trade and
invisibles gives the *current account balance*. For reasons which will be
explained below, at 9.4.1, it is normally this figure which is the focus of
attention within the balance of payments accounts, for both the Government and the media.

(b)   *Transactions in UK external assets and liabilities (capital account)*

The main components of this part of the balance of payments accounts may
be summarised as follows:

(i)   *Overseas investment in the UK*, which may be divided into *direct*
investment (for example, purchases of factory buildings, land and
capital equipment) and *portfolio* investment (for example, the
purchase of equity shares in UK business enterprises).

(ii)   *UK private sector investment overseas*, which again may be divided
into direct and portfolio investment.

(iii)   Foreign currency and sterling *borrowing and lending overseas by
UK banks.*

(iv)   *Deposits with banks overseas* by the UK non-bank private sector.

(v)   *Borrowing from banks overseas* by the UK non-bank private sector
and the public sector.

(vi)   *Changes in UK official reserves* (comprising mainly gold and
convertible currencies).

(vii)   *Transactions in other external assets and liabilities* by the UK
non-bank private sector and public sector. This item includes
official borrowing and the repaying of funds to the International
Monetary Fund, Bank for International Settlements and overseas
central banks.

(c) *Balancing item*

This element arises because of *errors and omissions* in the recording of payments. It is simply the difference between the total value of recorded transactions and the recorded flow of currency between domestic and overseas residents. If the item is positive, this means that more currency (in net terms) has come into the country than the recorded current account and capital account transactions show.

9.2.3 Official financing

Prior to 1987 the UK balance of payments accounts were divided into four parts. The additional part arose from the sub-division of 'transactions in UK external assets and liabilities' into '*investment and other capital transactions*' (which were effectively private sector capital flows and non-financial government capital flows), and '*official financing*' (which included net transactions with overseas monetary authorities, official foreign currency borrowing on international financial markets, and the usage of official reserves). Today, as explained above, there remains a separate category for changes in UK official reserves, but it is somewhat more difficult to identify the other elements of official financing within the general capital account. Nevertheless, it should still be recognised that if the overall value of *official financing is positive*, then it may be said that there is a *deficit on the balance of payments* (i.e. all other items of the account, taken together, have a negative value). Conversely, a *negative value for official financing* means that the *balance of payments is in surplus*.

Clearly, the possession of *official reserves* is of crucial importance to a country's ability to *finance balance of payments deficits*. For most countries, the major component of these reserves is *convertible currencies* (which are often held in the form of marketable interest-bearing securities denominated in foreign currencies). However, it must not be forgotten that official reserves may also include:

- *gold*, which is now rarely used in day-to-day official financing activities, but which is felt to give a secure 'second line of defence' within the reserves;
- *Special Drawing Rights* (SDRs), which are a form of reserve asset created by the International Monetary Fund (IMF) and distributed amongst member countries on the basis of a prescribed formula. SDRs cannot be spent directly, but they give immediate access to borrowed foreign currency through the IMF;
- *reserve positions in the IMF*, which are effectively overdraft facilities with the IMF, giving access to foreign currencies on demand.

The sum total of convertible currencies, gold, SDRs and reserve positions in the IMF gives a measure of a country's available stock of immediately usable reserves. This measure is sometimes referred to as the *narrow definition of international liquidity*. However, in recent years there has been an increasing tendency to look towards a *broader concept of international liquidity*, which embodies the elements included in the narrow definition and, in addition, various *borrowing facilities* made available to sovereign states from the IMF, commercial banks (especially via the euromarkets), multilateral sources (such as the World Bank) and central banks of other countries. While the narrow definition can be measured precisely (although the volatility of the gold price means that the value of total reserves changes constantly), the broad definition is not susceptible to accurate measurement. However, for creditworthy countries, the concept means that the amount of liquidity potentially at their disposal can be considerably greater than their published reserves.

In relation to the usage of *official reserves*, it is important to appreciate that when reserves are *drawn upon*, this appears as a *positive* value in the balance of payments accounts. If the authorities use these reserves to purchase sterling (in the case of the UK), they are effectively supplementing the available foreign currency on the exchange markets. Conversely, if the authorities buy foreign currency, in exchange for sterling, this *addition to official reserves* appears as a *negative* value in the accounts (as foreign currency is being removed from the exchange markets).

It should also be recognised that if the authorities borrow foreign currency from overseas, and then deposit it directly into the official reserves, there is no net effect on the overall official financing position. Quite simply, the positive value for borrowing (which is effectively currency being brought into the country) cancels out the negative value (of equal magnitude) on the change in official reserves element. However, if the official overseas foreign currency borrowing takes place, and the funds are used immediately to purchase domestic currency from the exchange markets, then the positive value for the borrowing will correspond to a negative value on the current account and/or the non-official financing elements of the capital account. Effectively, the authorities will have borrowed foreign currency in order to finance a deficit on the balance of payments.

9.2.4 Accounting equality and economic equilibrium

The balance of payments accounts are constructed on the principle of *double entry bookkeeping*, and hence they will *always balance in accounting terms*. In effect, each external transaction is entered twice into the accounts; first, to show the original transaction; and secondly, to indicate how it has been financed. Therefore, so long as the accounts have been compiled accurately, the sum of the individual items must equal zero. Thus:

current account balance
+ capital account balance
+ balancing item

= zero

Strictly, there is an *economic equilibrium* only when *official financing is zero*. When a balance of payments surplus or deficit occurs, a disequilibrium position (an economic imbalance) exists. A persistent deficit or surplus on the balance of payments is referred to as a *fundamental disequilibrium*, and this concept is of importance in determining whether or not policy actions are required. However, in recent years, there has been an increasing tendency for commentators to focus attention upon the *current account* of the balance of payments, in the light of its crucial importance in respect of *the country's ability to pay its way internationally*. Hence, both private and government sector capital items may be grouped together to give a broad measure of the level of *net borrowing* by the country as a whole (after appropriate adjustment for changes in official reserves), and equilibrium may be thought of in terms of a *zero balance on the current account*.

When a *deficit* occurs on the *current account* of the balance of payments, it must, by definition, be balanced by a *surplus* of equal size on the *capital account* and *balancing item* taken together. Clearly, within this surplus, it is quite possible that individual capital items may be in balance or in deficit. Thus, ignoring the balancing item, if the total of non-official financing elements is in balance or in deficit, then the source of financing for the current account deficit must be official financing. Indeed, these official funds will also have to cover any deficit on the remainder of the capital account. When official financing is required in this way, it may be provided either by running down official reserves, or by official borrowing overseas or both. However, if the current account deficit is covered by a surplus on non-official financing capital account items, the implication is that either net overseas debt of the private sector is rising, or net claims on foreigners are falling.

A *surplus* on the *current account* may be 'financed' in a similar way. Thus, there may be an off-setting *deficit* on the *capital account* (although not all individual elements need to be in deficit) and/or a negative value on the *balancing item*. If official financing is negative, this implies that either official reserves are raised or net overseas official debt is reduced or both.

Finally, it should be noted that where the authorities operate a *clean floating exchange rate regime* (i.e. they pursue a policy of not intervening within the foreign exchange markets, in order that the domestic currency's value may be determined by market forces), the balance of payments is by definition *always in equilibrium*, as there is no official financing undertaken. In this instance, it might be argued that the balance of payments is forced into an equilibrium position, and, notwithstanding any non-official financing government sector transactions appearing in the current or capital accounts, the private sector is obliged to cover its overseas expenditures through its overseas earnings or borrowing. However, even here there is the problem that whilst a large deficit on the current account balanced by a large surplus on the capital account may constitute a technical equilibrium, it can hardly represent a sustainable situation into the long term, and it is certainly not a healthy position for an economy, as there are always limits to private sector international borrowing power.

In fact, for Western nations, pure clean floating exchange rates are most unusual, as it is improbable that monetary authorities will wish to allow market forces to proceed unabated. The fluctuations in exchange rates which might occur under clean floating, together with the possible destabilising of interest rates (as financial institutions seek to defend their deposit bases against outflows of funds to overseas markets) could cause considerable harm to business confidence and domestic economic activity as a whole. (The determination of exchange rates and the relevance of balance of payments items are considered in detail in Chapter 10, at 10.3.)

9.3 THE TERMS OF TRADE

The terms of (visible) trade for any particular country relative to the rest of the world are defined as:

$$\frac{\text{index of export prices}}{\text{index of import prices}} \times 100$$

At a particular base date both indices are given a value of 100, and so the starting point of the terms of trade is also 100. If there is subsequently a rise in the average price of imports, whilst the average price of exports remains constant (all prices being expressed in a common currency value), the terms of trade will fall below 100, and conventionally this is described as a 'deterioration' in the terms of trade. A fall in the index of export prices relative to import prices would have the same effect. If the opposite adjustments occur, there is said to be an 'improvement' in the terms of trade. In effect, movements in the terms of trade show changes in *the real purchasing power of a given quantity of exports in terms of imports*. If the terms of trade improve, this means that for every unit of goods exported, the country will obtain a larger quantity of imports; the converse is true of a deterioration in the terms of trade.

Great care must be taken with the *interpretation* of movements in the terms of trade, for whether or not an improvement (or a deterioration) in its value is good (or bad) for the country will depend upon the *reason* for the change in value. Thus, for example, an improvement in the UK's terms of trade may be caused by foreigners demanding more UK manufactured goods, and hence bidding up the price of exports. In this case there is a favourable effect on the balance of trade, as higher export prices are accompanied by a higher demand for exports. There are also likely to be positive effects on domestic employment. However, an improvement in the terms of trade which arises due to higher domestic production costs may not be so favourable. The effect on the value of trade will depend upon the responsiveness of the demand for exports to changes in their price. A high price elasticity of demand will result in a reduction in demand which is proportionately greater than the increase in price. Consequently, not only will the balance of trade deteriorate, but also the total demand for domestic output will fall, along with the level of domestic employment. This effect may be supported by an increased domestic demand for the now relatively cheaper foreign goods.

Similar examples may be given in respect of a deterioration in the UK's terms of trade. Thus, if the deterioration is caused by falling export prices, and overseas demand for exports rises by a proportionately greater amount, the balance of trade and domestic output and employment are likely to benefit. Conversely, if there is only a low elasticity of demand for exports in overseas markets, the balance of trade may suffer (unless there is a significant reduction in imports into the domestic economy), although there may still be positive effects on output and employment in the domestic economy. Rising import prices may also cause a deterioration in the terms of trade, and again the impact on the domestic economy will depend upon the relevant elasticities of demand for traded goods. If the imported goods are regarded as necessities, with low elasticities of demand, then the effect on the balance of trade is likely to be adverse, and the economy as a whole may be depressed if expenditure has to be diverted to the purchase of the now more expensive imports.

As changes in the terms of trade have significant implications for the operation of the domestic economy, it would seem reasonable to suggest that the Government may seek to influence its value. However, the extent of this influence is likely to be limited, as in order to *alter the terms of trade* it is necessary for the authorities to *alter the relative prices of exports and imports*, and these are very much at the mercy of world market forces. Thus, whilst the Government may be able to alter the terms of trade via an adjustment in the domestic currency's exchange rate, subsequent changes in market conditions, altering the prices of traded goods, may wipe out the effect on the terms of trade. Nevertheless, by implementing policies which affect the level of domestic prices relative to prices overseas, the Government will have some influence on the terms of trade. As mentioned above, alterations in the *domestic currency's exchange rate* will affect the terms of trade, for given sets of domestic prices. Alternatively, the authorities may introduce policies to hold down the rate of *domestic price inflation*, with the view to keeping price rises below those experienced by overseas countries. This approach, which might involve a tightening of monetary or fiscal policies, would tend to cause the terms of trade to deteriorate, perhaps with the intention of stimulating overseas demand for domestic exports and hence improving the balance of trade (assuming that elasticities are sufficiently great). It seems unlikely that a government would attempt to cause domestic inflation as a means of improving the terms of trade. A far more sensible approach would be to encourage domestic industry to produce high quality output and undertake aggressive marketing in overseas markets. Thus, if overseas demand for domestic exports can be stimulated, the prices of these goods may be pushed upwards (and hence the terms of trade improved) as a by-product of a favourable shift in trading patterns.

9.4 THE ECONOMIC SIGNIFICANCE OF BALANCE OF PAYMENTS STATISTICS

9.4.1 The current account

(a) *Deficits*

At the very basic level, a current account deficit means that a country is not paying its way internationally. In technical terms, current overseas expenditures are not being covered by current overseas earnings, and hence, as explained at 9.2.4, there must be an *increasing level of debt to other countries* and/or a *running down of existing claims on other countries*. Therefore, as a continuing ability to import commodities from overseas is vital to the well-being of a country, a current account deficit must always be given careful consideration by the authorities. However, the extent to which a deficit is regarded as being unfavourable for a country will depend upon the *size and persistence of the deficit*, the *economic and financial strength of the country*, and *expectations on the country's future international financial prospects*.

Assuming that the current account deficit is expected only to be a *short-term phenomenon*, then, so long as it is not excessively large, there is no reason why it necessarily should be viewed as being unfavourable: first, to the extent that the deficit implies greater imports than exports of goods and services, consumers in the domestic economy are able to maintain a *higher living standard* than would otherwise have been the case. Secondly, the deficit may reflect a growth in the imports of raw materials and/or semi-manufactured goods, which may be processed and *re-exported* at some future date. Thirdly, the deficit may be more than covered by *capital account inflows* relating to portfolio or direct investment in the domestic economy (and these flows may help to raise the future production potential of the domestic economy, and hence enhance its ability to grow out of the current account deficit). Fourthly, *international borrowing facilities* may be readily available, and so long as the economy is inherently sound, the future servicing requirements should cause few difficulties. Finally, the country may be able to finance the deficit by *running down* its previously accumulated official gold and convertible currency *reserves*.

It must be emphasised that the implied acceptability of the current account deficit exists only because of the expectation that it is to be a short-term phenomenon. Thus, it is hoped that at some future date sufficient surpluses would be generated so as to allow overseas debt to be reduced, or at least stabilised, and for the country's official reserves to be replenished. In addition, for purposes of long-term economic stability, it would be useful to limit the net inflow of direct and portfolio investment; otherwise the country might find that large parts of its domestic economy are controlled by foreigners, without there being a comparable domestic ownership of productive resources overseas.

Once it is believed that a current account deficit is likely to *persist into the longer term*, the implications of its existence become somewhat more serious. Clearly, a country's *official reserves are finite*, and there are *limits to the extent to which foreigners will be willing to lend to a country with a current account deficit*. The larger is the deficit, and the weaker is the international financial position of the country to begin with, the more likely it becomes that a crisis will be precipitated.

As the current account deficit persists, the country is likely to become increasingly indebted to overseas nations. Irrespective of whether this takes the form of private sector or official borrowing, or whether it constitutes direct or portfolio investment in domestic industry and commerce, the fact remains that the growing debt will, in all probability, lead to *progressively more onerous servicing requirements*. In the case of borrowed funds, interest payments must be made, and funds must be earmarked for the eventual repayment of the capital sum.

In respect of direct and portfolio investments, overseas investors will normally expect to be able to repatriate profits and dividends. Thus, the build-up of debt is likely to undermine the interest, profits and dividends section of the current account; whilst the repatriation of capital funds, which becomes ever more likely as foreigners come to doubt the ability of the country to meet its international financial commitments, will tend to weaken the capital account. Indeed, the *undermining of confidence* in the domestic economy may force the government to *raise interest rates* in an attempt to ward off a precipitous withdrawal of foreign investment funds, and thus avoid a collapse of the domestic currency's exchange rate; although, somewhat ironically, a lower exchange rate may be seen as part of the necessary adjustment mechanism for the rectification of the current account deficit (as will be explained in 9.5.2).

The *international debt problem*, experienced during the 1980s, resulted largely from certain less developed countries borrowing huge amounts of funds on the international markets in order to sustain current account deficits. Major countries such as Mexico, Brazil and Argentina found that high real rates of interest and a general strengthening of the currencies in which much of their debt was denominated created unmanageable debt servicing burdens. It was only through major rescheduling exercises and the provision of additional funds by creditors (often on the understanding that policies would be implemented to deal with the underlying balance of payments problems), that a global financial crisis was averted. However, the cost to many debtor countries was high, especially in terms of the periods of retrenchment required within the domestic economy in order to bring about the balance of payments adjustments. On occasions the economic policies required led to social and political upheavals within certain debtor countries.

Finally, it should be recognised that in relatively special circumstances, sustained current account deficits may not augur long-term difficulties. This is when the current account deficit is largely due to high levels of imports of capital investment goods and materials (rather than consumer goods and services). Effectively, foreign investment funds are being used to build up the domestic economy's capital stock. If this leads to rapid rates of economic growth, and the building up of confidence in the economy, then the debt servicing commitments should create no major problems; although there must always be some doubt as to the length of time over which the requisite high rates of economic growth can be sustained. If international confidence does eventually wane, the country could still find itself in longer term financial difficulties.

(b) *Surpluses*

Whilst a persistent deficit on a country's current account tends to be viewed with some concern by that country's government, a persistent surplus is often regarded with a certain amount of favour. This is because the existence of a surplus allows a country to *build its overseas investments* (and hence its future overseas earnings) or *repay overseas debt* (thus reducing debt servicing costs), without causing official reserves

377

to be run down. Indeed, the authorities may take the opportunity to *accumulate official reserves* in order to provide security against future current account deficits. Nevertheless, there may be circumstances within which a country may seek to reduce a current account surplus, especially if it is large by international standards and it appears to be persisting. In particular, as every current account surplus is, by definition, matched by a current account deficit in at least one other country, the surplus country may find itself under *political pressure* to reduce the surplus. Quite simply, current account deficits, which imply increasing international indebtedness and/or falling official currency reserves, are likely to require some form of remedial action. Now, whilst a deficit country may seek to depress domestic demand for imports, it is generally agreed that a more attractive solution may be for the surplus country to increase the volume of its imports, thus avoiding any overall depression in the level of demand for traded goods and services. In fact, this solution to the payments imbalance may provide a stimulus to world economic activity, assuming that productive resources are available to meet any overall increase in the level of demand. In recent years, the USA has exerted political pressure on Japan and certain newly industrialised countries in Asia in an attempt to counter domestic calls for *protectionism* against foreign imports. The surplus country may, of course, act before explicit pressure is exerted, if it fears that *trade barriers* will be erected against its products.

A further reason for a country to wish to reduce its current account surplus is that it implies that current earnings from overseas are greater than current expenditures, and hence that domestic residents are consuming less than they might otherwise consume from their earnings. In other words, if a surplus can be reduced by increasing imports of goods and services, *domestic living standards may be raised* without any increase in international indebtedness. In addition, to the extent that current account surpluses are 'financed' by the accumulation of official reserves, an expansionary pressure is placed on the *domestic money supply*. Consequently, the authorities may seek to reduce the surplus in an effort to *ease inflationary pressures* within the domestic economy. The reduction of the surplus would effectively shift the balance of demand towards overseas producers.

9.4.2 The capital account

Given the rather varied nature of the individual component parts of the capital account, great care must be taken in respect of the *interpretation of capital flows*. Indeed, even if the capital account should be in balance overall, it is still necessary to consider the underlying components if a true picture of the balance of payments is to be achieved. For example, it may be argued that a net outflow of long-term direct investment overseas, balanced by a net inflow of short-term money market deposits, is not a desirable position for a country's balance of payments accounts. Short-term funds may be extremely volatile, and should the country's interest rates fall relative to those ruling overseas, there could be a reversal of the capital flow, leading to problems for the authorities (especially if official reserves were only modest).

(a) *Deficits*

A deficit on the capital account means that there is a *net outflow of funds* for overseas investment, lending to foreigners, the repayment of outstanding debt, and so on. If official financing is included within the capital account, there may also be an increase in official reserves and/or a reduction in overseas official debt. Therefore, at least on the surface, the implications of a capital account deficit are far less disturbing than those of a current account deficit. The capital account outflow is likely to imply *higher net interest, profits and dividends inflows* (or at least *smaller net outflows*) in the future; and if the capital outflow represents domestic residents undertaking capital investment overseas, then the country will be left with a *larger stock of overseas capital* which might be drawn down in future should the need arise. In addition, the outflows of foreign currency in respect of capital items are likely to hold down the domestic currency's exchange rate, relative to what it otherwise would have been, and hence may improve the international competitiveness of domestically-produced goods and services. (The determination of exchange rates is explained in detail in Chapter 10, at 10.3.)

A possible detrimental effect of a substantial capital outflow relates to the fact that it may serve to *raise productive capacity overseas*, and hence raise output and create jobs abroad at the expense of the domestic economy. Specifically, the investment may lead to a reduced dependence on imports in the foreign country, increased competition in overseas export markets, and an increase in import penetration in the domestic economy. Thus, in the longer term, overseas investment may tend to undermine the visible trade balance, although the trading effects may be dissipated through all countries which trade with the recipient of the capital.

(b) *Surpluses*

If a capital account surplus involves *long-term* capital investment by foreigners in domestic industry, then this might assist the country in future years by allowing for the *production of more goods domestically*, perhaps leading to a reduction in visible imports and an increase in visible exports.

However, it must never be forgotten that capital may be withdrawn at a future date, although its long-term nature does not normally make this a critical issue. In addition, capital inflows are likely to generate *interest, profits and dividends to be paid abroad*, and this will tend to undermine the invisibles balance on the current account. Thus, whilst capital inflows may be vital for a country experiencing current account deficits (in the face of limited official reserves), as time passes such inflows may lead to a weakening of the current account, if the adverse effect on invisibles outweighs any positive effect which may be generated for visible trade.

If capital inflows involve *short-term* ('hot' money) investments, perhaps stimulated by relatively high domestic interest rates, then there is not only the problem that future interest payments overseas will be raised, but also it may be the case that a certain amount of *instability* is introduced into the capital account. For example, foreign holders of sterling-denominated funds in the UK may fear a depreciation in the value of sterling, and hence they may wish to withdraw their funds (and switch into some other currency) at very short notice. The authorities may then feel obliged to allow domestic interest rates to rise in order to persuade foreign investors to maintain their holdings of sterling funds. If this does not occur with sufficient speed, it is possible that there may be damaging outflows of investment funds, and the depreciation that was feared may be brought about.

Clearly, a country which runs persistent and significant surpluses on its capital account is in a precarious position. It is effectively living on borrowed time, and sooner or later an *international payments crisis* is likely to occur. Official reserves are finite, and there are limits to the amounts which may be borrowed overseas by both the government and the private sector. Indeed, even before a country reaches the limits of its borrowing power, it is likely that foreign creditors will become increasingly reluctant to provide more funds, and the terms and conditions required are likely to become progressively more onerous. Should the net capital inflows cease, or, worse still, should a net outflow occur, the country simultaneously experiencing a current account deficit could find itself in serious difficulties.

9.5 CORRECTING A BALANCE OF PAYMENTS IMBALANCE

9.5.1 The basic payments problem

As suggested in 9.4, the occurrence of imbalances on either the current account or the capital account of the balance of payments may imply potentially serious problems for an economy, irrespective of whether those imbalances are in the form of deficits or surpluses. Consequently, governments may actively seek to influence specific elements within the balance of payments accounts in order to limit or to remove a disequilibrium position. However, before considering the policies which the authorities might implement in relation to the balance of payments, it should be recognised that there may be *natural mechanisms* operating within the economy, which, if left to run their course may lead to an automatic correction for an imbalance. For example, a shift in demand away from domestically-produced goods and towards foreign-produced goods will not only tend to cause the current account of the balance of payments to deteriorate, but may also lead to a reduction in domestic output and employment, and, other things being equal, a reduction in domestic disposable income. This latter occurrence is likely to lead to a reduction in the demand for imports, and downwards pressure on domestic inflation, which will aid the competitiveness of exports. Consequently, there may be an adjustment which pushes the current account back towards its equilibrium position.

Despite the possible existence of natural adjustment mechanisms within the economy, it may be the case that they do not act quickly enough to be of relevance for short-term policy decisions, and the ultimate effects may either be too weak to deal with the problem faced, or may be unpredictable in their precise impact. Therefore, the authorities may feel that they have little alternative but to introduce policies designed to deal with imbalances on the current account and/or the capital account. However, it must be emphasised that such policies may be prone to the problems of implementation and operation as examined in Chapter 8, at 8.2. In particular, the timing of policies will be crucial if their effects are to hit the economy when they are required, rather than at a time when the problem has subsided. Care will also have to be taken in respect of possible policy conflicts, in the sense that actions thought to be desirable for balance of payments purposes may have detrimental effects on other policy objectives.

9.5.2 A current account imbalance

(a) *Deficits*

Taking the UK as an example, the main measures which could be implemented with the view to reducing a current account deficit are basically as follows:

(i)   The authorities could seek to *reduce the sterling exchange rate*, as a means of reducing the foreign currency price of UK exports, whilst raising the sterling price of foreign imports, other things being equal. Whilst it is probable that the UK's demands for imported goods and services would be depressed, total expenditure on imports would only fall if the *price elasticity of demand* for these imports was greater than one (i.e. the proportionate reduction in the quantity demanded must be greater than the proportionate increase in the sterling price of the goods and services if total expenditure is to be reduced). Similarly, whilst the volume of exports would probably increase, overseas foreign currency earnings would only rise if the price elasticity of demand for exports was greater than one. Clearly, for there to be an overall improvement in the balance of traded goods and services, it is not necessary that both these elasticity conditions should be met. Strictly, if the sum of the two elasticities is greater than one, the balance of traded goods and services will improve (this is known as the Marshall-Lerner condition).

The adjustment in exchange rates may be brought about by the authorities allowing *market pressure* to depress the value of sterling (which would probably occur at some point if the current account deficit was large enough to undermine the confidence of overseas investors in the UK's international payments position). Alternatively, the downwards pressure could be intensified by *official exchange market intervention* involving sales of sterling, or by a loosening of monetary controls with the aim of pushing interest rates downwards and hence undermining the attractiveness of sterling deposits for foreign investors. However, a possible adverse side effect of this type of policy action is that domestic money supply growth may be stimulated, and hence the level of demand within the economy may be raised, thus counteracting at least some of the effect of the policy on the level of imports. In addition, it should also be noted that irrespective of the means by which the exchange value of sterling is reduced, there may be a *J-curve effect* to contend with. That is, as it takes time for trading patterns to adjust, in the short term it is likely that the deficit will be made worse. It is only as the demand for the now cheaper export goods and services begins to rise, that export earnings will recover; and it is only as the demand for the now more expensive imports falls that total expenditure on such items will fall back. The final outcome will, as explained above, depend upon the elasticities of demand for traded goods and services (once the trading adjustments have been completed).

(ii)   *Demand management policies* may be directed towards reducing the volume of imports, and hence improving the current balance. Specifically, the authorities could tighten monetary policy (although higher interest rates could place upwards pressure on the sterling exchange rate, through the attraction of foreign capital funds), reduce the level of government spending or raise taxes. The ensuing reduction in total demand would not only depress the demand for imports, but also would possibly lead to the creation of spare capacity in the domestic economy, thus providing industry with the ability (and the motivation) to service export markets more effectively. Unfortunately, any failure to raise the volume of exports by an amount sufficient to compensate for lost demand from the domestic market could lead to higher levels of unemployment and slower economic growth.

In practice, demand management and currency depreciation are the *only serious policy options*. Whilst other policies, of the types listed below, are theoretically possible, they are either of only marginal importance or are precluded under current international trading agreements.

(iii) *Direct controls* could be introduced as a means of making imports less attractive to the domestic consumer, or simply limiting the volume of such imports. For example, the authorities might apply *tariffs* to specific imports in order to raise their price within the domestic market, and hence improve the relative competitiveness of domestically produced products. So long as the elasticity of demand for the imports is greater than zero, demand would fall, and, other things being equal, total payments made to the foreign exporter would be reduced. The problem with this measure is that it may lead to retaliation by overseas countries, which may adversely affect the UK's exports. There is also the possible impact on domestic inflation rates to bear in mind. In consequence, the authorities may place *quotas* (physical limits) on imports, but again they would run the risk of possible overseas retaliation.

(iv) *Exchange controls* could be applied in order to limit the use of foreign currency by UK residents. This measure would effectively require the authorities to give their explicit permission before UK residents could spend foreign currency. Hence, the ability of UK residents to purchase goods and services from overseas could be severely restricted.

(v) *Overseas investment* by UK residents might be encouraged as a means of improving the net inflow of interest, profits and dividends in the longer term. However, the feasibility of this policy, in the face of current account deficits, would depend upon the availability of foreign currency reserves, and a willingness to see those reserves run down.

(vi) Any policy designed to *improve the quality of UK-produced goods and services* and their associated *marketing* on an international level, would help to improve the current account positon, although probably only in the longer term.

(vii)   The Government might seek to *reduce* its *net payments to official institutions and organisations overseas* (such as the EC and the UN), and its *expenditure on military and diplomatic commitments overseas*. However, the feasibility of such actions is severely restricted by political factors.

Clearly, the authorities have a wide range of means through which they may attempt to influence the current account of the balance of payments, and potentially their effects may be great. However, in practice, the degree of influence will depend upon the response of consumers to policy changes, and the extent to which overseas governments are willing to acquiesce in the face of possible adverse effects on their own balance of payments.

(b)   *Surpluses*

A large part of the debate in relation to current account adjustments is directed towards the deficit problem, but as outlined above, in 9.4.1(b), the existence of current account surpluses may also cause difficulties for a country. Consequently, the authorities may seek to reduce these surpluses, and may do this largely by *reversing the policies outlined above* as being appropriate for the treatment of deficits. Thus, to summarise, the following policies may be implemented:

(i)   The authorities may seek to *raise the exchange rate of sterling*, in order to make exports relatively less competitive in overseas markets, and make imports relatively more competitive in the UK market. This policy might involve official intervention on the currency markets, selling foreign currencies and purchasing sterling, in order to alter the balance of currency supplies and demands appropriately. Alternatively, the authorities might operate indirectly, by attempting to attract foreign currency capital inflows. This would not only put upwards pressure on the exchange rate, but also it would tend to raise interest, profits and dividends outflows in the longer term. To achieve this end, the authorities might offer fiscal incentives to foreign investors (tax allowances, grants, subsidies, and so on), or there might be a tightening of monetary policy in order to raise domestic interest rates. Unfortunately, the latter course of action would tend to depress the demand for imports. In any event, a raising of the exchange rate for sterling would only reduce the current account surplus if the price elasticities of demand for traded goods were high enough. However, if these elasticities were, in fact, low, then the appropriate policy would appear to be the reduction of the exchange value of sterling; imports would become more expensive in the UK, and exports would become cheaper overseas, but the quantities demanded would alter very little. In this case, intervention to raise the supply of sterling on the foreign exchanges, or policies to discourage foreign investment, would appear to be appropriate.

(ii) *Expansionary fiscal policy* (perhaps raising government expenditure and/or reducing levels of taxation) may be used to raise domestic demand, thus drawing in imports, and perhaps leading to the diversion of potential export goods to the domestic market. This policy may also create domestic inflationary pressures, thus helping to make export goods become less competitive in overseas markets, other things being equal.

(iii) *Expansionary monetary policy* (depressing interest rates and allowing the money supply to rise rapidly) may also stimulate domestic demand. There is also the longer-term inflationary impact, undermining overseas competitiveness of exports. Unfortunately there are two problems with this policy:

(1) if the elasticity of demand for domestic exports is low, then it is possible that export earnings may rise as a result of higher export prices (this issue is also relevant to any domestic price effects caused by the expansionary fiscal policy);

(2) lower domestic interest rates will mean that the outflow of funds for interest payments on foreign-owned financial assets will fall, thus raising net interest, profits and dividends inflows on the invisibles section of the current account. This effect may be supported in the longer term, to the extent that domestic capital is driven overseas.

(iv) If any *import controls* exist (in the form of tariffs or quotas or excessive paperwork requirements on importers), the authorities might dismantle these, thus making it easier for importers to carry out their business. Indeed, *export controls* might be introduced, in the form of physical limits on the volumes of specific types of goods which might be sold overseas, or perhaps through selective taxes applied to exports (to make them less price-competitive in the overseas market). Once again, any policy influencing relative prices of traded goods depends for its success on the price elasticities of demand for those goods being sufficiently high, so that the increase in export prices leads to a proportionately greater reduction in the quantity of exports demanded.

(v) Policies might be introduced to *encourage* domestic residents to take *holidays abroad* (perhaps via the removal of any government assistance to the domestic tourist industry; this would also probably lead to a reduction in the number of foreign tourists coming into the country); or to encourage students to study overseas, whilst discouraging foreign students from coming into the country, and so on.

(vi)   The *Government* might increase its own overseas *expenditure*, on embassies, armed forces serving abroad, and on foreign aid. It might also seek to reduce the level of foreign official expenditure in the domestic economy.

It should be clear from the above discussion that whilst there are many policies which might be applied to reduce a current account surplus, some bring with them *adverse implications* for the operation of the domestic economy as a whole. Policies to raise domestic demand may lead to higher levels of consumption for domestic residents, but the inflationary implications may cause difficulties in the longer term. Higher interest rates to attract foreign capital may undermine domestic investment in productive capital. Policies to discourage foreign visitors may cause political problems, as might excessive increases in certain types of official overseas expenditure. Therefore, policies to deal with current account surpluses must be formulated with as much care and attention to detail as policies to deal with current account deficits.

9.5.3   A capital account imbalance

(a) *Deficits*

In an attempt to stimulate inflows of capital funds, or perhaps stem outflows of such funds, the following policies may be implemented:

(i)   The authorities may use *monetary policy* as a means of raising domestic interest rates, and hence making domestic interest-bearing assets more attractive to international investors. This policy may also help to depress inflationary pressures, and hence give increased confidence to investors in respect of the holding of assets denominated in the domestic currency (sterling).

(ii)   An official commitment to the maintenance of a *stable currency exchange* rate will reduce the perceived risk of losses, in international purchasing power terms, from the holding of sterling-denominated assets.

(iii)   The broad stance of the *Government's economic policy* will be important to foreigners' expectations of the possible future development of the domestic economy. Therefore, policy may be formulated in a manner designed to calm fears in international financial markets, or even to stimulate hopes of favourable interest rate or exchange rate movements.

(iv)   *Direct controls* may be introduced in the form of limits on the amounts of foreign currency which may be withdrawn from the country for overseas capital investment purposes. Alternatively, direct limits may be imposed on the amounts of overseas investment which may be undertaken by domestic residents. Unfortunately, such policies may lead to retaliation by other countries, which may see a direct threat to their own capital account position.

(v) The Government may offer *incentives* for investment, in the form of grants, subsidies or tax free allowances, which may be directed either towards the potential foreign investor in the domestic economy, or towards the domestic investor on the brink of investing abroad. Indeed, the authorities may use the threat of taxation as a weapon to dissuade domestic residents from investing overseas.

(vi) The *Government* may attempt to reduce its own *capital expenditure outflows*, perhaps by drawing back from political and military commitments. It may also encourage foreign governments to undertake capital expenditure within the domestic economy. However, the nature of such expenditure could generate serious political problems for the Government.

(vii) In relation to the *official financing* elements of the capital account, the authorities might seek to lengthen the repayment period on any outstanding official overseas debt. They may also negotiate with international monetary institutions and overseas central banks to raise official overseas borrowing.

With any policy designed to influence capital flows, it is important to bear in mind that the effects may only occur with a *time lag*, and may, to some extent, be unpredictable in respect of both their timing and magnitude. This is likely to be a particular problem in respect of the longer-term capital flows, associated with direct investment and long-term lending. Thus, the relevance of some of the policy initiatives outlined above is likely to be only limited for the purposes of dealing with immediate balance of payments problems. Care must also be taken by the authorities not to cause a level of disruption to capital flows which would be likely to lead to *retaliation* from overseas governments. In addition, it must be remembered that capital account flows may have important implications for the position of the current account of the balance of payments. For example, policies which are successful in attracting capital inflows may serve to put upwards pressure on the domestic currency's exchange rate, and hence may undermine the country's trading position as domestically-produced goods are made relatively less attractive in international markets. There are also likely to be increased net outflows, or reduced net inflows, of interest, profits and dividends as a result of the corrective policies listed above; and consequently the invisibles section of the current account will probably be adversely affected.

(b) *Surpluses*

The policies which may be implemented in order to deal with a surplus on the capital account are basically the reverse of those outlined above, and hence may be dealt with fairly briefly. Thus, the authorities may attempt to *reduce domestic interest rates* or any existing *subsidies* or *grants* payable to investors, as a means of undermining the attractiveness of capital investments within the domestic economy. Any existing *direct controls* designed to limit the ability of domestic residents to invest overseas may be removed, and there might be the introduction of *taxes* on domestic investment earnings. In addition, although hardly likely in practice, the Government could attempt to *destabilise domestic financial markets* in an effort to undermine the confidence of overseas investors. A much less risky strategy would be for the Government to *increase* its own *overseas capital expenditure*, and, in relation to *official financing*, outstanding official debt could be repaid and the Government could become a net lender to overseas official institutions.

The extent to which any of the above-listed policies may be pursued will depend upon the current account position and the level of official reserves. Clearly, if the surplus on the capital account coincides with a deficit on the current account, then policies which are successful in reducing net capital inflows will sooner or later cause official reserves to fall. The effects of the policies on the current account must also be considered. For example, lower rates of interest may stimulate domestic demand and hence may cause the current account to deteriorate; although, counteracting this effect may be a lower exchange rate (and hence less competitive import prices) brought about by a weaker capital account position. Without doubt, the ultimate effects of policies may be complex, and hence it is important that the authorities recognise the full implications of their actions, if undesired side-effects are to be avoided.

9.6 THE UK BALANCE OF PAYMENTS

9.6.1 The current account

(a) *Visible trade*

Until the late 1960s, over half of UK *visible imports* were in the form of *basic materials, fuel, food, beverages, and tobacco.* However, even before this time the importance of imported *manufactured goods* had been increasing steadily, and this trend continued into the 1990s. By 1992, manufactured goods accounted for about 78% of total visible imports into the UK, having risen from 53% in 1975, and only 23% in 1955. This significant change in the composition of imports, which is clearly demonstrated in Table 9.1, is reflected in the UK's pattern of trade with other countries. Thus, since the 1950s, an increasing proportion of visible imports has come from other *developed countries*, and within that group the *EC* has shown a tremendous growth in importance. In 1955 imports from the EC and the rest of Western Europe accounted for 26% of the total; by 1992 the proportion attributable to the EC alone had risen to about 52%. Table 9.2 shows the pattern of visible trade by area in 1992.

Table 9.1   UK visible trade: Commodity pattern, 1992, percentage of total value

Category	Imports	Exports
Food, beverages and tobacco	10.7	8.0
Basic materials	4.1	1.9
Fuels	5.5	6.4
Finished manufactured goods	54.3	55.4
Semi-manufactured goods	24.1	26.4
Others	1.3	1.9

Source: *Monthly Digest of Statistics,* Central Statistical Office, March 1993.

Table 9.2   UK visible trade: Trading partners by area, 1992, percentage of total value

Category	Imports from	Exports to
European Community	52.4	56.4
Rest of Western Europe	11.6	8.0
North America	12.6	13.0
Other OECD countries	7.2	3.7
Oil exporting countries	2.5	5.6
E. Europe and former USSR	1.3	1.6
Other countries	12.4	11.7

Source: *Monthly Digest of Statistics,* Central Statistical Office, March 1993.

The commodity pattern in respect of *visible exports* has tended to be relatively stable in recent years. The most important element of visible exports has continued to be *manufactured goods*, which account for around 80% of total visible exports. It was only during the early years of the 1980s that the importance of manufactured goods diminished somewhat (to around 65% of the total); this being due largely to the rapidly growing exports of *North Sea oil* at a time of relatively high world oil prices. Once again, trade with *developed countries* has become increasingly important for UK visible exports, and within that group the *EC* has achieved a dominant position. In 1955 the EC took only 15% of the UK's visible exports; by 1992 that proportion had risen to around 56%. The recent patterns of visible exports and trading partners are summarised in Tables 9.1 and 9.2 respectively.

For much of the post-war period, UK *visible trade* has been in *deficit*. It was only during the years 1980 to 1982 that the UK experienced a sustained and substantial visible trade surplus, and this was largely due to a growing surplus on trade in oil. However, throughout the 1980s, the UK's visible trade balance worsened continually, with a record deficit of approximately £25b being generated in 1989. Table 9.3 illustrates clearly the overall deterioration in UK visible trade in recent years, and shows the significance of trade in manufactured goods for this trend. It should also be noted that since the mid-1980s the balance of trade in oil has also deteriorated sharply. (The factors underlying these very important trends are outlined below in part (c) of the present section.)

(b) *Invisibles*

The overall invisibles balances for the years 1983 to 1992 are shown in Table 9.3. It may be observed that whilst invisibles remained in *surplus* throughout this period, there was a significant *deterioration* in the overall balance between 1986 and 1990. Within the overall surplus figures, the performances of the individual component parts of the invisibles account have been quite varied. Table 9.4 shows the balances on the major components for 1991, and the aggregate balances for the three broad categories of components for 1992. The pattern of results illustrated is largely typical of that which has occurred in recent years, although net interest, profits and dividends for the private sector and public corporations were unusually low during 1991. The *substantial deficit* position for the *government sector* items is clear, with the transfers item reflecting the UK's net contribution to the EC budget. The major *surplus* items have tended to be *financial and other services* and earnings of *interest, profits and dividends* by the *private sector*. Until the mid-1980s, civil aviation also normally made a positive contribution to the accounts, with the travel item tending to fluctuate between deficit and surplus.

(c) *Current account balance*

In 1981, the UK experienced its largest ever current account surplus of £6.6b; by 1989 the position had *deteriorated* to one of a record deficit of £21.6b. The almost continual downwards trend over this period is clear from the figures given in Table 9.3. The major factors explaining this

Table 9.3   UK balance of payments current account, 1983 to 1992, selected sub-balances, £ billion

	1983	1984	1985	1986	1987	1988	1989	1990	1991	1992
Oil balance	7.0	6.9	8.1	4.1	4.2	2.8	1.3	1.5	1.2	1.5
Non-oil visible trade	−8.5	−12.1	−11.2	−13.5	−15.7	−24.4	−25.9	−20.3	−11.5	−15.3
of which manufactures	−2.7	−4.4	−3.6	−6.1	−8.3	−15.4	−17.2	−11.6	−3.6	−7.5
Visible balance	−1.5	−5.2	−3.1	−9.4	−11.5	−21.6	−24.6	−18.8	−10.3	−13.8
Invisibles balance	5.3	7.1	6.3	9.4	7.1	5.3	3.0	1.8	4.0	1.9
Current balance	3.8	1.9	3.2	–	−4.4	−16.3	−21.6	−17.0	−6.3	−11.9

Source: *Balance of Payments 'Pink Book'*, 1992, Central Statistical Office
Financial Statement and Budget Report, March 1993, HM Treasury
Monthly Digest of Statistics, Central Statistical Office, March 1993

Table 9.4   UK balance of payments invisibles account, 1991 and 1992, major sub-balances, £ billion

Category	1991		1992
Services:		4.9	3.7
General government	−2.4		
Private sector and public corporations	7.3		
Sea transport	—		
Civil aviation	−0.5		
Travel	−2.7		
Financial and other services	10.5		
Interest, profits and dividends:		0.4	3.2
General government	−0.1		
Private sector and public corporations	0.5		
Transfers:		−1.3	−5.0
General government	−1.0		
Private sector	−0.3		
Invisibles balance		4.0	1.9

Source: *Balance of Payments 'Pink Book'*, 1992, Central Statistical Office
Monthly Digest of Statistics, Central Statistical Office, March 1993

massive turnaround in the UK current account during the 1980s, and the modest improvement at the beginning of the 1990s, may be summarised as follows:

(i)   *Oil prices.* In 1981 the price of oil was around $34 per barrel; by 1989 the price had fallen to half of this amount. However, during the early years of the decade, the growth in the UK's oil production had allowed the UK to experience an increasing surplus on oil trade, which peaked at £8.1b in 1985. It was not until 1986 that the rapid deterioration in the oil market was reflected in the UK's trading position, with a reduction in the oil surplus to £4.1b. Since that time the oil market has recovered only marginally but the UK oil industry has experienced a number of severe production problems (including the Piper Alpha disaster) which have undermined the UK's oil trade still further. The recorded surplus for 1992 was only £1.5b.

(ii)   *Economic growth.* A price which the UK had to pay for the improvement in its rates of economic growth during the second half of the 1980s, was an expansion in the domestic demand for imported goods at a significantly faster rate than the growth in overseas demand for UK exports. Consequently, the difference in growth rates between the UK and other major Western countries had an adverse impact across a broad range of current account items. By contrast, the recession in the UK economy between 1990 and 1992 undoubtedly contributed to the improvement in the current account, by depressing the demand for imports.

(iii) *Consumer spending.* An important aspect of the more buoyant economic conditions in the UK during the second half of the 1980s, was a boom in consumer spending. (It may be argued that this factor was a major driving force behind the improvement in economic growth.) This boom was fuelled not only by greater confidence in the future health of the economy, underpinned by falling levels of unemployment and improved job prospects, but also by several rounds of *income tax cuts* and a *massive expansion in consumer credit* (encouraged by deregulation and increased competition within the financial services sector). Unfortunately, a substantial proportion of the increase in consumer demand was directed towards imported manufactured goods. In 1980 the UK had a surplus on trade in manufactured goods of £5.4b; by 1989 this had turned into a deficit of £17.2b. During the early 1990s, the reduced levels of consumer confidence in the UK, as a result of rising unemployment and uncertain economic conditions, under-mined the demand for imports of manufactured goods. In 1992, a substantial reduction was seen in the value of visible imports, and this helped to reduce the current account deficit to £6.3b. More recently, international trading conditions have deteriorated as many other major Western economies have recorded slow economic growth, and in some cases marked recessionary conditions. This development is reflected in the continuing weak position of the UK's current account.

(iv) *Capital goods imports.* It has been argued that the growth of the UK economy, together with improved business confidence during the second half of the 1980s, led to a marked expansion in the demand for capital equipment by UK business. At least part of this demand fed into increased imports of capital goods.

(v) *UK trading competitiveness.* Throughout the 1980s and the early years of the 1990s, the UK's *rate of inflation* remained somewhat higher than the rates experienced by most of its major trading partners. Between 1981 and 1985, the substantial *depreciation* in the value of sterling relative to most other major currencies offered some degree of compensation for this inflation, and allowed the UK to maintain (and, in some instances, improve) its competitive position in international markets. However, following the sterling crisis of January 1985, the UK Government directed increasing attention to the strength of sterling on the foreign exchange markets. As a result, during the remainder of the 1980s, the exchange value of sterling proved to be relatively stable overall; although this disguised a substantial strengthening in the value of sterling relative to the US dollar, at the same time as the deterioration in value relative to the deutschmark and the yen continued. In consequence, during the second half of the 1980s, the UK's competitive position overall was once again undermined. This situation not only made it more difficult for UK exporters to break into and hold overseas markets, but also made foreign goods appear increasingly attractive just at the time when UK consumers were keen to raise their levels of spending. The surge in the UK's inflation rate during 1989 and 1990, immediately followed by the placing of sterling within the ERM, merely exacerbated this problem, and probably helps to explain the deterioration in the visible trade balance and current account balance during 1992. The substantial depreciation of sterling experienced following its withdrawal from the ERM in September 1992, combined with the historically low rates of inflation recorded in the UK during the first half of 1993, should serve to enhance the UK's trading competitiveness; although the short-term effect may be to accelerate the deterioration in the UK's trading position, as it takes time for trading patterns to adjust to changes in relative international prices. (This so-called 'J-curve effect' is explored in Chapter 10, at 10.3.5(d).)

(vi) *Economic policy.* Whilst official policy actions are reflected in the factors outlined above, the Government's position on *monetary policy* has been of particular relevance, and should be identified separately. Of especial note are the *relatively high interest rates* in the UK between 1989 and 1991, which are believed to have damped down domestic demand, and hence reduced pressure for the growth of imports. The significant *relaxation of monetary policy* following the withdrawal of sterling from the ERM, in September 1992, is likely to have had the opposite effect on the level of domestic demand, and this may stimulate the demand for imports; although the concurrent depreciation in the exchange value of sterling, and hence the reduced attractiveness of foreign goods and services, may counteract this trend.

9.6.2 Transactions in UK external assets and liabilities

In each year between 1987 and 1992 *substantial net inflows of funds* were recorded on the capital account of the UK's balance of payments. This is in marked contrast to the earlier years of the 1980s when *large net outflows* occurred, and very much reflects the *shift of the current account from surplus to deficit* over the corresponding time periods. As is illustrated in Table 9.5, movements of capital funds have been extremely

Table 9.5 Summary of transactions in UK external assets and liabilities, 1987 to 1992, £ billion

	1987	1988	1989	1990	1991	1992
Transactions in assets						
UK investment overseas:						
Direct	− 19.2	− 20.9	− 21.5	− 9.6	− 10.1	− 8.6
Portfolio	5.2	− 11.2	− 35.5	− 15.8	− 29.2	− 27.9
Lending overseas by UK banks	− 50.5	− 19.7	− 28.6	− 41.2	32.4	− 25.7
Deposits/lending overseas by UK non-bank private sector	− 4.8	− 3.0	− 7.9	− 11.8	− 9.4	− 27.4
Official reserves	− 12.0	− 2.8	5.4	− 0.1	− 2.7	1.2
Other external assets of central government	− 0.8	− 0.9	− 0.9	− 1.0	− 0.9	− 0.7
Total transactions in assets	− 82.1	− 58.5	− 89.0	− 79.5	− 19.9	− 89.1
Transactions in liabilities						
Overseas investment in the UK:						
Direct	9.4	12.0	18.6	18.6	12.0	10.9
Portfolio	19.5	15.6	14.6	5.3	16.1	17.1
Borrowing from overseas by UK banks	52.4	34.1	44.7	47.6	− 24.2	22.6
Borrowing from overseas by UK non-bank private sector	3.3	5.4	27.5	18.2	24.9	41.8
Other external liabilities of general government	1.8	0.8	2.8	0.9	− 2.3	− 0.9
Total transactions in liabilities	86.4	67.9	108.2	90.6	26.5	91.5
Net transactions	4.3	9.4	19.2	11.1	6.6	2.4

Source: *Monthly Digest of Statistics,* Central Statistical Office, March 1993.

large in recent years, with *borrowing and lending overseas by UK banks* and *UK portfolio investment overseas* being particularly significant. More recently, *borrowing and lending transactions* associated directly with the *non-bank private sector* have grown significantly.

It is interesting to note that during much of the 1980s there were substantial net outflows of funds relating to direct and portfolio investment, which, to some extent, were balanced by large amounts of net borrowing overseas by UK banks. In other words, within the capital account, there tended to be *fairly large deficits on longer-term investment* in productive capital, which were balanced by *surpluses* in respect of generally *shorter-term bank deposits and lending*. In the light of the potential sensitivity of such short-term flows to changes in interest rate differentials between countries and to expectations of exchange rate movements, the observed pattern of capital flows was not the best that might have been hoped for in terms of the stability of the capital account.

Since 1989 there have been some important changes to the patterns of capital flows, although the broad balance of net longer-term outwards investment and net shorter-term borrowing overseas has remained. Specifically, following a period of retrenchment in international financing by UK banks, which saw reductions in both overseas lending and overseas borrowing in 1991, the flows of funds in this regard have been more closely balanced, and in 1992 there was recorded a *modest net lending figure for the banks*. However, during this period there was a *substantial upsurge in net borrowing from overseas by the UK non-bank private sector*. Whilst the average maturity of this debt in practice is uncertain, it still requires regular servicing and ultimately the funds must be repaid, with obvious implications for future interest and capital outflows. A somewhat more positive development since 1990 has been the occurrence of a *net inflow of direct investment*, reflecting significantly reduced outflows of UK direct investment overseas.

The observed values for capital account items reflect the often rapidly changing fortunes of the UK economy relative to those of other major economies. Hence, it is difficult to specify concisely the factors which have had the greatest influence on the capital flows. Nevertheless, it is generally agreed that, at least until 1992, the *high level of interest rates* within the UK economy relative to those ruling in other major financial centres, was a very significant factor in explaining the large inflows of shorter-term bank deposits and lending. In addition, the relatively *high level of economic growth* in the UK during the second half of the 1980s almost certainly both attracted and was encouraged by substantial amounts of overseas direct investment in the UK. By contrast, the *recession* of the early 1990s is reflected in the markedly reduced flows of both inwards and outwards direct investment. Indeed, a critical factor in respect of longer-term investment is *general business confidence* in the *growth prospects* for the UK economy, and in its ability to overcome its *weak current account position* and *inflation rates* often above the average for major Western nations. In this respect, the nature of the *Government's economic policy* is of especial relevance, as is the extent to which international investors believe that the policy is likely to achieve its objectives.

A significant occurrence in respect of portfolio investment was the *stock market collapse* of October 1987. The short-term impact of this crisis was to cause a moderate *net repatriation of portfolio funds* by UK investors. This was followed by a damping down of interest in such investment, at least at an international level. However, more recently, investor confidence would appear to have risen, and international flows of portfolio funds have returned to their former high levels. The stock market collapse provides a very good example of the type of shock which can occur from time to time within the world economy, and which makes the interpretation of capital account statistics difficult, and the prediction of future trends almost impossible.

9.6.3 Official financing

For many years, the levels of official financing have *fluctuated dramatically*, as *government policies in respect of sterling's exchange rate* have dictated the need to accommodate volatile movements in the combined current account and non-official financing capital account. Thus, although the Government made little explicit effort to interfere with the value of sterling during the early years of the 1980s, its repayment of some outstanding official overseas debt, taken with the significant private sector capital outflows registered at that time, led to a substantial reduction in the UK's official reserve holdings. However, between the beginning of 1986 and the beginning of 1989, the position improved markedly, largely as a result of *Bank of England exchange market intervention* designed to limit the rise in the value of sterling against other major currencies. The value of the UK's reserves peaked in January 1989, at US$51.7b, having stood at only US$15.5b at the beginning of 1986. More recently, following the need for official intervention to halt the slide in the value of sterling, the reserves have once again fallen. By July 1993 their value was around US$43.3b.

Table 9.6   UK official reserves, 1980 to 1992 (end year figures), US$ billion

	Gold	SDRs	Reserve position in the IMF	Convertible currencies	Total
1980	7.0	0.6	1.3	18.6	27.5
1981	7.3	1.0	1.5	13.5	23.3
1982	4.6	1.2	1.6	9.6	17.0
1983	5.9	0.7	2.2	9.0	17.8
1984	5.5	0.5	2.1	7.6	15.7
1985	4.3	1.0	1.8	8.5	15.6
1986	4.9	1.4	1.8	13.8	21.9
1987	5.8	1.2	1.6	35.7	44.3
1988	6.5	1.3	1.7	42.2	51.7
1989	5.5	1.1	1.6	30.5	38.6
1990	5.2	1.1	1.5	30.6	38.5
1991	5.0	1.2	1.7	36.1	44.1
1992	4.8	0.5	2.0	34.3	41.6

Source: *Bank of England Quarterly Bulletin*, various issues.

Table 9.6 shows the recent trends in the UK's official reserves position. It may be observed that convertible currencies dominate the reserves, and that they have borne the brunt of official transactions in recent years. (The changes in the value of gold holdings largely reflect the annual revaluation of the stock at market prices.)

9.6.4 The balancing item

The only issue which needs to be recognised in respect of the balancing item within the UK balance of payments accounts is that in most years since 1986 it has registered *extremely high positive values*. For example for the years 1988, 1990 and 1992 its values were £6.8b, £5.9b and £9.5b respectively. The significance of these figures is that they must cast some doubt on the *accuracy* of at least some current account and capital account items discussed above. However, until the quality of balance of payments statistics can be improved, the user of those statistics can only note the extent of errors and omissions, and take due care not to put too much weight on the fine details of the accounts.

9.7 EXAMINATION PRACTICE
9.7.1 Questions

The following questions are taken from past examination papers, and are intended to give students an indication of the type of questions which they are likely to face within the topic area of the Balance of Payments. Students may care to map out answers to these questions before consulting the guidance notes in 9.7.2. Each question carries 25 marks.

(1)   The media often talk of a balance of payments deficit. How can this occur if 'the balance of payments always balances'?

(October 1991)

(2)   (a)   Identify the components of the current account of the balance of payments.   (8)
      (b)   Discuss the problems associated with a large and persistent:
            (i)   current account deficit;   (13)
            (ii)   current account surplus.   (4)

(October 1990)

(3)   (a)   Distinguish between a country's 'terms of trade' and its 'balance of trade'.   (12)
      (b)   To what extent can a government influence its terms of trade and its balance of trade?   (13)

(May 1990)

(4)   Explain, with regard to a country's balance of payments:

      (a)   how overall balance is achieved if the current account is in surplus;   (12)
      (b)   why and how a country might seek to reduce its current account surplus.   (13)

(May 1989)

(5)   ‡(a)   How can the authorities influence the exchange rate of their country's currency?   (10)
      †(b)   Discuss the impact of a depreciating exchange rate on a country's economy.   (15)

(May 1991)

9.7.2 Guidance notes

(1) (i) This question requires a detailed knowledge of the *structure of the balance of payments accounts*, and, as a starting point, it may be useful to outline briefly the major sub-parts of the accounts. Excessive detail on the individual components should be avoided.

(ii) The key to answering this question is to differentiate between the *accounting balance*, which must always occur (as the accounts are compiled on double entry bookkeeping principles), and the *economic equilibrium* position, which relates to the balance on the sub-parts of the accounts.

(iii) Care should be taken in respect of the *balancing item*, which is included in the accounts to register *errors and omissions*. It is not included in order to make the accounts balance.

(iv) It should be recognised that conventionally a balance of payments deficit refers to the situation where there is a *negative sum* for the balances on the *current account* and the *non-official financing elements of the capital account*, plus the *balancing item*. In other words, a balance of payments deficit signifies a positive value for official financing. However, increasingly, and especially in the media, the term balance of payments deficit is used to denote a negative balance on the *current account* or even on the *visible trade account*.

(v) There is no need for any discussion of actual experience with the balance of payments in the UK or in any other country.

Source of relevant material:

9.2.2 (as background) and 9.2.4 (especially paragraphs 1 to 4).

(2) (i) Part (a) merely requires a brief outline of the component parts of both the *visible trade* and *invisibles* sections of the current account. There is no need to discuss the current UK position.

(ii) Do not confuse capital account flows with current account interest, profits and dividends.

(iii) The answer to part (b) must *recognise the significance* of a *large* and *persistent* current account deficit/surplus. Discussion of the causes of or cures for a deficit/surplus is not required, and neither is consideration of actual experience in respect of the current account of the UK or any other country.

(iv) Part (b)(i) requires an examination of the *problems related to financing a large and persistent deficit*. It is not enough merely to list the means by which the deficit could be financed. In addition, it is necessary to comment upon the *broader problems* which may arise, including those flowing from associated *exchange rate movements* and *inflationary pressures,* and from the impact of growing overseas debt on *interest, profits and dividends flows.*

(v) The answer to part (b)(ii) should emphasise the possible *political pressures* which may be faced by a country with a current account surplus, and should note the possible impact on the country's *money supply* and *inflation rate.*

Source of relevant material:

Part (a)   9.2.2(a).
Part (b) (i)   9.4.1(a) (especially paragraphs 4 to 8).
(ii)   9.4.1(b).

(3)   (i)   Normally, the concepts of balance of trade and terms of trade are interpreted as relating solely to *visible trade* (i.e. tangible merchandise trade). However, as this is not specified explicitly in the question, it would be acceptable to include invisibles in the discussion relating to the balance of trade.

(ii)   The answer to part (a) requires *clear and concise definitions* of the two concepts, bringing out clearly their *differences.* There is no need to discuss the balance of trade or terms of trade in practice for the UK or any other country.

(iii)   Do not confuse the balance of trade with the balance of payments as a whole.

(iv)   Part (b) requires an outline of the ways in which the Government may seek to influence the *flows of international trade* (and hence the balance of trade) and the *relative prices of exports and imports* (and hence the terms of trade). It is important to recognise the factors which may *limit* the Government's ability to influence the two concepts. There is no need to examine actual experience in relation to policies and problems, although examples of real world events may be used for illustrative purposes.

Source of relevant material:

Part (a)   9.2.2(a) and 9.3 (paragraph 1).
Part (b)   9.3 (paragraph 4) and 9.5.2(a) (parts (i) to (iv) and (vi)).

(4)   (i)   Part (a) requires a knowledge of the *broad structure* of the balance of payments accounts, and an appreciation of how the

accounts must always balance in *accounting terms*. It is important to understand that the balancing item (which picks up unrecorded transactions) is merely one element in the explanation of the accounting balance.

(ii) There is no need for excessive detail on the component parts of the current account, although a reasonable level of *detail* is required on the *capital account*. Also, it is necessary to explain *how* the capital account items may lead to a balance in the accounts; it is not enough just to list the capital account items.

(iii) Discussion of the history of the balance of payments in the UK or elsewhere is not required, and neither are observations on why the current account may be in surplus.

(iv) Part (b) requires an explanation of *why* the authorities might seek to *reduce a current account surplus*, as well as an outline of *how* they may go about achieving this goal. Take care to differentiate between *using* a current account surplus, and *reducing* the surplus.

(v) Do not confuse flows of capital funds (which appear in the capital account) with interest, profits and dividends (which appear in the current account).

Source of relevant material:

Part (a)   9.2.2 (especially parts (b) and (c)) and 9.2.4 (especially paragraph 4).

Part (b)   9.4.1(b) and 9.5.2(b).

(5) (i) This question relates to *theoretical possibilities*. Therefore, the answer must go further than just limited discussion of actual experience in the UK or in any other country.

(ii) The answer to part (a) requires a summary of the *means which may be used by the authorities to influence their country's exchange rate*. The *full range* of means should be recognised, including foreign exchange market intervention, manipulation of interest rates, and economic policy initiatives designed to influence international currency flows via both the current account and the capital account.

(iii) Discussion of the authorities' motives for influencing the exchange rate is not required.

(iv) The answer to part (b) should focus upon the impact of the *depreciating currency* on a country's *balance of payments position*, but it is important that the *broader implications for the economy* as a whole are recognised. It is necessary to discuss the relevance of the *elasticity of demand* for traded goods and

THE BALANCE OF PAYMENTS

services for the current account, and to note the possible occurrence of the *J-curve effect*. The capital account may also be affected, via the influence of the depreciating exchange rate on *investor confidence*. The impact of higher import prices on *domestic inflation*, and the possible boost to *domestic growth* and *employment* should be mentioned. Care must be taken to differentiate between *short-term* and *long-term* effects.

Source of relevant material:

‡Part (a) Chapter 10, at 10.6 (paragraphs 1, 2, 4 and 5).
†Part (b) 9.5.2(a)(i), 9.5.2(b)(i), 9.5.3(a)(ii) and (iii), and (as background) Chapter 8, at 8.3.1 (especially paragraph 6).

9.8 FURTHER STUDY

The Balance of Payments topic includes a significant amount of relatively detailed descriptive material. Consequently, it is important that students attempt to identify the *major concepts* and *key trends*, and to isolate the *substantive factors* which are believed to have influenced the UK's recent balance of payments performance. Also, recognising that items within the accounts, and the associated determinant factors, may alter relatively quickly, it is important that students keep up-to-date with the evolving balance of payments position. However, care must be taken not to place too much weight on the most recent statistics, as certain components of the accounts are often subject to quite substantial revisions as time passes.

The definitive publication on the structure and recent history of the UK balance of payments accounts is the annual *UK Balance of Payments (Pink Book)* (Central Statistical Office); although the degree of detail presented therein goes well beyond the level of knowledge required for the examination. A somewhat more concise presentation of the key elements of the accounts is to be found in the *Monthly Digest of Statistics* (Central Statistical Office). A regular authoritative statement on the factors influencing the UK balance of payments position is to be found in the Economic Commentary section of the *Bank of England Quarterly Bulletin*. This publication is also useful for periodic analyses of broader trends in the balance of payments position throughout the Western world. In addition, relevant articles in quality newspapers are also useful, especially those which tend to appear around the time of publication of the monthly current account statistics. However, students should be warned that even in some of the more reliable newspapers there is an increasing tendency to use sloppy and inaccurate terminology in respect of the balance of payments. In particular, care should be taken not to confuse the terms of trade with the balance of trade, and the latter with the current account balance or the overall position on the balance of payments.

10 EXCHANGE RATES

10.1 INTRODUCTION

In the early 1970s the Bretton Woods (adjustable peg) system for determining currency exchange rates collapsed. Since that time the operations of the currency exchange markets have become ever more crucial to the successful development of Western economies. The increasing importance of international economic relations in recent years has merely served to emphasise the markets' significance.

The basic idea of the supply of and the demand for a currency determining its price (i.e. its exchange rate) in terms of another currency, is relatively straightforward. However, the form of *exchange rate regime* within which this market operation is allowed to occur continues to generate considerable controversy. At the extreme, a government may take the view that its country's currency exchange value should be determined by *unimpeded market forces* (in a clean floating regime), and hence may decide not to interfere in any way in exchange rate determination. Despite there being certain advantages with this approach, it may also lead to serious problems in respect of the stability of exchange rates. Consequently, it is normal for some form of *official intervention* in the currency exchange markets to take place. It is the nature and extent of this intervention which is at the centre of the ongoing exchange rate debate.

This chapter considers the general nature of exchange markets and rates, and examines the operation of the various forms of exchange rate regime. It also discusses recent experience in relation to sterling exchange rates, as well as the currently topical arguments in respect of the UK's membership of the European Monetary System. Throughout it is important to remember that exchange rate determination may have crucial implications not only for the domestic economy, but also for the economic well-being of overseas trading partners. Hence, decisions relating to currency exchange markets cannot be viewed in isolation from the Government's *overall economic objectives*; neither can they be divorced from *domestic and international political considerations*.

10.2 THE NATURE OF CURRENCY EXCHANGE MARKETS

10.2.1 Background

Within the domestic economy, trading and investment transactions are normally settled by the payment of cash or by the transfer of bank or building society deposits. Today, there is little difficulty in making such payments, when all parties to the transactions are quite willing to use a common (domestic) currency. However, for transactions at an international level, the situation is more complex, as payment is often required in a foreign currency. Thus, for example, if a UK exporter sells goods to a company in Germany, the importing company may prefer to pay in deutschmarks, but the exporter will in most cases require payment in sterling. Thus, it may be necessary for the importer to obtain sterling (or, more usually, a claim to sterling bank deposits) in order to be able to discharge the debt. Alternatively, if the exporter accepts a transfer of deutschmark-denominated bank deposits, these will have to be exchanged subsequently for sterling deposits. But irrespective of the approach taken, at some stage it is most probable that *currencies will have to be traded* (or, more precisely, bank deposits denominated in different currencies will have to be traded), on one of the world's foreign currency exchange markets. It is the activities of these markets, reflecting the *interactions and the supplies of and the demands for currencies*, which determine the structure of currency exchange rates.

Currency exchange markets have no physical form, in the sense of there being an actual market place where people meet to trade in currencies. Rather, the markets exist through a sophisticated *network of communications*, involving telephone, telex and computer links. The markets in different countries are closely associated, and the nature of operations means that market activities are *truly international in character*. However, whilst such markets operate in most Western countries, as might be expected the main markets are based in the world's major financial centres, with London, Tokyo and New York dominating operations. An official survey conducted in April 1992 showed that the daily turnover in the London market was at that time a massive US$300 billion, compared with US$192 billion for New York and US$128 billion in Tokyo. Without doubt, these markets are a vital element of the world's financial system.

10.2.2 Market participants

Market participants may act as *dealers* or *principals* or both. A dealer buys and sells currencies on behalf of clients; often selling to the client at a margin above the market determined exchange rate, and buying at a margin below the market rate. Clients may also be required to pay fees or commissions on the transactions undertaken. For dealers, the currency markets provide a pool through which net purchases or sales of currencies may be accommodated. The *commercial banks* are important market players in this respect, effectively dealing on behalf of customers ranging from individuals wishing to obtain currency for overseas travel purposes, through to multinational companies engaging in international investment activities.

Principals in the foreign currency markets buy and sell currencies on their own account, and effectively *speculate* on favourable exchange rate movements. Thus, for example, a principal may buy a currency in the hope of being able to sell it at a future date at a higher exchange rate. Once again commercial banks are important participants in this aspect of market activity. Indeed, in practice, it is very difficult to separate out banks' transactions which are directed towards meeting the identifiable needs of individuals and institutions involved in international trading and investment operations, from those which are purely speculative in nature.

Within the market framework, some banks and investment houses act as *market makers*; meaning that their dealers will *quote both buying and selling prices for currencies at all times*. By adjusting these prices, market makers may attempt to manage their currency holdings so as to avoid excessive exposure to depreciating currencies, or to ensure sufficient holdings of appreciating currencies. Market makers deal directly with other banks, investment houses and major corporations. There are also *specialist brokers* which act as *intermediaries* between banks and other currency dealers. These brokers maintain contact with institutions dealing in currencies throughout the world, and hence should be aware of the rates on offer for any particular type of transaction. Brokers do not deal on their own account, rather they earn *commission* for providing market participants with information on the best rates available.

It should also be recognised that periodically in many countries, the *official monetary authorities* are important participants in the currency exchange markets. As will be explained below, in 10.6, the authorities may not wish to allow market forces to proceed unabated. Hence, either with the objective of *reducing undesired short-term fluctuations in exchange rates*, or in order to pursue specific policy objectives in respect of *raising or lowering currency exchange rates*, the monetary authorities (in the case of the UK, the Bank of England) may enter the currency exchange markets and *buy or sell currencies*. Where foreign currencies have to be sold, the authorities will either draw down official reserves, borrow from official international monetary institutions or UK or overseas banks and investors, or perhaps come to currency swap arrangements with overseas monetary authorities.

10.2.3 Types of transactions

Transactions may be divided into *spot* transactions, which occur at current market prices, and where settlement must take place within two business days of the deal being contracted; and *forward* transactions, where a price is agreed for currency to be delivered at a future date, and settlement is more than two business days after dealing. The 1992 official survey showed that just under half of all transactions in the London market were spot transactions; whilst forward transactions for up to one month to delivery accounted for 37% of the total.

A company which expects to pay or receive a fixed amount of foreign currency at a known future date may utilise the forward market in order to obtain a guaranteed exchange rate for the domestic currency. This form of transaction (which was discussed in detail in Chapter 2, at 2.8.3(a)) allows the company to *hedge exchange rate risk*, and hence improve its financial planning. However, forward transactions may also be used for speculative purposes. For example, dealers may sell currency forward that they do not possess at the time that the deal is struck, in the hope that they can subsequently purchase the currency, either forward or spot, at a lower rate of exchange than that applied to the agreed sale, and thus make a profit on the transaction.

As was explained in Chapter 7 (at 7.9.2), *the premium to be paid or the discount which may be obtained on a forward transaction*, relative to the spot exchange rate, *reflects the differential between the rates of interest which may be earned on funds* (with the same maturity as the forward transaction) *denominated in the two currencies* to which the transaction relates. Thus, for example, the higher the interest rate on sterling funds relative to the interest rate on dollar funds, the greater will be the premium which has to be paid for a forward purchase of dollars for sterling. Conversely, if the sterling interest rate falls below the dollar rate, a discount will apply on the forward purchase, relative to the current spot rate. Interest rate differentials are themselves affected by expectations of future economic conditions in the countries whose currencies are involved, and hence by expectations of future exchange rate movements.

10.2.4 Exchange rate regimes

There are many different forms of exchange rate regime which may be operated. At one extreme, there is the *clean floating* regime, where there is no deliberate official intervention in the determination of exchange rates; free market demands for, and supplies of, currencies are left to determine the structure of exchange rates. At the other extreme, there is the *rigidly fixed* exchange rate regime, within which currencies are given immutable parities by official edict. Between the two extremes there are many variants of the basic forms, each involving different degrees of *official exchange market intervention*. However, most economists would tend to argue that in the *longer term* it is *market forces* which determine the broad pattern of exchange rates, irrespective of the formal regime in force. This is because if the authorities seek to hold exchange rates above or below their market equilibrium levels (that is, the levels reflecting the real economic variables underlying the supplies of and demands for currencies), balance of payments problems are likely to emerge, which will either cause the system to collapse or cause the authorities to back down from their original exchange rate position. (These ideas will be developed below in 10.3).

At different times during the twentieth century, the UK authorities have operated most of the major forms of exchange rate regime. During the early years of the century a rigidly fixed system of rates, known as the *gold standard* was operated. This system set a value for each currency in terms of a quantity of gold, and hence the relative value of each currency was fixed absolutely by an administrative decision. Following the collapse of the gold standard, the value of sterling was allowed to float relatively freely on the currency exchanges, until the outbreak of the Second World War. Since 1945, the UK authorities have pursued policies which have involved varying amounts of official intervention in the foreign exchange markets, depending upon their overall policy objectives. Between 1945 and 1972, intervention was undertaken rigorously within the context of the *Bretton Woods Agreement*, which was directed towards maintaining the values of the world's major currencies to within a narrow margin of fixed United States dollar parities. Between 1972 and October 1990 the regime was the somewhat more relaxed one of *managed floating*, whereby, in theory at least, the market is left to determine the longer-term trend for the exchange rate, but the authorities are expected to intervene in the exchange markets in order to iron out short-term fluctuations in rates.

It is generally agreed that there is *no perfect exchange rate system*, and that the advantages and disadvantages of each form have to be evaluated against the background of the particular economic and financial environment within which it has to operate. As the environment alters, questions are raised as to the appropriateness or efficiency of the existing form of exchange rate regime. For example, throughout much of the 1980s there was an ongoing debate in relation to the UK's possible full membership of the European Monetary System (EMS). This eventually came about in October 1990, by which time the issue had become entwined with the broader arguments relating to Economic and Monetary Union within the EC. (The EMS debate is considered in detail in 10.4.5 below.) The enforced withdrawal of sterling from the ERM, in September 1992, saw the UK return to the managed floating regime.

10.2.5 Measuring the value of a currency

In a fixed exchange rate regime it is logical to express the international exchange value of a currency in terms of the base of the regime. Thus, under the gold standard each currency had a fixed value in terms of a weight of gold; whilst under the Bretton Woods system each currency was valued relative to the United States dollar. Through the common base, it is relatively easy to interpret the meaning of an exchange rate value. However, under regimes which involve at least some degree of floating rates, it may be misleading to judge the value of a currency merely by reference to its exchange rate for just one other currency. For example, sterling may fall in value relative to the United States dollar, which, of course, will have important implications for the UK's international trading position, given the significance of the dollar for international payments. But it must be remembered that the UK also undertakes large volumes of transactions denominated in other currencies. Indeed, today, over a half of all UK visible trade relates to other EC nations, and a high proportion of these transactions are denominated in European currencies. Therefore, if the fall in the value of sterling relative to the United States dollar occurs at the same time as the value of sterling rises relative to the deutschemark, the French franc and the lira, it is not immediately obvious what the implications are for the UK's trading position. In this instance, the practice of monitoring only the sterling-dollar exchange rate may be quite misleading.

Today, most major currencies are valued in terms of *trade-weighted indices*. For the UK, the *sterling exchange rate index* is calculated by taking a weighted average of the sterling exchange rate against 16 other major currencies. Since the basis for the index was up-dated in January 1989, the weights have been calculated according to the relative importance of other countries as competitors to the UK in both domestic and overseas markets. The current base date for the index is 1985 (= 100), and movements in its value are thought to give a reasonably good indication of changes in the UK's *overall international competitiveness*, for any given set of domestic prices. Nevertheless, *caution* must still be exercised in the interpretation of movements in exchange rate indices, for it is possible that simultaneous movements in individual exchange rates may have a biased effect on the overall trade position. For example, the value of sterling may fall relative to the United States dollar (thus making dollar-priced imports of basic commodities more expensive for UK industry and consumers), but at the same time its value may rise relative to major European currencies (thus making UK exports of manufactured goods less competitive in their major overseas markets). Consequently, the sterling exchange rate index may hardly alter, but it is most likely that the net value of UK trade flows will be adversely affected (depending, of course, upon the relevant elasticities of demand for traded goods).

10.3 THE DETERMINATION OF EXCHANGE RATES

10.3.1 Long-term trends in exchange rates

In the longer term it is the *relative economic performances* of different countries which determine the broad structure of exchange rates. The major factors in this context, which are generally referred to as the *'economic fundamentals'*, may be considered under the headings of relative inflation rates, relative interest rates, and the position of the balance of payments.

(a) *Relative inflation rates*

A well-known theory relating to the impact of differing inflation rates between countries on the structure of exchange rates is the *purchasing power parity (PPP) theory*. This theory states that the equilibrium exchange rate between any two currencies is that rate which equalises the domestic purchasing powers of those currencies. For example, if a particular bundle of goods has a price of £20 in the UK, and an identical bundle has a price of $40 in the USA, then according to the PPP theory, the equilibrium exchange rate should be £1 = $2. If this rate does not hold, it is argued that it will be worthwhile to import goods from the country with the relatively low prices (in international terms) into the country with the relatively high prices. The country with the relatively low prices would therefore experience a trade surplus, and hence upwards pressure would be exerted on the exchange rate of that country's currency (as there would, in effect, be an excess demand for the currency on the exchange markets). Conversely, the country with relatively high prices would find its trade balance moving into deficit, and hence its currency's value depreciating (as the supply on the exchange markets exceeded the demand from overseas residents). In theory, this exchange rate adjustment should continue until each currency has the same purchasing power within both countries (i.e. until purchasing power parity is achieved).

A fundamental weakness of the PPP theory is that it ignores the existence of *international capital flows*, which, at any given time, may influence the exchange rate between pairs of currencies. Thus, whilst the theory might give some indication of what the exchange rate should be in the *long-run equilibrium position* (when net capital flows are zero, where there is no government interference in the currency exchange markets, and when the

411

current account of the balance of payments is in balance), its power to explain the exchange rate in the short to medium term is very limited. In addition, the PPP theory is rather too simplistic for direct application to the real world. In particular, it ignores *transport and other trading costs*, which may drive a wedge between domestic prices and foreign prices, and thus although price differences may exist between countries, they may not be large enough to make it economically viable to shift goods between those countries.

The main relevance of the PPP theory is when trading partners' *inflation rates differ*. In this case, the theory suggests that the equilibrium exchange rate will be approached only if the value of the currency of the country with the higher rate of inflation falls relative to the currency of the country with the lower rate of inflation. If the exchange rate does not alter (or, at least, does not alter quickly enough), the relative prices of the high inflation country's exports will rise, and the relative prices of its imports will fall. The opposite effect will be felt in the low inflation country. Thus, over time, it is likely that balance of payments problems will emerge, which may necessitate explicit official policy actions (as outlined in Chapter 9, at 9.5).

(b) *Relative interest rates*

The level of real domestic interest rates (i.e. nominal rates adjusted for the effects of expected domestic inflation) relative to those ruling in overseas countries, is usually thought to be an important determinant of *international capital flows*, especially in relation to *short-term funds*. A higher level of real domestic interest rates, other things being equal, may not only attract directly a greater inflow of capital funds from overseas, but also it may build up investors' confidence in the Government's policies towards domestic inflation, which has clear implications for the real return on nominally-denominated assets in the longer-term. To the extent that net capital inflows are raised, this will create an increased demand for the domestic currency, and its exchange rate is likely to be pushed above the level which would have been found had interest rates within the domestic economy been relatively lower. In this respect, the Government's monetary policy position may be an extremely important factor in the determination of the level of exchange rates, as well as in influencing the position of the capital account of the balance of payments.

In the light of the discussion in Chapter 9, relating to the potential problems which may be generated for a country as a result of excessive net inflows of capital, there must be some doubt as to the extent to which the value of the currency may be maintained at a relatively high level on the basis of such capital flows alone. Nevertheless, if the authorities are willing to accept the *domestic implications* of holding interest rates at levels which are persistently high by international standards, it may be possible for the exchange rate to be influenced significantly into the longer term.

(c) *The position of the balance of payments*

The balance of payments accounts reflect the actual flow of currencies related to international trade and capital movements, and hence the *longer-term trends* within these accounts are of great importance to the patterns of exchange rates established. The *current account* is usually seen as being of especial relevance. The ability to finance current overseas expenditures with current overseas earnings is often taken as a sign of economic strength, and, other things being equal, a persistent current account *surplus* will tend to put *upwards pressure* on the exchange rate of the domestic currency. Current account *deficits* are likely to have the *opposite effect*. However, as mentioned above, *capital account flows* may also be of importance, and the effects of persistent current account deficits or surpluses on the exchange rate may, at least to some extent, be *counteracted* by capital flows. Consequently, any factor which has a sustained impact on balance of payments items is likely to be of relevance in respect of long-term trends in exchange rates. Thus, in addition to the key economic variables of inflation rates and interest rates, which have already been dealt with above, the following factors should also be recognised as being of importance to the determination of exchange rates:

(i) *Changes in consumers' tastes, real income levels and productive capacities*, both within the domestic economy and overseas, may have an important impact on international trading patterns and investment flows.

(ii) *Expectations* concerning future economic conditions within specific economies are likely to be critical to the pattern of international investment flows. These expectations may be affected by fundamental changes in government policies or by events such as the discovery of major reserves of natural commodities.

(iii) Actual or expected changes in the *political and social environment* within a country may have implications for its future economic and trading position, and hence for foreign currency flows. Political unrest can badly undermine business confidence.

(iv) Even without direct intervention on the foreign currency exchange markets, a government can have a significant influence on the exchange rate, not only through the general stance of its *economic*

413

policies (which is likely to affect the progress of the economy and investor confidence), but also via the specific effects of the policies on the demand for imports, supply of export goods, general inflation rate, and so on. Import controls, investment incentives, and government expenditure overseas might also be included here, as might policies designed to improve the quality and marketing of exports.

10.3.2 Short-term movements in exchange rates

Irrespective of the longer-term pattern of exchange rates, there may be shorter-term movements which accelerate or run against the long-term trends. These may be caused by *short-term changes* in the variables listed in the previous section. For example, for domestic political reasons, the authorities may reduce interest rates, which may have an immediate impact on short-term international capital flows. The consequent weakening of the capital account, perhaps supported by an increased demand for imports stimulated by cheaper consumer credit, can only serve to undermine the domestic currency's exchange rate. Similarly, the announcement of unexpectedly poor balance of payments results may shake the confidence of international investors, and hence may put downwards pressure on the exchange rate.

Of particular importance for short-term exchange rate movements is likely to be *official currency market intervention* by the monetary authorities, both within the domestic economy and overseas. Thus, large scale purchases or sales of currencies by the country's central bank may be sufficient to move the exchange rate, especially when such action is unanticipated by the market. Indeed, any changes in *government economic policies*, particularly those which are of direct relevance to international trade and investment matters, and those which have not been foreseen by participants in the currency markets, are likely to alter exchange rates. For example, the announcement of a change in the official view on the role of monetary policy may have an immediate effect on investor confidence, and hence on exchange rates. If policy changes are subsequently introduced, and it is believed that these are to be maintained into the longer term, the impact on the currency markets may be more than just transitory.

In addition, significant events may occur within a country the effects of which are almost always temporary, but which nevertheless may have a marked impact on the exchange rate. For example, a strike within the oil producing sector in a country such as the UK is bound to lead to increased imports of fuels, and is likely to raise fears about knock-on effects into other sectors of the economy. The domestic currency may weaken until the true impact of the strike becomes clear, or until the strike is resolved. General elections, fears concerning the health of leading politicians, major industrial accidents, and even the weather may have similar effects on exchange rates.

10.3.3 Clean floating exchange rates

If exchange rates are left purely to *market determination*, with *no direct or deliberate intervention from the monetary authorities*, then there is said to be a clean floating exchange rate regime in force. The pattern of exchange rates established will be determined by the *interaction of the supplies of and the demands for currencies on the open market*. Taking the UK as an example, credit items on the balance of payments represent a supply of foreign currencies (in effect a demand for sterling) from foreign residents wishing to purchase UK exports or to invest or make other payments in the UK. Conversely, debit items represent a demand for foreign currencies (and hence a supply of sterling) from UK residents wishing to purchase imports or to invest or make other payments overseas. It is the interaction of the supply of and the demand for sterling, and the supplies of and demands for foreign currencies, which will determine sterling's exchange rate against those other currencies. Therefore, any factor which increases (or decreases) the supply of sterling relative to demand is likely to push the exchange value of sterling downwards (or upwards) in terms of other currencies. The relevant factors, the effects of which are reflected in the country's balance of payments accounts, are those listed above in 10.3.1 and 10.3.2, with the exception, of course, of official intervention on the currency markets.

A major advantage of a clean floating exchange rate system is that it provides an *automatic mechanism* for dealing with balance of payments problems, at least in theory. Thus, for example, if a deficit appears on the current account, and this is not balanced by sufficient 'natural' inflows of foreign currency for investment purposes, the private sector will effectively have to borrow foreign currency in order to cover current expenditures. As foreigners will have no wish to hold claims denominated in an inherently weak currency without adequate compensation, this will tend to depress the exchange value of the domestic currency (as supply exceeds demand) and to push upwards the level of domestic interest rates. Whether or not these adjustments will actually lead to a reduction in the current account deficit, and hence a reduced pressure on the exchange rate, will depend upon the *price elasticities of demand for traded goods*. As was explained in Chapter 9 (9.5.2), so long as the elasticities are high enough, the current balance should improve. In theory, the exchange rate will continue to adjust until the demands for and supplies of currencies are brought into equilibrium. This means that the current account and capital account flows must be at their desired levels, given the ruling structure of prices and interest rates, and that these flows in aggregate generate a balance between the demands for and supplies of currencies.

Other advantages which may be identified for the clean floating exchange rate regime are that:

(a) *official international currency reserves* are not required, as exchange market intervention is not undertaken;

(b) as *market forces determine the exchange rate*, the Government is relieved of this task, which is inherently difficult, both economically and politically (given the implications for international competitiveness);

(c) the Government may direct its *economic policy* instruments towards dealing with domestic problems, such as unemployment, inflation and slow economic growth, without being constrained by the need to stabilise currency exchange rates.

Unfortunately, there are also several serious *disadvantages* associated with the clean floating exchange rate regime, which tend to undermine its attractiveness in practice:

(a) As there is no official intervention in the currency markets, even to stabilise short-term fluctuations in exchange rates, it is possible that the markets may become *unstable* and that business confidence on an international level may be undermined. Indeed, as exchange rates are likely to be very sensitive to changes in market conditions, pure currency speculation may be a cause of market instability.

(b) If the *price elasticities of demand* for internationally traded goods are low, then there is the possibility of persistent pressure on exchange rates in the face of a balance of payments problem. Thus, a depreciation of the domestic currency may merely serve to worsen a trade deficit; whilst a surplus may be exacerbated by an appreciating currency.

(c) A continually depreciating exchange rate may generate *inflationary pressures* within the domestic economy, as not only may higher prices for imported raw materials push up domestic production costs, but also higher prices for imported consumer goods may encourage demands for higher wages. Clearly, to the extent that such domestic inflation occurs, the competitive advantage gained in overseas markets by the depreciating exchange rate is eroded.

10.3.4 Managed floating exchange rates

As suggested above, there are *serious practical problems* involved with the operation of a clean floating exchange rate regime, particularly in relation to the economic instability and financial uncertainty which might be generated. However, allowing exchange rates to move broadly in line with market forces has the fundamental attraction of bringing about automatically a *gradual adjustment of exchange rates,* in order to reflect the *underlying real economic factors* within the relevant economies. Therefore, the logical compromise would appear to be a system within which *market forces* determine the *longer-term trend* in exchange rates, but which also allows the authorities to take *discretionary action* to iron out *short-term fluctuations* in exchange rates. This type of system is referred to as a 'managed floating exchange rate regime'.

Within the managed floating regime, *the authorities may buy and sell currencies* on the foreign exchange markets, drawing on official reserves and engaging in official borrowing from overseas as appropriate. For example, if there is upwards pressure on the domestic currency's exchange rate, and the authorities believe that this is a significant deviation from the longer-term trend for the currency, they will sell domestic currency, in an attempt to counter the original market pressure, and hence hold down its value. The authorities may also reduce *short-term domestic interest rates* in an effort to depress net inflows of short-term capital funds, and hence reduce the demand for the domestic currency relative to its supply. The degree of official intervention is very much a *matter of judgment,* and the authorities may have an *informal target* for the maximum exchange rate movement thought to be desirable within any given period of time. The obvious problem is how far an official action may be seen as a smoothing operation, and how far a deliberate attempt to manipulate exchange rates for reasons of economic self-interest; for it must never be forgotten that the structure of exchange rates may have important implications for domestic inflation rates, unemployment, and living standards in general.

It must be emphasised that irrespective of the degree of official intervention to smooth exchange rate fluctuations, there is no guarantee that balance of payments problems will automatically be solved within the floating exchange rate system. Indeed, experience has shown that *significant disequilibrium positions may persist*; although this is partly to be expected, for so long as there is net official financing over the accounting period, by definition, the balance of payments cannot be in equilibrium. Thus, the important issue is whether or not the balance of payments is brought closer to equilibrium than it otherwise would have been in the absence of floating. Obviously, there is no way that this question can ever be answered convincingly. It is impossible to know what would have

417

happened had the Western world remained on a fixed exchange rate system after 1972. However, many commentators have suggested that the tremendous shocks which have been experienced by the world's major economies since 1972 would have caused much more serious dislocation to the international financial system had floating not been in force.

10.3.5 Fixed exchange rates

Today, a fixed exchange rate system may be thought of as being one within which the authorities seek to hold the value of their country's currency to within a *narrow margin* of a *predetermined value* in terms of some other currency, by means of *exchange market intervention*. As there is normally some facility for the *adjustment of currency parities*, in response to changes in economic circumstances within the countries whose currencies are part of the regime, it is, in fact, not too far removed from the managed floating system as described above. The major difference is that within the fixed rate system there is an *overriding commitment to the stability of exchange rates within agreed narrowly defined margins*. Moreover, it is anticipated that adjustments in the parity bands will only occur *infrequently* and when it is absolutely necessary in order to accommodate *fundamental shifts* in the relative economic performances of the countries involved.

The Bretton Woods system, which operated between 1945 and 1972, provides a good example of a fixed rate regime. Within this system each of the world's major currencies was to be pegged to within a $\pm 1\%$ margin of a *fixed United States dollar par value*. Central banks were required to intervene in the currency markets in order to ensure that this objective was achieved on a day-to-day basis. However, the devaluation or revaluation of a currency relative to its dollar par value was allowed, but only when a country experienced serious balance of payments problems. Indeed, a major function of the International Monetary Fund, which was established to oversee the operation of the Bretton Woods system, was to provide financial support to countries experiencing balance of payments difficulties, in the hope that this would create a breathing space for the problems to be rectified without exchange rate adjustments being required. A somewhat more sophisticated example of the fixed exchange rate system is that which is currently operated within the EC under the name of the *European Monetary System*. (This system is examined in detail in 10.4 below.)

Important *advantages* may accrue to a country through the achievement of stable exchange rates. In particular, they help to underpin *business confidence* in international transactions by reducing an element of uncertainty within financial calculations, and this is of great importance for both current trading activities and short-term and long-term capital investment decisions. However, it is important to recognise that stable exchange rates do not necessarily mean stable prices for internationally-traded goods and services or for capital items. Clearly, movements in domestic prices are vital to the determination of prices in overseas markets. It is for this reason that periodic *devaluation* of a currency may be necessary, as a means of maintaining a country's *international competitiveness* in the face of *domestic inflation rates above the average rates of major trading partners.* Indeed, the excessive stabilisation of exchange rates by the authorities would be damaging to a country's competitive position in such circumstances.

Nevertheless, in most circumstances the avoidance of excessive fluctuations in exchange rates is seen as being a good thing for business planning decisions, and hence should *facilitate trade* and *encourage economic growth.* *Exporters* benefit from being able to set prices for their goods in foreign currency terms, in the knowledge that when the goods are sold the revenues in domestic currency terms will be sufficient to generate the desired profit on the transaction. Clearly, if rates are unstable, the exporter risks having the domestic currency appreciate on the currency exchanges after the price of the exports has been set, and thus may receive a reduced revenue in domestic currency terms. Similar problems would be faced by the *importer* of goods, except that in this case, a depreciation of the domestic currency could cause unexpected increases in the domestic prices of the imports, which would threaten the profitability of such transactions. Thus, where exchange rates are unstable there is an inherent pressure for both exporters and importers to operate on wide profit margins in order to cover exchange rate risks or to cover hedging costs, and hence there is a greater possibility that business may be lost.

It should also be recognised that if a country's currency exchange rate is *stabilised relative to the currencies of low inflation countries,* this will help in the *control of domestic inflation.* Quite simply, pressure will be placed on domestic producers to hold down their production costs or face being priced out of world markets. Inflation rates in the domestic economy which are above the average rates of major trading partners will necessarily translate into increasingly uncompetitive export prices. Similarly, import prices will be held down relative to what they otherwise would have been had the domestic currency's exchange rate been allowed to depreciate. In addition, the explicit commitment to stabilise exchange rates will impose a discipline on government policy actions, and in particular will emphasise the need for the control of inflation within the domestic economy. However, it must be emphasised that the stabilising of a currency's value relative to the currencies of high inflation countries is likely to have adverse effects, as there will be a tendency to import inflationary pressures.

Despite the clear benefits which may be generated by a system of fixed exchange rates, experience has shown that there are also significant *disadvantages* associated with the system, which eventually may come to undermine its usefulness. These disadvantages may be summarised as follows:

(a) The authorities must hold *sufficient official reserves* to make their exchange rate objectives appear credible to the currency markets. Otherwise, the emergence of balance of payments problems may lead to *speculative pressures* against the currency, which may eventually precipitate the feared devaluation of the currency. Speculation may also be a problem in respect of possible currency revaluations. The authorities may be forced to sell large amounts of domestic currency in order to hold down its exchange value, and this may have undesired implications for domestic monetary growth, and hence longer-term trends in inflation.

(b) Decisions must be made in respect of *how far a government should go in defending its exchange rate* against market pressures. The critical issue is obviously in relation to the occurrence of deficits on the balance of payments. Official reserves are finite, and there are limits to the amounts of foreign currency which may be borrowed from overseas institutions. Thus, if the deficits persist, the government may be forced to introduce severe domestic deflationary policies in order to damp down the demand for imports. Clearly, other economic policy objectives may have to be sacrificed in order to allow sufficient policy instruments to be brought to bear upon the balance of payments problem. In the shorter term domestic interest rates may also have to be raised as a means of attracting capital inflows, despite the effects which this may have on domestic consumption and investment.

(c) Even if the authorities conclude that there is a fundamental disequilibrium on the balance of payments, and hence that the defence of an existing fixed exchange rate would be futile, they still face the difficult choices of *when* and *by how much* the exchange rate should be altered. These choices are not only of economic importance, but also may have political overtones, as an explicit devaluation of the currency may be taken as a sign of weakness or even failure of the pre-existing economic policy. Overseas governments may also resent the sudden shift in competitiveness towards the devaluing country, and may *retaliate* by devaluing their own currencies should the original adjustment be perceived to have been needlessly excessive.

(d) The sudden and possibly substantial movements in exchange rates, which may be required within a fixed rate system, may not only cause *periodic destabilisation* in world financial markets, but also are more likely to lead to *J-curve effects* than are the gradual adjustments associated with floating rate systems. The J-curve effect occurs because the quantities of goods and services traded take time to adjust to the new structure of relative prices brought about by the alteration of exchange rates. Thus, in the short-term, following a devaluation of the domestic currency, the foreign currency price of exports will be lower, but demand may not be very much greater, and hence earnings from sales of exports are likely to fall. Conversely, imported goods and services will be more expensive in domestic currency terms, and demand may fall only slowly, thus raising expenditure on imports. Therefore, the current account deficit, which necessitated the devaluation, may become larger before it begins to diminish. The existence of the J-curve effect means that the authorities may have to arrange special overseas borrowing facilities, or at least be prepared to see official reserves fall even further in the short term.

(e)   Without the *convergence of economic performances* of international trading partners, especially in relation to inflation rates, it may be impossible to maintain fixed exchange rates for anything other than relatively short periods of time. Therefore, and in the light of the problems outlined above, the question is raised as to whether it is worthwhile even to attempt to fix exchange rates; although, if convergence of economic performances can be achieved, the gains from stable exchange rates are not to be dismissed lightly.

10.4   MONETARY ARRANGEMENTS WITHIN THE EC

10.4.1   Background

Since the time that the EC came into existence in 1957, there has been much debate on the view that the EC should move towards full *Economic and Monetary Union* (EMU). At the extreme, EMU may imply the introduction of a single EC currency, with monetary controls being implemented by a European central bank, and with a much greater power over economic policy being vested with EC institutions. However, as might be expected, substantial reservations have been expressed about such objectives, and in particular a number of EC governments have resisted strongly any proposals which would undermine their independent sovereign powers in respect of economic policy.

In 1970, *The Werner Report* put forward the first comprehensive plan for a movement towards EMU. This plan was accepted in principle, but due to adverse economic conditions during the first half of the 1970s, and with a general lack of practical support from several EC member states, the plan had only a limited impact. Its effect was felt mainly in terms of the establishment of a fixed exchange rate regime (referred to at one stage as the 'snake in the tunnel' arrangement), but even this structure had largely collapsed by 1976. Nevertheless, broad support remained for attempts to stabilise the exchange rates of EC currencies, and some member states were still very much in favour of an eventual movement towards EMU. An important step forward was taken at the *Bremen Summit* of EC Heads of Government in July 1978, when proposals for the formulation of the *European Monetary System* (EMS) were adopted.

10.4.2 The components of the EMS

The EMS may be divided into three broad aspects: the Exchange Rate Mechanism; the exchange rate stabilisation fund; and the Very Short-Term Financing Facility.

(a) *The Exchange Rate Mechanism (ERM)*

The objective of the ERM is to limit the fluctuation of exchange rates between EC currencies. The mechanism operates on the basis of two criteria:

(i) *A 'parity grid' arrangement* sets upper and lower *'intervention rates'* for each pair of currencies. Initially, the grid allowed a maximum movement of $\pm 2\frac{1}{4}\%$ of the fixed par values for most pairs of currencies (with a small number of currencies being allowed $\pm 6\%$). However, following extreme turbulence on the currency exchange markets, in July 1993, the band was widened to $\pm 15\%$ for most currencies (officially as a temporary expedient). Once any two currencies reach their respective intervention limits, the central banks of the countries involved are expected to *intervene in the foreign currency markets*, buying the weaker of the currencies and selling the stronger. These purchases and sales of currency, which may be supported by currency swaps between the central banks if required, continue until the currency values are pushed away from their intervention limits. In practice, central banks are likely to take action before their currencies reach the parity grid limits. This action may be in the form of *intra-marginal intervention* (that is, buying and selling currencies before formal intervention obligations are triggered) or adjustment of monetary controls in order to alter *short-term domestic interest rates*.

(ii) *The European Currency Unit (ECU) indicator* is intended to provide an *early warning* of when a country is likely to get into difficulties in relation to its currency's exchange rates, relative to all other EC currencies taken as a group. Each currency is initially given a *central exchange rate* expressed in ECUs (the ECU being a weighted 'basket' of all EC currencies – see 10.4.3 below). If the actual ECU rate for a currency diverges from its central rate by more than *75% of its divergence limit* (which is calculated to be well within the parity grid limits), it is presumed that the relevant government will take some form of *remedial action*. For a country with a weak currency, this may involve the raising of domestic interest rates or perhaps a tightening of fiscal policy. For a strong currency country, some form of expansionary policy might be expected. It is hoped that by taking action in good time to correct a broad drift in the currency's value, full-scale central bank intervention at the parity grid limits may be avoided.

Within the ERM there is also a facility for parity grid values and ECU central rates to be *realigned*, if the *fundamental economic relationships* underlying the exchange rates alter. Thus, if a particular currency shows signs of persistent weakness, which requires excessive amounts of exchange market intervention, and which does not appear to respond to appropriate remedial action, then the currency may be devalued against some or all of the other currencies within the ERM. Conversely, a persistently strong currency may be revalued within the mechanism. But as EMS rules are intended to impose a certain amount of financial discipline on member states, it has been argued that realignments should only take place as the very last resort.

Whilst all EC states are members of the EMS, at August 1993 Greece had still not joined the ERM, and the memberships of the UK and Italy were still suspended following the September 1992 EC currency crisis.

(b)　*The exchange rate stabilisation fund*

This fund provides a *Short-term Monetary Support* arrangement and a *Medium-term Financial Support* facility for EMS members facing international payments problems. Members pool 20% of their gold and dollar reserves with the *European Monetary Co-operation Fund* (EMCF) in return for ECUs. These 'official' ECUs, created as a bookkeeping exercise by the EMCF, may be used for transactions between members' central banks (and certain other monetary institutions), for example, for settling debt incurred as a result of ERM operations. The swaps of reserves for ECUs are renewed every three months, and, in fact, the reserves do not actually change hands, and hence the fund depends upon commitments to provide the reserves should they be called upon.

423

As at August 1993, all EMS members participate in the EMCF swap arrangement, although members which are not a party to the ERM are not formally required to do so.

(c) *The Very Short-Term Financing Facility*

This facility relates to arrangements whereby participants in the ERM open to each other *very short-term credit facilities* in their own currencies. The credit is provided for purposes of exchange market intervention, and is made available automatically and in unlimited amounts when currencies reach their official intervention limits. Repayment of funds is normally required within three months, but may be temporarily deferred if the borrower's international payments position deems this to be appropriate. This facility may also be used in support of intra-marginal intervention, although funds are not available automatically or in unlimited amounts. All transactions under the facility are channelled through the ECMF, and repayments may be made partly, and in some cases wholly, using official ECU.

10.4.3 The European Currency Unit

The ECU is a *'basket'* of EC currencies, and may be regarded as a form of *international money*, performing all the functions which are normally associated with money assets. Thus, for example, the ECU is used as a means of payment between EC central banks; it is used as the unit of account for both the intervention and credit elements of the EMS; and it may be used for its medium of exchange, store of value, unit of account and standard of deferred payment properties in private sector financial transactions.

The value of the ECU is calculated as a *weighted average of all EC members' currencies.* The weights are set to reflect each member's relative economic size in terms of gross national product, the importance of its trade within the EC, and the access which it has to short-term financing from the EMCF. In the past, the weights were reviewed every five years, but following the ratification of the EC Treaty amendments agreed at Maastricht in December 1991, these revisions will cease, and the basket will be frozen at its current composition, which was determined in June 1989.

It should be recognised that since its introduction, in March 1979, the ECU has developed along two distinct routes. The *official ECU*, as explained above, is a key element in the operation of the EMS. This is quite separate from the *private ECU* which is created by private institutions out of the ECU's component currencies, and may be bought and sold on the foreign exchange market. Both individuals and companies may hold ECU assets (such as bank deposits and marketable securities) and incur ECU liabilities (such as bank loans and securitised debts). The major advantage in using the ECU is that its value, in terms of international purchasing power, is likely to be more stable than the corresponding values of the individual component currencies.

10.4.4 The objectives of the EMS

In the medium term, the EMS is intended to create a *zone of exchange rate stability* within the EC. In other words, it is desired that exchange rate fluctuations between the currencies of EC members should be kept to a minimum, in the interests of providing a sound base for trade and payments between members. In the longer term, the successful operation of the EMS is seen as an important means of promoting the movement towards *full EMU*.

In order to achieve the objectives of the EMS it is necessary that the *economic performances* of EC member states should be *broadly similar*. If this does not occur, then it is likely that the countries with relatively strong economies would tend to have persistent surpluses on their trade with the countries whose economies are relatively weak. The resulting international payments imbalances would then tend to destabilise exchange rates, as market adjustments brought the supplies of and the demands for the various EC currencies into equilibrium. In consequence, the successful operation of the EMS is likely to require a high level of *economic policy co-ordination* between EC governments, with a view to bringing about a convergence in individual members' economic performances. In particular, policies will have to be aimed at:

- bringing *inflation rates* in member states to similar low levels;
- reducing differentials between the levels of *interest rates* ruling in comparable financial markets in the respective countries;
- limiting the extent of *balance of payments* imbalances.

If these economic conditions are not met, then it is unlikely that exchange rate stability will be maintained in the medium term. Whilst central bank intervention on the foreign currency exchange markets may be able to limit exchange rate fluctuations in the shorter term, such intervention is unlikely to be successful over longer periods, in the face of persistent market pressures for exchange rate adjustments.

10.4.5 The UK and the EMS

The UK was a full member of the EMS between October 1990 and September 1992, with sterling being placed in the ± 6% fluctuation band

425

of the ERM. As at August 1993 the UK Government appeared to be in no hurry to return sterling to the ERM, despite the relative freedom given by the (temporary) ±15% fluctuation band. However, if the system was to revert to relatively narrow bands of fluctuation, the arguments in favour of the UK's full participation are likely to be heard once again. These may be summarised as follows:

(a) As the EC now accounts for over a half of all the UK's overseas trade, a stable relationship between sterling and other EC currencies would help both *exporters and importers* in their business planning and pricing decisions. For both exporters and importers there should be less pressure to operate on wide profit margins (in order to cover exchange rate risks or hedging costs), and hence there should be a greater chance of gaining business.

(b) By stabilising the value of sterling relative to a strong currency, such as the deutschmark, the *control of domestic inflation* is likely to be assisted. Pressure would be placed on domestic producers to hold down their production costs, or face being priced out of their markets. Inflation rates in the domestic economy above the average rates of EC trading partners would necessarily translate into increasingly uncompetitive export prices; and import prices would be held down relative to what they otherwise would have been had sterling been allowed to depreciate. Thus, membership of the ERM would effectively provide an *exchange rate target for UK monetary policy*. However, it must be emphasised that these anti-inflation benefits would only accrue so long as other members of the ERM maintained low rates of inflation.

(c) The influence of the UK in *EC decision-making* at a time of great economic and political change in Europe can only be enhanced by the UK's full commitment to the EMS. Without this, it is argued, the UK will become *isolated politically*, and may miss out on important opportunities, such as having a future EC central bank based in the UK.

Full membership of the EMS is not, of course, without its *problems*. Indeed until October 1990 the UK Government argued strongly that the difficulties which might be created by ERM membership were likely to outweigh the recognised benefits, as listed above. The major difficulties, which are still pertinent to any decision to return sterling to the ERM, may be summarised as follows:

(a) The need to co-ordinate economic policies within the EC, if the EMS is to operate successfully, implies that *domestic policies* within individual EC countries may have to be *subordinated* to this purpose. This suggested *loss of sovereignty* over economic policy decisions has often been used as an argument, by the UK Government, for keeping sterling out of the ERM. It is feared that the effective loss of economic independence would deny the authorities the power to respond to events which might be unique to the domestic economy, or which might be regarded as being less urgent by other EC governments.

(b) When sterling was placed within the ERM, the question arose as to the *appropriateness of the exchange rate* on entry. There would appear to be little agreement on this issue, and yet it is a critical factor in determining not only the UK's competitive position but also the chances of stability being maintained with the ERM. It would make little sense to re-enter the mechanism at an unrealistic rate which required an early realignment of parities.

(c) If the UK failed to achieve an economic performance on a par with the other major EC states, the relatively fixed exchange rate structure could prove to be *damaging* to both UK *output* and *job prospects*. (The essential economic conditions which would have to be satisfied are outlined above in 10.4.4.)

(d) It is sometimes argued that the importance of sterling in world trade and finance makes it an inherently unstable currency; or, perhaps more strictly, makes its exchange rate *vulnerable* to changes in certain economic and financial conditions. Consequently, there may be friction generated between sterling and other EC currencies, which may be affected differently by *external events*. In this context, the position of the deutschmark is of particular significance, given its growing importance in world financial affairs. Indeed, some commentators have argued that attempting to bring together two such important currencies within the ERM could undermine its basic stability. Also, to the extent that sterling does not settle down easily within the ERM, the authorities may be required to undertake excessive amounts of exchange market intervention, which, as implied above, could have adverse effects on the well-being of the domestic economy.

At a meeting of the European Council (comprising EC Heads of State or Government) in June 1989, the UK Government made clear that it was its wish that sterling should join the ERM, but that this would only be feasible when the *level of inflation* in the UK had *fallen significantly*, when there had been *complete liberalisation of capital movements* within the EC, and when real progress had been made towards *completion of the single European market* (the 1992 initiative), *freedom of operation for financial services firms*, and a *strengthening of EC competition policy*. Critics of this position argued that the UK Government was merely playing for time, as it was not prepared to make the political commitments which full membership of the EMS would undoubtedly require. As events turned out, sterling was taken into the ERM despite the fact that the Government's own pre-conditions had not been met, especially in respect of the inflation objective. It is generally accepted that the Government's decision was risky in economic terms, and was not without political motivation.

Following sterling's entry into the ERM, the generally perceived rigidity of exchange rate parities within the ERM initially allowed the UK authorities to *reduce UK interest rates*, without any apparent detrimental effect on the exchange value of sterling. By the Summer of 1992, UK interest rates were little more than those ruling in Germany, having been around 5% higher at the time of entry. However, it was widely believed that UK interest rates could not be reduced any further without undermining the stability of sterling's value within the ERM. The key relationship in this respect was between *sterling and the deutschmark*, recognising the underlying relative economic circumstances of the UK and Germany. Thus, in effect, *UK economic policy became linked to German interest rate policy*. Moreover, as German interest rates were being maintained at *a relatively high level*, as a counter-inflationary measure in the face of the expansionary fiscal policy associated with German reunification, UK interest rates had to be held at a level which was widely regarded as being *excessively high* against the background of *deepening recession* and a *rapidly falling rate of inflation*. In consequence, increasing domestic political pressure for the UK Government to take action to deal with the rising level of unemployment and generally depressed economic conditions, reinforced by the serious implications of the initial rejection of the Maastricht Treaty (relating to EMU) by the Danish people (discussed below in 10.4.6), *eroded confidence* in the UK Government's willingness and ability to maintain the exchange value of sterling within the ERM.

By mid-September 1992, market sentiment appeared to be that a devaluation of sterling was inevitable. This was despite *massive foreign currency exchange market intervention* within the ERM support framework, and ultimately a substantial (although very short-lived) *increase in UK interest rates* (as was explained in Chapter 8, at 8.7.3). In fact, rather than seek a devaluation of sterling within the ERM, the UK Government *withdrew sterling entirely*, and allowed its exchange value to float downwards relative to most other major currencies. By the end of 1992, sterling had depreciated by about 13% against a trade-weighted basket of other major currencies. Since that time, the value of sterling has strengthened slightly, but it is generally agreed that the sterling exchange rates ruling as at August 1993 are probably more in keeping with the *fundamental economic conditions* than was the case during the two-year period when sterling's value was fixed within the ERM.

10.4.6 The operation of the EMS and the evolution of EMU

Between its launch in March 1979 and the EC currency crisis beginning in September 1992, which involved both sterling and the lira being withdrawn from the ERM, and several other EC currencies being put under substantial pressure on the currency exchange markets, the EMS would appear to have operated *reasonably successfully*. Whilst there were a number of realignments, the exchange rates of currencies of ERM participants were *more stable* than those of the other main Western currencies, and to the extent that this helps to support business confidence this is clearly a positive outcome. However, it must also be recognised that some critics of the ERM have argued that its operation tended to *undermine economic growth* within the participating countries. The key point here is that the convergence of economic policies and performances, required for the stability of exchange rates, may have tended to hold back the potentially faster growth economies within the EC. It may also be argued that until economic convergence is largely attained, the strains created within the restrictive framework of the ERM will make further realignments almost inevitable. Moreover, official resistance to realignments necessitated by the *economic fundamentals* underlying international currency flows, may merely create the type of situation which led to the crisis of September 1992.

The debate on the future development of the EMS was given a renewed urgency with the formal presentation of the *Delors Report* to the European Council in June 1989. This Report made the explicit proposal that all EC member states should participate in the ERM by the end of the first stage of a three-stage transition to full EMU. The *progressive reduction in exchange rate fluctuations* between EC currencies is seen to be critical if a truly integrated EC economy is to be achieved. As might be expected, the Delors Report generated a great deal of *controversy*, not least because of the implied *concentration of power over economic policy at a Community level*. Nevertheless, the European Council agreed to set up an *Inter-Governmental Conference*, the objective of which was to propose amendments to the 1957 Treaty of Rome to allow for progress to be made towards EMU. In October 1990 the European Council agreed in principle that Stage 2 of the transition to EMU, as defined by the Delors Report, should begin on 1 January 1994. Treaty amendments were agreed at a summit meeting in *Maastricht* in December 1991. These amendments allow for Stage 3 (which involves the *irrevocable fixing of exchange rates* as the precursor to the introduction of a *single EC currency*) to begin as early as 1997, subject to a qualified majority of EC states being in favour (meaning that no one member state can prevent the others from entering Stage 3) and at least seven member states meeting the economic convergence criteria.

However, as part of the Maastricht agreement, the UK Government reserved the right to decide nearer the time whether or not the UK would proceed to Stage 3.

An important aspect of the Maastricht Treaty is the proposal that a *European Central Bank* (ECB) will be established, and will take up its full powers with the commencement of Stage 3. It is intended that the ECB will be *politically independent*, and will have as its main objective the *maintenance of price stability within the EC*. Each member state's own central bank will be maintained as part of the *European System of Central Banks*, and will be expected to support the ECB in the implementation of agreed policy. Each individual central bank will also be required to be *politically independent* of its own country's government. As well as having responsibility for *EC monetary policy and control*, the ECB will *conduct foreign exchange market operations*, will *hold and manage member states' foreign exchange reserves*, and will *promote the smooth operation of payments systems*. There may also be tasks conferred upon the ECB relating to the *supervision of credit and other financial institutions*.

Without doubt, the implications of the Maastricht Treaty are profound. However, as mentioned above, the implementation of its conditions will only come about when various *economic convergence criteria* are met by a minimum of seven member states. The main elements of these criteria are that each member state is required to *avoid excessive government budget deficits* (specifically, deficits should not exceed 3% of GDP in any one year, and the outstanding stock of government debt should not exceed 60% of GDP); the *rate of inflation* in the country must be within 1½% of the average of the three best performing states for a period of at least one year; the exchange value of the country's currency must be maintained within the *narrow fluctuation band of the ERM* for at least two years without realignment; and *long-term interest rates* must be within 2% of the three best performing member states in terms of price stability for a period of at least one year. These criteria are felt to be *vital*, as the locking together of EC states' currency values (with ultimately the introduction of a single EC currency), and the application of a common EC monetary policy, means that individual member states will *lose the ability to adjust their own exchange rates and interest rates* in response to adverse economic conditions. Consequently, unless prices and wages are sufficiently flexible, and labour and capital sufficiently mobile, whole regions (including whole countries) of the EC could find themselves suffering from *prolonged high unemployment and generally depressed economic conditions*. The political and social implications of this occurrence would be extremely serious, particularly if there was lacking an appropriate intra-EC resource transfer mechanism to support depressed regions. Clearly, these risks are minimised if all EC member states have similar economic performances and market characteristics, thus allowing the ECB to take appropriate remedial action, in concert with other EC bodies, to deal with what should be viewed as EC-wide economic problems.

As things have turned out, the path to implementing the Maastricht Treaty has not been smooth. France, Denmark and Ireland each held a referendum on whether the Treaty should be ratified, but only Ireland returned a convincing positive result, whilst the people of Denmark initially rejected the Treaty, and then subsequently accepted it with modifications. In the UK, the required enabling legislation was introduced in July 1993, after making tortuous progress through Parliament, reflecting the unease felt by many people in the UK at the full implications for the UK's *economic independence* of going ahead with EMU, despite the so-called opt-out clause relating to the UK's participation in Stage 3. There has also been some underlying criticism of the Government's tactics in handling the UK's relationship with the rest of the EC and of its attitude to social policy matters. Somewhat ironically, the national debates precipitated by the Maastricht Treaty, and the inconclusive referendum results, served to highlight doubts about the prospect of closer EC integration. This development was crucial in *unsettling the foreign exchange markets*, which in September 1992 led to a collapse of confidence in sterling and the lira, causing both currencies to be withdrawn from the ERM. Several other ERM currencies were subsequently forced into realignments, and, as mentioned above, in July 1993 it was felt necessary to broaden the ERM fluctuation bands for most participants in response to market pressures. This was undoubtedly a backwards step in respect of satisfying the convergence criteria. Indeed, during 1992 only Luxembourg met all four criteria, and four other member states met three of the criteria. Therefore, even assuming that the required ratification of the Maastricht Treaty is secured in all member states, there will remain much *uncertainty* as to the likely *timing* of the implementation of the EMU provisions, and the *precise extent of their application across the EC*. The UK Government's commitment to the concept of EMU will only be proven when the UK has moved to Stage 3, and full political independence has been given to the Bank of England.

10.5 STERLING EXCHANGE RATES

Table 10.1 shows the movements in the exchange value of sterling, since 1980, relative to the United States dollar, the deutschmark and the yen, and in terms of the sterling exchange rate index. It is clear that the exchange value

continued on next page

of sterling altered dramatically during this period. The trends against the deutschmark and the yen and in terms of the exchange rate index are unmistakably downwards. An important factor in this context has undoubtedly been the UK's poor performance in respect of inflation, and hence international trading competitiveness, relative to Germany and Japan. The predictions of the purchasing power parity theory would appear to be borne out by this experience. By contrast, the much more volatile relationship between sterling and the United States dollar is partly explained by the importance of the financial markets based within the UK and the USA, and the sensitivity of capital flows to interest rate movements. The unique characteristics of economic and financial developments within the USA since the early 1980s also have had an important impact on the structure of exchange rates.

Table 10.1 Sterling exchange rates against the US dollar, the deutschmark and the yen, and the sterling exchange rate index, 1980 to 1992

| | Exchange value of sterling | | | Sterling exchange |
	US$	DM	Yen	rate index (1985 = 100)
1980	2.328	4.227	525.6	117.7
1981	2.025	4.556	444.6	119.0
1982	1.749	4.243	435.2	113.7
1983	1.516	3.870	359.9	105.3
1984	1.336	3.791	316.8	100.6
1985	1.298	3.784	307.1	100.0
1986	1.467	3.183	246.8	91.5
1987	1.659	2.941	236.5	90.1
1988	1.780	3.124	228.0	95.5
1989	1.638	3.079	225.7	92.6
1990	1.786	2.876	257.4	91.3
1991	1.769	2.925	237.6	91.7
1992	1.767	2.751	223.7	88.4

Source: *Bank of England Quarterly Bulletin,* various issues.

The trends in sterling exchange rates reflect closely the evolution of the UK's balance of payments. In particular the general depreciation in the value of sterling during the 1980s runs parallel to an almost continuous deterioration in the current account. In this respect, the importance of the UK's inflation rate has already been emphasised. A further factor was the significant reduction in world oil prices during the middle years of the 1980s, which not only undermined the UK's visible trade balance, but also most probably dented the confidence of international investors in the longer-term strength of the UK's international trading position.

continued on next page

During the later years of the 1980s, the deterioration of the current account was made worse by the high levels of economic growth experienced within the UK (relative to most other Western nations) and by the associated rapid expansion of consumers' expenditure. However, the current account's generally depressing effect on the value of sterling was periodically countered by relatively strong capital inflows, at least some portion of which was heavily influenced by official exchange market intervention, and the increasingly explicit use of short-term interest rates as an instrument to influence exchange rates. (For a detailed examination of the factors which have affected the UK's balance of payments position, and hence sterling exchange rates, in recent years, see Chapter 9, at 9.6.1 and 9.6.2.)

10.6   OFFICIAL INTERVENTION IN CURRENCY EXCHANGE MARKETS

The crucial importance of official intervention in the currency exchange markets has been identified within several different contexts in the foregoing sections of this chapter. However, it is useful to draw together the motives for such intervention and to consider the possible limitations which might exist in respect of its usefulness.

At the outset, it should be recognised that, at least potentially, there are three *approaches* which might be included under the heading of exchange market intervention:

(a) *Official purchases and sales of currency*, which have a direct impact on the supplies of and demands for currencies on the markets.

(b) *The manipulation of domestic interest rates*, using standard monetary control instruments, as a means of affecting the flows of short-term international investment funds, and hence currency flows through the markets.

(c) *The application of exchange controls*, which place direct limits upon the private sector's ability to hold or trade in foreign currencies.

Since 1979, exchange controls have not been used in the UK; rather the emphasis has been placed upon items (a) and (b).

The main *motives* for official intervention in the currency exchange markets may be summarised as follows:

(a) The authorities may be committed to holding a fixed parity for their country's currency within a *fixed exchange rate system*.

(b) Within a *floating exchange rate regime*, the authorities may intervene in order to *smooth* exchange rate movements. This action is directed towards the avoidance of abrupt destabilising shifts in rates, which might undermine business confidence and damage the financial framework.

(c) Devaluation (within a fixed exchange rate regime) or depreciation (within a floating exchange rate regime) of the domestic currency will enhance the *competitiveness* of domestic exports, other things being equal, and this should help the domestic output and employment position. Furthermore, so long as the elasticities of demand for traded goods are sufficiently high, the current account of the balance of payments itself should be strengthened.

(d) Revaluation or appreciation of the domestic currency will tend to reduce the domestic price of imports and act as a restraint on the price-setting behaviour of domestic firms, thus depressing the *rate of inflation*. The terms of trade are also improved, thus meaning that more imports may be purchased with each unit of exports.

Official intervention in the currency markets is normally regarded as being a *short-term* means for stabilising exchange rates. If a country's exchange rate is under pressure due to an *underlying strength* or *weakness* in the country's *basic economic position*, then it is most unlikely that central bank intervention could hold the exchange rate against market forces in the long term. For example, if the country is persistently performing badly in relation to the current account of the balance of payments, then it may seek to support its currency's value by selling foreign currency reserves on the exchanges. However, *reserves are finite* and there are *limits to the amounts that overseas lenders are willing to provide* to a country which is getting deeper and deeper into debt. Indeed, whilst interest rates may be raised to attract capital funds from overseas (and hence counterbalance the current account deficit), there are domestic factors constraining the extent to which the Government is willing to countenance such action (especially in relation to the impact of the policy on mortgage interest payments and business cash flows).

It is generally agreed that exchange rate stability in the *long term* is dependent upon *comparable economic performances* between a given country and its major trading partners. In particular, if a country experiences a *rate of inflation* which is markedly out of line with its trading partners' rates, its relative competitiveness will alter over time, and the current account of its balance of payments will tend either towards deficit (placing downwards pressure on its currency value) or towards surplus (placing upwards pressure on the value). Indeed, differences between countries in respect of factors such as the productivity of labour and capital, the rate of technical innovation, and longer-term growth prospects are likely to have fundamental effects on the balance of payments, and hence trends in exchange rates. A policy of keeping real interest rates high by international standards may succeed in holding up the value of the exchange rate in the face of downwards pressure, but, as indicated above, there is serious doubt that this policy could continue indefinitely. Similarly, in the face of a fundamentally strong current account, sales of domestic currency or reductions in interest rates might hold down the domestic currency's exchange rate, but as this would tend to cause excessive monetary expansion in the domestic economy, the consequent inflationary pressures would probably undermine the currency's strength in the long term, thus removing the need for central bank intervention. Thus, in the longer term, if the authorities wish to influence exchange rates, it is necessary for them to direct their policies towards the *economic fundamentals* which influence the general pattern of exchange rates. Policies should be aimed at ensuring that the *performance of the domestic economy remains basically in line with that of the country's major trading partners*, especially in respect of relative inflation rates and the overall balance of payments position.

10.7 EXAMINATION PRACTICE
10.7.1 Questions

The following questions are taken from past examination papers, and are intended to give students an indication of the type of questions which they are likely to face within the topic area of Exchange Rates. Students may care to map out answers to these questions before consulting the guidance notes in 10.7.2. Each question carries 25 marks.

(1) (a) To what extent does the theory of purchasing power parity explain a change in a country's exchange rate? (13)
(b) Examine the consequences of a depreciating exchange rate on a country's
†(i) current account of the balance of payments; (9)
(ii) inflation rate. (3)

(October 1988)

(2) †(a) Under a floating exchange rate regime, what is the link between money supply, inflation and the exchange rate? (13)
(b) How does a fixed exchange rate regime help to control inflation? (12)

(October 1992)

(3) (a) What are the fundamental economic factors affecting exchange rate movements? (6)
(b) Explain the relevance of these factors to the ability of a system such as the Exchange Rate Mechanism (ERM) to operate successfully. (10)
(c) What are the advantages of keeping exchange rates in close relationship? (9)

(October 1991)

(4) (a) Outline the main objectives of the European Monetary System (EMS). (5)
(b) What economic conditions are essential for the objectives of EMS to be achieved? (8)
(c) Discuss the case for and against full UK entry into EMS. (12)

(May 1989)

(5) (a) Outline the reasons which might lead a central bank to intervene on the foreign exchange markets. (11)

(b)   Apart from imposing exchange controls, how might a central bank intervene to influence the exchange rate?   (6)

(c)   Can central bank intervention succeed in stabilising a country's exchange rate in the long term? Give reasons for your answer.   (6)

(October 1989)

10.7.2   Guidance notes

(1) (i)   Part (a) of the question requires something more than just a brief outline of the PPP theory. It is necessary to comment upon *the extent to which* the theory is able to explain movements in a country's exchange rate. The key to this issue is to be found in the *time period* over which exchange rate movements are to be considered. Strictly, the PPP theory is only relevant in respect of *long-run movements.*

   (ii)   Part (b)(i) relates to the *current account* of the balance of payments, and hence the emphasis of the answer must be placed upon the *relative competitiveness of internationally-traded goods and services.* The importance of *elasticities of demand* should be noted, as should the possible J-curve effect. Capital account items should only be mentioned to the extent that they may have implications for flows of interest, profits and dividends.

   (iii) There is no need to discuss the structure of the balance of payments or components thereof.

   (iv) The answer to part (b)(ii) should concentrate on the effects of currency devaluation on the *domestic price of imported goods and services.* Other things being equal, these items will become more expensive. There may also be second round effects as the cost of raw material inputs is raised, and pressures for higher wages are increased.

Source of relevant material:

Part (a)   10.3.1(a).
†Part (b)(i)   10.6 (paragraph 3(c)) and Chapter 9, at 9.5.2(a)(i).
   (ii)   10.6 (paragraph 3(d)) and 10.4.5 (paragraph 1(b)).

(2) (i)   The answer to part (a) should begin with a *concise statement* of what is meant by a *floating exchange rate regime.* It is then necessary to explain how *changes in the money supply* are likely to affect the *rate of inflation* (using the Fisher formula) and the *international competitiveness* of domestic output, and hence the *exchange rate* (mentioning the PPP theory). The relevance of inflation for *real interest rates* and international capital flows should also be noted.

   (ii)   A general discussion of the nature of exchange rates or the cases for and against fixed and floating exchange rates is not required.

   (iii) The key to part (b) is in recognition of the *direct link* established between *domestic prices* and *international competitiveness* when exchange rates are fixed. Thus, a *discipline is imposed* upon domestic producers and the monetary authorities to avoid inflation rates going above those experienced by major trading partners. However, it should be noted that high overseas inflation could be 'imported' through the use of fixed exchange rates.

(iv) There is no need to consider the UK's, or any other country's, experiences with money supply growth, inflation and exchange rates.

Source of relevant material:

†Part (a) Chapter 1, at 1.10.1 and 1.10.2, 10.3.1 and 10.3.3 (especially paragraphs 1 and 2).

Part (b) 10.3.5 (especially paragraph 5).

(3) (i) The answer to part (a) requires a brief outline of the influence on exchange rate movements of *relative inflation rates, relative interest rates,* and the *balance of payments position* (with particular reference to the current account). The importance of inflation rates may be highlighted by reference to the *PPP theory.*

(ii) Part (b) of the question focuses upon the economic conditions necessary for a fixed exchange rate system to operate successfully. An explanation should be given of how *divergence of economic performance* between countries, in terms of the factors identified in part (a), may *undermine a fixed exchange rate system.*

(iii) The question does not require examination of the ERM, either in theory or in practice.

(iv) The answer to part (c) should offer a discussion of the *advantages* of fixed exchange rates including *reduced uncertainty* in trading and investment, imposition of *financial discipline* on governments, possible *downwards pressure on inflation rates,* and the *movement towards EMU* (in the case of EC countries).

(v) It is not necessary to discuss actual experience with exchange rates in the UK or in any other country.

Source of relevant material:

Part (a) 10.3.1.
Part (b) 10.3.1, 10.4.4 and 10.6 (paragraph 5).
Part (c) 10.3.5.

(4) (i) Part (a) of the question requires a brief outline of the *main objectives of the EMS* in both the *medium term* and the *longer*

term. Discussion of the mechanisms of intervention or the operation of the EMS in practice is not required.

(ii) The EMS should not be confused with Economic and Monetary Union (EMU), or with the EC's internal markets (1992) initiative.

(iii) Part (b) involves a discussion of the *economic conditions* required for the objectives of EMS to be achieved. The *economic fundamentals* underlying the patterns of exchange rates must be emphasised. There is no need to consider the political factors which might interfere with the operation of the EMS.

(iv) It is important to recognise that the EMS comprises several different elements. Whilst all EC states are technically members of the EMS, sterling was placed within the *Exchange Rate Mechanism* (ERM) only between October 1990 and September 1992. Part (c) of the question requires a *balanced examination of the cases for and against the UK's participation in the ERM.* The discussion of the benefits for the UK should be on the basis of the assumption that the objectives of the EMS are actually achieved.

Source of relevant material:

Part (a)   10.4.4 (paragraph 1).
Part (b)   10.4.4.
Part (c)   10.4.5.

(5) (i) Part (a) requires a summary of *all the major objectives* which a central bank *might seek to achieve* via intervention on the foreign exchange markets. The answer should not simply deal with the objectives which are currently emphasised in the UK (or any other country).

(ii) It is important to remember that whilst the exchange rate might be manipulated as an end in itself, such action is usually seen as a *means to achieving other policy objectives.*

(iii) Do not waste time explaining about economic policy in general.

(iv) Part (b) requires a brief discussion of the *ways* in which the *central bank* might influence the exchange rate. Broader government policy actions, such as fiscal policies aimed at affecting trade flows, are not relevant for this question.

(v) The answer to part (c) involves an explanation of the *economic fundamentals* which determine the *long-term trend* of exchange rates. The limits to currency reserves and international borrowing power, and the extent to which it is practical to manipulate interest rates should be noted, but these factors form only a part of the answer.

(vi) There is no need to explain the arguments for and against fixed or floating exchange rates, and discussion of individual countries' experiences is not required, other than by way of illustration of the theoretical points.

Source of relevant material:

Part (a)   10.6 (paragraph 3) and (as background) 10.3.4 and 10.3.5 (paragraph 1).

Part (b)   10.6 (paragraph 2).

Part (c)   10.6 (paragraphs 4 and 5).

10.8 FURTHER STUDY

The debate concerning the appropriate degree of official intervention in currency exchange markets (or, as it is often termed, the issue of fixed versus floating exchange rates) is well-established. The major challenge for students is, therefore, to relate this debate to the on-going evolution of exchange rate regimes in the Western world. In particular, it is important that students come to terms with the difference between the (more or less) managed floating system, and the relatively fixed exchange rate regime as formalised within the European Monetary System (as initially formulated). As the full impact of the UK's recent decision to withdraw from the ERM remains uncertain, students should remain alert for developments in this area, but should rest assured that, in quality newspapers at least, headline status will be afforded to the major issues.

For general up-dating on currency exchange market developments, and assessment of the broad factors influencing exchange rate movements, publications such as *The Economist, Bank of England Quarterly Bulletin* and *IMF Survey* should be consulted. Statistical information may also be accessed from *Monthly Digest of Statistics* and *Economic Trends* (both published by the Central Statistical Office). Students should also watch out for relevant commentaries, in the quality press, and should consult the regular 'Economics' feature in *Banking World*.

Finally, students should bear in mind that the Exchange Rates topic is very closely linked with the Balance of Payments topic (Chapter 9). Therefore, it is advisable to take these two areas of the syllabus together when revising for the examination. A clear understanding of the factors affecting the major components of the balance of payments is crucial to a full appreciation of the determination of exchange rates and their movement over time. Examination questions may exploit this linkage, as well as that between exchange rates and the Government's economic policy in general (Chapter 8).

INDEX